REDUCTION AND GIVENNESS

Northwestern University
Studies in Phenomenology
and
Existential Philosophy

Translated by

Thomas A. Carlson

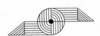

REDUCTION AND GIVENNESS

Investigations of Husserl, Heidegger, and Phenomenology

Jean-Luc Marion

Northwestern University Press
Evanston, Illinois

Northwestern University Press
625 Colfax Street
Evanston, Illinois 60208-4210

Copyright © 1998 by Northwestern University Press
All rights reserved
Printed in the United States of America

ISBN 0-8101-1216-7 cloth
    0-8101-1235-3 paper

Library of Congress Cataloging-in-Publication Data

Marion, Jean-Luc, 1946–
    [Réduction et donation. English]
    Reduction and givenness : investigations of Husserl,
Heidegger, and phenomenology / Jean-Luc Marion ; translated
by Thomas A. Carlson.
        p.   cm.—(Northwestern University studies in
phenomenology and existential philosophy)
    Includes bibliographical references (p.   ) and index.
    ISBN 0-8101-1216-7 (cloth : alk. paper).—ISBN 0-8101-
1235-3 (pbk. : alk. paper)
    1. Heidegger, Martin, 1889–1976.   2. Husserl, Edmund,
1859–1938.   3. Phenomenology—History.   I. Title.   II. Series:
Northwestern University studies in phenomenology &
existential philosophy.
B3279.H49M27413   1998
142'.7—dc21   97-52350
                                                  CIP

Contents

Translator's Acknowledgments

Translation can indeed seem a thankless and isolating labor wherein the translator is checked, over and again, by the severe limits of his or her own language and thought, knowledge, and creativity. At the same time, translation demands that those limits be expanded or ruptured—which they are, when they are, thanks to the incalculable generosities of language, the surprise of unforeseen insights, and the friends and colleagues who open us to such generosity and surprise. From among those whose expert aid and good-humored encouragement were indispensable to the completion of the present project, I thank especially John D. Caputo, Patrick Clemens, Jeffrey L. Kosky, and the author, Jean-Luc Marion. My gratitude also to my parents, Rosanne Lee Carlson and Joseph Carlson II, who continue to give me more than they know, and to Ashley T. Tidey, who sustains me in all things essential.

Preface

The investigations whose results we present here aim to place givenness at the center of reduction, and therefore of phenomenology. In this sense, they maintain an indirect but no doubt necessary tie with older works which, without knowing it, presupposed them. They should, in principle, render possible other advances which aim to determine what, without Being, comes after the subject.

Although autonomous, this work owes much to many. I would like first in particular to thank J.-F. Courtine and D. Franck, who have aided me by their works and by their practice of phenomenology, which is older and better than mine, but also by the activity of the prestigious Archives Husserl de Paris (unité associée au CNRS no. 106), which since 1985 they have reestablished at the Ecole Normale Supérieure. Next, I would like to recognize Samuel Ijsseling and Rudolph Bernet, whose cordial welcome at the Husserl-Archiv de Leuven confirmed my project more than a little. Finally, I would like to say to Michel Henry how much his faithful friendship and his example of philosophical probity have sustained me.

English-language Editions Cited

English-language editions of the following works will be cited in brackets as [Eng. trans., p. #]. In order to capture the emphases of Marion's language, we have often modified the established English translations, and such modifications are indicated by a "mod." following the pertinent references. In cases where Marion's language differs so significantly from established English translations that we do not use those translations, such is indicated by [see Eng. trans., p. #].

Derrida, Jacques

La voix et le phénomène

Speech and Phenomena and Other Essays on Husserl's Theory of Signs. Translated by David B. Allison. Evanston: Northwestern University Press, 1973.

Heidegger, Martin

Brief über den Humanismus (in *Wegmarken*, GA, 9)

"Letter on Humanism." In *Basic Writings.* Edited by David F. Krell. New York: Harper and Row, 1977.

Einführung in die Metaphysik (GA, 40)

An Introduction to Metaphysics. Translated by Ralph Mannheim. New Haven: Yale University Press, 1959.

Einleitung zu "Was ist Metaphysik?" (in *Wegmarken*, GA, 9)

"The Way back into the Ground of Metaphysics." In *Existentialism from Dostoevsky to Sartre.* Edited and translated by Walter Kaufmann. New York: Penguin, 1975.

Grundbegriffe (GA, 51)

Basic Concepts. Translated by Gary E. Aylesworth. Bloomington: Indiana University Press, 1993.

Die Grundbegriffe der Metaphysik: Welt— Endlichkeit—Einsamkeit (GA, 29/30)

The Fundamental Concepts of Metaphysics: World, Finitude, Solitude. Translated by William McNeill and Nicholas Walker. Bloomington: Indiana University Press, 1995.

Die Grundprobleme der Phänomenologie (*GA*, 24)

The Basic Problems of Phenomenology. Translated by Albert Hofstadter. Bloomington: Indiana University Press, 1982.

Identität und Differenz

Identity and Difference. Translated by Joan Stambaugh. New York: Harper and Row, 1969.

Metaphysische Anfangsgründe der Logik (*GA*, 26)

The Metaphysical Foundations of Logic. Translated by Michael Heim. Bloomington: Indiana University Press, 1984.

Nachwort zu "Was ist Metaphysik?" (in *Wegmarken, GA*, 9)

Postscript to "What is Metaphysics?" In *Existentialism from Dostoevsky to Sartre.*

Prolegomena zur Geschichte des Zeitbegriffs (*GA*, 20)

History of the Concept of Time: Prolegomena. Translated by Theodore Kisiel. Bloomington: Indiana University Press, 1985.

Sein und Zeit

Being and Time. Translated by John Macquarrie and Edward Robinson. Oxford: Basil Blackwell, 1962.

Was ist Metaphysik? (in *Wegmarken, GA*, 9)

What Is Metaphysics? In *Existentialism from Dostoevsky to Sartre.*

Vom Wesen des Grundes (in *Wegmarken, GA*, 9)

The Essence of Reasons. Translated by Terrence Malick. Evanston: Northwestern University Press, 1969.

Zur Sache des Denkens

On Time and Being. Translated by Joan Stambaugh. New York: Harper and Row, 1972.

Husserl, Edmund

Cartesianische Meditationen (*Hua*, I)

Cartesian Meditations: An Introduction to Phenomenology. Translated by Dorion Cairns. The Hague: Martinus Nijhoff, 1960.

Entwurf einer Vorrede zu den Logische Untersuchungen

Introduction to the Logical Investigations. Edited by Eugen Fink, translated by Philip J. Bossert and Curtis Peters. The Hague: Martinus Nijhoff, 1975.

Formale und Transzendentale Logik (*Hua*, XVII)	Formal and Transcendental Logic. Translated by Dorion Cairns. The Hague: Martinus Nijhoff, 1969.
Die Idee der Phänomenologie (*Hua*, II)	*The Idea of Phenomenology.* Translated by William P. Alston and George Nakhnikian. Dordrecht: Kluwer Academic Publishers, 1990.
Ideen I (*Hua*, III)	*Ideas Pertaining to a Pure Phenomenology and to Phenomenological Philosophy.* First Book. Translated by F. Kersten. The Hague: Martinus Nijhoff, 1983.
Ideen III (*Hua*, V)	*Phenomenology and the Foundations of the Sciences.* Third Book: *Ideas Pertaining to a Pure Phenomenology and to a Phenomenological Philosophy* (*Collected Works.* Vol. 1). Translated by Ted E. Klein and William E. Pohl. The Hague: Martinus Nijhoff, 1980.
Die Krisis der Europäischen Wissenschaften und die Transzendentale Phänomenologie (*Hua*, VI)	*The Crisis of European Sciences and Transcendental Phenomenology.* Translated by David Carr. Evanston: Northwestern University Press, 1970.
Logische Untersuchungen	*Logical Investigations.* 2 vols. Translated by J. N. Findlay. London: 1970.
Phänomenologische Psychologie (*Hua*, IX)	*Phenomenological Psychology.* Translated by John Scanlon. The Hague: Martinus Nijhoff, 1977.
Philosophie als Strenge Wissenschaft (in *Hua*, XXV)	*Philosophy as Rigorous Science.* In *Phenomenology and the Crisis of Philosophy.* Translated by Quentin Lauer. New York: Harper and Row, 1965.

Bibliographical Note

Husserl's works are cited according to the *Husserliana: Edmund Husserl Gesammelte Werke* (abbreviated as *Hua*), edited under the responsibility of the Husserl-Archiv de Leuven (dir. S. Ijsseling), published by M. Nijhoff, the Hague. However, for the *Logical Investigations* (abbreviated as LU), I used the text of their second edition, which appeared in three volumes (Tübingen: Niemeyer, 1913) (reprinted in 1968).

Heidegger's texts are cited according to the volumes of the *Gesamtausgabe*, which are published under the direction of F.-W. von Herrmann (Frankfurt: Klostermann, 1975–) (abbreviated as *GA*). We make an exception for *Sein und Zeit*, which is cited following the 10th edition (Tübingen: Niemeyer, 1963), according to page and lines. Except when modifying them, we use the usual translations. Thus *Etre et Temps* is always cited following the translation (for restricted circulation only) of E. Martineau, "Authentica" (Paris, 1985).

We thank the journal *Philosophie*, the *Revue de Métaphysique et de Morale*, and the *Tijdschrift voor Filosofie* for having allowed us to reprint and modify certain materials whose first versions they had welcomed (respectively, "La percée et l'élargissement. Contribution à l'interprétation des *Recherches logiques*," nos. 2 and 3 [April and September 1984]; "L'*ego* et le *Dasein*. Heidegger et la 'destruction' de Descartes dans *Sein und Zeit*," vol. 92, no. 1 [January, 1987]; and "Différence ontologique ou question de l'être. Un indécidé de *Sein und Zeit*," vol. 49, no. 4 [December, 1987]).

Introduction:
Phenomenology as Such

I n an essential way, phenomenology assumes in our century the very role of philosophy. In fact, after Nietzsche had brought to an end and completed all the possibilities—even inverted—of metaphysics, phenomenology, more than any other theoretical initiative, undertook a new beginning.

The same year of 1887 sees Nietzsche drawn definitively by his last god and Husserl give his first class on "The Ends and the Tasks of Metaphysics";[1] the same year of 1900 sees Nietzsche disappear entirely and the first part of the *Logische Untersuchungen* appear. But their encounter, free of any anecdote, has to do with only one question: Can the conditions of presence be extended to the point that all beings reach it, beyond the limits fixed by previous states of metaphysics, or even by any metaphysics at all? Can the givenness in presence of each thing be realized without any condition or restriction? This question marks Nietzsche's last advance and Husserl's first point of arrival. Around it, philosophy swings from a positively and negatively completed metaphysics toward a thought that is perhaps already postmetaphysical—at least in the sense that phenomenology can claim to fulfill the "nostalgia of all modern philosophy"[2] at the very moment of passing beyond it. In undertaking to free presence from any condition or precondition for receiving what gives itself as it gives itself, phenomenology therefore attempts to complete metaphysics and, indissolubly, to bring it to an end. Phenomenology therefore remains exactly on the line—the watershed: by soliciting the liberation of presence, it fulfills the expectations of metaphysics, but in thus stealing from it the object of its quarrel, it abolishes it.

Or at least it claims to do so. For presence, thus given without any of the metaphysical restrictions that were placed on its former usage, imposes in its turn a number of requirements. The "breakthrough"

1

accomplished by Husserl in 1900–1901 in fact remains extraordinarily ambiguous: first, because it extends the field of presence beyond any limits, so as to dissolve the very notion of presence; then, above all, because it thereby repeats the constitutively metaphysical definition of presence—objectivity. Does not the reestablishment, or better the irrepressible consecration of objectivity by Husserl indicate the extreme difficulty that phenomenology has in remaining faithful to its own endeavor? More than the conventional debates over "realism" and the "transcendental turn," the ideal of objectivity calls into question the very objective of phenomenology—the return to things in question. For it is not at all self-evident that the things in question are given only in the form of their constituted objectification.

The objective of phenomenology does not coincide with objectivity —this expresses Heidegger's point of departure. The recent publication of the courses prior to or just following *Sein und Zeit* (as much from the first Freiburg period, and that of Marburg, as from the second Freiburg period) allows us to establish firmly a decisive point: Being became the stake of phenomenology for Heidegger only first and definitively within a critique of the ideal of objectification pursued by Husserl. The conflict that opposed Heidegger to Husserl thus appears absolutely exemplary: a perfect reciprocal understanding is combined—as in all the great philosophical confrontations—with a total mutual lack of understanding, so as to make phenomenology, in a second surge, cross its watershed. Henceforth the question is stated thus: Does the return to the things in question lead back to their objectivity or to their Being? Does that which effects the re(con)duction act in the capacity of transcendental *I* or in that of *Dasein*? It is not simply a matter here of transforming the phenomenological method, nor even first of posing anew the question of Being, but rather—much more radically—of determining whether and to what extent phenomenology truly opens a "new beginning" for philosophy as such.

It remains that Heidegger no doubt did not accomplish what he nevertheless attempted, more than anyone else, to attain through and for phenomenology. This is so, first, because, whatever the case may be, *Dasein* still remains haunted by the *I*; next it is so because the "phenomenon of Being," even in the already attenuated form of the ontological difference, never shows itself; and finally it is so because the "phenomenology of the unapparent" henceforth called for never gets beyond either its programmatic status or its contradictory formulation. But if the horizon of Being in its temporality thus becomes highly problematical, as Heidegger is the first to admit as early as 1927,[3] then phenomenology would have to confront the following dilemma: either disappear as a philosophical discipline or else admit that its method—if a term so marked by the history of metaphysics can be suitable here—does not have to depend on the question of Being any more than it was previously able to limit itself to the objective of objectivity. There is no doubt that the great majority of recent phenomenologists (and thus, to begin in France, from Emmanuel Lévinas and Paul Ricoeur to Jacques Derrida and Michel Henry) have chosen the second path: the phenomenological way of thinking rests solely on its own protocols, beyond or short of both the object in its constitution and beings in their Being.[4]

In the following pages we have attempted nothing more than to free the phenomenological way of thinking as such, without confusing it with its successive, and, in a sense, provisional objectives. If in phenomenology—as opposed to metaphysics—possibility in truth surpasses actuality,[5] then we must push this principle to its end, as far as eventually to wield it *against* phenomenology as already actualized. For one does not overcome a true thinking by refuting it, but rather by repeating it, or even by borrowing from it the means to think with it beyond it. Then even failure succeeds.

1

The Breakthrough and the Broadening

1. Two Interpretations and a Broadening

"A breakthrough work, *ein Werk des Durchbruchs*"—it is with these words that Husserl salutes the *Logical Investigations* thirteen years after their first edition of 1900–1901. This turn of phrase barely conceals a depreciation under the praise. In the same year, Husserl publishes the first volume of the *Ideen,* and if he still salutes the *Investigations,* he does so in the way that a traveler salutes, from a boat that withdraws, the land forever left behind. In 1913 the breakthrough fades before that which it rendered possible; Husserl confirms this straightaway: "a break-through work and, just as well, less an end than a beginning."[1] Hence the paradox that does not cease to dominate the interpretation of the *Logical Investigations*: the breakthrough is recognized only in order to serve immediately as a beginning for the later phenomenology; whether this shift appears as a questionable deviation (as it is for Ingarden and his disciples[2]) or the only correct path (as for Husserl himself) matters little since in both cases the breakthrough of 1900–1901 can be understood only in relation to what it does not yet state. Now, even supposing that the whole theoretical achievement of the breakthrough of 1900–1901 can be found again, in its entirety, in the later texts (which remains to be proved, as Sartre, among others, has shown), one must in any case admit that it was won without the array of the later phenomenological orthodoxy. And therefore, if there is a breakthrough, we should be able to read it solely according to the discourse of the *Investigations.* This work does not consist first in identifying the theses and the authors that they critique in the measure of their advance; some excellent studies[3] have shown that Husserl's adversaries remain largely unaware of the metaphysical situation that determines them, so that we cannot expect more of them than a doxographical identification of the first theoretical decisions of the *Investigations*. The breakthrough can receive its properly metaphysical dignity only from an interpretation that is itself awake to the essence of metaphysics. Thus, it has found only two problematics powerful enough to put us on the trail of their metaphysical situation. But these two problematics, following two opposite directions, radicalize the breakthrough to the point of abolishing what is at stake in a real effort to situate it. In one case—Heidegger—Husserl reaches in the *Investigations*, and especially in the Sixth, the categorial intuition of Being; he therefore extracts himself from the Neo-Kantian dissimulation of the ending metaphysics, in order to open himself to a givenness of Being: "In order even to lay out the question of the meaning of Being, it was necessary that Being be *given*, so that one be able to ask after its meaning. Husserl's tour de force consisted precisely in bringing Being to presence, making it phenomenally present in the category. Through this tour de force," Heidegger adds, "I finally had a ground: 'Being' is not a simple concept, a pure abstraction obtained thanks to a deductive operation."[4] To be sure, Husserl does not really unfold the question of the meaning of Being (*Sinn des Seins*); it nonetheless remains that, once accomplished, the breakthrough does allow one to pose the question of Being, as it were, already beyond metaphysics. Hence the direct filiation, which Heidegger never explicitly formulates but ceaselessly suggests, between, on the one hand, the *Logical Investigations*, which lead to the categorial intuition that gives Being, and, on the other hand, *Sein und Zeit*, which constructs the question of Being starting from the analytic of Dasein. According to this topic, the breakthrough of 1900–1901 anticipates the destruction of ontology and thus accomplishes the end of metaphysics. The breakthrough breaks beyond metaphysics.

The other approach—which we owe to J. Derrida, who thus acquired a definitive phenomenological merit—inverts this perspective entirely. The breakthrough of the *Investigations* certainly does consist in freeing up signification (*Bedeutung, meinen*) in its a priori ideality. But far from drawing the consequences of this—namely, that signification signifies by itself, without in any way having to go back to an intuitive presencing—Husserl would have ceaselessly led signification back to a fulfilling intuition, which secures it in evident presence. Thus phenomenology would perpetuate, even against its intention—against the intentionality of signification—the primacy of presence, and it would founder in a final "adventure of the metaphysics of presence"; in short, "the adherence of phenomenology to classical ontology"[5] would be betrayed by its recourse to intuition to secure presence for signification, but above all by the unquestioned primacy of presence itself in and over signification. To overcome metaphysics as a "metaphysics of presence" would require that one overcome phenomenology, by playing against it one of its potentialities that had been censured as early as the First Investigation—by playing the indication (*Anzeichen*), the sign foreign to all presence, against the sign that is endowed with a signification that awaits its intuitive fulfillment. Within this topic, according to the development that leads it to the "principle of principles" of 1913, the breakthrough of 1900–1901 restores metaphysics by extending the ontological primacy of presence. The breakthrough does not pass beyond metaphysics but rather leads back to it.

The conflict of these two interpretations orients the *Logical Investigations* in two opposite directions. Either, reading them on the basis of the Sixth and final Investigation, one can retain the categorial givenness of Being, and it then becomes possible to pass on to ontological difference by carrying out the "destruction of the history of ontology." Or else, reading them on the basis of the First Investigation, one retains the primacy of presence which is all the more clear insofar as the intentionality of the a priori allows one to contest it; then it becomes necessary to move on to *différance*, in order to work at deconstructions without end or beginning. This conflict, which is in fact unavoidable, gives rise to two main difficulties among many. (1) In Husserl's own eyes, and putting aside the continuation of the *Ideen*, in what did the breakthrough of the *Logical Investigations* consist? Does the consciously Husserlian motive for the breakthrough, if there is one, concern—either directly or indirectly—metaphysics as eventually thematized by the primacy of presence? (2) Heidegger retains from the Sixth Investigation the categorial *givenness* of Being; Derrida stigmatizes in the First Investigation the presentifying *intuition*. Supposing that it is founded in the texts, would this distinction not offer a conceptual range sufficient enough that the two readings, instead of being in confrontation, might be arranged more subtly? In short, if it is a matter of defining metaphysics in order to put it in question, is the characteristic of givenness equivalent to the characteristic of presence through intuition? It is at some peril that we must now risk an examination of these questions.

If Husserl does not understand the *Investigations* as a "breakthrough work" until 1913, he very consciously recognizes as early as 1900 the "difficulties of pure phenomenological analysis," and he indicates the reason for this: "The source of all such difficulties lies in the unnatural direction of intuition and thought which phenomenological analysis requires," or again in "an anti-natural *habitus* of reflection."[6] Such a *habitus* requires that one not take objects as actual but rather the acts that underlie them. The "things in question" are not those that we would naturally be inclined to consider actual, but rather those that we overlook—the acts. In order to substitute for things (*Dinge*), which are perhaps only words, the corresponding actuality, in order to return each time to the thing in question (*Sache*), one must lead reflection back toward its own acts, and therefore lead conceptions back toward the intuition that corresponds to them (or not): "Logical concepts . . . must have their origin in intuition." To return to the things in question implies turning thought toward intuition, in return: "We must go back to 'the things themselves' [*auf die 'Sachen selbst' zurückgehen*]. We desire to render self-evident in fully developed intuitions [*vollentwickelten Anschauungen*] that what is here given in actually performed abstractions is what the word-meanings in our expression of the law truly and actually stand for."[7] The return to the thing at stake demands that thought lead its words to their intuition. The verification of statements presupposes their repetition on the basis of the actually performed intuition, and therefore on the basis of acts: "It is purely on the basis of internal intuition [*Innenschau*] and of the analysis of the intuited [*Geschauten*], and in an intuitive [*intuitiven*] reascent to general necessities, that affirmations will be gained as affirmations of essences. These are not essential necessities that are only supposed or claimed, but rather the necessity and the unconditioned universality of their validity will come to be intuited itself [*selbst zum Geschauten*]."[8] Such a return to the things themselves as a leading-back [*reconduction*] to intuition has force only if it is a matter of thus bringing to its eventual evidence what, according to the natural orientation of thought, precisely does *not* offer any intuition. Moreover, Husserl admits the phenomenological difficulty only because he demands intuition in logic—what he does not hesitate to name "the intuitive fulfillment [*Vollzug*] of our abstraction."[9] The rule of the return to intuition, and therefore of the reversal of the natural direction, is thus developed " . . . in general. Each thought, or at least each consistent thought, can no doubt become intuitive."[10] In the preface essay to the *Investigations*, itself also written in 1913 (and published by E. Fink in 1939), Husserl can explain the breakthrough by the unqualified return to intuition: "my method is strictly 'intuitive' [*intuitiv*], that is to say radically *intuitive* [*anschauliche*] in the broadened sense that I give to this term [*in meinem erweiterten Sinne*], and . . . it is precisely this that constitutes the very profound difference that separates my rationalism and my idealism from those that have preceded them and from all the scholastic ontologies."[11] One must speak of a "breakthrough" because one must lead every thought back to its intuitive actualization (its acts). This later self-interpretation does not deviate from the intitial intention, since as early as 1901 Husserl claimed in a self-presentation "to have discovered a corner-stone [*ein Grund- und Eckstein*] for all phenomenology and for any future theory of knowledge" in what he already named "a fundamental broadening, until now . . . not accomplished [*fundamentale und bisher nicht vollzogene Erweiterung*], of the concepts of perception and of intuition."[12] We therefore conclude: the breakthrough of the *Investigations* has to do with the elevation of intuition, as the worker of evidence, to the level of an "adequate phenomenological justification" of all statements, that is, to the absolutely "decisive [*massgebend*]" role of the "descriptive character of phenomena, as experienced by us."[13] The overture and the finale match: the phenomenological breakthrough is accomplished by leading back to intuition everything that claims to be constituted as a phenomenon. This result gives rise to two confirmations.

First, it appears difficult to maintain that the "principle of principles" formulated in the *Ideen* of 1913 would orient the phenomenological enterprise in a new direction, or even contradict the original injunction of the "return to the things themselves." The preface that remained unpublished (written in 1913, to be sure, but for the *Investigations*) in fact does not hesitate to recognize that they "radically profess the principle of all principles," namely the "right of what is seen clearly, which precisely, as such, is what is 'originary,' what is before any theory, what gives the ultimate norm." This de jure principle is carried out when, "following the evidence of experience and ultimately of originarily giving perception in its harmonious progression, we speak straightforwardly about things that are," for "then precisely we accept what is immediately given to us as something that is and we question it concerning its properties and its laws." This principle contradicts the "return to the things themselves" all the less insofar as it explicitly includes it: "This intuitive method, appealing as it does to 'the things themselves' here in question, that is, to the knowledge 'itself' (precisely in its direct, intuitive givenness), is what the second volume of these *Logical Investigations* employs, which, in my opinion then, was not written for nothing [*nicht umsonst*]."[14] For Husserl at least, the "principle of principles" does not limit the "return to the things themselves," but rather constitutes its accomplishment and truth: to return objects to acts implies that "the originarily giving intuition is a source of right for cognition."[15]

Couldn't one nevertheless object to this conciliation of the two principles that it appeared precisely in 1913, in a rereading of the *Investigations* that was contemporaneous with the turn taken in the *Ideen*? This objection loses a great deal if one notes that several texts from the *Investigations* themselves anticipate the "principle of principles." Let us cite two. First, this extreme argument from the Sixth Investigation: "If the peculiar character of intentional experiences is contested, if one does not want [*will*] to admit what for us is most certain [*was uns als das Allersicherste gilt*], that being-an-object consists phenomenologically in certain acts in which something appears, or is thought as our object, it will not be intelligible how being-an-object can itself be objective to us."[16] What is most certain, what Descartes named the *inconcussum quid*, and which alone renders possible the Being of the object as object, has to do with this: the object consists only in certain acts, acts whose primacy stems from their ability to allow the given to appear as an intentional lived experience. Whoever refuses here the "legitimate source" of any appearance, namely lived experiences, cannot be refuted since he excludes himself from the terrain of givenness, where alone an argument becomes possible. If the conditions of possibility of the Being-object, namely intuition in its lived experiences, are rejected, then the eventual objects of experience are also rejected. But another text immediately presents itself, a text that closes the introduction to the second volume of the *Investigations* under the unambiguous title of "principle of the absence of presuppositions [*Prinzip der Voraussetzunglosigkeit*]." It demands that one ensure the return to the things themselves by means of respect for the sole authority of intuition: "If such a 'thinking over' of the meaning of knowledge is itself to yield, not mere opinion, but the evident [*einsichtig*] knowledge it strictly demands, it must be a pure intuition of essences, exemplarily performed on an actual *given* basis of experiences of thinking and knowing." Intuition itself cannot be understood as a last presupposition, since it is neither presupposed, nor posited, nor given, but originarily giving. Intuition sees what theories presuppose of their objects; as intuition gives, with neither reason nor condition, it precedes the theories of the given, in the capacity of a "theory of all theories,"[17] perhaps in the sense that, according to Aristotle, the impossibility of securing science solely by the repetition of science (οὐδ᾽ ἐπιστήμης ἐπιστήμη) requires admitting the *nous* within the principle of principles (νοῦς ἂν εἴη τῶν ἀρχῶν). It remains the case that in order to take on such a function, intuition must free itself from the limits that theory commonly imposes on it.

Hence the second confirmation of the breakthrough: what Husserl thematizes as an intuitive return to the things themselves requires "a new notion of intuition" that is freed from "the usual notion of sensuous intuition."[18] Intuition becomes the principial recourse of every concept only by being the first to undergo the phenomenological reform, in this case by submitting itself to a "fundamental broadening," by becoming "intuitive in the broadened sense that [Husserl] gives to this term."[19] One could not deny that the phenomenological redeployment of intuition, although announced as early as the Second Investigation, is not accomplished until the Sixth Investigation; as early as its introduction, it announces "an *unavoidable broadening* [*Erweiterung*] *of the originally sense-turned concepts of intuition and perception,* which permits us to speak of *categorial,* and, in particular, of *universal intuition.*"[20] In fact, as if the essential decision that makes the breakthrough actual did not cease to delay its true accomplishment, the Sixth Investigation will fulfill the promises of the prefaces of the First and the Second Investigations only in the second part; the first part still hesitates, as it were, to enter into the ultimate debate: "In our next chapter, which deals generally with categorial forms we shall show the need to widen [*Erweiterung*] the concepts of perception and other sorts of intuition." In fact, one will have to wait until § 45, explicitly entitled "Broadening of the Concept of Intuition [*Erweiterung des Begriffes Anschauung*]," for Husserl to dare to admit before the categorial object that "we cannot manage without these words, whose broadened sense [*erweiterter Sinn*] is of course evident"—the words, unavoidably, of "'intuition,' or . . . 'perception' and 'object.' "[21] If one recognizes the guiding thread of intuition, then the direct unity of the First Investigation with the Sixth becomes clear. The First Investigation (and its prefaces) posits as the principle of principles the universal and intuitive return to the things themselves. In order to exercise the right of the concrete, intuition itself must become fit for its principial phenomenological function, in a final and most difficult effort which mobilizes the whole of the Sixth Investigation: to render even the domain of the categories intuitively given. The First Investigation "therefore has only a preparatory character [*vorbereitenden Charakter*]," since it does not yet have at its disposal the concept of intuition that it claims to put into operation; on the contrary, the Sixth Investigation, "the cornerstone of all phenomenology," must be recognized as "the most extended, in fact the most mature, and also the richest in its results, of the entire book [*aufgereifteste und wohl auch ergebnisvollste*]."[22] Should we be surprised that the path of the *Investigations* proceeds in the reverse of an analytic order, and that the point of departure already implies results that are still to come? We can certainly be surprised by this, but on the condition that we admit that Husserl had warned that phenomenology cannot not advance in this way: "we must, in our exposition, make use of all the concepts we are trying to clarify. This coincides with a certain wholly irremovable defect which affects the systematic course of our basic phenomenological and epistemological investigations. . . . We search, as it were, in a zig-zag fashion, a metaphor all the more apt since the close interdependence of our various epistemological concepts leads us back [*zurückkehren*] again and again to our original analyses, where the new confirms the old, and the old the new."[23]

We can therefore respond to the first question: the breakthrough of the *Investigations* consists in leading concepts and objects back to intuition, and thus in radically broadening the scope of intuition itself. The breakthrough implies that intuition gives more than it seems, at least more than it seems to a nonphenomenological gaze. In other words, because intuition is broadened, there appears more than it seems; namely, exactly as much as intuition in its broadened sense gives to be seen by the phenomenological, and therefore antinatural, gaze.

2. The Domains of Intuition

But what does the thus broadened intuition give to be seen? A quick response to this corollary of the first question will allow us to conceive exactly how far the broadening, and therefore also the breakthrough, proceeds. In the preface to the *Investigations,* Husserl underscores a second aspect of the unique breakthrough: we know evidently "something objective [*ein Gegenständliches*] that is, without, however, being in the mode of the thing [*Reales*]"; in other words: " 'ideas' themselves are and count as objects [*Gegenstände*]."[24] In fact, in 1900–1901, it is a matter of understanding that "ideal objects veritably exist," for example that "the seven regular solids are seven objects just as much as the seven Wisemen; the principle of the parallelogram of forces is *one* object just as much as the city of Paris."[25] In order to attain the non-natural orientation that is demanded by the breakthrough, it is necessary to consider as objects those acts taken heretofore as nonobjective—"it is precisely these acts, until now lacking in any objectivity [*nicht gegenständlich*], that must henceforth become the objects of apprehension and of theoretical position; it is these that we must consider in new acts of intuition and thinking, analyze according to their essence, describe and make the objects [*zu Gegenstände . . . machen*] of an empirical or idealistic thought."[26] Objectivity surpasses the mode of Being of the thing, frees itself from reality (*Realität, real*), and therefore is itself also broadened: "I often make use of the vaguer expression 'objectity' [*Gegenständlichkeit*], since here we are never limited to objects in the narrow sense [*im engeren Sinn*], but have also to do with states of affairs, properties, with real forms or dependent categorials, etc."[27] Commenting on the *Investigations* in 1925, Husserl will clearly posit that "there are thus without doubt *irreal* objectities and *irreal truths* belonging thereto."[28] Here it is first necessary to bring up the fact that objectity is extended beyond real objectivity, in a manner parallel to the broadening of intuition beyond the sensible; and it is necessary to note above all that these two broadenings lead to the same—categorial—horizon. Moreover, in the note cited from the First Investigation, the broad objectity immediately concerns the categorial forms. It is therefore necessary to understand that to begin with the breakthrough works in favor of and with a view to the categorial, as much through broadened intuition as through broadened objectity.

The broadening of intuition is opposed to its Kantian finitude, according to whom "our nature is so constituted that our intuition can never be other than *sensible*."[29] It is therefore a matter "of submitting the very concept of intuitiveness [*Anschaulichkeit*], against its Kantian acceptation, to an essential broadening [*wesentliche Erweiterung*],"[30] a matter of admitting that the concept affects us, and therefore that the concept is given to us, in its categorial figure. The transgression of the Kantian prohibition is accomplished in three moments; each of these sets into operation a new meaning of the categorial as such, with the result that we can suppose that for Husserl *all* intuition is to some degree categorial.

1. Kant clearly stated it: sensible intuition would remain "blind" if no concept subsumed it. Husserl uses this as a reason to posit that "the goal, true knowledge, is not mere intuition, but adequate intuition that has assumed a categorial form and that perfectly adapts itself thereby to thought, or conversely, the thought that draws its evidence from intuition."[31] The most elementary intuition, hence the sensible, would not have any validity unless to begin with it had a signification whose fulfillment it assures; its function is deployed only in being restricted to the fulfillment of a categorial form. It can presuppose it only if this categorial form is given.

2. This givenness is itself realized in the mode of intuition, at least in "the evident [*einsichtige*] ideation in which the universal is given to us 'in person.' " For "one and the same intuition" in fact delivers to us two objects that are irreducible to one another: indeed, "on the basis of the same intuitive foundation [*desselben anschaulichen Untergrundes*],"[32] two acts, and not one, are accomplished. On the one hand, intuition serves as a foundational presentation for an act of individual intention—we aim at *a particular* house, or *a particular* shade of red, a particular little patch of yellow wall and not another, according to a singularity that is so irreplaceable that in order to reach it one must go "directly before the model" ["*sur le motif*"] at the risk of thereby dying like Bergotte; intuition then functions, as in its first acceptation, by fulfilling a singular aim. But on the other hand we can also aim, through the first intuition utilized as a simple medium, at *the* house as the essence of any empirically possible or impossible house, *the* universal color of red which no shade among all the reds in the world could exhaust or approach, since *this* essential red never shines therein, even though all the particular reds

shine on the basis of it. In this way, upon sensible intuition rests "an act of apprehension and aim directed to a species [*spezialisierenden*]," such that "a new mode of apprehension has been built upon the 'intuition' of the individual house or of its redness, a new mode that is constitutive for the intuitive datum of the idea of *red* [*intuitive Gegebenheit der Idee*]."[33] Of the categorial, as universal essence, there is datum and intuitive datum: the first intuition is used in order to render the categorial intuitive because it allows itself to be turned away from the individual (and therefore from itself, which is first given *hic et nunc* in the mode of a 'this' [*dieses*]), under the possessive fascination of the categorial. "On the other hand, ideal objects truly exist. . . . we also apprehend *evidently* [*einsichtig*] certain categorical truths that relate to such ideal objects."[34] Evidence [*Einsicht*] completes, in ideation, the intuition of essences. The Kantian limit yields to evidence—evidence of the essences that are *intuitively* given. We do not need to insist on this well-known point, but on what makes it possible. The intuition of essences becomes unavoidable by mobilizing already—which is absolutely remarkable—the couple of founding and founded acts, anticipating the Sixth Investigation.[35] Above all, it mobilizes the instance of the categorial. Thus, the difference between particular (founding) acts and universal (founded) acts is "categorial," for "it pertains to the pure form of possible objects of consciousness as such. (See also the Sixth Investigation, chap. 6)." Thus the "nonsensuous acts" have to do with a "categorial" thought. And thus above all, when it envisages the "categorial functions," the First Investigation defines the different significations that are attributable to one *same* intuition with variations solely in the "categorial point of view."[36] In other words, the orientation of intuition toward the universal categorial forms (the essences) rests entirely on the itself categorial interpretation of intuition—heretofore taken as sensuous. As early as the opening of the *Investigations*, the decisive step of a broadening of intuition is accomplished only on the basis of the authority of the "categorial," and thus on the basis of the Sixth Investigation. Once again, the breakthrough remains incomprehensible and unjustifiable if the whole is not read on the basis of its end. This reversal of the order in which to read the *Investigations* does not simply correspond to the methodological paradox of their "zig-zag" movement; it answers above all to the phenomenological paradox of the return to the things themselves, such as Heidegger will formulate it again in 1925:

> These acts of ideation, *of the intuition of the universal*, are categorial acts which give their object. They give what is called an idea, ἰδέα, *species*. The Latin term *species* is the translation of eidos, *the aspect under which something shows itself* [*Aussehen von etwas*]. The acts of universal intuition give what

is seen in the matters first and simply. When I perceive simply, moving about in my environmental world, when I see houses, for example, I do not first see houses primarily and expressly in their individuation, in their distinctiveness. Rather, I first see universally: this is a house.[37]

I see *the* house, *as* house, before seeing (and in order to see) *a* house; or rather, the *as* of the house precedes a particular house and allows it to appear as such. The intuition of essences does not double sensuous intuition by a weak extension, but precedes it in rendering it phenomenologically possible.

3. Whence the last step: categorial intuition in the strict sense. In following the precise moment when, in § 45, the Sixth Investigation completes "the broadening of the concept of intuition," and thus the initial (and unique) plan of the breakthrough of 1900–1901, the manner of proceeding cannot but surprise, as much by its economy of means as by the rapid conclusion. Hence a principle: "the essential homogeneity of the function of fulfillment"; in other words: whatever be the intentions of signification, they all require, in principle, at least the possibility of their intuitive fulfillment. A question is connected to this principle: In an expression like *the gold is yellow,* can all the categorial forms receive the corresponding fulfilling intuition, if we stick to the two types of intuition already recognized? It is clear that sensuous intuition (and therefore the founding acts) cannot fulfill the categorial forms of essences, like *gold* or *yellow*; therefore they receive their intuitive fulfillment only from intuitions of essence. There remains the simple *is*. Now the *is* "is itself placed under our eyes . . . is not only thought, but precisely *intuited* [*angeschaut*], perceived." In fact, we do not mean here only *gold,* and then *yellow,* but indeed their connection, and therefore we affirm their unity; more than that, we affirm that the predicative unity is doubled by an existential declaration: we do not mean simply *the gold* (is) *yellow, yellow-gold,* but also *the yellow-gold is.* Therefore we can note that these strictly categorial aims require an intuition and a corresponding fulfillment. We finally obtain confirmation that *is* is properly meant and therefore awaits its own fulfillment when this aim does *not* find an adequate intuitive fulfillment: just as the signification *the yellow-gold* obviously does not coincide with the signification *the yellow-gold is,* so the absence of the intuitive fulfillment of *is* is clearly distinguished from its presence—which would give us the *yellow-gold being* in person. Both positively and negatively, the ultimate categorial form sets into operation the play of intention and of intuition, of aim and of fulfillment. Thus all significations, even categorial, in the end "unavoidably come upon 'intuition' (or upon 'perception' and 'object')."[38] Categorial intuition does not at all impose itself through

some mystical initiation that would open a suspect third eye of the mind. It results from the pure and simple return to the things themselves, which verifies that the *is* itself also offers a signification and therefore requires an intuition. It therefore constitutes one particular, though polemically remarkable, case of the "great class of acts whose peculiarity it is that in them something appears as 'actual,' as 'self-given' [*etwas als 'wirklich,' und zwar als 'selbst gegebenen' erscheint*]."[39] Categorial intuition marks the determination of all intuition by the categorial requirement of the givenness in person of the phenomenon. Intuition results from givenness without exception. Another confirmation of this dependence comes from the curiously "analogical" status that is reserved for categorial intuition—analogy with all the other intuitions in relation to the requirement of a universal givenness of the phenomenon.[40]

The limit fixed upon intuition by Kant must be transgressed in various ways—but for one reason: the phenomenological requirement of the givenness in presence of every phenomenon with neither remainder nor reserve, the categorial not being an exception. We thus come upon the last corollary of the first question: Does the breakthrough of 1900–1901, now identified with the broadening of intuition, concern, directly or indirectly, metaphysics—itself definable by the primacy of presence?

3. The Completion of Presence

If metaphysics is defined by the absolute and unquestioned primacy of the presencing of beings, and if that presencing is never completed except through intuition, then one must conclude, without beating around the bush, that metaphysics was never completed as perfectly as with the breakthrough of 1900–1901, since it ends up, at the end of the Sixth Investigation, opening "the field of *universal intuition* [*der allgemeinen Anschauung*]—an expression which no doubt will not seem better to many than 'wooden iron.' "[41] Presencing covers a field with neither limit nor remainder, because the intuitive placing-in-evidence becomes universal. The powerful originality of the Husserlian institution of phenomenology can be imagined only if one measures the audacity of the thesis of the *Investigations*: nothing constitutes an exception to intuition, and therefore nothing escapes its reconduction into the full light of presence; neither the sensuous, nor essence, nor the categorial form itself—nothing will remain invisible from now on, since a mode of intuition tracks and hunts down each of these objects as so many modes of presence. Less than seven years after the breakthrough, the Göttingen *Lessons* enumerate at the end of their itinerary "the diverse modes of authentic givenness"; the list is stretched so far that it becomes obvious that no remainder of darkness or withdrawal resists the evidence of appearing [*l'apparaître*]. Husserl indeed takes an inventory successively of "the givenness of the *cogitatio*," the givenness in recent memory, the givenness of the phenomenal unity in flux, the givenness of the variation of the latter in flux, the givenness of the thing "exterior" to the flux, the givenness specific to re-memberance and imagination, the givenness of logical entities, the givenness of the universal, and even the givenness of absurdity and of logical nonsense. Hence the ultimate but inevitable consequence that "givenness is everywhere [*überall ist die Gegebenheit*]."[42] Like the flow of a tidal wave, givenness submerges all beings and all thought, since the invisible (ἀόρατον) par excellence, the intelligible as λόγος and *idea*, allows itself in a sense to be staged by an intuition that from now on is without limit (in the Kantian sense), without condition (in the Leibnizian sense), and without reserve. Without reserve here means: without keeping anything in the invisibility of withdrawal, but also without maintaining the least self-restraint. Intuition inspects everything and respects nothing; it fulfills the theoretical requirement with a strange sort of barbarism—the flood of presence. One should not be mistaken about the ever more programmatic character of Husserlian phenomenology: it is not a question of any indecision concerning the final direction, nor concerning the means to reach it; the direction is presencing; the sole means is universalized intuition. If the undertaking becomes programmatic, it is because the excessive scope of givenness delivers such a material to constitution that the *Sinngebung* discovers a task that is almost truly infinite—in the measure of the continent opened by the breakthrough. Hence Husserl's troubled and almost anguished appeal to "teams" of investigators, to "generations" of phenomenological workers who would busy themselves in all the available "regions." In this extremely sober way, phenomenology reaches a sort of ὕβρις before the presence that is overabundantly given by intuition. We should cite as confirmation not only what the Second Investigation evokes under the title of the "divine intuition of all [*göttliche Allerschauung*],"[43] but also a text from 1925, which, after having recalled "the task and the significance of the *Logical Investigations*," defines the "method of intuitive generalization [*intuitiven Verallgemeinerung*]" in the following way:

> First it is necessary to disclose what is experienced as a world only in a narrowly limited way [*nur eng begrenzt*] and with unclarified horizons, in such a way that we put possible experience into play, progress from possible evidences to ever new possible evidences and, so to speak, form for ourselves a total picture [*ein Gesamtbild . . . bilden*], an actually

explicated though also openly progressing *total intuition of the world* [*Gesamtanschauung der Welt*]: namely as how it would look all in all [*alles in allem*] and would have to look [*aussehen*] if we fill out the open indefinite horizons with possibilities of experience which fit together harmoniously, whether it be by actually experiencing or by immersing ourselves in any experience by fantasy.[44]

Intuition does not only make objects of the world present, it makes *the* world itself present; intuition does not simply fill in the world, it superimposes itself on the world in order to coincide with the whole worldliness of its presentification. Intuition covers the world only in totalizing it according to a *Gesamtanschauung*, which shows its total picture (*Gesamtbild*) in forming it (*bilden*): it fills the world with presence only inasmuch as it is itself constituted as a world. It makes (*bilden*) the world only in making itself a world. The world is worlded through intuition, which one must therefore recognize as literally universal. Intuition deposits the world into presence, without withdrawal, without remainder, without restraint. The metaphysics of presence is completed in absolute appearance (*Aussehen*)—the world as intuition of the whole, the intuition of the whole as a worlding.

The breakthrough therefore opens only onto the completion of the metaphysics of presence. We rediscover, by a different path, the interpretation proposed by Derrida. On this path, which was not his, the comparison of Husserl with Nietzsche becomes unavoidable, at least in a late (1888–89) and essential fragment, strangely entitled "Wherein I recognize my twin [*meines Gleichen*]."[45] Nietzsche claims to reveal therein "the *hidden* [*verborgene*] history of philosophy," not without some similarity to Husserl, who sets up phenomenology as "the secret [*geheime*] nostalgia of all modern philosophy."[46] Why has there been such a secret, such a hidden face in philosophy up until now? Because in both cases the last metaphysician makes obvious what metaphysics could not, and did not dare, allow to appear. Nietzsche defines his own innovation in quasi-phenomenological terms: "Philosophy, as I have hitherto understood and lived [*erlebt*] it, is a voluntary quest for even the most detested and notorious sides of *Dasein*." Now, does not Husserlian phenomenology aim at the frenzied investigation of the most hidden faces of *Dasein*, in order to submit to the presentifying evidence of intuition what previously no philosophy had even been able to *see* face to face? This undertaking in Nietzsche often passes for negative and, in one sense, rightly so: "Such an experimental philosophy as I live [*lebt*] anticipates experimentally even the possibilities of the most fundamental nihilism; but this does not mean that it must halt at a negation, a No, a will to negation." Similarly, in order to see, and therefore in order to return to the things themselves, Husserlian phenomenology already in 1900–1901 must negate any presupposition, to the point that it soon will carry out, under all its forms, the reduction of thought to the evidence of the given. In both cases, plenary presence first demands the destruction of the shadows that restrict or limit it and therefore obfuscate it. But just as the reduction—that other nihilism that is in the first place negative—leads to constitution and the *Sinngebung*, so Nietzsche completes the "no" with a "yes," the great *Amen*: "It wants rather to cross over to the opposite of this—to a Dionysian affirmation [*Jasagen*] of the world as it is, without subtraction, exception or selection—it wants the eternal circulation:—the same things, the same logic and illogic of entanglements. The highest state a philosopher can attain: to stand in a Dionysian relationship to *Dasein*—my formula for this is *amor fati*." For its part, the phenomenological breakthrough wants "universal intuition," which makes the totality present in an "overall intuition of the world." The evidence of Husserlian givenness also brings about the "sunrise," and leaves but "the shortest shadow," and even eliminates all nonevidence from the world. To the Nietzschean noon corresponds phenomenology's intuition without remainder, just as to Zarathustra's "uncanny and unbounded Yes and Amen [*ungeheure unbegrenzte Ja- und Amen-Sagen*]" there corresponds the originary givenness of the "principle of principles."[47] For in the principle that fixes the highest state that a phenomenologist might attain, it is indeed a question of maintaining that "*everything originarily offered* to us *in 'intuition'* (so to speak, in its carnal actuality) *is to be accepted simply as it gives itself*, but also *only within the limits in which it is given there.*"[48] To receive what is given in the noon of intuition as it is given, neither more (Husserl) nor less (Nietzsche)—exactly, according to the sole "legitimate source of cognition," intuition, in both without limit, remainder or withdrawal. Also, in another fragment devoted to the "highest will to power," and therefore echoing the "highest state," Nietzsche explicitly thinks "'being' as phenomenon ('*Das Seiende' als Schein*),"[49] not without announcing Husserl's end point: "Under the blow of the reduction . . . all the ontologies fall," such that "pure phenomenology as well seems to harbor within itself all the ontologies."[50] Beings find their "legitimate source" only in allowing themselves to be reduced to intuition, and therefore made present, with neither remainder nor withdrawal, in the (just) measure that they are given—in short, in appearing as phenomena. Destruction and monstration are spoken equally by the ambivalence of *Schein*, "mere semblance" but also "appearance." Nothing is that does not appear, nothing appears that is not. Therefore the "broadened" intuition and/or the "unbounded yes" set the norm for the Being of beings by ensuring its perfect presence. In order to complete the metaphysics of presence, Nietzsche can therefore recognize as his most strange but no doubt most unavoidable twin—Husserl.

At least in outline, we have thus attained the answer to our first question: the breakthrough of the *Investigations* completes the "metaphysics of presence" by broadening intuition to the point that it manages, in an echo of Nietzsche's "great *Amen*," to place the totality of beings in presence.

4. A Misunderstanding of Signification?

There remains a second question: the completion of the primacy of intuition as universal presentification, a primacy that indisputably characterizes the breakthrough of the *Investigations*, a primacy that we have underscored even more clearly (if that is possible) than did Derrida, a primacy, finally, that affiliates a nascent phenomenology with a Nietzsche coming to his end—does this completion suffice to make the breakthrough of 1900–1901 fall entirely, immediately, and forever back into metaphysics, itself understood as a "metaphysics of presence"? This question can be understood correctly only by adding two remarks to it.

1. The definition of metaphysics by the primacy of presence in it and the claim to identify metaphysics as a unifying form of all philosophy sends us back to Heidegger's thought, without which these ideas would have remained unworkable; therefore, any use of these notions implies taking a position with respect to their initiator. Now it happens that, in returning the breakthrough of the *Investigations* to the closed field of metaphysics, Derrida makes use of the Heideggerian notions without justifying their tactical reprise and without admitting their intrinsic pertinence. Should we speak in general of a "metaphysics of presence"? Should we speak of one in Husserl? Can we speak of one as early as the *Investigations*? These prejudicial questions are not posed. Nor would they so much need to be if Derrida took up the entire Heideggerian strategy for his own use. But precisely, Derrida himself thinks too originally to do so without reservation. For if he accepts the notion of the "metaphysics of presence," he rejects just as radically Heidegger's understanding of the *Investigations*: far from seeing in them the first fruits of a "new beginning," he unveils in them the pure and simple completion of metaphysics—as, precisely, the unveiling of beings in presence. This double and strongly contrasted usage of Heideggerian theses is surprising; it can without any doubt be justified, but it also no doubt does not receive an explicit legitimation in *Speech and Phenomena*.[51] In other words, one needs to ask

about this paradox: In reading the *Investigations*, how can we play one Heideggerian thesis (the "metaphysics of presence") against another (the categorial intuition of Being as the outline of a "new beginning")? We will not claim to resolve this paradox, but we will allow its strange light to illuminate our argument.

2. Besides, Derrida's interpretation largely escapes the simplism that we are attributing to it. For Derrida, the *Investigations* in fact fall back into metaphysics only inasmuch as they have first attained the outer edge of the field of presence; they return to metaphysics only because they fail to transgress that field, for "Husserl describes, and in one and the same movement effaces, the emancipation of speech [*discours*] as nonknowing." By such a "speech as nonknowing" one must understand more precisely—and this distortion might appear as surprising as it is remarkable—the status of signification (*Bedeutung, meinen*), which is valid without the confirmation of an intuition and therefore without the foundation of a presencing; Husserl was no doubt the first (which, by the way, Derrida does not specify) to have understood that "it belongs to the original structure of expression to be able to dispense with the full presence of the object aimed at by intuition"; or again, that "the absence of intuition . . . is not only *tolerated* by speech, it is *required* by the general structure of signification, when considered *in itself*."[52] Husserl's step forward would liberate signification from presence. The step back—for Husserl would recoil before his own audacity within the *Investigations* themselves—would reestablish for signification an obligatory confirmation by intuition, and therefore it would censure the autonomy of signification, or rather, to say it with Derrida, "the sign would be foreign to that self-presence, the foundation of presence in general." In order thus to reconstruct the double but simultaneous movement of a breakthrough (toward ideal signification) and of a retreat (before the originally nonoriginal *différance* of the sign), Derrida must implicitly introduce, skillfully, two crucial decisions. First he must lead the definition of signification back to that of the sign or of "speech" [*discours*]; this equivalence, moreover, governs his interpretation much more profoundly than that to which he nevertheless gives priority between the sign endowed with signification (*Zeichen*) and the indication deprived of any "quality of figuration" (*Anzeige*); for before deciding whether indication constitutes the ultimate truth of the significant sign, or the inverse, it remains to be demonstrated that the essence of signification plays first and completely in the figures of the sign. This is self-evident for Derrida but not for Husserl.[53] Next, Derrida must presuppose that intuition governs the "metaphysics of presence" through and through, and therefore that intuition alone completes presencing.

But does intuition constitute the last word concerning presence, at least for Husserl?

It seems to us that these two decisions sustain Derrida's entire reading of the *Investigations*. They would equally merit a close discussion. Nevertheless, since they in fact first determine the point of departure proper to Derrida's itinerary (if "property" didn't sound *here* like the impropriety par excellence), and since we are concerned only with the assignation of its stakes to the Husserlian breakthrough, we will occupy ourselves only with the second of these decisions, without concealing how much the first is worthy of question, and without forgetting it entirely. Indeed, the equivalence maintained by Derrida between intuition and presence raises a formidable difficulty in situating signification within phenomenology itself. What status can Husserl grant to signification when, on the one hand, he establishes it apart from any confirming intuition, and when, on the other hand, thanks to its "broadening" to the level of a "total intuition, *Gesamtanschauung*," intuition becomes the universal presencing? In other words, if signification signifies without intuition (such would be the breakthrough according to Derrida), if presence is given universally through intuition (such seemed to us Husserl's breakthrough), what remainder of presence, what mode of Being, in short what place would still belong in particular to signification? The step back would result almost necessarily from this aporia, which Derrida renders unavoidable, whereas Heidegger seems not even to divine it. It is necessary to pose *one* question to the *Investigations*: Does the "broadening" of intuition to the dimensions of a world not radically contradict the autonomy (the ideality) of signification? What presence can still accommodate "intentional" and especially significant "nonexistence" when intuition exhausts all presence? In short, since signification dispenses with presence, and therefore with Being, signification could do without intuition only in doing without itself. This is the aporia. Derrida leads us to it, and Derrida alone. Nevertheless, it seems to us that he responds to it with an elegance that is in some way too quick and too easy to do justice to the question which thus arises. According to that response, encountering "the *différance* . . . that is always older than presence," Husserl would have "turned away from" the "consequences" thereof, as one turns away from an obstacle. The "intuitionist imperative," the authentic categorical imperative of metaphysics, would have held back the breakthrough at the threshold of *différance*, and from the beginning "the originality of meaning as an aim is limited by the telos of vision. To be radical, the difference that separates intention from intuition would nevertheless have to be *pro-visional*."[54] Do such a self-contradiction on Husserl's part and such a half-conscious repentance offer the only possible picture? No doubt, at least if intuition constitutes the last word of presence; within this hypothesis alone signification must either turn toward *différance* or else fall back under the intuitionist yoke. This hypothesis—which Derrida indisputably presupposes as the horizon of the aporia that he constructs—characterizes metaphysics precisely as a "metaphysics of presence": Being amounts to being present, and presence amounts to intuition. Before this hypothesis, two paths still open up for interpretation. Either Husserl can only go back on his decision in contradicting the autonomy of signification by the "broadening" of intuition; and he would admit thereby to recognizing as unsurpassable the metaphysical hypothesis of presence through intuition. Or else Husserl would confront the status of signification only because he would have *already* transgressed the primacy of intuition with regard to presence in a manner all the more decisive in that it would liberate signification from intuition only after having completed the most metaphysical "broadening" of the latter; in this case, the irreducibility of signification to intuition would not contradict the universality of the mode of intuitive presence but would attest, by transgression, that intuition, as universal as it might be, does not constitute the ultimate name of presence. Even without being seen through intuition, signification could still *be*. Could Being therefore be made manifest, already in the *Investigations*, otherwise than through intuition, even categorial, in a mode that is attested above all in signification?—Since this interpretative path was not followed, even by the one who *a contrario* renders it possible, let us take it.

5. Presence without Intuition

Whatever the universality of intuition might be, it admits an exteriority that is all the more irreducible in that it is preserved by "a phenomenologically irreducible difference," which, through a "total separation," leads to "the opposition between intuition and signification."[55] Of all the oppositions to which the *Investigations* lead, that which separates signification from intuition precedes those that follow, all three of which concern the diverse forms of intuition alone. The couples of sensuous/categorial intuition, adequate/inadequate intuition, and general/individual intuition do not place in question the isolation of signification; they place it in evidence, inasmuch as they presuppose it. The intuitive extraterritoriality of signification is indicated at the end of the *Investigations*, when the last Investigation has just gained the categorial intuition, which, far from bringing signification back under the intuitionist yoke, underscores, in extending itself to the most extreme significations, that it never "fulfills" and "coincides with" them except in granting them the a priori right to delimit the spaces to be saturated thus with presence. The phenomeno-logical possibilities of error and deception, of adequate or partial fulfill-ment, etc., imply that signification precedes intuition and that, even when filled with an intuitive given, it receives therefrom first a confirmation of itself, and therefore of its sense. The convenient formula $i + s = I$, with its extreme variations according to whether $i = o$ or $s = o$, should not lead us into error: signification does not vary in inverse proportion to intuition; intuition can give only what it has, and it can give that only to what it is not—the always earlier signification.[56] Thus the irreducibility of signification to intuition is affirmed as early as the First Investigation, which announces "important [distinctions] that concern the possible relations between signification and the intuition that illustrates it and perhaps renders it evident." It next recognizes that in this way "there is constituted . . . an act of signification which finds support in the intuitive content of the representation of the word, but which differs in essence (*wesentlich verschieden*) from the intuitive intention directed upon the word itself."[57] Signification is opposed irreducibly to intuition and there-fore, by that negation, is itself defined as the other of intuition, from the beginning to the end of the *Investigations*. Before intuition, as universal as it may be, there remains, irreducible, signification. How was this actual decision thinkable?

Because an act of signification "is constituted without need of a fulfilling or illustrative intuition," signification displays an autonomy of which intuition offers only an "eventual" complement.[58] In expression or in perception, signification is always fulfilled, and contrary to the convictions of natural consciousness, intuition either lacks totally or else is partially missing and, in any case, comes to offer itself as an addition. "Each assertion, whether representing an exercise of knowledge or not—whether or not, i.e., it fulfills or can fulfill its intention in corresponding intuitions and the categorial acts that give them form—has its intention [*ihre Meinung hat*] and constitutes in that intention, as its specific uni-fied character, its signification [*die Bedeutung konstituiert*]."[59] Intention depends so little on intuition to complete itself as the aim of a signi-fication that it precedes fulfillment; intention dispenses with intuition and therefore can "eventually" render its addition possible. The clearest confirmation of the "inadequacy [*Unangemessenheit*] of illustration [*Veran-schaulichung*] even in the case of consistent significations,"[60] comes with examples from geometry: no mathematical ideality can find an adequate fulfillment in actually experienced space; inadequacy, and therefore the surpassing of intuition by intention, and its being exceeded by signifi-cation, far from constituting an exception, announces an absolute rule:

the signification of *straight line*, or of *curve of the equation ax + b*, or even of *triangle*, will never meet an adequate fulfillment in the experiences of intuition that are actually realized by a consciousness. No doubt, the equation will continually find fulfilling intuitions, but in each case that will be for a particular value of unknowns, never for its abstract, universal essence as such. As for figure, it is clear that no empirical line will ever come to fulfill its signification intuitively; even more, it will very quickly become impossible even to have an imaginary presentification of it (the chiliagon that Descartes can no longer imagine and that he must simply understand). Mathematical understanding, on the contrary, is properly characterized by its capacity to think significations that remain irreducible to any intuition. This capacity is all the more remarkable in that the paradox grows deeper: not only is it a matter of thinking mathematical idealities as such, and therefore as significations that in principle extend beyond any intuitive fulfillment, but even more, it is a matter of thinking them as evident and as more evidently thinkable than intuition could ever make them; not only are mathematical significations thinkable, or better thinkable *only* without adequate intuition, but they are so in full evidence:

> we are appealing [*in Anspruch nehmen*] to this state of things as to an immediately graspable truth, following in this the evidence [*Evidenz*] that is the final authority in all questions of knowledge. I see evidently [*ich sehe ein*] that in repeated acts of representation and judgment I mean or can mean [*meine, bzw. meinen kann*] identically the same [*dasselbe*], the same concept or proposition; I see evidently [*ich sehe ein*] that, for example, wherever there is talk of the *proposition* or *truth* that "π *is a transcendental number*,' there is nothing I have less in mind [*im Auge*] than an individual experience, or a feature of an individual experience of any person. I see evidently [*ich sehe ein*] that such reflective talk really has as its object what serves as a signification in straightforward talk. Finally, I see evidently [*ich sehe ein*] that what I mean [*meine*] in the mentioned proposition or [when I hear it] what I grasp as its signification [*als seine Bedeutung*] is the same thing, whether I think and exist or not, and whether or not there are *any* thinking persons and acts to think them.[61]

Phenomenological evidence is realized, at least here, without a fulfilling intuition or an intuition-experience, because the ideality of the object—in fact and in principle, the ideality of any signification—depends neither on an intuition nor on an intuiting agent. As early as the First Investigation, signification attains an evidence that is strictly autonomous because definitively ideal and intentional. Does not the "confusion of signification with fulfilling intuition" that is stigmatized by Husserl in Erdmann and Sigwart, for example, anticipate more clearly the diagnostic that Derrida thinks himself able to formulate—"The originality of meaning is limited by the *telos* of vision"?[62] Doesn't Husserl immediately criticize as nonphenomenological the confusion that Derrida nevertheless attributes to him, according to an anachronism that is as exemplary as it is ideal?

The autonomy of intention, of meaning, and therefore of signification can even find an indisputable confirmation in the very text that Derrida invokes to denounce the "subtle displacement" through which, finally, for Husserl "the true and genuine meaning [*vouloir-dire*] [would be] the will to say the truth [*le vouloir dire vrai*]." At issue here is a passage from the First Investigation, § 11, which, by the way, is significantly entitled "The ideal distinctions between expression and signification as ideal unities." In fact, the passage quoted by Derrida contradicts the presumed ideal status of signification, which it is supposed to illustrate; let us therefore cite the chosen sequence: "If 'possibility' or 'truth' is lacking, an assertion's intention can only be carried out symbolically: it cannot derive any 'fullness' from intuition or from the categorial functions performed on the latter, in which 'fullness' its value for knowledge consists. It then lacks, as one says [*wie man zu sagen pflegt*] a 'true,' a 'genuine' *Bedeutung*."[63] From this Derida immediately concludes that *for Husserl* signification holds its genuine and final truth, at least *here*, from the fullness of the intuition that serves as a foundation. But Husserl's text seems to us to say just the opposite, as the following points prove. (1) The thesis stated here is not that of the phenomenologist, but indeed that of natural consciousness, explicitly named in a central phrase: "as one says [*wie man zu sagen pflegt*]." (2) The terms brought up by Derrida to establish the subjection of signification (meaning) to signification fulfilled by intuition (true meaning) only appear in quotation marks: "true," "genuine," "symbolic," "possibility," and "truth" are here used *wrongly* by those who, precisely, do not follow the ideal distinctions; *Husserl's* thesis will therefore consist, conversely, in refusing to refuse a signification its "truth" under the pretext that it lacks a fulfilling intuition. (3) Moreover, this is precisely what he does in the immediately following text, which is omitted by Derrida's quotation. He does this first in announcing the next developments: "Later we shall look more closely into this distinction between intending and fulfilling signification. To characterize the various acts in which the relevant ideal unities are constituted, and to throw light on the essence of their actual 'coincidence' in knowledge, will call for difficult, comprehensive studies." As is often the case in the First Investigation, here we find a reference to the Sixth, in this case to the first chapter of the first part, actually entitled "Signification-Intention and Signification-Fulfillment." Next, and in anticipation of the complete argument, Husserl dogmatically posits his own thesis, which absolutely contradicts the opinion of natural consciousness and therefore also the thesis that Derrida wrongly attributes to him: "It is certain, however [*Sicher aber ist*], that each assertion, whether representing an exercise of knowledge or not—whether or not, i.e., it fulfills or can fulfill its intention in corresponding intuitions, and the categorial acts that give form to these— has its intention [*ihre Meinung*] and constitutes its signification [*die Bedeutung konstituiert*] in that intention as its specific unified character." Unless one wants to claim that Husserl contradicts himself word for word within a couple lines, one must acknowledge that if, finally, it is "certain" that every expression has an intention, and therefore a signification, whether *or not* it has an intuitive fulfillment, then the converse opinion, mentioned above in an intentionally loose language—signification becomes "true" only by finding its foundation in intuition—must be taken not as Husserl's conclusion but as the error that he criticizes. (4) The passage whose integrity we have just reestablished is framed by formulas that leave no room for any doubt. A few lines lower, Husserl invokes "the evidently grasped ideal unity" that one must not confuse with real judgment. A few lines higher, he evokes the "ideal content, the signification of the statement as a unity in diversity," in order to add the decisive point: "we do not arbitrarily attribute it to our statements, but discover it in them [*sondern finden sie darin*]."[64] We conclude therefore that if "displacement" there must be in § 11 of the First Investigation, it is not "subtle" but on the contrary fairly crude, as is suitable to a position that is explicitly *rejected* by Husserl.

If this text leads to what must indeed be called a misinterpretation, the reason for it could not be a run-of-the-mill oversight. On the contrary, it is through an overly selective attention that Derrida isolates the antithesis in order to turn it into one of Husserl's own theses; indeed, he proceeds starting from the interpretation of another text of decisive importance and difficulty: § 26 of the First Investigation, which is dedicated to "essentially occasional and objective expressions." Husserl here stresses that any expression including a personal (or a demonstrative) pronoun ceases to intend *one* signification; for the meaningful sign there is substituted a meaningless sign, whose "indicative [*anzeigende*] function," or whose "universally effective indication [*allgemein wirksames Anzeichen*]," indicates an infinity of possible significations only because it does not signify (and show) any that are self-identical. Here the sign lacks signification. Husserl adds a sequence that Derrida privileges: "The word *I* names a different person from case to case, and it does so by way of an ever new *Bedeutung*."

But then can one legitimately ask about the source of a signification that is always arising because never given in the statement? Husserl's answer is cited immediately by Derrida: "What on each occasion constitutes its *Bedeutung* can be gleaned only from the living discourse [*lebendige Rede*] and from the intuitive data [*anschaulichen Umständen*, intuitive circumstances] that are a part of it. When we read this word without knowing who wrote it, we have a word that is, if not lacking *Bedeutung* [*bedeutungslos*], at least foreign to its normal *Bedeutung*." Signification therefore does indeed depend *here* on intuition; and it is Derrida who concludes that "Husserl's premises should sanction our saying exactly the contrary."[65]

And yet this objection seems to us weak for several reasons. (1) The absence of signification, in fact indisputable here, and therefore the eventual recourse to intuition to fix it, here has to do with a very particular case: the indeterminacy of the *this* (or of the *I*), such as Hegel, for example, already pointed it out; this type of expression is characterized not by the reduction of signification to intuition, but by the absolute and radical absence of signification itself; it is called an "essential" absence by Husserl, who makes of it less a particular and privileged case of *all* expression (as is supposed by the generalization undertaken by his critic) than an exception to the normal system of expression, or even a veritable nonexpression; if there is no expression without signification—for "the essence of an expression lies solely in its signification"[66]—the essentially occasional expressions must be understood as essentially *non*expressive. They therefore could not call the doctrine of expression into question because they simply do not pertain to it. (2) One should be surprised that the *I* cannot in itself have a signification at its disposal all the less insofar as, in the *Investigations* at least, the *I*, reduced to a simple "complex of experiences," has no ideal signification (as transcendental *I*), with the result that "there is nothing to remark" about the *I* as the meeting point of completed acts.[67] One would have to oppose another paradox to the alleged paradox denounced by Derrida: Husserl's premises concerning the status of the *I* would have to force us to acknowledge the essentially nonexpressive character of the occasional expressions where it occurs. (3) The weakness of the signification of the *I*, irremediable in the First Investigation, is nevertheless not Husserl's last word in 1901; interpreters cannot remain silent about the resumption of the same question in § 5, addendum, of the Sixth Investigation, which explicitly retrieves § 26 from the First Investigation; in this text, which we will not take up here in all of its difficulty, Husserl attempts at least partially to reintroduce signification into indication. He does this first by opposing to the hearer of the *I*, who receives only a "universal and indeterminate thought" and therefore depends on an intuition to constitute signification, the speaker who himself receives the indication as given and immediately possesses "the 'indicated' signification [*die 'angezeigte' Bedeutung*]": he does not have the indication of a signification that is not given, but the givenness of a signification in the sole mode of indication; in short, indication does not always exclude signification, inasmuch as indicated. He does so next by sketching a phenomenology of "indicated intention," as much in mathematics as in the simple deictics of the *this*.[68]

In short, the text privileged by Derrida, while certainly difficult, does not fundamentally call into question the ideal autonomy of signification; it would even be necessary to stress that, at the very moment one meets an objection that is as old (Hegel) as it is formidable, Husserl—even if he concedes at first (and how could he avoid it?) that the expression including an *I* does not offer by itself any "normal signification"—warns nevertheless, even before this step back, that it is in any case not a matter of a "meaningless word [*nicht ein bedeutungslos*]."[69] Without, obviously, claiming to exhaust all the arguments that would support it, and without refuting all those that would challenge it, we will hold to a single thesis: in the *Logical Investigations*, signification is given evidently without depending on fulfilling intuition. Even without intuition, "we find it there," to speak like the First Investigation. Similarly, it does not owe anything either to the "phonic complex," to speak like the Sixth Investigation, for "signification cannot, as it were, hang in the air, but for what it signifies, the sign, whose signification we call it, is entirely indifferent."[70] Without intuition, signification is nevertheless not disseminated according to the anomic rhythm of the differences of the signifier. In other words, signification offers a "content" that is sometimes characterized as an "ideal content," sometimes understood "as intending sense, or as sense," sometimes identified with a "theoretical content" or a "logical content"—in all cases, "the essence of signification is seen by us, not in the meaning-conferring experience [*bedeutungverleihenden Erlebnis*], but in its 'content,' which presents [*darstellt*] an identical intentional unity."[71] Signification has a content (*Inhalt, Gehalt*); it holds it in itself and by itself; it does not hold this content like the tenure it possesses so much as it maintains itself in it, and in order to maintain itself in it it holds in and to it alone. The maintenance of signification, without intuition, indication or enunciative act, is sufficient for it to present itself (*sich darstellt*) in presence. But is it really legitimate to speak here of presence, without any presentation instituting it? Perhaps it would be suitable to reverse the question: What mode of presence is deployed sui generis when signification, by itself and itself alone, presents itself?

6. The Evidence of Givenness

Thus, according to a mode of presence that is still undetermined and that, for this very reason, might not be defined exactly by the word "presence," "each signification can be thought completely [*vollzogen*] without the least correlative intuition." This thesis from the Sixth Investigation is confirmed by another that explicitly takes up again the conclusions of the First Investigation: "*What is here the act in which signification resides?* I think we must say, in harmony with points established in our First Investigation, that it does not reside in perception, at least not in perception alone."[72] In other words, "signification cannot first [*nicht erst*] have been acquired [*sich vollzogen*] through intuition," because, conversely, "first there is given, and given for itself, the signification-intention; only then [*dann erst*] does the corresponding intuition come to join in."[73] The anteriority of signification over any intuition, ensured by signification's independence, alone explains the *last* word of the First Investigation: whatever be the broadening of intuition, "there are [*es gibt*] . . . countless significations which . . . can never be expressed."[74] The signification that "we find there" is constituted by itself, in a mode of advance that is without condition because, even though pure of intuition, it attains "the final authority in questions of knowledge: evidence." The decisive point here is this: as an actual though nonreal object, signification ultimately appears in full evidence, in the form of "an evidently [*einsichtig*] grasped ideal unity . . . which evidently stands before us [*mit Evidenz . . . gegenübersteht*] in its unity and identity [*als Eine und Selbige*]."[75] Phenomenologically, evidence can allow itself anything—in the capacity of final authority—and therefore it can also allow anything—in its capacity as universal choreographer of the visible. It allows itself to make known that significations "must necessarily *exist*, that is, present [*darstellen*] a unitary sense." The autonomy (*Selbige*) in which the unity of sense culminates stems from its sufficiency for entering into visibility (*darstellen*); therefore, since Being is phenomenologically reduced to evidence, signification exists insofar as it signifies by itself: " . . . significations that actually are—that are as significations [*wirklich seiende Bedeutungen—seiend als Bedeutungen*]." In his breakthrough, Husserl reaches Being *before* the Sixth Investigation, and therefore before the categorial intuition, when the Fourth Investigation manages to distinguish the "independent [*selbständigen*]" significations in their specificity; for because of its independence, "signification itself exists in person."[76] The phenomenological placing-in-evidence reaches Being as existence as soon as it reaches signification as independent, precisely because its independence qualifies it as an actual being. Signification is broadened not only to meaning offered without intuition, but even to its acceptation as the actuality of a being. Meaning, as such, has the validity of a being, which consecrates the absolute independence of signification against any presupposition—including and especially intuition. Would it be necessary to go so far as to take intuition as a presupposition to be reduced, in order that there appear the final given of signification?

We thus approach what nevertheless could indeed open up an understanding of the breakthrough of 1900–1901. If it is definitively established that the breakthrough first accomplishes the universal broadening of intuition, we would nevertheless have to envisage the hypothesis that signification also (even especially) is broadened to the point of actually existing as a strictly autonomous being. Everything happens as if intuition were liberated from sensuousness only—according to a paradox still to be considered—in order to allow signification then to be liberated from intuition. And natural consciousness no doubt puts up as much resistance to this second broadening as to the first. Nevertheless, it is necessary to yield to the evidence—to the evidence of evidence—that a text confirms: *"The realm of signification is, however, much wider [sehr viel umfassender] than that of intuition."*[77] The difficulty of such a thought does not result from its lack of evidence but, quite the opposite, from an excess of evidence in it. There is an excess first of the evidence of intuition over the limits of sensuousness, so far as to be established as a total universal intuition (*Gesamtanschauung*). Next there is an excess of signification that exists beyond intuition, with which it essentially dispenses—the "draft drawn on intuition" is regularly honored by signification all the less insofar as, in principle, the latter is not held to draw it. Finally, and especially, there is an excess of the second excess over the first: incomprehensibly, signification surpasses—by far—the total field of intuition; but how can a field that is *already* broadened and *already* total be transgressed? How are we to avoid the contradiction between the broadening of intuition and the broadening of signification? "The unresolved tension of the two major motifs in phenomenology: the purity of formalism and the radicality of intuitionism"[78] becomes insurmountable as soon as one admits that, in principle if not in fact, intuition here completes metaphysics by no longer tolerating any remainder—any fringe still available to mark the vastness of the realm of signification. To where would this realm extend itself if intuition already covers and discovers everything, including the categorial, in evidence alone? For, precisely, evidence could seem here to spring from *two* sources: intuition or signification—two sources that are autonomous to the point of competing for primacy. In the last phase of his own continual reinterpretation of the *Investigations*, Husserl characterizes them according to a feature that, through its very indeterminacy, easily lends itself to such a contradiction:

> What is new in the *Logical Investigations* . . . is found not at all in the merely ontological investigations . . . , but rather in the subjectively directed investigations (above all the fifth and sixth, in the second volume of 1901) in which, for the first time, the *cogitata qua cogitata*, as essential moments of any conscious experience . . . come into their own and immediately come to dominate the whole method of intentional analysis. Thus "self-evidence" (that petrified logical idol) is made a problem here for the first time, freed [*befreit*] from the privilege given to scientific evidence and broadened to mean original self-giving in general [*zur allgemeinen originalen Selbstgebung erweitert*].[79]

That evidence is freed from the limits of natural consciousness for the first time with the breakthrough of the *Investigations*, very well; that it is broadened to the point of coinciding with any self-givenness, originally and universally, very well again; but must the ultimate "broadening" of evidence be understood as the "broadening" of intuition (to the categorial, such as the mention of the Fifth and Sixth Investigations invites us to believe) *or* as the broadening of the realm of signification, "more vast—by far—than that of intuition"? The broadening seems so wide—an unconditional amnesty that would free indiscriminately everything that, like so many captives, metaphysical requirements had fettered—that it "does not want to know" what it frees, or at the very least does not identify or declare it. To what exactly does the "broadening" give free rein? The simple mention of a universal *Selbstgebung* does not answer this question: to the contrary, the indeterminacy of the universality in it underscores the unresolved ambiguity of the evidence. Does the breakthrough of 1900–1901 remain obscure due to an excess of evidence? Would phenomenology, far from resolving the conflict between them, merely exacerbate the irreducibility of formality and intuitionism, by confusing them within an obscure evidence that is universal but vague?

The same interpretation of the *Investigations* that confirms the aporia no doubt also opens the way out. A little beforehand, in fact, a note from the *Krisis*, a note that is decisive in other respects, fixes the breakthrough of 1900–1901 in its origins: "The first breakthrough of this universal correlational a priori of the object of experience and of the modes of givenness [*dieses universalen Korrelationsapriori von Erfahrungsgegenstand und Gegebenheitsweisen*] (while I was working on my *Logical Investigations*, around 1898) struck me so profoundly that, ever since, my whole life's work has been dominated by this task of elaborating the correlational *a priori*." The body of the paragraph confirms this interpretation: "Never before (that is, never before the first breakthrough [*durchbruch*] of 'transcendental phenomenology' in the *Logical Investigations*) has the correlation of the world (the world of which we speak) with its modes of subjective givenness [*subjektiven Gegebenheitsweisen*] provoked philosophical amazement." The *Investigations* accomplish their breakthrough not first by broadening intuition or by recognizing the autonomy of signification, but by being amazed, as by a "wonder of wonders," by a correlation. Which one? One should not rush here to find the noema/noesis correlation (dominant in the *Ideen),* nor the intuition/intention correlation (prevalent in the *Investigations);* these correlations, decisive as they are, are rendered possible by a more essential relation, about which Husserl belatedly discovered that it governed the breakthrough of 1900–1901 from the beginning: "the correlation between *appearing and that which appears as such.*"[80] Appearing (*Aussehen)* no longer counts as a datum [*une donée*] for the single conscious subject, but first as the givenness of what thus appears: the appearing, through the correlation that merits the full title of "phenomenological," *gives* that which appears. Or again, that which appears, nothing less than an actual being, appears in person in the appearance, because, according to a necessity of essence (the correlation), it gives itself therein. Phenomenology begins in 1900–1901 because, for the first time, thought sees that which appears appear in appearance; it manages to do this only by conceiving the appearing itself no longer as a "given *of* consciousness," but indeed as the givenness *to* consciousness (or even *through* consciousness) of the thing itself, given in the mode of appearing and in all of its dimensions (intuition, intention, and their variations): "Beings, whatever their concrete or abstract, real or ideal sense, have their own modes of self-givenness in person [*Weisen der Selbstgegebenheit*].”[81] The phenomenological breakthrough consists neither in the broadening of intuition, nor in the autonomy of signification, but solely in the unconditional primacy of the givenness of the phenomenon. Intuition and intention, as liberated as they may be, are so only through the givenness that they illustrate—or rather that never ceases to illuminate them—and of which they deliver only modes—the "modes of givenness" of that which appears. Intuition and intention would give nothing (and therefore would not have themselves to be given) if everything did not have first, by virtue of the principle of correlation, to be given in order to appear. Givenness precedes intuition and intention because they make sense only for and through an appearance, which counts as the appearing of something that appears (a phenomenon being) only by virtue of the principle of correlation— and therefore of givenness. From now on, seeming [*paraître*] no longer belongs to the domain of semblance [*apparence*], since, in the capacity of an arrival at seeming [*paraître*], it issues from appearing [*apparaître*] and therefore from something that appears. This thing that appears, correlated to its apparition [*apparition*] through the appearing itself, does not deceive in its apparition—as tenuous as the appearance may be (partial intuition, empty intention)—because it gives itself therein. Givenness alone—as it operates in the correlation—loads semblance [*apparence*] with its seriousness as an apparition: there is never an appearing without something that appears, and there is never something that appears (something appearable, if we might risk the neologism) without an apparition. Givenness is thus executed phenomenologically through the strict play of the correlation between what appears (given to give) and the apparition in the semblance. Givenness alone is absolute, free and without condition, precisely because it gives. In 1907 Husserl will say it clearly: "Absolute givenness [*Gegebenheit*] is an ultimate." Or, reciprocally: "The 'seeing' or grasping of what is self-given in person [*Selbstgegebenes*], insofar as it is actual 'seeing,' actual self-givenness [*Selbstgegebenheit*] in the strictest sense, and not another sort of givenness [*Gegebenheit*] which points to something that is not given—that is an ultimate. That is *what is understood absolutely by itself* [*Selbstverständlichkeit*]." The reduction itself would exercise no priority if it did not lead the phenomenon to its final givenness: "*the givenness* [*die Gegebenheit*] *of any reduced phenomenon is an absolute and indubitable givenness.*"[82] In 1913, the "principle of principles" privileges intuition only to the extent that it interprets intuition first as "originarily giving" and admits as one of its formulations a definition that starts directly from givenness: "We see indeed [*Sehen wir doch ein*] that each theory can only again draw its truth from originary data (or: givennesses? [*Gegebenheiten*])."[83] Already in 1900–1901 givenness preceded ("eventual") intuition as much as it did signification, since "for consciousness the given remains essentially equal [*das Gegebene ein wesentlich Gleiches*], whether the represented object exists, or is made up and even perhaps absurd."[84] For both must allow themselves to be reinterpreted as two modes of the one givenness which alone is originary.

Intuition is opened to its "broadening" only inasmuch as it is given first as a mode of givenness: "Thus, when the signification-intention is fulfilled in a corresponding intuition, in other words, when expression, in the current operation of naming, is related to the given object [*auf den gegebenen Gegenstand*], the object is then constituted as 'given' [*als 'gegebener'*] in certain acts, and in truth [*zwar*] it is *given* to us in them—if at any rate the expression actually fits the intuitive given [*dem auschaulich Gegebenen*]—in *the same mode* according to which it is aimed at by signification."[85] In such a text, givenness very clearly marks its anteriority by defining each of the terms to be considered: the object, already "given" in signification, is found " 'given' " anew by intuition, in "the same mode" as the latter; the subtle play of quotation marks alone indicates the divergence between two givennesses, as discretely as is required by the unique dative character of the originary phenomenality. The "object at once intended and 'given,'" or the "meant objectity (which is 'given' to us in evident cognition)"[86] always remains given in the fulfilling intuition because it was in fact *already* in the signification. The "broadening" of intuition does not contradict the autonomy of signification but rather implies it: in both cases it is a question solely of the originary givenness, which can increase one of its modes only by increasing the other—which conditions the first. Intuition can be broadened only by broadening its fulfillment, and therefore by depending on the meant spaces to be fulfilled. If intuition must give, it is therefore already and especially necessary that significations be released, and therefore that they be already given, without intuition and in full autonomy. And in fact, "first there is given, and given for itself, the signification-intention; it is only then that there intervenes, in addition, the corresponding intuition," for "there are significations [*es gibt also . . . Bedeutungen*]."[87] Nothing precedes givenness, which is modulated in all the modes of the phenomenon, whatever they might be. More "broadened" than intuition, more autonomous than signification, givenness gives the phenomenon through itself because it falls thoroughly to givenness to deal the thing in person. In their ultimate advance, the *Investigations* will equate the *Selbstdarstellung* or the *Selbsterscheinung des Gegenstandes*[88] with its *Selbstgegebenheit*, where "something appears as actual and as *given* in person [*als selbst gegeben*]." We should understand the syntagm *aktuelles Gegebensein*[89] in its strictest acceptation: only given Being is fulfilled, as a presencing in the metaphysically insurmountable mode of the act. To the question concerning the mode of presence that is irreducible to intuition, or even concerning the legitimacy of the term "presence," we can therefore outline a response: already in the *Investigations* Husserl determines presence by going beyond intuition to the point of attributing it to signification only because he passes beyond both in favor of givenness. Everything that reveals itself as given, inasmuch as already given, appears, because inasmuch as given to seem, it is. To be—to be in presence, since in metaphysics the two are equivalent— amounts to the givenness that gives to the given the opportunity to appear. One must no doubt recognize here one last figure of the "metaphysics of presence," and confirm Derrida's interpretation. But with two small remarks. (1) Presence is nevertheless not reduced to intuition, to the detriment of autonomous signification; presence triumphs as much in signification as in intuition; the whole of the *Investigations* therefore belongs to the domain of metaphysics. Derrida's interpretation remains, paradoxically, *not* radical *enough* (supposing signification to be broken off from presence, and therefore excepted from metaphysics), because it still contributes to an overly narrow understanding of presence which misses the properly Husserlian deepening of presence as a givenness. It remains the case that, without that interpretation, the Husserlian deepening of presence as givenness would itself have no doubt remained unapproachable. We must therefore confirm Derrida's conclusion—phenomenology remains a "metaphysics of presence"—all the while contesting its principal argument—the reduction of presence to intuition alone. *Here,* and precisely because it is realized in the name of all metaphysics, presence yields to givenness. (2) But if presence culminates in a givenness where the given appears, if therefore the "metaphysics of presence" is completed without remainder with the breakthrough of the *Logical Investigations,* how are we to understand the fact that Heidegger was able to recognize in them his own point of departure, as much during his Marburg courses as during his last seminar, in 1973? Would he have missed givenness as the completion of the primacy of presence? Would he have taken for a break with metaphysics that which seems to us, with Derrida, its unreserved realization? Thus arises the last question.

7. Givenness as a Question

Heidegger himself at least twice recognized in the breakthrough of the *Investigations* the necessary (although insufficient) condition of the "new beginning" that was *Sein und Zeit.* In 1925, in his summer semester course, he salutes "what is decisive in the discovery of categorial intuition" in the fact that it "gives a ground." In 1973, in the final so-called Zähringen seminar, he confirms that "by this *tour de force* [of Husserl] . . . I finally had a ground."[90] It thus seems to be self-evident, as much for Heidegger as for his interpreters, that categorial *intuition,* by fixing the Being itself at work in the expression, defines the hyphen—tenuous but obstinate—between the last metaphysician and the first "thinker." If such is the case, then Derrida's critique would be victorious: even with Heidegger, presence, ceaselessly reinsured by the primacy of intuition, would discover the Being proper to every being, and it would therefore cover over the originarily nonoriginary *différance.*[91] But the sanctioned interpretation (or indeed self-interpretation) of Heidegger, as right as it seems literally, perhaps masks the essential. According to these two texts, what is essential does not have to do with the intuition of categorial Being, which, moreover, neither one formulates in these terms. For, in fact, categorial Being is never said here to be intuited, nor intuitable, but only and more radically *given* according to categorial intuition. In 1973, categorial intuition is thought explicitly by *analogy* with sensible intuition, an analogy that is rendered inevitable by the fact that Being *is given* as much as the sensible: "For Husserl, the categorial (that is, the Kantian forms) is *given* just as much as the sensible. Therefore there is indeed CATEGORIAL INTUITION. Here the question bounces back: by what path does Husserl arrive at categorial intuition? The answer is clear: categorial intuition being *like* sensible intuition (being giving), Husserl arrives at categorial intuition by the path of analogy." According to Heidegger, the Husserlian path would be reconstructed as follows: givenness surpasses the limits of sensible intuition, and therefore, by analogy, one must admit a giving intuition that is nonsensible, that is, categorial. The decision that leads to categorial intuition therefore *does not* arise from intuition itself, but from the excess of givenness over the sensible, over the giving intuition in the sensible. If intuition becomes categorial, it is because Being gives itself, and not because Being is given by virtue of categorial intuition. Categorial intuition does not give Being, but Being makes inevitable the admission of something like categorial intuition due to its own givenness. Let us reread the decisive passage in order to be convinced: "In order even to develop the question of the meaning of Being, it was necessary that Being be *given*, so that one might question its meaning. Husserl's *tour de force* consisted precisely in this presencing of Being, phenomenally present in the category. By this *tour de force*," Heidegger adds, "I finally had a ground: 'Being' is not a simple concept, a pure abstraction obtained thanks to the work of deduction. The point that Husserl nevertheless did not pass is the following: having more or less obtained Being as *given*, he does not question any further."[92] The decisive step of the *Investigations* consists in reaching "Being as *given*." Husserl manages to take it, at least "more or less." What constitutes the weakness? No doubt this: that he contents himself, too easily, with naming that givenness without truly thinking it. How does he name it? Through the finally very rough analogy of a categorial intuition, which, by a new (or rather very old) syntagm, dissimulates the abyss of the givenness of Being. Could one risk saying, without declaring it, that Heidegger opposes categorial intuition to givenness? The breakthrough goes as far as the givenness of Being, but recoils in face of its abyss, by closing it again through the unquestioned because problematic, but structurally traditional, concept of categorial intuition. If categorial intuition results from givenness, then far from provoking givenness, the thought that does no more than stand in categorial intuition flees the enigma of givenness. Heidegger, as opposed to Husserl, will seek to think givenness, and therefore he will destroy categorial intuition—indeed, he will no longer evoke it either in *Sein und Zeit* or later.

This paradoxical conclusion finds confirmation in the 1925 course. Analyzed as one of the "fundamental discoveries" of the *"fundamental book of phenomenology"* that ensures its "breakthrough," categorial intuition is there thought straightaway as an intuition, and therefore as a *"pure and simple grasp of the given in the flesh [von leibhaftig Gegebenem], such as it shows itself,"* it being well understood that *"the flesh is a signal mode of the self-givenness of a being [der Selbstgegebenheit eines Seienden]."* It imposes itself, beyond sensible intuition, as soon as one notices that some categories, like "totality," "and," "but," etc., in fact arrive at an *"originary self-givenness [originären Selbstgebung]"* in the same way as significations fulfilled through sensible intuition.[93] Categorial intuition can be admitted only in response to a categorial givenness, and therefore in being thought first as giving. The categorial acts, "in regard to their character as giving [gebende] acts . . . are intuitions, they *give* objectity [*sie* geben *Gegenständlichkeit*]"; and therefore the categorial act "brings the being in this new objectity to givenness [zur Gegebenheit]," precisely because that objectity is defined by self-givenness, as "self-giving [sich gebende] objectity."[94] Categorial intuition is never—and this is already true in 1925—directly related to being (still less to Being) as some "intuition of Being"; it always mediates its relation to being through givenness, which originarily determines them both. The breakthrough does not consist here, either, in the broadening of intuition alone, but in the broadening of the concept of reality or of objectity to the dimensions of givenness: "Rather, by way of understanding what is present in categorial intuition, we can come to see that the objectivity of a being is not absolutely exhausted by reality in the narrow sense, and that objectivity [*Objektivität oder Gegenständlichkeit*] in the broadest sense [*im weitesten Sinne*] is much richer than the reality of a thing, and what is more, that the reality of a thing is comprehensible in its structure only on the basis of the total objectivity of the purely and simply experienced being."[95] The stake of the *Investigations,* particularly of the Sixth, has less to do with categorial intuition than with what it points to without itself realizing it—the broadening of presence, understood as objectivity, according to the excessive measure of givenness. The broadening must be understood not only as an extension (*Erweiterung*) of intuition and of signification through givenness, but especially as "the demand for a liberation of the [phenomenological] ground [*Freilegung des Bodens*]."[96] Givenness broadens presence in that it frees it from any limits of the faculties, as far as to let beings play freely—eventually beings in their Being. And only such a liberating broadening will be able to claim to surpass the "metaphysics of presence," which, in fact, does not cease to *restrain* the present and to *hold back* its givenness.

The privilege thus accorded by Heidegger to givenness over categorial intuition allows one first of all to free his interpretation of the
Investigations from Derrida's objection. It also allows one to free Husserl
himself, at least in a certain measure, which it will suffice for us to point
out without going any further (we have already advanced *too far* on uncovered terrain). Heidegger in fact does justice to the Sixth Investigation
on two decisive points. (1) Husserl never declares in it that Being or
beings are intuited by the least "intuition of Being" or its equivalent. On
the other hand, the evidence of the "object given [*gegebener Gegenstand*]
in the mode of the meant" implies that "here *Being* in the sense of
truth . . . is realized, here the truth in person is given [*gegeben*], to be
seen [*erschauen*] and grasped directly," such that even the "little word *is*,"
finally, "is *itself given* or, at least, presumed given . . . in the fulfillment."
For each correlate of representation, even its sensible correlate, requires
that one name "its actual 'Being-given,' or even its appearing inasmuch
as 'given' [*sein aktuelles 'Gegebensein,' bzw. als 'gegeben' Erscheinen*]."[97] The
completed apparition gives what appears in it in person; now, the expression claims to give even in the copula, or indeed the position; it
is therefore necessary to admit that the *is* is given in person since it
appears as such. Categorial intuition does not itself give the *is*, nor does
it even see it: it marks, as an index (such would be the paradox), the in
fact anonymous givenness of the *is*. (2) Husserl always infers categorial
intuition starting from sensible intuition, by analogy and in order to
respect the advances of givenness: "If 'Being' is taken to mean *predicative*
Being, some *state of affairs* must be given to us, and this by way of an act *that
gives it—the analogue of ordinary sensible intuition* [*einen ihn gebenden Akt—
das Analogon*]."[98] Categorial intuition remains in need of givenness, far
from givenness being in need of it in order to be achieved as a givenness
of the *is*, and therefore of being in its beingness. Categorial intuition
only allows one to take the measure—henceforth without measure—of
givenness. It marks the open abyss of givenness, without covering it over—
at least in Heidegger's eyes, if not in Husserl's. For here, the one who is
most sober before the fascination of overabundant and unconditional
presence is doubtless not the one expected. Husserl, indeed, completely
dazzled by unlimited givenness, seems not to realize the strangeness of
such an excessiveness and simply manages its excess without questioning
it. That is, unless bedazzlement doesn't betray—by covering over—a fear
before the broadening of presence by givenness.

It is here no doubt that there arises the question that Husserl
could not answer, because he perhaps never heard it as an authentic
question: What gives? Not only: "What is that which gives itself?" but,
more essentially: "What does giving mean, what is at play in the fact that

all is given, how are we to think that all that is is only inasmuch as it is given?" It seems permissible to suppose that Husserl, submerged by the simultaneously threatening and jubilatory imperative to manage the superabundance of data in presence, does not at any moment (at least in the *Logical Investigations*) ask himself about the status, the scope, or even the identity of that givenness. This silence amounts to an admission (following Jacques Derrida's thesis) that Husserl, leaving unquestioned the givenness whose broadening he nevertheless accomplished, does not free it from the prison of presence, and thus keeps it in metaphysical detention. Heidegger, to the contrary, seeing immediately and with an extraordinary lucidity that the breakthrough of 1900–1901 consists entirely in the broadening of givenness beyond sensible intuition, assumes precisely the Husserlian heritage by making the entire question bear on what such a givenness means—and therefore in being careful not to reduce it too quickly to presence, even under the figure of categorial intuition. It will be a question—much further on—of understanding how and why that which is is only inasmuch as given: Being comes down to Being given, from a givenness that is achieved only in the play of the phenomenon with itself—of the appearing with what appears. Such a question, however, presupposes two preliminaries: (1) a step back in face of givenness itself—simply in order to come to consider it worthy of question, instead of forgetting it by dint of inhabiting its evidence; (2) the recognition that, in the henceforth universal givenness, what is at issue is the Being of what thus appears in the very measure that it is given. These two preliminaries amount to asking (1) whether a phenomenological reduction would achieve the step back that allows one to consider givenness as such, and (2) whether the breakthrough of givenness does not inevitably and immediately lead phenomenology toward the question of Being. In fact if not in principle, these two questions amount to one: Does the reduction lead phenomenology to see Being as a phenomenon?

2

Beings and the Phenomenon

1. Putting Ontology out of Play

"*Es gibt keine Ontologie* neben *einer Phänomenologie, sondern* wissenschaft-liche Ontologie ist nichts anders als Phänomenologie [There is no ontol-ogy *alongside* a phenomenology, but rather *ontology as a* [*rigorous*] *science is nothing other than phenomenology*]," Heidegger was stating as early as 1925. In doing so he was opposing Husserl's declaration of 1912: "*Denn an sich, wir werden davon sprechen, ist* Ontologie nicht Phänomenologie [For in itself—and we will have more to say about this—*ontology is not phenomenology*]."[1] The radicality of this opposition could not in any way be dulled. Not only because so many other texts confirm it; not only because it rendered both possible and necessary, among other things, Heidegger's deviation with respect to Husserl, and this well before 1927, or a fortiori, 1933; not only because it covers, at least in appearance, the debates that fed the different post-Husserlian phenomenological "schools" with their divergences; but above all because it puts into play, along with the relation between phenomenology and ontology, the turning that forces one both to leave and to rediscover the question of Being through the principal, if not to say the only, attempt at a radical founding of philosophy en-gendered by the twentieth century, which means the century that thinks with and after Nietzsche. We shall therefore interrogate successively the definition of phenomenology, then the definition of the phenomenon, and finally the definition of being, in order to measure whether and to what degree each of these terms reaches an understanding of Being, or depends on one—according Husserl or according to Heidegger.

The transgression of ontology by phenomenology certainly can, and even must, be related to the final determination of phenomenology as transcendental idealism: "Transcendental phenomenology is *ipso facto* a *transcendental idealism*," posits the *Cartesian Meditations*, or a "phenomeno-logico-transcendental 'idealism.' " This is very clearly explained and jus-tified by the afterword to the *Ideas*: "Transcendental-phenomenological idealism is not a particular thesis or a theory among others, but transcendental phenomenology, taken as a concrete science, and even when not a word is said about idealism, is in itself *universal idealism*, developed as a science."[2] Transcendental and universal idealism here signifies: an idealism that is nonsubjective because nonempirical. Idealism can claim to be universal (καθόλου) and transcendental (anhypothetical, ἀνυπόθετον) only in the strict measure that, before any other condition, it determines everything that presents itself to be seen. It is idealism, for only the *idea* can be seen. To be seen means to be experienced as a lived-experience (*Erlebnis*). Rereading the *Logical Investigations,* Husserl was rightly able to declare (even, no doubt, for the Sixth Investigation, although his reservations concerned, in this case, the Third as well) that, taking into account what is given *rein als die Erlebnisse* and following "ideation," "the investigations of this work, insofar as they have non-ontological themes [or: inasmuch as they do not have ontological themes] . . . were purely phenomenological."[3] Why does phenomenology authentically begin when the consideration of ontological themes ceases? Why must one conclude, following the example of the last paragraph of the *Ideen I,* that "the connections between constitutive phenomenologies and the corresponding formal and material ontologies *in no way imply that the former ground the latter. The phenomenologist does not judge ontologically* [*urteilt nicht ontologisch*] when he recognizes in an ontological concept or proposition the index of a constitutive eidetic connection, when he sees in them a guiding thread that carries in itself its right and its validity"?[4] The right and the validity (*Recht und Geltung*) of an ontological concept can certainly be recognized phenomenologically, but to that very extent they concern phenomenology and reflect in no way on ontology itself. The meeting remains a crossing without ever becoming an alliance.

In other words, "the task of an *a priori* ontology of the real world—which is precisely discovery of the Apriori belonging to the world's universality—is inevitable but, on the other hand, one-sided and not philosophical in the final sense." Why? Because the "factual world" remains an "ontic fact" totally stripped of "philosophical—that is, transcendental intelligibility."[5] Ontology attempts (and must attempt) to bring the a priori of the world to light; but it could not in principle succeed in doing so, once it does not reach the full intelligibility of the world, or rather of its fact. That Husserl here takes "ontology" in an extremely narrow sense in no way weakens his questioning; not only because, once his question is satisfied, the Husserlian acceptation of "ontology" (ontologies, regional ontologies, etc.) will not be broadened; but especially because the requirement of a "phenomenological intelligibility" of that which ontology claims to treat—and which here remains indeterminate for a reason—will become all the more inevitable for the later enterprise that would claim to reestablish—if only through a "destruction"—the enterprise of a classical ontology. The distinction between phenomenology and ontology is based on the "theoretical reflection that also produces the separation between natural science and philosophy. It is only through this separation that it comes to light that the natural sciences of Being are not the definitive sciences of Being [*nicht endgiltige Seinswissenschaften*]. We still need a science of beings in the absolute sense [*vom Seienden in absolutem Sinn*]."[6]

It falls to the Göttingen lessons, given in 1907, to take the step, or more exactly to indicate the step to be taken outside of ontology. There, universal and transcendental idealism does not reproach classical ontology for attempting to think the Being of the world or of any other region, but quite on the contrary for not thinking it radically; that is, for not thinking it all the way through by not thinking it in its origin. For before organizing Being in the management of the a priori, one must still secure it, which means that one must apprehend it with certitude; now, only phenomenology obtains certitude concerning Being, by assigning to itself as its sole object the absolute givenness under the gaze of intuition: "*in diesem Schauen ist es absolute Gegebenheit. Es ist gegeben als ein Seiendes, als ein Dies-da, dessen Sein zu bezweifeln gar keinen Sinn gibt.* [in this seeing is an absolute givenness. It is given as a being, a this-here, whose Being it makes no sense to call into question]."[7] Only the *epoché*, and therefore the phenomenological reduction attained in 1907, allows one to reach being as such, namely as absolutely given in and to the pure intuition of a transcendental gaze. One must go far beyond classical ontology, far beyond the "natural sciences of Being [*natürliche Seinswissenschaften*]," as far as the universal principle of "the [absolute] givenness of any reduced phenomenon,"[8] to reach this point of departure that ontology lacks because it does not even imagine that it needs to reach it. The very quest of being becomes a particular case of the search for absolute givenness— an absolute givenness that does not take up again, at a more secure level, ontology's field of investigation, but forcefully displaces it. For if certain beings traverse, so to speak, the reduction to the point of being rediscovered in a state of absolute givenness, others do not manage to do so. Conversely, numerous absolute (immanent) givennesses exceed what ontology recognized as beings. Not only do "all ontologies . . . fall under the blow of the reduction and disappear therein [*verfallen der Reduktion*]," but again, far from their being able to expect a relief [*relève*] from it that would reestablish them beyond the reduction with a perfect security, "this *epoché* signifies the putting-out-of-operation of the belief in Being as concerns the world of experience."[9]

Let us measure well the radicality of the dismissal that Husserl is effecting with the reduction: what he names *das Ausser-Vollzug-Setzen des Seinsglauben* prohibits not only maintaining the old regency of the world by ontology, not only reestablishing something like an ontology on the basis of absolute givenness, but above all the "belief in Being." For once the reduction is carried out, or rather—since the reduction does not cease to be carried out and deepened—in the experience that is opened by the constant practice of the reduction, it is no longer useful *nor allowable* to appeal to Being or to accord it the least theoretical confidence. In the realm of reduction it is no longer a question of Being. Why? Because Being never intervenes in order to permit the absolute givenness in which it does not play the slightest role; because beings either disappear or else are reduced to that same givenness (in the capacity of the lived and of essences); because the world unfurls henceforth as a world of experience—only experience, which the reduction opens, makes a world. If one still wants to insinuate that "phenomenology *seems* to harbor in itself all ontologies," because "the roots of all ontologies are their basic concepts and axioms," that restoration can remain legitimate only inasmuch as one well sees that "everything that the sciences of beings, the rational sciences and empirical sciences, offer us (in the enlarged sense they can all be called 'ontologies,' insofar as it becomes apparent that they are concerned with unities of the 'constitution') 'resolves itself into something phenomenological,' ['*löst sich in Phänomenologische auf*']—a figurative expression that must not be misunderstood and whose more precise sense is still to be established."[10] Ontologies do not raise themselves to phenomenology through the reduction any more than beings coincide, in the reduction, with the absolute noematic and immanent given. Another world—absolutely other, without any vestige or restoration of the old one—appears. Under the sun of its evidence, beings and the belief in Being definitively lose their visibility and their validity. In itself, ontology is not phenomenology and, no less, in itself, phenomenology is not, does not have to be, and could not be, ontology.

2. The Method of Ontology

To contest this prohibition was obviously the original plan and thus the first turn of Heideggerian thought. To contest, however, means to attest in the mode of subversion, and thus indeed to admit. At the very heart of its "parricide," Heidegger's first turn therefore preoccupies itself faithfully with the last word of the *Ideen*: with the articulation between phenomenology and ontology. In 1927, *Sein und Zeit* § 7 posits a reciprocal relation between the two instances: if *Ontologie ist nur als Phänomenologie möglich*, phenomenology nevertheless does not encompass ontology as one of its regions or possibilities, since in return *Sachlich genommen ist die Phänomenologie die Wissenschaft vom Sein des Seienden.*[11] In 1927, in the summer semester course, this equivalence also plays openly: "The basic components of *a priori* knowledge constitute what we call *phenomenology*. Phenomenology is the name for the method of ontology, that is, of scientific philosophy. Rightly conceived, phenomenology is the concept of a method." Here, three terms are articulated, and not only two: phenomenology, ontology, and philosophy. How do they correspond to one another? At bottom, it is a matter of philosophy searching for its proper scientificity, in a sense parallel to its "rigor" according to the Husserlian project; the scientificity of philosophy consists in its unfolding in and as an ontology: "Philosophy must legitimate by its own resources its claim to be universal ontology."[12] But ontology becomes universally accessible to philosophy only if the latter has at its disposal the method to reach it—method: the path indicated as well as the strength to traverse it. The method that opens ontology to philosophy is called, for Heidegger, phenomenology. *Sein und Zeit* condenses this relation in speaking, more than of philosophy as universal ontology or of ontology as phenomenology, of philosophy as "universal phenomenological ontology."[13] As a methodological approach, phenomenology renders possible the properly ontological enterprise of philosophy. Phenomenology does not have the task of constituting itself, even if in subsuming philosophy—in the sense that, for Husserl, philosophy expects nothing more, since "phenomenology is, so to speak, the secret nostalgia [*geheime Sehnsucht*] of all modern philosophy."[14] Phenomenology's task is rather, strangely, to lead philosophy to that which completes it as such, ontology; for Heidegger, not only does phenomenology lose the rank of an autonomous and of itself final science to the benefit of ontology, but above all this regression to the ancillary status of method serves the restoration of ontology. In fact the two inversions merge: phenomenology, having entered into the service of philosophy and not of itself, works in the capacity of method with a view to ontology. Phenomenology serves methodologically to render philosophy ontological—it serves as a method opening a path to philosophy, in order that the latter give way to ontology.

The violence thus done to the Husserlian definition of phenomenology by the Heideggerian texts of 1927 should nevertheless not fascinate to the point of concealing another question. For phenomenology becomes a method for philosophy only in that, first, phenomenology becomes a method toward ontology. Where and when does Heidegger decide, or rather where and when does he see decided under the gaze of thought, the ontological charge of phenomenology? Why and how does Heidegger come to recognize as "*the basic phenomenological question*" that which asks: "*What does Being mean?* [*Was besagt Sein?*]"[15] The answer to these questions (like their ultimate formulation) can be read as early as this same summer semester course of 1925:

> *Phenomenological research is the interpretation of beings with regard to their Being [auf sein Sein hin].* For such an interpretation, what is put into prepossession is what it has in advance as its thematic matter: a being or a particular region of Being. This being is interrogated with regard to its Being, that is, with regard to that with a view to which what is put into prepossession [*das in die Vorhabe Gestellte*] is interrogated—the very-consideration-of-the-relation [*die Hinsicht*]; that with regard to which it is and must be seen is Being. Being is to be read upon (the face of) being; that is to say, what phenomenological interpretation puts into pre-view [*in die Vor-sicht stellt*] is Being.[16]

Let us pay attention: phenomenology, to be sure, establishes a being as the goal of its advance (method); but that advance nevertheless no longer stops at that being; for phenomenology interprets it with a view to what it intends and sees as in relation (*Hinsicht*) with it, but also and for that very reason as beyond it (method), namely Being. As early as 1925 what *Sein und Zeit* states in 1927 is accomplished at least in outline: "Taken at the level of the thing itself [*sachhaltig*], phenomenology is the science of the Being of beings." The "things itself" to which phenomenology makes philosophy return is no longer called being (nor essence, the category, noema, etc.), but radically being *with a view to* Being. Phenomenology becomes a method in the strict sense only in that it displaces the "thing" beyond being as far as Being. Much more, as early as 1925, phenomenology becomes, thanks to Heidegger, a path beyond itself, a sort of methodological self-overcoming. It would even be necessary to envisage applying to this inaugural transition what Heidegger nevertheless did not declare until the end of his *Denkweg*, when he wrote in 1962: "But if we understand 'phenomenology' as: to allow the most proper 'question' [*Sache*] of thought to express itself, then the title would have to be 'a path *through* phenomenology into the thought of Being.' This genitive then says that Being as such [*Sein als solches (das Seyn)*] shows itself at the same time as what is to be thought, what is in need of a thinking that answers to it."[17] Like the a priori, which in 1925 constitutes one of its principal traits (along with intentionality and categorial intuition), phenomenology itself bears the "character of the Being of being, and not of being itself."[18] Ontology means here (and inadequately) this displacement of phenomenology from beings to Being. Whereas for Husserl phenomenology renders ontology null and void because it concerns itself, in its place and better than the latter, with beings, for Heidegger, phenomenology takes up the title of ontology because it moves from beings to Being. The *Hinsicht* has radically changed; or rather, the simple view (*Sicht*) that can only fix itself on permanent and available evidence—and therefore on beings—is replaced by the *Hinsicht*, which sees being only in its relation with Being and in its prepossession of that Being. The debate over the agreement or the antagonism between phenomenology and ontology therefore deepens into a debate over the very status of ontology: does it concern being (Husserl) or rather the Being of being and its mode of encounter (Heidegger)? The phenomenological method remains the same, without question; the debate concerns its point of application. Between Husserl and Heidegger the difference at once concerns the difference between beings and Being. But, one will immediately ask, how did this second view become possible, which sees being otherwise than as a pure being? How does phenomenology thus slip beyond its own evidence? Here is the criterion that frees up the authentic phenomenological method: "*Phenomenological* signifies everything that belongs to the mode of such an exposition of phenomena [*Aufweisung von Phänomenen*] and phenomenal structures, everything that becomes thematic in this kind of research. The *unphenomenological* would be everything that does not satisfy this kind of research, its conceptuality and its methods of exposition." Whence this strange but inevitable consequence, that phenomenology "never [*nie und nimmer*] has to do with phenomena and even less with mere phenomena."[19] The paradox here is indeed one, but it is the very paradox of apparition: phenomenology does not treat of phenomena that have appeared and are apparent, it treats of the "mode of exposition [*Art der Aufweisung*]" of those phenomena; in short, not of the phenomena, but, through them, even though directly, of their very phenomenality.

Whence two questions: (1) Would the displacement of phenomenology from beings to (the) Being (of beings) coincide with its displacement from the "mere phenomena" to their phenomenality? (2) Does Husserlian phenomenology completely satisfy the definition of phenomenology by phenomenality (since it ignores the first displacement from beings to Being)? The answer to the first question must be put off until a later moment of our study, if only because it implies an at least provisional elucidation of the answer to the second question. In fact, what the course of 1925 locates as a "missing" (*Versäumnis*) of the meaning of Being originates in a "missing" of the Being of the intentional. Husserl no doubt applies himself persistently to moving back from the transcendent objects to the immanent acts, by following in reverse the thread of intentionality; he no doubt calls into question through the *epoché* the naive acceptance of the supposed Being of the world; but in this advance (or rather in this regression), he aims first at the results of the acts, namely the disengagement of an absolute givenness in the immanence of the lived experiences that are given perfectly to and as consciousness. The acts act as the means by which to arrive at the immanent givenness of the lived experiences, without they themselves, as such, becoming the stake of an authentic questioning; in short, "the kind of Being of acts is left undetermined."[20] Why charge Husserl here with having "missed the question of Being" (*Versäumnis der Seinsfrage*)? Why impute to him as a failure what, in fact, was not for him a question having any priority? What legitimacy does a reproach have if its object was of no importance to the one accused? But precisely, why wasn't the question of the kind of Being of the intentional, and therefore of the reductive consciousness, of importance to Husserl? Why is the reproach addressed precisely to the wrong address? Answer: because

> Husserl's primary question is simply not concerned with the character of the Being of consciousness. Rather, he is guided by the following concern: *How can consciousness become the possible object of an absolute science?* The primary concern that guides him is the *idea of an absolute science.* This idea, that *consciousness is to be the region of an absolute science,* is not simply invented; it is the idea which has occupied modern philosophy since Descartes. The elaboration of pure consciousness as the thematic field of phenomenology is *not derived phenomenologically by going back to the matters themselves* [*Rückgang auf die Sachen selbst*] but by going back to a traditional idea of philosophy.[21]

The guiding thread of phenomenology is not followed by Husserl all the way to its end, namely the *Seinsfrage*, because Husserl, having conquered intentionality and the reduction (for which, by the way, Heidegger always recognized himself as Husserl's "disciple"),[22] employs them only to divert them, in order to accomplish the philosophical ideal of an absolute science of and through consciousness.

We should note that it is not a question, on Heidegger's part, of deploring the overly famous Husserlian movement from the supposed "realism" of the *Logical Investigations* to the confirmed "idealism" of the *Ideas.* It is a question of contesting the common and tacit basis of these two works: first that the mode of Being of consciousness does not constitute a specific or primary question, and then that that mode of Being might be likened to the mode of Being of the things of the world: "What is retained then is always only the Being of an already given objective datum, of a real object. This means that it always only comes down to Being as objectivity, in the sense of Being an object [*Objektivität im Sinne des Gegenstandseins*] of a reflection."[23] One will no doubt set the "unbridgeable essential difference"[24] that Husserl posits between the phenomenal Being of the transcendent and the absolute Being of the immanent, between Being as reality and Being as consciousness, against §§ 44 and 42 of the *Ideen I*; for the moment, let us limit ourselves to underlining that the Being of consciousness remains nonetheless defined, precisely in order to oppose it to the Being of the world, as the "sphere of absolute position," and therefore starting from position, from permanent presence, from objective subsistence—the very same that allowed Kant to define the Being of the world.[25] The distinction of regions in Being does not suffice to think a difference of the ways of Being; on the contrary, to establish consciousness as a region, even as an original region (*Urregion*), implies, at the foundation of its singularity in face of the phenomenon, that it also occupies a region, and therefore a position, and therefore an objectivity. Now, it is precisely the treatment of the Being of consciousness as a region that prohibits the questioning concerning the Being of consciousness as a nonobject, since it allows one, through a quick and therefore effective response, to fix on the inventory of the intentional acts (and therefore of the phenomena in the capacity of noema) and to neglect the nonscientific question concerning the mode of Being of consciousness as an instance of the intentional. Husserlian phenomenology goes back to the things themselves, *but only to a certain point*. That point has a name: the Being of consciousness as such. This stopping point is imposed by an authority: the traditional idea of philosophy (which Heidegger will later name "metaphysics"). Related to the *discrimens* of the phenomenological— to consider not the phenomena, but the "mode of their exposition [*Art ihrer Aufweisung*]"— one must therefore conclude—as violent as the paradox may seem— that Husserl's phenomenology remains unphenomenological: "In the basic task of determining its ownmost field, therefore, phenomenology is *unphenomenological* [*unphänomenologisch*]!—that is to say, *phenomenological only in intention* [*vermeintlich phänomenologisch*]! But it is all this in a sense which is even more fundamental."[26] There remains a long path for phenomenology to travel in order for it to become itself, namely the return to the things themselves. Phenomenology must become radically a method—not, to be sure, a method for science, but indeed a method for itself toward that of which it is a question. A method for itself—a transgression of itself, as far as its own intention, which is called the Being of the intentional.

The turn that is taken by the very idea of phenomenology from Husserl to Heidegger, and this even before *Sein und Zeit*, can be located according to a sign—the inversion of its relation to ontology; instead of abolishing it by substituting itself for it, phenomenology attempts to reach ontology by becoming a method. This sign refers to an underlying displacement: phenomenology no longer concerns the knowledge of the phenomena, but the knowledge of their mode of exposition, and therefore it no longer aims at the foundation of the sciences, but at the thought of phenomenality. This turn will become really conceivable, however, only from the moment when we will have cleared up how thought can go beyond (method) the phenomenon in the direction of its phenomenality. In other words: How and in what way is phenomenality distinguished, other than verbally, from the phenomenon? The mere access to this question implies a debate with the competing definitions of the phenomenon according to which Husserl and Heidegger confront each other.

3. The "Phenomenon Reduced" to Present Objectivity

To determine the phenomenality of the phenomenon does not seem to present any insurmountable difficulty, since as a science of the phenomena phenomenology must manage to do so as soon as it defines its own principle. This principle, Heidegger does not cease to repeat, has to do with the enterprise of returning to the things themselves, or rather of orienting oneself in thought only according to the things themselves— according to that of which it is each time a question.[27] But Husserl does not respect this principle—not only because Heidegger tells us, but especially because, in the *Ideas*, this principle enters into competition with another principle, which is extolled by the exceptional title of "principle of all principles"; before the return to the things themselves, even before the reduction (§§ 31–32) it is posited that "*all originarily giving intuition* is *by right a source of knowledge*, that what *offers itself originarily* to us in '*intuition*' (in its fleshly actuality, so to speak) *must be taken wholly as it gives itself*, but also *only in the limits within which it gives itself [as being] there.*" In order better to grasp the stakes of this principle par excellence, we must read its negative formulation: "the *norm* that we should follow as phenomenologists: *to claim [in Anspruch zu nehmen] nothing that we cannot render essentially evident to consciousness itself* in its pure immanence."[28] Nothing can exert a claim (*Anspruch*) over consciousness except that which gives itself in full evidence to consciousness; and conversely, everything that gives itself in full evidence to consciousness (through and as originary intuition) can validate its claim absolutely and incontestably. To return to the things themselves means: to return to the evidence given by intuition to consciousness; the certitude of that givenness anticipates the reduction itself (understood as the exemplary case of givenness, intuitive because immanent).

Commenting on this displacement of the principle, and according to its double formulation, Heidegger will conclude in 1962: "In its negative and also in its positive sense, the call *zur Sache selbst* determines the securing and development of method, as the procedure of philosophy through which alone the thing itself [*Sache selbst*] reaches an attested givenness. For Husserl, the 'principle of all principles' in the first place does not concern the content [of the thing], but is a methodological principle." And to continue: "If one wanted to ask: Where does the 'principle of all principles' get its unshakable right, the answer would have to be: from the transcendental subjectivity that has already been presupposed as the matter of philosophy."[29] The critique that Heidegger formulates here amounts to denouncing the displacement of phenomenology from the status of a science of the phenomena—as the matter of thought and as its stake—to that of a science of and by consciousness—taking up again the metaphysical project of a certain science and an absolute knowing. But, one cannot fail immediately to object to this objection, doesn't Husserl here ensure, on the contrary, the right and the primacy of the phenomenon which, precisely through the principle of all principles, can finally be taken as it gives itself? Moreover, does not the text that Heidegger continually designates as the Husserlian deviation from phenomenology, the article that appeared in *Logos*, in 1910–11, under the title *Philosophy as a Rigorous Science*, postulate already that "one must . . . take the phenomena as they give themselves"?[30] The principle indeed contains a definition of the absolute givenness of the phenomena, and it therefore aims at their phenomenality and manifests the unconditionality of that phenomenality. In this way, moreover, Husserl limits himself to confirming here a thesis that appeared in the appendix of the Sixth Investigation, and thus of the privileged text par excellence in Heidegger's own eyes: "the only and uniquely determining [*massgebend*] thing here is the descriptive character of the phenomena, such as we experience them [*so wie wir sie erleben*]."[31] Would it not therefore be suitable to recognize in the principle of all principles the highest Husserlian determination of the phenomenality of the phenomena, since the principle states that phenomenality's absolute mode of givenness to consciousness? Let us be clear on this: there is no doubt whatsoever that the principle must be so understood. But it is precisely for this reason that the Heideggerian challenge is right on target; for here, according to Husserl, the phenomenality of the phenomena is interpreted as givenness, but givenness itself is interpreted in turn as the givenness of an actual presence for consciousness with a view to a certitude. In other words, phenomenality is indeed at stake here, but it is understood starting from consciousness—which is presupposed to be prevalent. Consciousness therefore determines phenomenality by reducing every phenomenon to the certitude of an actual presence, far from phenomenality requiring that consciousness be itself determined by the conditions and the modes of givenness—which are always multiple and disconcerting.

This can be established with three remarks. First, the givenness of the phenomena, taken as they give themselves, presents them in the present in the form of actuality (*leibhafte Wirklichkeit*), and therefore in accordance with what is required by the project of a rigorous science, that is, a rigorously certain science. Indeed, "it belongs to the mode of Being of the lived that a gaze of intuitive [*erschauender*] perception can be directed quite immediately to each actual and living experience as an originary living present [*auf jedes wirkliche, als originäre Gegenwart lebendige Erlebnis*]." The mode of Being of the lived, namely that wherein the thing appears, must turn toward the originary present, which is actual and therefore certain, since it is a matter of appearing to a gaze that aims only at certitude. For the preeminence of the present develops its uncontested rule over the lived only inasmuch as, first, it characterizes— or better issues from—the mode of Being of the consciousness that perceives through intuition: "*My* intropathy [*Einfühlen*], *my* consciousness in general is, in the capacity of a flowing present [*strömende Gegenwart*], given originarily and absolutely, not only according to essence, but also according to existence."[32] The interpretation of the mode of Being of the phenomena as actuality ensues from the actuality that is necessarily induced by the presence of consciousness in the present. The transition from one term to the other (lived experience/consciousness) in the same evidence in the present does not contradict the opposition of immanence and transcendence, but indeed offers its theater: the objectivity of the transcendent object can only result from the acts of the consciousness immanent to itself, according to intentionality. For, since the *Logical Investigations*, "what for us is most certain [*das Allersicherste*] is that Being-an-object [*Gegenstand-sein*] consists phenomenologically in certain acts in which something appears or is thought as an object."[33] The objectivity, and therefore the actual presence imposed on any phenomenon, follows from the intentional acts of consciousness; consciousness therefore also predetermines, in advance and in conformity with the prevalence of pure presence in it, the mode of Being of the phenomena: these give themselves as they appear only on condition of appearing in the mode that consciousness silently imposes on them, that is, on condition of satisfying the actuality of presence—which reigns unquestioned.

We should add a second remark: what appears is accepted as such not because it appears but because it appears to an authority that is established to begin with as originary; one could still suspect that the apparition offers only an appearance if the authority that it satisfies were not itself held to be originary. That authority, the satisfaction of which is law, bears the name of intuition. That intuition should be originary means that the origin of the givenness of phenomena has less to do with their apparition than with the very intuition that, originarily, claims to be "giving." We know the difficulty to which the interpretation of this adjective still gives rise: Who gives, the intuition or the apparition? The intuition no doubt, because it *legitimates* the apparition, in that no other faculty or instance of consciousness behind it can judge the apparition in its appearing. If one can posit "*seeing in general as an originarily giving consciousness*," it is because it constitutes "by right the ultimate source of all reasoned affirmations"— of any presence. One must speak, as of a whole, of "originarily giving intuition and of its own original right [*ihr ureigenes Recht*]."[34] At the origin of any appearing stands intuition, which originarily gives the apparition, not, to be sure, in taking its place, but in authenticating, by right, that its appearing has nothing apparent about it, since it, intuition, established as the principle of all vision, sees nothing therein that deceives it. Intuition is established as the tribunal (the tribunal of intuition, more originary than that of reason) of apparition as the actual presence of what gives itself. Consciousness thus receives what appears to the extent that intuition determines its validity. Phenomena give themselves absolutely only to the absolute of intuition—which reigns unquestioned.

Finally, we should indicate the clearest sign of the submission of phenomenality to consciousness; it is provided by the very definition of the phenomenon starting from the "lived," *Erlebnis*; to be sure, Husserl firmly denounces "the equivocation that allows one to give the name of phenomenon [*Erscheinung*] not only to the lived, in which the appearing of the object is constituted [*Erlebnis, in dem das Erscheinen des Objekts besteht*] . . . , but also to the appearing object as such." In the *Investigations*, this distinction even secures the closing, since the appendix to the Sixth Investigation finally concedes that, even after the whole journey,

the term *Erscheinung* is, of course, beset with equivocations, whose extreme dangers are seen precisely in this case. It will not be useless at this point to list these equivocations explicitly: we have already touched on them in passing in the text of these Investigations. The term *Erscheinung* has a preferred application [*vorzugweise*] to acts of intuitive representation [*Vorstellen*], to acts of *perception*, on the one hand, and to acts of *presentification* [*Vergegenwärtigung*], on the other. . . . *Erscheinung* accordingly means: 1. The concrete lived experience [*Erlebnis*] of intuition (the fact of having a certain object intuitively present or presentified to the mind [*das anschaulich-gegenwärtig—oder vergegenwärtigt—Haben eines gewissen Gegenstandes*]. . . . 2. The intuited (appearing) object, inasmuch as it is the one that appears here and now.[35]

This equivocation requires that the phenomenologist not confuse the *Erlebnis* and the appearing thing. "Sensations . . . are lived [*erlebt*], but they do not appear objectively. . . . Objects appear and are perceived, but they are not lived [*erlebt*]."[36] The vigorousness of this warning, however, would have no justification if, precisely, two acceptations of *Erscheinung* did not enter into competition. But then why maintain the duality of acceptations if, on Husserl's own admission, it gives rise to an equivocation, and then to a confusion? Wouldn't it be fitting to stick with what Husserl in the same appendix recognizes as the "originary concept of *Erscheinung*," "that which was indicated above in second place: namely, the concept of what appears [*des Erscheinenden*] or of what can appear, of the intuition-able as such"? The equivocation must nevertheless absolutely remain, because the duality of the term "phenomenon" constitutes, paradoxically, the fundamental achievement of Husserlian phenomenology: the term "phenomenon" does not apply first, nor only, to the object that appears, but indeed to the lived experience in which and according to which it appears; this duality alone will allow one to think absolute givenness, intentionality, and the couple of noesis/noema. Even and especially if one takes intentionality into account, *Erscheinung* is approached on the basis of the immanence of *Erlebnis*—and therefore, inevitably, never on the basis of the appearing of the object itself, which is by definition conditioned.

One should not object here with the preceding text; to be sure, the "concept of what appears" is expressly held to be the "originary concept of *Erscheinung*"; but from the fact that *Erscheinung* must be understood as the appearing object, it does not follow that lived experiences can no longer claim to appear as phenomena; quite the contrary, the same text immediately continues, "the lived experiences, whatever they might be, can become . . . objects of reflexive, internal intuitions," such that the phenomenality of lived experiences itself becomes that of objects, and "phenomenology is accordingly the doctrine of lived experiences in general."[37] Phenomenology could not be called equally the doctrine of the phenomena that appear and the doctrine of lived experiences if the phenomenality of the phenomena were not thought on the basis of lived experiences. The equivocation of the term *Erscheinung* results purely and simply from an addition to the traditional sense (phenomenon: appearing object) of the properly Husserlian sense (phenomenon: *Erlebnis* in and as which the object appears). *Erlebnis* is rightly translated by "lived experience [*vécu*]"; one would also have to hear in this lived experience the affective charge that colloquial language retains ("he has lived through a lot"); lived experience implies a test or proof [*épreuve*]; proof in the sense of proof of the actual, encountered world; proof also in the sense of photography or printing: *Erlebnis* signifies, for the mind, undergoing the test of phenomenality; but conversely, proof signifies that the phenomenality of the appearing object is inscribed and attested first in the fabric and according to the flux of consciousness. The appearing object is outlined and adumbrated (*Abschattung, adumbratio*) on the sensible plate of consciousness, which thus becomes the first and unique proof of the phenomenon—undergoing the test of the phenomenon. The regency of the phenomenon by the *Erlebnis* is confirmed—beyond the equivocal splitting of the very notion of the phenomenon—by its hold over the definition of truth: "Evidence is the '*Erlebnis*' of truth."[38] Truth, and therefore the completion of phenomenality (full and entire manifestation), opens up against the background of the *Erlebnis*, shows through it as through a filter, is recorded in it as on film, is outlined in it, finally, as in the threads of a preestablished network. The phenomenon appears only in and through the test and the *Erlebnis* of its consciousness—which reigns, unquestioned.

Consciousness thus radically determines phenomenality by imposing upon it the actuality of presence, the absoluteness of intuition, and the test of lived experience. The return to the things themselves is limited to a "return to the sources of intuition."[39] The phenomenon that so emerges receives, with its purity, its limit—the "reduced phenomenon,"[40] Husserl often says; by this we understand, to be sure, the phenomenon that is obtained through the reduction, but also and indissolubly the phenomenon whose mode of Being is reduced by the reduction to what the primacy of consciousness imposes upon it. For "the basic point is that one must not overlook the fact that evidence is this consciousness which is truly [a] 'seeing' [consciousness] and which has a direct and adequate grasp of itself and that signifies nothing other than adequate presence-in-person [*Selbstgegebenheit*]."[41] Self-givenness in person, if we might so translate *Selbstgegebenheit*, becomes the phenomenon's sole correct mode of Being because it alone satisfies the requirements of direct grasp, permanent presence, and immediate evidence which are imposed by consciousness on anything that would claim to appear to it. Consciousness in fact expects only one benefit from the phenomenon: presence; for "each *Erlebnis* in general (when it is, if one might say, actually living) is a lived experience 'being in the capacity of a present [*gegenwärtig seiendes*].' "[42] By the constraining grace of the reduction as the instance of givenness in presence, the reduced phenomenon is reduced to the being that is present here and now (*Dies da!*). Or again, if "absolute givenness is an ultimate,"[43] then absolute presence becomes a primary term—short of which we could not speak of a phenomenon, still less of a lived experience. The primacy of presence is deployed as a horizon that is all the less surpassable inasmuch as it does not give itself as such a horizon, inasmuch as it keeps itself and conceals itself, so to speak, in its neutral evidence. Thus the gap between the (appearing, transcendent) thing and (immanent) lived experience (in which the thing would appear) is created, in an opposition that Husserl does not hesitate to characterize as the "culminating point" of his meditation, only by comprehending both terms of the opposition according to givenness in the flesh and in person, and therefore according to presence: "Any thingness given in person [*leibhaft gegebene*] can, despite that givenness in person, also not be, whereas no lived experience given in person [*leibhaft gegebenes Erlebnis*] can also not be."[44] More essential than this "essential law" that separates the transcendent from the immanent, the constraint of presence becomes unavoidable: from near or far, nothing enters into the field of an even possible phenomenality that must not subscribe first to givenness in person, in flesh and body; that givenness itself has the sole function of offering to the gaze of consciousness the present object implied by the reduced phenomenality; the primacy of the immanent over the transcendent flows only from a better and more immediate satisfaction of the requirements of consciousness: "It belongs to the mode of Being [*Seinsart*] of the *Erlebnis* that the gaze of an intuitive perception can be directed quite immediately to any actual *Erlebnis*, which is living as an originary present [*als originäre Gegenwart*]."[45] Lived experience prevails only as the object par excellence, because originally present; lived experience attests the privilege of accomplishing, before all the (transcendent) world, the perfection of presence which is enduring, immediate, and intuitionable—in short, available. Why qualify it as immanent? Because consciousness can be led back to the Cartesian definition of *substantia*,[46] inasmuch as it knows itself to be present in permanence and apprehends in the lived experience of the "consciousness region" an originary presence of the same type as itself. It has only to remain (*manere*) in (*in*) it in order to discover a presence of equal permanence. Thus the reign of presence as permanence is extended to every region: "Immanent or absolute Being and transcendent Being are, certainly [*zwar*], both called 'being,' 'object,' and both certainly [*zwar*] have their objective determining contents."[47]

But is it self-evident that objectivity offers the only face of being? Is it self-evident that objectivity can be attributed equally (*beides*) to the immanent being of consciousness and to the transcendent being of the world? Is it self-evident, finally, that the phenomenon must reduce its phenomenality to objectivity, itself understood as an assured permanence? The reduction of the phenomenon to a phenomenality of objectivity is indicated and fully operative in the Husserlian impossibility of considering the nonpresent: "The perception of a thing does not presentify something nonpresent [*vergegenwärtigt nicht ein Nichtgegenwärtig*] as though it were a memory or an imagination; it makes present [*gegenwärtigt*], it seizes [a thing] even in its carnal present [*ein Selbst in seiner leibhaftigen Gegenwart*]. It does this according to *its own peculiar sense*, and one would violate its sense if one supposed something else of it."[48] Perception can deploy itself only in the mode of the presentification that seizes and grabs hold of a presence in person and objectively awaiting (*Gegen-wart*) that grasp; every approach to the thing as stealing away from permanent presence must therefore abandon itself to the imagination and to memory, for it does not belong to the domain of the general grasp of presence. In a word, as the phenomenality of the "reduced phenomenon" is reduced to objective and permanent presence, every phenomenon that is not reduced to that presence is of itself excluded from phenomenality. Of the Husserlian phenomenon one would have to say that, reduced without remainder to the evidence of presence, it eliminates the disequilibrium of appearing; the only function of adequation (between intentionality and fulfillment, between evidence and truth) is to lead such disequilibrium back to strict equality. Without remainder, indeed; since no remainder comes to trouble the final equation, the Husserlian phenomenon, as a perfect apparition of presence, can be called a flat phenomenon.

4. From the Unapparent Phenomenon to the "Phenomenon of Being"

But can one understand the phenomenon in another sense? Can the phenomenon be defined otherwise than by permanent presence under the gaze of consciousness? The *index* that is decisive for responding to such a question stems from the authority that one grants, as concerns phenomenality, to presence itself; in other words, it is a question of knowing in what measure the phenomenality of the phenomenon is defined in terms of presence—better: at the term of presence. To this question, Heidegger seems at first to respond in strict conformity with Husserl, since, in the famous § 7 of *Sein und Zeit*, he maintains that "the expression 'phenomenon' signifies *that which shows itself in itself* [*das Sich-an-ihm-selbst-zeigende*], the manifest." To be sure, he mentions some deviant cases: the phenomenon as "mere appearance" or as "sign," or as "deceptive appearance"; but in every case, he clearly indicates that these acceptations depend on a confusion that "cannot be disentangled unless the concept of the phenomenon is understood from the beginning [*von Anfang an*] as that which shows itself in itself [*das Sich-an-ihm-selbst-zeigende*]*.*" Must we not conclude that Heidegger purely and simply repeats the Husserlian determination of being on the basis of presence, and therefore of evidence for intuition? Not at all, and for at least two reasons.

1. It is not a question here of presence, even in person; it is a question of the showing of the phenomenon on the basis of its own initiative. The phenomenon gives itself by itself and on the basis of its own visibility, far from being reduced to presence for a consciousness. The possible deviations of phenomenality attest, in fact, that one is dealing with a characteristic initiative of the phenomenon to enter into visibility, according to a path that conceals, proportionately, caches of possible dissimulation. Likewise, Heidegger does not here mention anything like consciousness: not because nothing is required in order to see that which rises to its proper visibility, but because in a sense that visibility—whatever its modes may be—is decided beyond any evidence and therefore any consciousness; visibility is not represented, it presents itself. And precisely because it presents itself by itself, it can also be absent. From deviant acceptations of that which is defined as showing-itself-by-itself, and therefore from nonshowings of the phenomenon, Heidegger does not conclude the necessity of a drastic reduction to presence that is given absolutely for consciousness; he concludes, against Husserl, that "Covered-up-ness is the counter-concept to 'phenomenon' [*Verdecktheit ist der Gegenbegriff zu 'Phänomen'*]."[49] *Gegenbegriff* does not signify the contrary or the contradictory so much as the counterplay, the fire-back, the buttress that inscribes manifestation in the very orbit of concealment, such that in arriving at its own manifestation, the phenomenon only covers up the covered, takes up again in the mode of the manifest that which remained concealed in the mode of the covered-up. The phenomenon manifests only inasmuch as it manifests that which remained nonmanifest before that very manifestation, and which still obscurely governs its brilliance.

2. Consequently, for Heidegger, phenomenology surpasses the "vulgar" usage of the phenomenon only inasmuch as it renders manifest not simply the manifest, but indeed the nonmanifest.

> What is it that phenomenology is to "let us see"? What is it that must be called a "phenomenon" in a distinctive sense? What is it that by its very essence is *necessarily* the theme whenever we exhibit something *explicitly*? Manifestly, it is something that proximally and for the most part does *not* show itself at all: it is something that lies *hidden*, in contrast to that which proximally and for the most part does show itself; but at the same time it is something that belongs to what thus shows itself, and it belongs to it so essentially as to constitute its meaning and ground.[50]

The phenomenon has to come to manifestation only inasmuch as it *is not* at first apparent. The phenomenon is first characterized by its unapparentness. Let us cite some other texts in order to confirm this surprising inversion:

> Being-covered-up [*Verdecktsein*] is the *counterconcept to phenomenon,* and such concealments through covering up [*Verdeckungen*] are really the immediate theme of phenomenological reflection. What can be a phenomenon is first and foremost covered up, or known in a tentative form. . . . There are *accidental concealments* and there are *necessary* ones, given in the very Being of their way of discovery and its possibilities. Every phenomenological proposition, though drawn from original sources, is subject to the possibility of concealment when it is communicated as an assertion. . . . This possibility of petrification of what it has drawn out and demonstrated in an original way is implied in the concrete labor of phenomenology itself.

Or again:

> The critical reflection at this point showed us that phenomenological questioning can begin in the most obvious of matters [*im Selbstverständlichen*]. But this "matter of course" means that the phenomena are not really exposed to the light of day [*offen zutage*], that the ways to the things themselves are not without further ado ready-made, and that there is the constant danger of being misled and forced off the trail—which precisely and in general constitutes the sense of phenomenology as a research that clears.

In short, if "φαινόμενον is that which shows itself," there remains "the astonishing possibility that a being may show itself as something which it nevertheless is not," such that, properly speaking, "the phenomenon is experienced as enigmatic."[51] The Husserlian phenomenon is defined by, and therefore confined to, evidence, such that any residue of nonevidence must disappear from the "reduced phenomenon." On the contrary, the Heideggerian phenomenon, originating in the rise to visibility of the not-yet visible, implies by right and in principle what is unapparent in apparition. In one case evidence reduces apparition to presence (and thus to objectivity for consciousness), and in the other case apparition reveals *as such* the unapparent whose contrast haloes the apparent. Instead of offering the certain evidence of an object for consciousness, the phenomenon offers itself as the enigma of the forever unobjectifiable play of the apparent with the unapparent. Phenomenon no longer signifies the certain object, but a certain play of the apparent in its apparition. Consequently, the work of phenomenology is to render apparent not only the unapparent, but even the play between the apparent and the unapparent within apparition: " 'Behind' the phenomena of phenomenology there is essentially nothing else; on the other hand, what is to become a phenomenon can be hidden. And just because the phenomena are proximally and for the most part *not* given, there is need for phenomenology. Covered-up-ness is the counter-concept to 'phenomenon.' "[52]

The question that aimed at determining the relation of phenomenology to ontology had led us to an interrogation concerning the phenomenality of the phenomenon. At the end of the first question, the break between Husserl and Heidegger concerned the phenomenological pertinence of a project of ontology. Here, at the end of the second question, the break falls between the reduction of the phenomenon to presence and the recognition of the enigma of its apparition outlined by unapparentness. What relation can we recognize between these two breaks? In other words, in what way does the thought of the phenomenon as enigma allow one to advance toward the thought of phenomenology as an ontology? For the moment, let us limit ourselves to an indication that expressly confirms the intimate connection between the two thoughts. At issue is a formula from the 1925 course which is taken up again in *Sein und Zeit*: "*Soviel Schein—soviel Sein* [so much appearance—so much Being]."[53] *Schein* counts here for the appearance that does not comply directly with apparition because it covers over an unapparentness that, if it appeared, would offer a completely different appearance; thus the appearance of the *Schein* attests to the enigma of the phenomenon as a play of the apparent and the unapparent. How then are we to understand the fact that where the enigma of the phenomenon arises there arises also nothing less than Being? First, without any doubt, in the sense that the enigma of the phenomenon has nothing illusory about it, since on the contrary it puts into question everything that presents itself, and thus eventually—if it presents itself—Being. Next and above all, in the sense that the play of the phenomenon concerns Being—directly. Because "that which, in the most proper sense, remains *hidden*, or which falls again into the state of *covering-over concealment* [*Verdeckung*], or which shows itself only '*in disguise*' ['*verstellt*'], is not just this being or that, but rather the *Being* of beings, as our previous observations have shown."[54] The ultimate matter to which the return to the things themselves must return has a name: the phenomenality of *Being* itself. For Heidegger the repetition and radicalization of the Husserlian watchword had no other goal than to succeed in formulating this incomparably ambitious and paradoxical task—to return to Being as Being and, in the same movement, to return to it as to a phenomenon. The phenomenon had to pass from evident presence to the enigma of the play within it between the unapparent and the apparent only in order to be able to give rise to the phenomenality of Being, which, par excellence, is covered over in the very uncovering of beings—since it brings about that uncovering. On the condition that the phenomenon open up to its own enigma, it becomes possible to dare to qualify Being itself with the title of phenomenon. Heidegger had that audacity at least once: "this phenomenon of 'Being' [*dieses Phänomen, 'Sein'*] . . . must be elaborated."[55] Let us elaborate it, then, with Heidegger and without Husserl.

We have therefore come to the situation where, as the Zähringen seminar will put it in 1973, "this phenomenology is a phenomenology of the unapparent."[56] Before retorting a bit too quickly that one must choose between, on the one hand, a phenomenology, and therefore the apparent, and, on the other hand, the unapparent, and therefore an impossibility for phenomenology, let us ask why this paradox—a phenomenology of the unapparent *as such*, and not simply of the not-yet appearing—is here fully required by the necessity of thought. The answer, in fact, offers no difficulty at the level of formulation (if it does offer a difficulty at the level of thought). Phenomenology must bear on the unapparent because Being does not appear, "is not perceivable"; Being is never perceived within the horizon of presence as a perfectly obedient and lawful phenomenon. Why? Because the presence uncovered in evident permanence receives, and is suitable to, beings alone; only a being can remain here and now in order to respond "present!" to the command of evidence; but "this Being itself is nothing of a being [*nichts Seiendes*]. Likewise what belongs to the Being of a being remains in obscurity." These two texts, one from 1925, the other from the summer of 1927, rigorously frame a fundamental thesis of *Sein und Zeit*: "The Being of beings 'is' not itself a being."[57] That which the gaze sees and knows in full assurance alone is—is a being; Being itself does not show itself precisely because it is not: "For what we experience first and foremost is beings, that which is; we recognize Being only later or maybe even not at all."[58] Being, at least from the point of view of the present phenomenon, and therefore of evident beings, is nothing of a being, and it is nothing visible. Nothing? It is known that in 1929 the lecture *What Is Metaphysics?* will finally no longer hesitate to radicalize what *Sein und Zeit* already urges and will strictly identify Being with the nothing/nothingness.[59] For the moment that concerns us, it is sufficient to note that, since the phenomenon ever admits only beings, the most perfect uncovering in presence will also ever be able to present nothing except the evidence of a being; the most evident phenomenon in the world gives only what it has—namely, the evidence of a being. Any inquiry in the direction of the Being of beings will therefore have to set out itself in search of a goal other than uncovering; for Being can never be found as uncovered or exposed; only beings can and must be. Consequently: "We therefore distinguish not only terminologically but also for reasons of intrinsic content between the *uncoveredness of a being* [*Entdecktheit eines Seienden*] and the *opening of its Being* [*Erschlossenheit seines Seins*]. A being can be uncovered, whether by way of perception or some other mode of access, only if the Being of this being is already open—only if I already understand it."[60] It should not be surprising here that Heidegger talks about an opening in which Being deploys itself, as if it were a matter of Being imitating the entrance into presence proper to uncovered beings; that very surprise only indicates that *we* still spontaneously think Being and that which concerns it on the basis and in the mode of the uncoveredness of beings. But precisely, Being does not open like beings are uncovered, if only because its opening precedes uncoveredness and renders it possible. This also means that the opening does not open Being like uncoveredness uncovers beings—in and according to presence. In opening, to be sure, Being opens the orbit of the uncoveredness of present beings, but for that very reason it does not itself enter into evident presence. If we want to maintain the title of phenomenon for Being—at the risk of an extremely dangerous ambiguity—it would be necessary to think a phenomenon that is not exhausted in presence here and now, since it is defined only by being able to refuse itself to such presence. To render phenomenal not that which, being invisible, could become visible, and therefore become a being, but, paradoxically, to render phenomenal that which, invisible as such, could not in any way become visible in the mode of a present being—can this task be taken on, or even formulated?

5. The Two Senses of the Reduction

Concerning the phenomenon in its Husserlian acceptation we concluded that it gave itself as a *flat* phenomenon (without remainder, slack, superficial) and therefore as perfectly present. We are now seeking a mode of the phenomenon that frees it from the requirement of presence; might one not suspect that, in this new case, it would also escape flatness? In a certain way, it would be a question here of sounding (and not of uncovering) what we could name the *depth* of the Heideggerian phenomenon. Depth, because it is a question of envisaging that phenomenon according to two layers and not just one. How? By interpreting being as being precisely in its Being. Being doubtless never offers itself to any direct reading for the gaze of evidence, and therefore this gaze by definition never uncovers (*entdeckt*) anything other than present beings. However, outside (beyond) their presence, those beings give to be read that which they themselves ignore, or even conceal—the mode of their entrance into presence, their very phenomenality: "Being must be read starting from/on the surface of beings [*am Seienden soll ablesen werden*]; in other words, what phenomenological interpretation puts into fore-sight [*in die Vor-sicht stellt*] is Being."[61] *To read starting from/on the surface of . . .* poorly translates *ablesen*, which indicates first a gleaning, a nonsystematic but nevertheless select picking; it is not simply a question of reading the evidence of the phenomenon in its flatness (which the Husserlian constitution already accomplishes perfectly); beyond that, in this case, it is a question of reading, between the lines, so to speak, between the bursts of evident presence, that from which that very presence proceeds; the text next says *Interpretation*, a word of Latin origin whose German equivalent would be, precisely, *Auslegung*. It is therefore a question of reading the phenomenon in such a way that one *departs* from it, or at least that one transgresses the unquestioned evidence of its presence. To depart does not mean that one forgets it in order better to move on to something else; it is indeed a question of moving, but not at all to something other than the thing. To what, then? To what one sets in view; here the text writes *Vorsicht*, or rather *Vor-sicht*, *Vorsicht* indicates, in one word, attention and precaution; but in order to pay attention, it is necessary, precisely, "to look beyond the end of one's nose," to look ahead of oneself with a forward look; this look that looks out looks, precisely in order to look out for it, beyond what it has before its eyes; it looks not only at the evident and present beings before itself, but, above all, beyond, before, far off. What does it look at in that view beyond (*Vor-sicht*)? Something else? Not at all, since it is a question of keeping this present thing, this being here and now. Sight looks at the horizon from which danger might come and where every new situation will arise. The phenomenological look looks in this way: it looks at being according to its horizon—in short, with a view to its Being. Interpretation does not consist in seeing another being, but in seeing being otherwise. However, it is not a question of seeing the being otherwise than as that being; on the contrary, it is a question of seeing it, for the first time, as a being, namely, as uncovered in presence, in short, of seeing it as a phenomenon. The phenomenon appears: it issues from its own exit from unapparentness into evident apparition; to see it as such therefore means seeing it inasmuch as it does not stop appearing and therefore freeing itself from unapparentness in order be fixed in presence. Before the apparition of the phenomenon, phenomenological interpretation indeed has an idea in the back of its head; or rather, because it does not seek the "reason for effects," one has to say that it has an attention (*Vorsicht*) in mind behind its vision (*Sicht*)—behind, or better, at the very heart of its vision. The vision of the presence of the phenomenon discovers in it, through its attention, a depth. Depth here does not indicate that "behind" the phenomenon some*thing* else would be waiting to appear, but that the very appearing of the phenomenon—as a way (of Being) and therefore as a nonbeing—reveals a depth. The depth does not dub or betray [*double*] the phenomenon (in the cinematographic or detective sense of *doubler*); it reveals it to itself—namely, it shows that it *is* inasmuch as Being first opens as the phenomenality in which, only then, it can itself be discovered.

Thus, the depth of the phenomenon relaunches phenomenology as a knowledge not only of the phenomena but, much more radically, of their phenomenality. Being can be opened by (and thus become the stake of) phenomenology only inasmuch as the phenomena are seen as beings entering into presence. Being opens on the basis of the uncoveredness of beings only in the sense that phenomenality is discovered on the basis of the enigma of the phenomenon. We can henceforth glimpse that the redefinition of the phenomenological method for Heidegger is of a piece with the establishment of the question concerning the Being of beings— an encounter announced by the identification of the phenomenon with being and accomplished by the accession to Being as phenomenality. In this way Heidegger specifies what he names "the phenomenological tendency—to clarify and to understand Being as such [*Sein als solches*]," or again, "the interpretation of beings with regard to their Being [*auf sein Sein hin*]."[62] In the two couples, phenomenon/phenomenality and beings/Being, and in order to allow their superposition or intersection, thought carries out the same act—a transgression. Transgression here means not some arbitrary and barbarous violence, but the performance of the return to the things themselves; the things of thought do not coincide with the things of life; thought must not only return to beings and phenomena, that is, to evident and permanent presence; it must step up its impetus in order to enter into the (immanent) depth of that presence, by opening immanence itself according to phenomenality, and therefore Being: "The question of Being can be reached only when the questioning is guided by a *questioning to the very end* [*Zu-Ende-fragen*], namely, a *questioning that returns to the beginning* [*in den Anfang Hineinfragen*], that is, when it is determined by the sense of the phenomenological principle radically understood—that of the thing itself—*to allow being to be seen as being itself in its Being* [*Seiendes als Seiendes selbst in seinem Sein sehen zu lassen*]."[63] The transgression does not undo being, nor does it contest the phenomenon, since it is a question of *allowing* being *to be seen* as being itself. The transgression consists in questioning to the end, and therefore in breaking through (*Hineinfragen*) all the way to the radical beginning—namely, all the way to what is at play in being appearing as such: Being in the capacity of phenomenality. The transgression moves *in* the phenomenon/being itself, because transcendence, for Heidegger, does not pass beyond the immanence of the phenomenon; on the contrary, if the phenomenon is valid as a being, then the Being that offers being to itself becomes, in the capacity of phenomenality, the transcendent par excellence. *Sein ist das transcendens schlechthin.*[64] The transcendence of Being does not leave being behind it, but rather pushes it to the end. The transcendence of phenomenality does not pass through the immanence of the phenomenon, but much rather leads it to its end.

The transcendence of Being pushes being to the end in such a way as to return truly to the things themselves. The thing to which thought must return depends on nothing among beings, but on the nothing *of* beings, namely Being. This first fulfillment of the phenomenological precept through the transgression of beings sets us on the path of a second fulfillment, obtained equally through transgression—the fulfillment of the reduction:

> *For Husserl*, phenomenological reduction, which he worked out for the first time expressly in the *Ideas Toward a Pure Phenomenology and Phenomenological Philosophy* (1913), is the method of leading [*Ruckführung*] phenomenological vision from the natural attitude of the human being whose life is involved in the world of things and persons back to the transcendental life of consciousness and its noetic-noematic experiences, in which objects are constituted as correlates of consciousness. *For us* [on the contrary], phenomenological reduction means leading [*Ruckführung*] phenomenological vision back from the apprehension of a being, whatever may be the character of that apprehension, to the understanding of the

Being of this being (projecting upon the mode of its unconcealedness [*Unverborgenheit*]).⁶⁵

Heidegger therefore remains a phenomenologist, since he resumes the reduction. This resumption, to be sure, does not occur without a profound displacement; nevertheless, that displacement still leads to freeing up in a certain sense a certain phenomenon: henceforth the reduction does not lead from the thesis of the world (of beings) to the immanence of an immobile presence of the phenomenon, but from the phenomenon as an uncoveredness of a being to its deep comprehension with regard to its Being. Far from provoking the dismissal of the *Seinsglaube*, the reduction, thus relaunched by the radical return to the thing itself, clears up the meaning of Being of beings:

> This bracketing of the being takes nothing away from the being itself, nor does it purport to assume that the being is not. This switching [*Umschaltung*] of perspective has rather the sense of making the being's kind of Being present. This phenomenological switching-off [*Ausschaltung*] of the transcendent thesis has the sole function of making the being present in regard to its Being. The expression "bracketing" is thus always misunderstood [*missverständlich*] when it is thought that in bracketing the thesis of existence [*Daseinsthesis*] and by doing so, phenomenological reflection would have nothing to do with being; quite the contrary: in an extreme and unique way, what really is at issue now is the determination of the Being of the being itself.⁶⁶

To bracket the position of the world, and therefore of being, does not at all amount to calling being into question, but to calling into question that being might be discovered without the horizon of Being opening first. To suspend the thesis of being does not eliminate being but prohibits one from seeing it otherwise than according to the thing itself, and therefore compels one to see it as it is—namely as being according to Being. It is therefore especially necessary not to conclude, as Husserl confided to Ingarden, "that Heidegger . . . did not seize this path and thus also did not seize the entire meaning of the method of the phenomenological reduction"; nor that the objections made to Husserlian phenomenology "all rest on misunderstandings and finally on the fact that one interprets my phenomenology by bringing it back down to the level that its entire meaning consisted in overcoming; or, in other words, on the fact that one has not understood the principial innovation of the 'phenomenological reduction' and therefore also the elevation from worldly subjectivity (man) to 'transcendental subjectivity'; on the fact that one remains bogged down in an anthropology, whether it be empirical or *a priori.*"[67] For the Heideggerian transgression does not distinguish itself from the Husserlian reduction by a retrogressive return toward the naive position of the world; it distinguishes itself by passing beyond, toward the meaning of the Being of being.

But if Husserl commits the error of attributing an error to Heidegger, it is necessary to seek his theoretical motive. We propose the following: Husserl envisages only two terms that constitute the two sides of one reduction (thesis of the world/reduced phenomenon), without suspecting that Heidegger sees three, worked out in two reductions: thesis of the world/phenomenon through a purely Husserlian phenomenological reduction, and then being/meaning of Being through phenomenological interpretation. Why does Husserl not see this resumption, to the point of reading in the interpretation of being with regard to its Being only the regressive inversion of the first reduction? Answer: because Husserl does not gain access, or rather from the start prohibited himself from gaining access to the phenomenon *as to a being.* For Husserl, the reduced phenomenon in its most evident presence offers but a (noematic) correlate to consciousness; it never appears as a being, in its turn susceptible to referring not to consciousness alone (transcendental idealism), but to the meaning of Being. Thus it clearly appears that Husserl's misunderstanding of the ontico-ontological status of the reduction ensues directly from his misunderstanding of the return to the thing itself, which he nevertheless first took as his goal and his method. Conversely, the shift from the reduction to interpretation goes hand in hand, according to Heidegger, with the resumption of the principle of a return to the thing itself, since in both cases it is only a question of passing beyond being toward its Being; but that transgression itself implies first the recognition of the phenomenon as a being. On the basis of that achievement, Heidegger's enterprise, which was phenomenological from the beginning, though in an original way, can be deployed as an illumination of being in the direction of its Being (and not only of the phenomenon on the basis of a consciousness that gives). Phenomenality as the Being of the phenomenon in the capacity of a being will be put into play according to two distinct tactics: the analytic of *Dasein*, on the one hand, and, on the other, the ontological difference.

6. The Redoubled Reduction—"*Dasein*"

The analytic of *Dasein* renders null and void the suspicion of an anthropology as soon as one sees that it responds to the radical injunction according to which "the question of Being must be constructed (*gestellt*)."[68] It is a matter of constructing the frame of a question that passes beyond (transcends) every being: therefore it cannot be a matter of any return to naive consciousness, to the position of the world, in short, of a regression that falls short of the phenomenological attitude; the frame to be established here (*Gestell* resonates in *gestellt*) leads the whole of the given back, and therefore reduces it, to what precisely is not immediately given, or is never mediately giveable (because it is giving)—Being. Thus, not only does the intervention of a frame exclude a regression that falls short of the reduction, but the intention of the question constructed by that frame, namely Being, which by definition cannot give itself as a being, demands that the requirement of a *certain* bracketing here be fundamentally at work. From the very beginning, and for two fundamental reasons, it is a matter of practicing, in a *certain* way, to be sure, the reduction.

Let us summarize again those two reasons for the reduction: The frame of the question is established quite rigorously according to three terms precisely insofar as one is dealing with a question taken in its most complete sense.

> Questioning, inasmuch as a questioning with regard to [*als Fragen nach*] . . . , has *something that it asks* [*sein Gefragtes*, what one asks]. But all questioning with regard to . . . is in one way or another the posing of a question to [*Anfragen bei* . . .]. To questioning belongs, in addition to that with regard to which it questions, *that which it questions* [*ein Befragtes*]. In an investigative question, that is, a specifically theoretical question, what one asks [*Gefragte*] must be determined and conceptualized. In what one asks, then, is found what one properly aims at [*das eigentlich Intendierte*], namely what one wants to know [*das Erfragte*], that toward which the questioning advances.[69]

In other words, an authentic question calls into action a frame that is not binary (reduction in the Husserlian sense), but indeed ternary (reduction in the Heideggerian sense): first what one asks, then to what or to whom one asks it, and finally what one wants to end up knowing by the asking. Transposed into detective language, it would be a matter of posing a question (where, when, how, *quibus auxiliis?*) to a witness (or suspect) in order to uncover the truth concerning an event. It is especially important to distinguish here the irreducibility of what one asks (of the one whom one is interrogating) with what, in the last instance, one wants to know; it is this gap that we have already encountered with the notion of *Ablesung*: a secondary reading that gathers what it finds with a view to something else than the very thing that it has just found. The ternary question becomes, strictly speaking, an investigation: it wants information, obtained from a being, with regard to what that being itself does not know, or at least conceals. The question asks the being much more than it can or wants to say; the question wants to know not what can be known, but indeed what cannot at first (and perhaps ever) be uncovered. Related to the section that the 1925 course devotes, much more explicitly than will *Sein und Zeit*, to the *Fragestruktur der Seinsfrage*, to the structuration that renders the question truly questioning, one might gloss, the three elements at play within the investigation each take a name: "Thus, to begin with, we have elicited a threefold distinction in the structure of the question and the questioning. Very formally, these are: 1) What *one seeks to know by interrogating* [*das Erfragte*]: the meaning of Being. 2) What *one asks for by questioning* [*das Gefragte*]: the Being of beings. 3) What or whom one *interrogates by questioning* [*das Befragte*]: the being itself."[70] This formal result will suffice for us, here at least, in order to understand Heidegger's own practice of the phenomenological reduction. The latter assigns itself the task—we have seen—of questioning *deeply*. Deeply? Clearly we understand that it is a matter of questioning in two moments, in order to raise being in two rounds, and no longer one. In the first round (in the sense of a fight in several rounds) or the first raise (in the sense of gambling or, if one prefers, of amorous bids) being is interrogated (*Ausweis*, in the sense of the indication that refers to . . . , but in the sense also and first of the identity that one must state and, eventually, prove with identification papers); in this questioning, something else (than itself, than its immediate identity) is asked of it: the being identified as such (inasmuch as being: a metaphysical, even Aristotelian, moment) is asked to explain its Being; to explain the Being of being could even constitute a reminder of the Husserlian reduction; whatever the case may be, being is enjoined to delimit (*Anweisung*, which also means the instruction that one gives to a subordinate) its Being: How do things stand, for it, with its Being? The being is not asked what it is, but of what it is (genitive: Being *of* beings; relation: *Sein des Seienden*). This is the first round, the first raise. But then there is also a second, which the interrogated being cannot, and moreover must not, reach; the second raise concerns the being only indirectly; it belongs properly to the question itself, inasmuch as it is practiced authentically. What the question, or more precisely the questioning, finally wants to know can in no way be confused with what the interrogated being wants to say or can know; the questioning has in the back of its head another "idea": it is in search not only of the Being of beings but indeed of the "meaning of Being" itself. Explicit as early as 1925, the gap between the *Sein des Seienden* and the *Sinn des Seins* points immediately, against any hasty acceptance of the *Kehre*, toward what *Zeit und Sein* names the attempt to "think Being without beings."[71] Beings are dismissed from the questioning (*Verweisung*, dismissal)—which is pursued, so to speak, without them—of the Being of beings as far as the "meaning of Being," in a rigorous movement from the ontic to the ontological which alone opens the horizon proper to—at least—the phenomenological intention of *Sein und Zeit* according to its initial formalism. One could risk saying that, from the very beginning and therefore already in the confrontation with the reduction taken in Husserl's strict sense, Heidegger has but one intention: to interrogate being through a question concerning its Being, such that finally Being alone is at stake—the "meaning of Being." It is in fact not a question of the meaning *of* Being, as if Being as yet intervened only indirectly (genitive of its meaning), but of Being directly as meaning, of meaning directly as Being. Such then is the second raise: to raise the Being of beings beyond beings as far as the "meaning of Being." The reduction is redoubled: it no longer aims only at showing of what Being beings are (Being as consciousness or indeed Being as world) but, starting from this first result and this first reduction, it aims finally to disengage Being as such. One can show that *Sein und Zeit* does not arrive at the completion of such an undertaking; for the moment we are concerned only to establish the intention and the structure of its questioning: the redoubled reduction attempts, through a strictly but originally phenomenological method, to lead being to the meaning of Being—to Being without regard for being.

But what being? What being could have such regard for Being that it should lead us back, *volens nolens*, to Being without regard for being? Does not the choice of human being, of *Dasein*, constitute the proof of a regression toward anthropology, and therefore of the concrete impossibility of setting the redoubled reduction into operation? In order to respond to this objection, if only formally, there is only one way: to seek the criteria that allow one to privilege *Dasein* in order to attempt the double phenomenological raise. For finally, Heidegger himself asks with rigor, "As what is this being , of which we say that it questions, looks upon, considers as, relates, etc.—already given [*als was ist . . . —vorgegeben*]? It is the being that we ourselves are; this being, which I myself am in each particular instance (*je*), we call *Dasein*"; but then isn't this an admission of anthropology, or even worse of "existentialism"? The preceding page, however, cautioned against this mistaken sense: "The questioning is itself a being which is given with the question of the Being of a being in the act of carrying out the questioning—whether it is expressly noted or not."[72] Let us be clear: *Dasein* does not constitute one of the beings that are susceptible to bearing the redoubled reduction, the one among others that only an unfortunate and irresistible propensity toward anthropology would have led us to privilege; on the contrary, it does not come, after the fact, to serve a questioning that was previously constructed; it itself, to begin with, constitutes the questioning as its flesh and body, its place and its call. *Dasein* as such is always already not only appointed to the double reduction but indeed realizes the double reduction itself. Why? Because "*Dasein* is here not only *ontically* decisive but also *ontologically* so for us as phenomenologists." It is not only necessary to say, with *Sein und Zeit*, here set in the background, that "*understanding of Being is itself a definite characteristic of Dasein's Being. Dasein* is ontically distinctive in that it *is* ontological";[73] it is necessary to say it from the phenomenological point of view. The privilege of *Dasein* is strictly phenomenological, not anthropological. Indeed, it is characterized ontically as having access to Being, as having Being for its stake, as having Being for its depth. Of itself, as a being, it refers, or better refers *itself*, back to Being: "*Dasein's* essential determination by which it intrinsically *transcends* [itself] is likewise connected with the ecstatic-horizonal character." It transcends, indeed, ceaselessly transcends itself not through an irrational, unspecifiable grace, but through its specific phenomenological characteristic, intentionality: "intentionality is the *ratio cognoscendi* of transcendence."[74] Thought through to its roots, intentionality implies a world, or more exactly *In-der-Welt-Sein* (and it is known that this was another breaking point with Husserl); therefore, in the beings which it thus transcends, it aims at the Being of beings; a fortiori, in the being that it first is for itself, *Dasein* aims intentionally at Being in its beingness. For this reason, *Dasein* could never, so to speak, stop with the consideration of itself (even in inauthenticity) and must always aim through transcendence at the Being of being. By nature, its ontological identity makes of it the principal witness (if not more) of the investigation that seeks the "meaning of Being." It is indeed necessary therefore to characterize it as such, as "that being in whose Being it is a question *of* that very Being,"[75] on condition, however, of understanding the Being of *that* being as Being *tout court* (*überhaupt*) according to its meaning—the "meaning of Being": "to comprehend the understanding of Being means first and foremost to understand *that* being to whose ontological constitution the understanding of Being belongs," "*Dasein*—as we have said over and over— is the being to whose existence the understanding of Being belongs," according to "what is distinctive about *Dasein*, namely, that it relates itself to beings while understanding Being [*als Sein-verstehend*]," the later texts will say.[76] The privilege of *Dasein* comes to it only from its disposition to undergo a redoubled phenomenological reduction; the latter passes from being to the "meaning of Being" only by working *that* being which is determined above all by the Being of being. Thus, according to a first tactic, the analytic of *Dasein* is accomplished as a redoubled reduction and thus permits the reference from being as phenomenon back to Being ("meaning of Being") as phenomenality.

7. The Redoubled Reduction—the Nothing

There still remains the second tactic which establishes a second phenomenological frame whose broad traits are established by the 1929 lecture, *Was ist Metaphysik?*—with even more clarity if one includes the corrections made to the later editions. It does not seem possible here to unfold its entire approach (see chap. 6, below). But for our purposes it will suffice to bring out its essential traits, which allow one to recognize therein a sort of phenomenological reduction—even a metamorphosis of what, with regard to the analytic of *Dasein*, we risked naming a redoubled reduction. A first trait: just as the analytic of *Dasein* resulted from the three dimensions according to which "the question of Being must be constructed [*gestellt*]," likewise here it will be a matter of "the elaboration of the question of the Nothing [*Ausarbeitung der Frage nach dem Nichts*]."[77] To elaborate a question means to identify the acts (and to determine their conditions of possibility) that are able to assure the givenness of the Nothing as such. Just as in *Sein und Zeit* it is a matter of attaining, and therefore of giving, the "meaning of Being," so here it is a matter of attaining, and therefore of giving, the Nothing—which in fact the lecture accomplishes: "And indeed, the Nothing itself—as such—was there."[78]

Hence a second trait: in the frame of 1929, as, moreover, in that of 1927, the reduction is carried out in the case of anxiety.[79] However, a notable difference here opposes the two roles held by anxiety. In 1927, this anxiety affects *Dasein* so as to make it reach the full rigor of *In-der-Welt-Sein*, which characterizes it as *Da-sein* for all the other beings; thus, anxiety is limited to *Dasein* alone, in opposition to the whole of being in face of which anxiety radically singularizes *Dasein*. In 1929, on the contrary, anxiety exerts itself without any particular reference to *Dasein*, or, more exactly, it exercises *Dasein* in the encounter with being in general, on the basis of the result already obtained by boredom: "This boredom shows being as a whole [*Das Seiende im Ganzen*]."[80] How are we to understand the fact that anxiety's field of application is broadened to the point of no longer operating the reduction on a being, *Dasein*, which is led back to its principial trait as *In-der-Welt-Sein*, but indeed on all being—which is led back to its originary Nothing? Two interpretations suggest themselves. Either Heidegger in 1929 leaves behind the supposedly narrow and limited rigor of a strictly phenomenological reduction; but in this case, why maintain so ostensibly one of the most famous analyses from *Sein und Zeit?* Or else the broadening of the ontic field (from *a* being to *all* being) would become possible as the consequence of, precisely, an enhanced phenomenological power of the reduction; that power would have become strong enough to operate the *same* reduction, not only on *Dasein,* but also on being in its totality. Just as, if one allows us the comparison, atomic physicists attempt to move from fission (where the chain reaction can be produced only by using enriched uranium) to fusion (where the reaction would be produced for any other material), so Heidegger's phenomenological reduction attempts, between 1927 and 1929, to operate upon all of being, and thus upon every being. To be sure, even in 1929, it still operates starting from *Dasein,* but it is deployed nonetheless resolutely beyond its field. It is true that that field consists in *In-der-Welt-Sein* and therefore concerns, immediately and in principle in 1927, being in its totality. But then it remains to be shown that the generalized reduction of 1929 aims, through stages that are no doubt different, at the givenness and phenomenalization of the very term that the 1927 reduction called the "meaning of Being."

The third trait allows, at least in outline, for the satisfaction of this requirement. What in fact does anxiety effect upon being in its totality, such as natural (here: scientific) consciousness naively posits it? Let us read the text:

> In anxiety there is a withdrawal before . . . which, assuredly, is not a flight but a fascinated repose. That withdrawal before . . . receives its exit from the Nothing. The latter does not attract toward itself, but on the contrary assigns essentially to expulsion [*abweisend*]. The assigning expulsion [*Abweisung*] is therefore as such the dismissal that makes slip [*entgleitenlassende Verweisen*] in the direction of beings as a whole which thus founder. This dismissal which, as a whole, assigns to expulsion [*abweisende Verweisung*] in the direction of beings which, as a whole, slip, such that the Nothing holds *Dasein* in anxiety, is the essence of the Nothing [*Nichts*]: the reduction to Nothing [*Nichtung*].

Let us take up this description, which is obscure in appearance but clear in fact. Anxiety abolishes the distinction among beings: I can no longer specify what being it is that I am afraid of; I am therefore afraid of whatever being it may be, and therefore of being in its totality; anxiety therefore imposes repulsion against being in its indistinct totality; it effects the expulsion of being, but an expulsion that at the same time designates it all the better as such since it assigns it in its threatening beingness: an expulsion that sees being and makes it slowly slip, and finally founder in a long immobile movement (like a ship that, vertical at the moment of foundering, seems to freeze between sky and sea); the expulsion distances being from the world—literally, "shows it the door" (such is the scholarly and general meaning of *abweisen*!). A note added by Heidegger in 1949 to this phrase comments on the expression *abweisende Verweisung*: "*Ab-weisen: das Seiende für sich; verweisen: in das Sein des Seienden.*"[81] Let us translate: to assign in expelling concerns being taken for itself (thus without relation to Being); to refer means to refer in and to the *Being* of being. In other words, the expulsion of being outside of the world constitutes only the first moment of anxiety, which pursues its work through the reference—henceforth rendered possible by the slipping and the shipwreck of being—to Being. Not that Being appears once the shipwreck of being in its totality is completed, as the "supreme one amidst the wreckage" (Mallarmé)—Being is not uncovered as the ultimate wreckage from the "sepulchral shipwreck" of being, nor, to speak like Husserl, as a "residue." Being shows itself here in a pure and simple movement of reference (*Verweisung*) that signals, in return, only to the strict (and inversely proportional) degree that being is assigned to expulsion (*Abweisung*). Thus Being appears not as the end of anxiety (result, residue, and therefore still being), but as the completion of its movement. Anxiety produces Being by setting itself forth as expulsion of being *and*, indissolubly, reference to Being. Anxiety thus carries out a phenomenological reduction by leading being in its totality back toward Being. That reduction therefore repeats some of the most fundamental traits of the 1927 reduction, as is confirmed moreover by the use of *Verweisung* as early as 1925 and 1927 to define the phenomenon as such: "The possibility of the phenomenon as reference [*Erscheinung als Verweisung*] is founded in the phenomenon in the proper sense, namely, self-showing [*im Sich-zeigen*]"—"Phenomenon [*Erscheinung*], for its part, signifies a reference-relation [*Verweisungsbezug*] which itself is in the direction of a being."[82]

However, an objection becomes unavoidable which compels us to bring out a fourth trait. First the objection: the 1929 reduction diverges from the analytic of *Dasein* in the identity of its outcome; trusting a later rereading of his own text by Heidegger, we have attributed the "*Being* of being" as an outcome to the reduction of being in its totality by anxiety. Now, as concerns the outcome, there returns more explicitly and more frequently the Nothing itself. What relation are we to establish between the one and the other? Even more, how could we find again, in 1929, the essential triplicity of terms, such as it alone had seemed to us able to permit the redoubled reduction specific to the Heideggerian innovation?

In order to attempt a response, it is necessary to take up again the stages of the phenomenological reduction by anxiety. The stages, we say: in fact, there are at least two, which set three terms (and not only two) into operation. The first stage leads from being (in its totality) to the "Being of being" through a dismissal that expels or, conversely, a "dismissal" that refers to . . . (*abweisende Verweisung*); one should not too quickly object here that this first stage leads only to the Nothing; for the Nothing itself constitutes the transgression (transcendence) of being toward the Being of being; and this is explicitly the case in the first reduction of 1929: "In the Being of being occurs the reduction to nothing of the Nothing [*Nichts*]"; or: "The Nothing does not remain the indeterminate opposite of being but is discovered as belonging to the Being of being."[83] The Nothing therefore undoubtedly does occur first as the nothing of being (as its ontic annihilation); but the reduction to nothing (*Nichten, Nichtung*) of the Nothing immediately reverses the relation: the annihilation itself would remain impossible and inconceivable if the Nothing, as the Nothing of being, did not itself reveal the first brilliance of another relation of being—namely: the Being of being. The Nothing as such does not only annihilate being, but above all it annuls being through a transcendence that shows being's role as a mouthpiece of the Being of being. We therefore do find again, this time transposed from *Dasein* as *the* privileged being to being in its totality, the first raise and round of the reduction that was being carried out, in the frame of 1925 and 1927, from being to the Being of being. In 1929, what one interrogates (*das Befragte*) is called being in its totality; what one asks for (*das Gefragte*) keeps the same identity as in 1927: the Being of being (unveiled in the Nothing of being in general). But how do things stand with what one wants to know (*das Erfragte*)? In order to satisfy the third dimension of the questioning, one would have, in disengaging a second round and raise of the reduction, to indicate the new name given in 1929 to what was being aimed at in 1925 under the title of "meaning of Being."

We should note before any other investigation that in 1927 *Sein und Zeit* obviously does not manage to decide on the "meaning of Being," still less to present it concretely at the end of the incomplete analytic of *Dasein*. The "meaning of Being" thus remains more the horizon of a project than the completion of a journey. This indetermination allows one to approach more carefully the difficulty that we experience in clearly determining the third term required in order to show completely, in 1929, a redoubled phenomenological reduction. As a simple hypothesis, we risk the following equivalence: what in 1927 *Sein und Zeit* designates (without really attaining it) under the title of "meaning of Being" the lecture of 1929 aims at—without including it explicitly—under the name of ontological difference. Without any doubt—at least to our knowledge—the lecture does not mention, in the body of its first draft, the phrase "ontological difference"; but as early as 1927 for the courses, and as early as 1928 for the published texts (*Vom Wesen des Grundes*),[84] the ontological difference determines the horizon of investigation, to the point that it became possible, in 1931, for Heidegger to complete his 1929 text, so as to introduce into it, in a self-commentary, some mentions of ontological difference. For example, "What essential discord unveils itself here?" is made more explicit by "ontological difference"; or: "it [i.e., the Nothing] differs radically [*schlechthin*] from it (i.e., being)" is set forth by these equivalents: "difference, *der Unterschied, die Differenz*"; and again, the formula: "We would prefer to say that, in anxiety, the Nothing is met *at one and the same time* with being. What is signified by this 'at one and the same time'?"—the gloss admits "difference"; and finally the conclusion of the description: "The essence of the Nothing that originarily reduces to nothing resides in this: it brings *Da-sein* for the first time face to face with being as such," is confirmed by: "Properly before the Being of being, before the difference."[85] Starting from 1928–29, the watchword and the guiding thread of the analyses will become more and more explicitly the clarification of the ontological difference; to the point of excess, the latter will play the canonical role of the *Erfragte*, that which one is seeking to know thanks to but also beyond everything that one asks of any being whatsoever. There is therefore nothing surprising in the fact that, even in the 1929 text, where it does not yet appear explicitly, it already thoroughly determines the whole of the question to be constructed. Within this hypothesis—since in fact we are dealing only with a hypothesis—the third element of a developed phenomenological question would be attained. Through it, one would also attain the goal of the second raise and round of the phenomenological reduction: it would be a matter of leading the Being of being back to the ontological difference, and therefore, what amounts to the same thing, it would be a matter of showing the gap between being and Being (the *of*) from the point of view not of being (even already reduced to nothing), but of Being as such.

These two rounds of the phenomenological reduction by Heidegger therefore converge toward a single goal: to receive Being itself in pure givenness and as a phenomenon. Heidegger attempts to include in the phenomenological placing-in-evidence not only being (eventually lead back to objectivity), but the Nothing that transcends every being—Being. "Being means appearing. Appearing is not something subsequent that happens from time to time to Being. Being displays itself precisely as appearing (*Sein west* als *Erscheinen*)."[86] Of course, one still needs to determine whether each of the two rounds of the phenomenological reduction by Heidegger accomplishes the plan that it set for itself; above all, one still needs to understand why Heidegger mobilizes successively *two* operations of the phenomenological reduction extended to Being; it is not self-evident that these questions can find a coherent answer. But before giving ourselves over to these questions,[87] it is necessary to stress that, at the very moment when he rejects and claims to overcome as nonphenomenological the reduction as Husserl practiced it, Heidegger can still legitimately acknowledge himself to be Husserl's "disciple"; for it is still by virtue of the method of phenomenology and of the principle of a "return to the things themselves" that the second and radical reduction is developed—that of all beings to the Being of beings. Heidegger does not abandon Husserlian phenomenology any more than he refutes it—he revives its temporarily slackened impetus, because he dares to ask of its possibility what its actuality no longer allowed one to give—Being as a phenomenon. Indeed, concerning phenomenology, "what is essential is not that it be *actual* in the capacity of a philosophical 'orientation.' For higher than actuality stands possibility."[88] That Being should appear—this ultimate accomplishment befalls phenomenology only in the mode of possibility. But can that possibility be accomplished in fact?

3

The *Ego* and *Dasein*

1. The Figure of Descartes within Heidegger's Path

Just as it is self-evident that Heidegger did not cease to confront Nietzsche, Hegel, Kant, or Aristotle, so his relation to Descartes can appear to be secondary. Thus, neither the commentators of Heidegger nor, to be sure, the historians of Descartes insist on the relation, when they do not ignore it altogether. Whatever the—bad or all too understandable—reasons for this misappreciation, they cannot lessen one massive fact: if only chronologically, Descartes appears already at the beginning of Heidegger's career and occupies it almost all the way to its end. If we stick to the texts already available in the present state of the publication of the *Gesamtausgabe* (in 1985), and unless we are forgetting something, the extreme evidence of a debate with Descartes intervenes as early as 1921 and right up to 1974.

In the course that he gives as *Privatdozent* in Freiburg during the winter semester of 1921–22, under the title of *Phänomenologische Interpretationen zu Aristoteles: Einführung in die phänomenologische Forschung* [*Phenomenological Interpretations of Aristotle: Introduction to Phenomenological Research*], a course therefore prior to the Marburg period, Heidegger does not treat Aristotle so much as he outlines a whole introduction to phenomenology; however, that introduction does indeed approach a philosopher: but instead of Aristotle, it is Descartes. Examining in fact "the metaphysics of the *I* and the idealism of the *I* [*Ich-metaphysik, ichlicher Idealismus*]," first in its Kantian and phenomenological forms, he ends up finally at Descartes, whose limits he already very clearly marks:

> The "*sum*" is, to be sure, also first for Descartes, but it is precisely here already that the failure lies: he does not stop there, but already has the pre-conception of the meaning of Being in the mode of simple observation [*Feststellung*] and even of the indubitable [*Unbezweifelbaren*]. The fact that Descartes was able to deviate toward the posing of a theoretical question

of knowledge and even that, from the point of view of the history of spirit [*geistigeschichtlich*], he inaugurated it, simply expresses [the fact] that the "*sum*," its Being and its categorial structure, were in no way a problem to him, but that the significance of the word "*sum*" was [for him] understood in an indifferent sense [*indifferenten . . . Sinn*], absolutely not related [properly] to the *ego*, formally objective [*formal gegenständlich*], uncritical and unclarified.

Already with this outline of an interpretation, Descartes appears as having privileged the ego in its certitude and as having assumed the *sum* without any real mediation: in other words, the mode of Being illustrated by the *sum* remains caught in its supposedly obvious, common, and indisputable sense and is therefore thought in fact on the basis of the acceptation of *esse* that is suitable to objects. Descartes privileges the question of the ego (hence the establishment of a theory of knowledge) and remains silent on the question of the *sum* (hence an objectivizing interpretation of all *esse*). Paradoxically, under the gaze of the young Heidegger, Descartes already poses the question of the mode of Being of the *sum* precisely by remaining silent on it in favor of a question concerning the status and the power of the *I*: "the weight of the question is placed immediately, without any motive and following the traditional standpoint, upon the 'I,' whereby the meaning of the 'I' remains essentially undetermined [*unbestimmt*], instead [of being placed] upon the meaning of the 'am.' "[1] Right away the essential is marked out: the *I* in the "I think" of the "I think, therefore I am," must be determined on the basis of the meaning of Being, and not on the basis of its own meaning as *I*.

The confrontation with Descartes, outlined so early, unfolds largely during Heidegger's stay in Marburg. In fact, that stay both opens and closes with a course explicitly dedicated to Descartes. That of the first winter semester of 1923–24 (still unpublished) undertakes an introduction to modern philosophy (*Der Beginn der neuzeitlichen Philosophie*); it must have evoked the figure of Descartes, at least if one accepts the testimony from the last course given in Marburg, in the summer of 1928: "This class, during the summer semester of 1928, set itself the task of assuming a position opposed to Leibniz. . . . The first semester of 1923/1924 risked taking the corresponding position with Descartes, which is then surpassed in Sein und Zeit (§§ 19–21)." We should underscore that the last course not only confirms that the first was dedicated to the study of Descartes and also that it thus anticipated nothing less than *Sein und Zeit*, §§ 19–21, but also itself concerned Descartes inasmuch as he persists in Leibniz, who, "like Descartes, sees in the *I*, in the *ego cogito*, the dimension from which all the fundamental metaphysical concepts must be drawn. One attempted to resolve the problem of Being as the fundamental problem of metaphysics through a return to the subject. However, in Leibniz as well as in his predecessor [i.e., Descartes] and successors, this return to the *I* remains ambiguous because the *I* is not grasped in its essential structure and in its specific mode of Being."2 From these texts, which frame the stay at Marburg but also precede it, it is necessary to conclude—and all the more so, no doubt, insofar as others will come to confirm this clear preoccupation—that Heidegger discerns from the beginning of his "path of thinking" the decisive importance of Descartes; but he does not see it where, following the tradition, his contemporaries saw it—in the establishment of the ego at the level of transcendental or quasitranscendental principle. He locates it, on the contrary, in what Descartes hides behind the evidence and the dignity of the *ego cogito*—in the indetermination of the way of Being of that ego, whose *sum* remains so indeterminate that it falls under the hold of the mode of Being of objects. Heidegger interrogates the *ego cogito* no longer concerning the cogitative origin of its primacy, but first concerning the ontological indetermination of its *esse*, and thus concerning what it conceals of itself and not what it proclaims of itself. This concealment, originally located in the indetermination of the Being of the *I*, in some way calls first for a phenomenological examination—since phenomenology bears above all on what, of itself, does not show itself. Thus the conversation with Descartes marks more than do other confrontations Heidegger's strictly phenomenological point of departure.

But it characterizes just as well his last texts. Sticking to a narrowly chronological criterion, one could stress the fact that Descartes remains an essential preoccupation right up to the end. (1) In 1969, the second seminar at Le Thor recalls the historial position of Descartes: "What happened between Hegel and the Greeks? The thought of Descartes"; or: "With Fichte we witness the absolutizing of the Cartesian *cogito* (which is a *cogito* only in the measure that it is a *cogito me cogitare*) in an absolute knowing."3 (2) In 1973, the Zähringen seminar carries to its highest point the interpretation of the Cartesian ego on the basis of the question of Being: " . . . subjectivity itself is not questioned as to its Being; indeed, since Descartes it is the *fundamentum inconcussum*. Throughout all modern thought, issuing from Descartes, subjectivity consequently constitutes the barrier to the beginning of the question in search of Being."4 (3) In 1974, one of the very last texts, *Der Fehl heiliger Namen* (*The Lack of Divine Names*) again signals this "barrier" in taking up again the theme of the first Marburg course: "At the beginning of modern thought are / According to the order before any clarification of the matter of the / thought of the treatises on method: / from Descartes the *Discourse on*

Method and the / *Regulae ad directionem Ingenii.*"[5] If only chronologically, Heidegger's thought does not cease to encounter that of Descartes, in a confrontation at least as constant as those that tie Heidegger to Nietzsche or Aristotle. This textual datum, which will be confirmed by the great number of instances concerning Descartes in the mature works, nevertheless does not suffice to clarify the encounter between Heidegger's thought and Descartes's. At the very most it allows us to establish the fact of that encounter and to require an understanding of it. The abundance and constancy of the Cartesian references will themselves become intelligible, moreover, only to the extent that concepts come to motivate and justify them. What conceptually identifiable reason leads and therefore constrains Heidegger, from the beginning to the end of his path, to argue over and with Descartes?

2. The Phenomenological Motif of the Original Confrontation

At the very moment Heidegger was expounding and critiquing Descartes at Marburg, Husserl was expounding and agreeing with Descartes at Freiburg, in a course during the 1923–24 winter semester, from which the work *First Philosophy* issues: even when he happened to maintain a "false theory," the "philosophical genius" of Descartes led him to sow the "seeds of transcendental philosophy."[6] In fact, Husserl had not awaited that date (nor, a fortiori, the *Cartesian Meditations* of 1929) to place Descartes at the center of his reflection; well before the *Ideen*, the Göttingen lectures had done so in 1907, after, to be sure, other texts.[7] At least in its Husserlian form, phenomenology had already before Heidegger tied its destiny to that of its interpretation of Descartes, in such a way that nothing phenomenological could any longer be decided, regarding principle, without a discussion with Descartes. Such as Heidegger encounters him, Descartes already has the status of a phenomenological motif, if not the rank of a phenomenologist. For Heidegger, through the intermediary of Husserl, Descartes first appears positively as a phenomenologist. In other words, the authority of Husserl, especially after the reversal of 1907, invested Descartes with a phenomenological dignity of such a kind that any discussion concerning Descartes amounts to a discussion with Husserl; more exactly, any discussion of the Cartesian theses that were legitimated by Husserl is equivalent to a theoretical discussion of Husserl himself. The equivalence between Descartes and (Husserlian) phenomenology can thus be developed in two absolutely opposed directions; either Descartes is a phenomenologist because he anticipates Husserl; or else Husserlian

phenomenology is not fully phenomenological because it remains imprisoned by uncriticized, even undiscerned, Cartesian decisions. Very early
on, Heidegger will follow the second direction: his departure from the
Husserlian interpretation of phenomenology is carried out through a
critique of the Cartesian presuppositions in it. Descartes will undergo a
critique, but a critique that is addressed also and first at Husserl, who is
all the less a phenomenologist insofar as he remains more a Cartesian.
Descartes thus arises as the nonphenomenological motif in Husserl.

Thus, in the summer of 1925, the *History of the Concept of Time: Prolegomena* attempts an "immanent critique of phenomenological research"
by examining how the latter determines pure consciousness. In other
words,

> Our [i.e., Heidegger's] question will be: Does this elaboration of the
> thematic field of phenomenology, the field of intentionality, raise the
> question of the *Being of this region*, of the *Being of consciousness*? What does
> *Being* really mean here when it is said that the sphere of consciousness is a
> sphere and region of *absolute* Being? What does *absolute Being* mean here?
> What does Being mean when we speak of the Being of the transcendent
> world, of the reality of things? . . . Does phenomenology anywhere really
> arrive at the methodological ground enabling us to construct [*stellen*] this
> *question of the meaning of Being*, which must precede any phenomenological
> deliberation and is implicit in it? . . . As the basic field of intentionality, is
> the region of pure consciousness determined in its Being, and how?![8]

One should notice that here, in 1925, Heidegger addresses to Husserl
and to the region of consciousness the same question and, in fact, the
same critique that he addressed already in 1921 to Descartes and to
the *ego cogito*: to establish the epistemological priority of the ego and
of consciousness is an achievement, but it does not free one from having
to determine the ego's mode of Being. Descartes is repeated with Husserl,
not only positively with the illumination of the condition for any certitude
in knowledge, but also negatively, with the forgetful evasion of the mode
of Being peculiar to originary certitude. To be sure, Husserl encountered
and noted, between consciousness and the reality of the world, "an unbridgeable difference of essence [*ein unüberbrückbar Wesensunterschied*],"
"a veritable abyss of meaning [*ein wahrer Abgrund des Sinnes*]." But for
all that, can he see therein only the divergence from "a necessary and
absolute Being [*ein notwendiges und absolutes Sein*]"? In short, in order to
think an epistemic divergence is it sufficient to name an ontic-ontological
divergence, as if from the irreducibility of consciousness to what it constitutes there ensued, for this very reason, "the principial difference among

ways of Being, the most important that there is in general, that between *consciousness* and *reality* [*die prinzipielle Unterschiedenheit der Seinsweisen, die kardinalste, die es überhaupt gibt, die zwischen* Bewußtsein *und Realität*]"?[9] It would have been necessary that Husserl not at all restrict himself to repeating the epistemic terms of the opposition—the absolutely certain because knowing consciousness, opposed to the reality that is contingent and relative because known—and undertake to elaborate the respective ways of *Being* of the two terms; but he reasons, in order to outline these two ways of Being, within a pair—certitude, contingency—that belongs entirely to the mode of Being which is solely that of the reality of the world, and which therefore has to do entirely with Being understood as permanent subsistence in the present. Like Descartes, Husserl is confined within the Being of the reality that is proper (or rather *im*proper) to consciousness, such that he evades the supposedly principial question of its way of Being; for its epistemic primacy, consciousness thus pays, so to speak, the price of an implicit but total submission to the way of Being of reality, and therefore of the world. Husserl carries out such a desertion of the question of the Being of consciousness only by relying explicitly on Descartes. Indeed, he cites Descartes textually in order both to define and to obscure consciousness' way of Being: "Immanent Being is also indubitably in the sense of absolute Being, in that in principle *nulla 're' indiget ad existendum* [*Das immanente Sein ist zweiffellos in dem Sinne absolutes Seins, dass es prinzipiell nulla 're' indiget ad existendum*]."[10]

Several remarks are necessary here. (1) Husserl undoubtedly does claim to define consciousness' way of *Being*, since he deduces absolute Being from immanent Being. (2) In order to reach his end, he cites the authority of Descartes, *Principia Philosophiae*, I, § 51: "*Per substantiam nihil aliud intelligere possumus, quam rem quae ita existit, ut nulla alia re indigeat ad existendum* [By *substance* we can understand nothing other than a thing which exists in such a way as to depend on no other thing for its existence]."[11] The meeting between these two thinkers certainly owes nothing to chance, since, already in agreement in recognizing the epistemic primacy of the ego, they meet again to define its way of Being by substantiality. (3) Husserl, however, modifies Descartes's formula: he omits *alia* in "*alia re*" and accepts *res* only between quotation marks: "*nulla 're.'* " Why? Obviously because *alia* (*res*) would imply that consciousness was itself and first a *res*; but Husserl undertakes here precisely to oppose consciousness to *realitas*; therefore, in defiance of any philological probity, he must modify what, in the quotation from Descartes, would implicitly extend *realitas* to the *res cogitans*, in order to retain from it only the application of substantiality to the ego. (4) This adjustment and therefore this difficulty already prove that Husserl utilizes in Descartes an insufficient and unsuitable definition; and in fact, for Descartes substantiality covers not only the *res cogitans* but even (although not without difficulties) all of the *res extensa*; therefore, it contradicts—far from confirming—the Husserlian privilege of consciousness: " . . . *substantia corporea et mens, sive substantia cogitans . . .* [. . . corporeal substance and mind, or thinking substance . . .]" (*Principia Philosophiae*, I, § 52).[12] A second contradiction might be added, moreover: all finite substance, thinking as well as extended, admits, for Descartes, a radical indigence with regard to the ordinary support of God; because of this, substantiality, which the ego must share with extension (first disagreement with Husserl), has only a relative validity (with respect to God) and not at all an absolute validity (second disagreement with Husserl). (5) These gaps do not call into question Husserl's intimate familiarity with Descartes; they prove, on the contrary, that the fundamental convergence had more power than any divergence in detail.[13] Such an exemplary encounter— Husserl citing Descartes to attempt to determine consciousness' way of Being—could not have escaped the attention of Heidegger. In fact, the same course from 1925 points out Husserl's formula and identifies it with precision as a reprise of Descartes. It can then stigmatize the ontological insufficiency of the reprise: immanence, indubitability, and absoluteness in no way allow one to think the *Being* of consciousness: "This third determination—absolute Being—is not in its turn such that it determines being itself in its Being, but such that it grasps the region of consciousness within the order of constitution and assigns to it in this order a Being that is formally anterior to any objectivity."[14] The Cartesian definition does not allow one to ground the difference of regions—which is ontological. Heidegger reduces to nothing the effort and the textual adaptations that Husserl imposes on Descartes's formula; here, it is Heidegger who defends the orthodoxy of the Cartesian text, precisely because it is conceptually opposed to Husserl. And what is more, Heidegger continues: not only does Husserl lose his way in reprising and forcing an unsuitable answer from Descartes, not only does he shy away from the authentic determination of consciousness' way of Being by believing himself to satisfy such a determination through the simple reprise of Cartesian certitude, but he goes astray even more radically in assuming a Cartesian question that he has not legitimated phenomenologically.

> Husserl's primary question is simply not that concerning the character of the Being of consciousness [*nach dem Seinscharakter des Bewußtseins*]. Rather, he is guided by the following concern: *How can consciousness in general become the possible object of an absolute science?* What guides him primordially is the *idea of an absolute science*. But this idea, that *consciousness*

must be the region of an absolute science, is not simply invented; it is the idea which has occupied *modern* philosophy ever since *Descartes.* The elaboration of pure consciousness as the thematic field of phenomenology is *not derived phenomenologically by going back to the things themselves* but by going back to a traditional idea of philosophy (nicht phänomenologisch im Rückgang auf selbst gewonnen, *sondern im Rückgang auf eine traditionelle Idee der Philosophie*).[15]

Let us measure the scope and acuity of Heidegger's critique of Husserl. (1) The question of the way of Being of consciousness receives no answer, because Husserl remains dependent on Descartes. (2) Husserl, evading the authentically phenomenological difficulty of the Being of consciousness, privileges the nonphenomenological ideal of a certain science of consciousness; we are therefore not far here from the parricidal declaration put forth by the same course: "In the basic task of determining its ownmost field, therefore, phenomenology is *unphenomenological!*"[16] (3) If Husserl distances himself from phenomenology, he owes this to the persistence in him of the Cartesian ideal as *mathesis universalis* and *universalissima sapientia,* defined already in the *Regulae.*[17] Far from guiding him along the phenomenological path, as Husserl thinks, Descartes played the notable role—from Heidegger's point of view—of *holding* Husserl *back* on the phenomenological path; between Husserl and full phenomenology, thus between Husserl and Heidegger, stands Descartes, a unique obstacle and stumbling block. The "affinity" that unites Husserl with Descartes[18] therefore designates a unique phenomenological obstacle, which phenomenology must surmount in order to remain itself; henceforth, in order to advance along the phenomenological path that Husserl leaves, Heidegger will have not only to leave Husserl but to "destroy" the one who held Husserl back—Descartes himself.

Thus can we better understand why Descartes occupies so much of Heidegger's attention: the chronological importance of the debate that he provokes ensues from the phenomenological radicality of the question that he poses—precisely by not posing it. To think Descartes means, for Heidegger, certainly not to repeat the establishment of the ego, as was attempted, each in his own way, by Hegel, Schelling, and Husserl, or even to overturn it like Nietzsche, but to destroy it in order to make appear, as the phenomenon that it hitherto concealed, the mode of Being of the ego (or of what is supposed to take its place) such as it is distinguished from the mode of Being of inner-worldly beings. Destroying the ego is not reducible to abolishing it ontically, but undertakes to free its ontological dignity—in short, destroying the *ego* opens access to *Dasein.* In this sense, within Heidegger's thought Descartes has no other privilege than that of the obstacle par excellence that prohibits the ontological fulfillment of phenomenology by blocking it with the ego and by thus masking *Dasein*.

3. The First Omission: The Indetermination of the *"Ego Sum"*

In 1927, and consistent with what has been outlined since 1921, Descartes intervenes in *Sein und Zeit* as "a supreme counter-example." A counterexample, exactly an extreme countercase (*Gegenfall*) of the ontological problematic of worldhood, Descartes therefore pushes phenomenology to its final extremity by failing to recognize the way of Being of the beings of the world; but this being the case, he calls into question—such as we shall see—the way of Being of all beings, beginning with *Dasein*. Indeed, "since the interpretation of the world first begins with an intra-worldly being, in order then to lose sight completely of the phenomenon of the world, let us try to clarify ontologically this point of departure by considering perhaps the most extreme development to which it ever led [*in seiner vielleicht extremsten Durchführung*]," namely the Cartesian ontology of the world. In this extremity, moreover, it is also a question of "the phenomenological destruction of the '*cogito sum*,' " which Heidegger announces, as the third part of his debate with Descartes, after §§ 19–20, just outlined in § 21 and put off to the unpublished "Second Part, Division 2."[19] In fact, the reproach addressed to Descartes applies to two omissions, that with respect to the world, and that also with respect to the ego, whose two ways of Being are missed equally, if in different ways. It is necessary to remark, moreover, that the reproach made to Descartes precedes the famous analysis of the *res extensa* from §§ 18–21,[20] where there is only a first confirmation, appearing first with regard to the *cogito sum*, already in the introduction to *Sein und Zeit*; this one holds, let us stress, for the entire plan announced in § 8, and therefore also for the unpublished part. The principle that institutes subjectivity within all of modern philosophy displays two characteristics: it claims to announce an absolutely certain beginning and, at the same time, it misses the thought of Being by masking the *esse* in the *sum* which is itself still left unthought under the shadow cast by the ego, which is alone thought in evidence: "In the course of this history, certain privileged domains of Being have come into view and have served as the primary guides for subsequent problematics (the *ego cogito* of Descartes, the subject, the *I*, reason, spirit, the person). But these domains, consistent with the complete omission [*Versäumnis*] of the question of Being, remain uninterrogated as to Being and the structure of their Being." Or again:

In taking over Descartes' ontological position Kant made an essential omission [*ein wesentliches Versäumnis*]: he failed to provide an ontology of Dasein. This omission was a decisive one in the spirit of Descartes' ownmost tendencies. With the "*cogito sum*" Descartes had claimed that he was putting philosophy on a new and firm footing. But what he left undetermined [*unbestimmt*] in this "radical" beginning was the mode of Being of the *res cogitans*, or more precisely the *meaning of the Being of the "sum"*. The elaboration of the implicit ontological foundations of the *cogito sum* is what marks the second stage along the path of the destructive return toward the history of ontology. Our interpretation not only proves that Descartes had necessarily to omit [*versäumen*] the question of Being in general, but it even shows why he was able to suppose that the absolute "Being-certain" of the *cogito* exempted him from raising the question of the meaning of Being of that being.[21]

Several remarks become unavoidable here. (1) In its § 6, *Sein und Zeit* questions Descartes first and above all with regard to the meaning of the Being of the *sum*; or rather, the Cartesian omission of the meaning of Being in general is indicated first and above all in the *ego cogito*; only the order of the first part and the absence of the second can give the reader the feeling that, within his debate with Descartes, Heidegger privileges the doctrine of the *res extensa*. With regard to this, one is dealing only with a particular failure (to think the phenomenon of the world), which is inscribed in the universal failure to think the way of Being of beings and, to begin with, of *Dasein*. (2) Nevertheless, the *ego cogito* and the *res extensa* offer to the phenomenological destruction undertaken by *Sein und Zeit* the case of two comparable "omissions": Descartes fails to recognize the ego's way of Being because he sticks to the certitude of its existence, without distinguishing a particular epistemic category from an ontologically determined existential; and if he sticks here to certitude, it is because he limits himself to transposing it into the ego starting from the domain where he first experienced it epistemically, the object of methodical science, extension. For if epistemically the object depends on the ego according to a tacit and undefined ontology (a gray ontology, let us say), the ego borrows from the *res extensa* in order to carry out its own interpretation through certitude. In all cases, the two "omissions" go hand in hand, displaying the same insufficiency: the indetermination of the meaning of Being. (3) The two dimensions of this single insufficiency anticipate exactly the two regions distinguished by Husserl: the absolute region of consciousness, on the one hand, and the relative region of worldly things, on the other. And just as Descartes fails to think them as such, so Husserl fails to think their respective meanings of Being. It is therefore suitable

to take up and to specify the two failures of which *Sein und Zeit* accuses
Descartes as integral parts of the "destruction" of the history of ontology
and therefore, positively, to understand them again as a breakthrough
beyond the phenomenological obstacle presented by Descartes.

Habitually taken as the thinker of the *cogito sum*, Descartes could
therefore more properly be characterized by a radical inability to think
that very same *cogito sum*, or at least to think the *sum* on the basis of the
esse; on the contrary, Descartes reduces *sum* to *cogito* and *cogito* to *sum*.
The ego itself is characterized only by an epistemic determination—that
of the absolutely certain first principle which renders possible the certain
knowledge of other beings. The extension of certitude, which goes from
the known being back to the knowing ego, satisfies the generalized
requirements of method only by leaving proportionally indeterminate
and shadowy the question of the meaning of Being for the ego. The
more that epistemic certitude invades ever more extended domains of
being so as to render them homogenous as so many *cogitata*, the more
the whole of being betrays the deep indetermination in which it is left
by the forgetting of any interrogation concerning what, each time, *Being*
means for each being or each domain of beings. This first affects the ego,
which, by absorbing, so to speak, the *esse* in the *sum* and the *sum* in itself,
assures in itself only its own ontological failure. This indetermination
marks the first and radical omission of Descartes: " . . . a total ontological indetermination of the *res cogitans sive mens sive animus*"; or again:
"Descartes, to whom one attributes the discovery of the *cogito sum* as the
point of departure for modern philosophical questioning, examined—
within certain limits—the *cogitare* of the *ego*. On the other hand, he leaves
the *sum* totally unelucidated [*unerörtet*], even though he posits it just
as originally as the *cogito*."[22] By stigmatizing such an indetermination,
Heidegger in no way contests, however, the certitude of the knowledge
of the ego as *cogito*; it is even very remarkable that he never engages in the
debate, as common as it is facile and lazy, to call into question the certitude
of the reasons that end up demonstrating the first, absolutely indubitable
and necessary existence of the *ego* as *cogito*. Heidegger contests an entirely
different point—namely, that epistemic certitude, which delivers the ego
as the first certain object for the knowledge that, finally, the ego itself
is, should suffice to determine ontologically the ego's characteristic way
of Being. Through his very silence on this point, Descartes postulates
the univocity of certitude (which keeps the same meaning and the same
validity when it goes from known objects back to the knowing subject);
that univocity is founded (like, moreover, the medieval *univocatio entis*)
only on a deep indetermination. Or better: the certitude remains not only
ontologically undetermined, but above all indifferent to the question

bearing on the ways of Being of the meaning of Being. Descartes first claims that certitude applies in the same sense to the whole (nevertheless heterogeneous) series of *cogitatum-cogito-ego*; then he postulates that, just as the *cogitatum* is, ever since the gray ontology of the *Regulae*, supposed to find the correct determination of its mode of Being in certitude, so the ego requires no determination of the meaning of its Being other than, again, certitude alone. The certitude of the *ego cogito* therefore does not abolish the indetermination in it of the *sum* and of the *esse* but rather reinforces that indetermination. The evident certitude of the ego allows Descartes only to desert any interrogation of the mode of Being implied by that very certitude and leads him to consider the meaning of its Being as self-evident, evident by itself. "*Nota est omnibus essentiae ab existentia distinctio,*" he responded to Hobbes.[23] Descartes thus not only omits the question of the meaning of Being of the *sum*; he masks this omission itself, in blinding himself with the epistemic evidence of the *cogito*. Descartes's first omission is accomplished by omitting itself.

This omission of the omission nevertheless decides the ego's way of Being, precisely because it does not explicitly determine that way of Being: if Descartes does not think its *sum* as such, he will think it implicitly on the model of intra-worldly being, following a "reflection [*Rückstrahlung*] of the understanding of the world on the explication of *Dasein*," for "*Dasein* . . . is inclined to fall [*verfallen*] upon the world where it is and to interpret itself reflectively [*reluzent*] on the basis of that world."[24] The way of Being of intra-worldly being thus becomes, precisely because there lacks any approach to the meaning of Being of the ego, the pole of attraction and of interpretation of the way of Being of intra-worldly being. The Cartesian ego (like, moreover, its substitutes and derivatives within the metaphysical tradition, up to and including its Husserlian avatar) differs essentially from *Dasein* in this: it is not according to its proper way of Being, and therefore it is not thought according to its proper way, but, first and always, it runs aground on intra-worldly being and imports upon itself intra-worldly being's improper way of Being. It is certainly an ego only by not being according to its Being—epistemic certitude, ontologically undetermined. The Cartesian ego is lost the very instant it finds itself and precisely because it finds itself in the mode of certitude.

4. The Second Omission: The Permanence of Intra-Worldly Being

The impropriety is here doubled, for just as the Cartesian interpretation of the ego omits its way of Being and also fails to understand this first omission; just as the absence of that interpretation delivers the ego to engulfment in the mode of Being of intra-worldly beings to which it nevertheless does not in principle belong; so finally the interpretation of the mode of Being of intra-worldly beings omits, in Descartes, the phenomenon of the world so as to substitute for it the univocal and minimal subsistence of presence-at-hand (*Vorhandenheit*). According to an analysis that is as well known as it is ambiguous and ephemeral,[25] the worldhood of the world is manifested less by the subsistence of beings present-at-hand (*vorhanden*) than by their play in the capacity of equipment that is manipulable and ready-to-hand; in this play, beings are defined by that for which they can serve (*um zu*), in a finality that, under the diverse aspects of interest, of utility, of function, of organization, etc., ultimately depends on "what it is all about" (*Bewandtnis*), and therefore on *Dasein* itself, which thus opens the world in its worldhood. The subsistence of being present-at-hand (*Vorhandenheit*) follows from *Zuhandenheit* only through the reduction and impoverishment of being ready-to-hand to the sole requirements of theory; the object required by the theoretical attitude must only remain, isolated as an atom of evidence, permanent as a perfect subsistence, neutralizing all finality as purely objective. The object of the theoretical attitude is obtained through reduction, abstraction, and method; it does not precede the being that is usable and ready-to-hand, but follows from it through impoverishment and elimination. That operation, which thus reverses the phenomenological preeminence of *Zuhandenheit* over *Vorhandenheit*, results from Descartes. The privilege that method accords to mathematical knowledge in fact does not rest for him on some intrinsic excellence of that science, but on its aptitude for reaching the certitude and permanent subsistence of an object; the primacy accorded to mathematics results, according to Descartes, from the privilege, immediately conceded to permanent subsistence alone, of certain objectivity as the sole meaning of intra-worldly being.

What has a mode of Being of the kind that measures up to the Being that is accessible to mathematical knowledge *is* in the proper sense. That being is *what always is what it is*; this is why what constitutes the real Being of beings experienced in the world is that which has the character of *constant remaining* [*des ständigen Verbleibs*], as *remanens capax mutationum*. . . . Far from allowing the mode of Being of intraworldly beings to be given beforehand by those beings, Descartes, on the contrary, prescribes to the world its "veritable" Being on the basis of an idea of Being (Being = constant Being-present-at-hand [*Sein = ständige Vorhandenheit*]) that is no more legitimated in its own right than it is unveiled in its origin.

The permanence of being as an object present-at-hand, "*ständige Ding-vorhandenheit*,"[26] establishes the meaning of Being of intra-worldly being only by degrading it in an acceptation that imposes certitude upon it, at the expense of the phenomenality of the world. The interpretation of being in general as permanent subsistence present-at-hand (*Vorhandenheit*) does not only omit the meaning of the Being of the ego by leaving the *sum* in it undetermined as such; it omits also and to begin with the meaning of the Being of intra-worldly being, of which it nevertheless claims to assure perfect knowledge. The two omissions come together in a common and more originary failure to think the Being of *any* being.

What assessment can the historian of philosophy—if at least, by a fragile hypothesis, he can be isolated from the philosopher—give of such an analysis and "destruction" of Descartes? Without launching into a more ample discussion that it would be necessary to carry out in another framework, we shall stick to three remarks.

1. Heidegger confirms that the *ständige Vorhandenheit* obfuscates and occupies the meaning of Being by raising the Cartesian interpretation of the *res extensa* as *substantia*, itself reduced to what *remanet* (= *verbleibt*) in any reduction.[27] This reference is obviously very exact; however, it masks another reference, which attributes permanence (*remanet*) first and directly to the ego before the *res extensa* itself; for, before asking "*Remanetne adhuc eadem cera?*" and responding "*Remanere fatendum est,*" thus before encountering the *res extensa* (which, it is necessary to repeat, does *not* intervene in the analysis of the piece of wax), Descartes had already reduced the ego to the *cogito* " . . . *ut ita tandem praecise remaneat illud tantum quod certum est et inconcussum.*"[28] If permanence characterizes certitude as the (missed) way of Being, then it would have to intervene already with the first certitude, and, in fact, it does indeed intervene with the existence of the ego; thus it is with respect to the ego that it would have been necessary to carry out the diagnostic of permanent subsistence: each time that it thinks, the ego remains. To miss such a Cartesian reference is surprising on the part of one who knows Descartes as precisely as Heidegger, and all the more insofar as this first remaining confirms, far from weakening, the whole thesis put forth by *Sein und Zeit*: *Vorhandenheit* does not determine only intra-worldly being, but flows back, through reflection (*Rückstrahlung*), upon the ego itself and closes all access for it to its true Being. One might respond, and quite rightly, that §§ 19–21, treating worldhood only such as Descartes misses it, did not have either to know or to mention a text treating the *Vorhandenheit* of the ego. However, even if one accepts this response, another question arises: Did Heidegger have to use the remaining of the ego, in the Second Part, Division 2, dedicated to the "ontological foundation of Descartes' 'cogito

sum' "?[29] Within this hypothesis alone, he would have taken more from a text that backs him up at the very moment when, apparently, he ignores it.

2. The omission of the meaning of Being in general is indicated in the Cartesian texts by the insufficiency of the doctrine of substance. On the one hand, Heidegger notes pertinently, substance is reputed as not affecting us directly, "... *non potest substantia primum animadverti ex hoc solo, quod sit res existens, quia hoc solum per se nos non afficit.*"[30] Thus, the investigation concerning substance turns straightaway toward an investigation concerning its principal attribute, while substance itself remains in principle unknown in itself. There follows a fundamental "equivocity" of the term,[31] which confuses its ontological acceptation with its ontic acceptation, so as to evade all the more easily the complete desertion of the first and take refuge in the treatment of the second. The debate, to which Descartes gives priority, concerning the distinction between finite and infinite substance only reinforces the fundamental orientation toward the solely ontic acceptation of *substantia*; in no way does the Cartesian treatise on *substantia*, in *Principia*, I, §§ 51–54, take up the discussion, which is ontological at least in intention, of οὐσία by Aristotle in *Metaphysics* Z. This reproach of Heidegger to Descartes seems to us essentially justified.

The debate becomes deeper in a second critique, which is less visible but more important. In submitting the ontological to the ontic in *substantia*, Descartes necessarily confuses the ontological difference: "The ontic being substituted for the ontological, the expression *substantia* functions sometimes in the ontological sense, sometimes in the ontic sense, but most often in a confused ontico-ontological sense. But what is harbored in this imperceptible difference [*Unterschied*] of signification is the inability to master the fundamental problem of Being." To this *grundsätzliches Grundproblem*, Heidegger adds a note in his personal copy, a simple phrase, *ontologische Differenz.*[32] A decisive addition! For it reveals that by obscuring the ontological within *substantia* Descartes first gave rise to the aporia wherein Husserl was supposed to be caught when he imagined himself able to distinguish substances (or "regions") solely by ontic criteria, without undertaking to distinguish their respective modes of Being (ontologically). It reveals, next, that Descartes failed to confront the difference between Being and beings, which alone would have allowed him to establish ontologically the distinction between beings or substances. The convergence of these two omissions—of the meaning of Being of the *ego*, and of the meaning of Being of intra-worldly being— flows finally from the original evasion before the ontological difference. The reintegration of Descartes within the history of metaphysics, through what *Sein und Zeit* as yet names only the "destruction of the history of ontology," had, moreover, to finish by revealing in him the essential trait of metaphysics: the failure to recognize the difference between Being and beings. Since in *Sein und Zeit* this difference remains implicit, though really at work, it stigmatizes Descartes only under the form of the two omissions of the meaning of Being of beings. That, however, is sufficient to bring out the ontologically Cartesian genealogy of Husserl's phenomenological insufficiencies—which it was a matter of showing.

3. Could one not, however, object to the analysis of *Sein und Zeit* that Descartes does indeed elaborate a thought of the world? Is not the worldhood of the world set up as an explicit problem to begin with when the *ego* asks itself whether it is alone in the world, "*me solum esse in mundo*,"[33] and then when it undertakes to prove the existence of the world in the Sixth Meditation? From these two references, one must on the contrary draw an argument in favor of the thesis of *Sein und Zeit*. In the first case, the ego reaches other possible beings only starting from itself, that is, from the *ideae* that it can have of such beings; thus representation determines them in advance as certain objects, and therefore according to subsisting persistence (*Vorhandenheit*), with God constituting no exception to this determination and, symptomatically, the other person finding in it no free place.[34] In the second case, the very fact that the "existence of the external world" must be proved constitutes—more than the absence of convincing proof which Kant deplored in taking up the Cartesian plan[35]—the real phenomenological "scandal"; for the world can owe its existence to such a proof only inasmuch as it is first reduced to the level of a representation that awaits actuality, that is, the level of *Vorhandenheit*. To prove (or not) the existence of the world presupposes that one has already neglected the worldhood of the world—its appearance within the phenomenological horizon.

The two omissions in Descartes therefore constitute only one— to have grasped "the Being of 'Dasein' . . . in the very same way as the Being of the *res extensa*—namely, as substance." Thus he determines Kant: "'Consciousness of my *Dasein*' means for Kant a consciousness of my Being-present-at-hand [*Vorhandensein*] in the sense of Descartes. When Kant uses the term '*Dasein*' he has in mind the Being-present-at-hand of consciousness just as much as the Being-present-at-hand of things [*sowohl das Vorhandensein des Bewußtseins wie das Vorhandensein der Dinge*]."[36]

5. "*Dasein*" as a "Destruction" of the "Ego"

Descartes's two omissions of the thought of the meaning of Being lead back therefore, in the end, to a single inability to think the Being of

beings without recourse to *Vorhandenheit*; that inability itself results from
the failure to recognize the ontological difference—at least understood
according to its negative formulation: "Being can never be explained by
beings."[37] The ego is set up by Descartes, and after him by Kant no less
than by Hegel, as a being which is privileged to the point that it must
account for all other beings and take the place of any meaning of Being
in them; in short, it must guarantee them ontically and legitimate them
ontologically. But at the same time, and in an increasing measure, its
own meaning of Being remains, first of all, completely undetermined.
The indetermination of the *ego cogito* in its mode of Being overruns
all the other beings and deprives them of any ontological solidity—"the
ontological groundlessness [*ontologische Bodenlosigkeit*] of the problematic
of the Self [*Selbst*] from Descartes' *res cogitans* to the Hegelian concept
of spirit." In other words, "if idealism signifies tracing every being back
to a subject or to a consciousness having the distinctive privilege of
remaining *undetermined* [*unbestimmt*] in their Being and of being able
at the very most to be characterized negatively as 'non-things,' then that
idealism is no less naive on the methodological level than the crudest
realism."[38] Consequently, what separates Descartes (and those whom he
made possible) from the question concerning the meaning of Being is
exactly equivalent to what separates the *ego cogito* from *Dasein*. *Dasein*
maintains within itself an echo of what the *ego* [*cogito*] already exhibits:
Da-, here, in this unique place where all the rest can then take place;
but with the *ego cogito* the rest has the status only of *cogitatum*, because I
limit myself, or rather *I* is limited in the capacity of ego, to *cogitare*; on
the contrary, starting from *Dasein*, the *Da-* accords to the rest of being
nothing less than *sein*, nothing less than to be. There where the ego gives
to be thought, or rather to make itself be thought (or even to make
itself simple thought) without ever giving Being in a determinate and
determining sense, *Dasein* gives Being by determining the way of Being
of the other beings, because it itself, in advance and according to its
privilege, determines *itself* to be according to its own way of Being. To
be sure, the ego is, but it is without thinking about it, since it thinks
only about thinking its thinkable things, whose respective ways of Being
it does not establish any more than it is itself determined in its own way
of Being; in thinking itself as being only through and for the exercise of
the *cogitatio*, it masks, through the epistemic evidence of its nevertheless
ontologically loose existence, and then through the certitude of the other
subsistent truths, the total absence of decision concerning the Being of
beings, which are reduced to the level of pure and simple *cogitata*. *Ego
cogito*, not *ego sum*, nor *Dasein*—the very formula that Descartes privileges
betrays what indetermination disqualifies it ontologically and the two

omissions that it commits. From this point on, the whole interpretation of Descartes by *Sein und Zeit* would have to be thematizable within the sole opposition between the *ego cogito* and *Dasein*, consistent with the declaration of principle that "the *res cogitans*, which does not coincide with *Dasein* either ontically or ontologically. . . ."[39]

These oppositions remain to be developed. According to the first, ontically, the *res cogitans* does not coincide with *Dasein*; indeed, the *res cogitans* has only an ontic consciousness of itself (from the point of view of *Dasein*), whereas *Dasein* is not identified (from the point of view of the *res cogitans*) as being itself another *res cogitans*. Although Heidegger never presents this opposition explicitly, it can nevertheless be reconstructed, in at least three ways.

1. The ego is a *res* that shares the *realitas* of intra-worldly beings, whether they be present-at-hand or ready-to-hand; on the contrary, "the Being of *Dasein* was at the same time delimited in relation to [*abgegrenzt gegen*] modes of Being (Being-ready-to-hand, Being-present-at-hand, reality [*Zuhandenheit, Vorhandenheit, Realität*]) that characterize the being that is not to the measure of *Dasein*."[40] The *res* of the ego leads to the Husserlian impossibility of distinguishing effectively the region of consciousness from the region of the world; on the contrary, *Dasein* does not count among the real terms, nor does it admit anything real in itself, because it precedes and renders possible the mode of Being of reality.

2. The ego is defined by the absolute primacy in it of the theoretical attitude; it is born from doubt; but this very doubt becomes practicable only inasmuch as every immediate, urgent, useful, and necessary relation has disappeared: " . . . no conversation . . . no cares or passions," " . . . *curis omnibus exsolvi*." On the contrary, "scientific research is neither the only, nor the closest possible mode of Being of this being [i.e., *Dasein*]"; indeed, *Dasein* relates to the world in the mode of preoccupation, which manipulates and utilizes beings as ready-to-hand, and therefore without the least disinterest; the theoretical attitude befalls *Dasein* only after the fact and as through subtraction: "In order for knowing [*Erkennen*] to become possible, as a circumspective determination of the present-at-hand [*des Vorhandenen*], there must first be a *deficiency* in our preoccupied having-to-do with the world."[41] *Dasein* is not limited to maintaining the theoretical attitude, in rejecting the so-called "natural" attitude (in fact, the preoccupation that makes use of being inasmuch as ready-to-hand), but assures and passes beyond both, because, more radically, it is *Dasein* that, ontologically, first renders them possible.

3. Finally, the *res cogitans* is confined to the domain of the *cogitatio* and relegates to other *res* that of *extensio*, according to an almost irremediable caesura; consequently, the *res cogitans* escapes space, which it also

lets escape. *Dasein*, on the contrary, because it is not first defined by the representation of present-at-hand (*vorhanden*) being, does not exclude a fundamental spatiality. The "spatiality of *Dasein*" has to do with the de-severing (*Entfernung*) through which it abolishes the distance of a being with respect to itself; such a nullification of distance, and thus a de-severing, modulates the original ecstasy of *Dasein*, its Being-in-the-world. As opposed to the subject of idealism, issuing from the *ego cogito*, "the 'subject,' if well understood ontologically, *Dasein*, is spatial."[42] *Dasein* is neither nonextended in the way of the *ego cogito*, nor is it extended in the way of the material *res*: it is spatial, or, in other words, not nonextended. Thus, *Dasein*, by refusing to take on the common title of *res*, is not restrained in face of the *res cogitans* but on the contrary surpasses it, in not being limited either to the theoretical attitude or to nonextension. It is perfectly confirmed that, taken as a being, *Dasein* does not coincide with the *res cogitans*.

But, as the "ontic characteristic of *Dasein* consists in the fact that it *is* ontological," its ontic opposition to the *res cogitans* can only prepare the ontological distinction that distinguishes it from the *res cogitans* (this time on the basis of itself and not at all of the *res cogitans*). No doubt, the *res cogitans* can claim, like *Dasein*, a multifarious "primacy," but not such an "ontological primacy." On at least three points the opposition between them becomes irreducible.

1. In *Dasein*, its Being is at issue; it is peculiar to this being to have to decide on its mode of Being and, in that decision, not only is *its* (mode of) Being at issue, but *Being* as such, and therefore the mode of Being of other beings, which themselves do not have to decide on the one or the other.[43] *Dasein* maintains with itself a surprising relation of uncertainty: far from assuring itself of itself in knowing itself as such, it knows itself only in admitting what play is at play in it—the play of its Being or more exactly the play of Being put into play, always to be decided in the case of this privileged being. *Dasein* knows itself authentically only by recognizing itself as an undecided and all the more uncertain stake, which will never and must never be rendered certain. *Dasein* plays—in the sense that wood has play: it maintains a gap, an articulation, a mobility, in order that the fold of Being, everywhere else invisible, should unfold, turning on that being like a panel on a hinge. Such a play, in the end beyond both incertitude and certitude, decidedly opposes *Dasein* to the *ego cogito*. No doubt, Heidegger is textually wrong to characterize the *ego cogito* as *fundamentum inconcussum*; however, Descartes does indeed aim in it at a "*fundamentum, cui omnis certitudo niti posses*," at some "fairly solid foundations"; and Descartes does indeed wish it to be unshakable: "*minimum quid . . . certum et inconcussum*"; it is even notable that he thinks it

according to the persistence of *Vorhandenheit*: "*quid firmum et mansurum*"; even more, the ego itself immediately takes the form of a foundation, or better an autarchic and sufficient fund: "a fund that is entirely my own."[44] In thinking itself, the ego takes hold of itself as full owner; not only is incertitude overcome, but the certitude of the *fund*, henceforth definitive, will be extended to every other *cogitatum* to come; the ego, to be sure, decides itself, but in order to abolish all play in the certitude of self; and if in the future the ego decides other beings, it will be in order to reduce them, as so many *cogitata*, to its own certitude. Thus *Dasein* opens a play, that of the Being of other beings, through its own, there where the ego closes all incertitude, first in itself, and then in the *cogitata*.

2. *Dasein* exists, but existence is defined in its turn as possibility: "*Dasein* always understands itself in terms of its existence, in terms of a possibility of itself to be itself or not to be itself." To exist means: to be outside of oneself, in such a way as to be only in the mode of being-able-to-be, in accordance with the stakes that essentially establish *this* being in a fundamental play with its Being, and therefore with Being itself; existence implies the ecstasy of *Dasein* outside of itself in the play of Being on which it is up to *Dasein* to decide. When the *res cogitans* grabs hold of itself with certitude in saying "*ego sum, ego existo*,"[45] it immediately interprets its *sum*, and therefore its Being, as an existence. Is it a matter of the existence that characterizes *Dasein*? On the contrary, specifies Heidegger: "if we choose existence to designate the Being of this being [i.e., *Dasein*], this term does not and cannot have the ontological signification of the traditional term *existentia*; *existentia* is ontologically [exactly] tantamount to Being-present-at-hand [*Vorhandensein*], a mode of Being that is essentially foreign to the being that has the character of *Dasein*." Is it necessary to prove that Descartes in fact understands *existentia* as the counterpart simply of possible essence, which it abolishes in certain and univocal permanence? He himself does not even define existence, insofar as he considers it as self-evident. "*Neminem enim unquam extitisse tam stupidum crediderim, qui prius quid sit existentia edocendus fuerit, antequam se esse concludere potuerit atque affirmare.*"[46] For the *ego cogito, existentia* means entrance into *Vorhandenheit*; for *Dasein*, existence signifies exit from self and transcendence with regard to *Vorhandenheit*, in order to enter into the possibility that, definitively, it is.

3. Finally, "it belongs essentially to *Dasein* to be in the world." Contrary to its Husserlian limit, intentionality is not restricted to the theoretical attitude because the relation to the world does have to do first with the constitution of things; intentionality is broadened and radicalized to the point of opening the *I*, immediately and from itself, to something like a world; thus alone can the Being of other beings be

at issue in a being. This critique of Husserl, which in an important way motivated the publication of *Sein und Zeit* and which runs throughout the whole work, is also valid against Descartes, by virtue of the "affinity" that unites them. Descartes, indeed, reaches the *ego cogito* on the hypothesis of its independence with respect to the whole possible world; the ego appears in fact when and on condition that the beings of the world disappear under hyperbolic doubt; the ego is thus defined as "a substance whose whole essence or nature is simply to think, and which does not require any place, or depend on any material thing, in order to exist."[47] Thus Heidegger is perfectly well founded in speaking (with regard to Husserl and Kant, and thus also with regard to Descartes) of a "worldless I [*weltlose Ich*]," of a "worldless subject [*weltlose Subjekt*]."[48] The classic difficulties of an opening to the world in Cartesianism do not have to be recalled here; they would sufficiently confirm the diagnostic given by Heidegger. Thus *Dasein* in no way rediscovers itself in the *res cogitans*, since the ego could be defined on the basis of *Dasein* as its strict reverse: the being for whom its own Being is *not* an issue. Reciprocally, *Dasein* could be defined, on the basis of the *ego cogito*, as its reverse: the being that is *not* inasmuch as it thinks (itself). *Dasein* therefore maintains with the *ego cogito* a relation of "destruction."

6. "*Dasein*" as a Confirmation of the "Ego"

Such a relation of "destruction," however, would not make any sense if there were not in the ego, such as it limits itself to thinking, already an ontology; for the "destruction" always bears on "the history of ontology." It is therefore necessary to presuppose for the ego a metaphysical situation, which inscribes it within the history of the ignored ontological difference; there follows a reexamination of the case of the *ego cogito* such as it still deploys a figure of the Being of being, although in an obscure and forgetful mode. But this historical (or rather historial) presupposition would not have any legitimacy if the *ego cogito* could not establish its ontological pertinence, even inauthentic and obfuscated, no longer in the course of the history of ontology but in the "new beginning"; if only to maintain its hermeneutic role toward and within metaphysics, the *ego* must keep in itself a reserve and potentiality of Being. It remains to be examined, therefore, whether *Sein und Zeit* does justice, if only partially, to these two postulations of the *ego cogito*.

From the—dominant—point of view of its "omission," the Cartesian ego is absolutely denied the manifestation of the meaning of Being, a property that characterizes *Dasein* alone. The ontico-ontological antagonism between the *ego cogito* and *Dasein* appeared clearly enough (§ 5 above) that, without insisting on it or weakening it, we would nevertheless counterbalance it with the remark of another relation between these same antagonists. To be sure, the *ego cogito* presents itself to *Dasein* as its most rigorous adversary; and yet *Dasein* would not have such an urgent need to destroy it if *Dasein* did not find in it, as in a delinquent outline, some of its own most characteristic traits: indeed, *Dasein* cannot not recognize itself in at least four characteristics of the *ego cogito*, according to a rivalry that is all the more troubling insofar as the similitudes only sharpen it.

1. *Dasein* "does not have an end [*Ende*] at which it just stops, but it *exists finitely* [*existiert endlich*]"; finitude is not added as if from the outside to an existence which, thus, simply would not have an indefinite (*endlose*) duration; it essentially determines *Dasein*, which is only for a term, its own death, according to a temporality of the future; marking Being-toward-death, finitude opens access for *Dasein* to its characteristic ecstatic temporality, according to the privilege of the future, in opposition to the temporality of *Vorhandenheit*, which privileges the present as remaining. But the *ego cogito* is just as well characterized by finitude: "*cum sim finitus*";[49] this finitude does not have only an anthropological function (the ego has to die, it lacks several perfections, etc.) but a quasi-ontological function; indeed, finitude alone provokes doubt, and thus opens up the *cogitatio*, which in its turn establishes the beings of the world as so many *cogitata* to be constituted; the finitude of the ego thus directly determines the meaning of Being for beings other than the ego. The pertinence of this *rapprochement*, of course, remains hidden to and by Heidegger, since he envisages the finitude of the ego only within the horizon of "the anthropology of Christianity and the ancient world"[50] and reduces the relation between finite substance and infinite substance to an efficient production, so as to deny Cartesian finitude an originary validity. It nevertheless remains that the ego can establish both itself as *cogito* and, indissolubly, the beings of the world as *cogitata*, only because it *is* according to an essential finitude; moreover, Heidegger's later meditation on the *cogitatio* (representation, *Vorstellung*) will continually develop this implication. Therefore, *Dasein* confirms the ego according to finitude.

2. There is more: *Dasein* is that being for whom Being is an issue only on the express condition that that Being be its own, in person: "its essence lies rather in the fact that in each case it has its Being to be, and has it as its own [*es je sein Sein als seiniges zu sein hat*]"; or again: "That Being which is an issue for this being is in each case mine. . . . Because *Dasein* has *in each case mineness* [*Jemeinigkeit*], one must always use a *personal* pronoun when one addresses it: 'I am,' 'you are.' "[51] *Dasein*

could not be itself, namely the one to whom it characteristically belongs to put itself into play as a being with Being for its stakes, except in a personal capacity; no one can play the role of *Dasein* in place of anyone else; the function of *Dasein* does not allow any failure to appear; even if it is a "you are" that is the *Dasein*, this *you* will itself also have to say "I am"; *Dasein*, even and especially played by another than myself, is played in the first person because it must be played in person. Thus, even if *Dasein* does not say *ego cogito* to begin with, it can say *-sein* only by saying "ich bin," and therefore "*ego sum*." *Dasein* therefore inevitably speaks, at least once, *like* the *ego cogito*: "*ego sum*," "I am." This meeting appears absolutely decisive. Indeed, Descartes did not simply inaugurate the tie between *cogitatio* and existence in a "subject"; he tied them in a "subject" that itself is always interpreted (in the theatrical sense of the term) in the first person, or better, as a character (*persona*, also theatrical) that one must perform in person (still theatrically) by assuming the function of an "I"—by *saying* "I," "hoc pronunciatum, *Ego*."[52] The successors of Descartes will tend, on the contrary, to eliminate this involvement of and with the ego; either by replacing the first formula with another, which no one any longer has to perform exclusively: "*Homo cogitat*" (Spinoza); or else they will abolish it, either by subtraction (Malebranche), or by generalization (Leibniz). Descartes is distinguished, therefore, not only by the necessary relation between the two simple natures (*cogitatio* and *existentia*), but above all by the performance of their necessary tie by the irreplaceable ego. Existence befalls man only inasmuch as he thinks, but above all inasmuch as he thinks in the position of the ego. Thus Descartes approaches fairly well the irreplaceability that characterizes *Dasein*. Therefore, *Dasein* confirms the ego according to mineness (*Jemeinigkeit*).[53]

3. The finitude and irreplaceability of *Dasein* befall it as the being for whom its Being is an issue; that way of Being falls to it by virtue of its Being-toward-death, for death is its ownmost, its most absolute, and its least surmountable possibility; indeed, "death [is] the possibility of the pure and simple impossibility of *Dasein*."[54] For its death, *Dasein* finds itself exposed to its own and final impossibility, as much because death remains to us ontically inconceivable (unimaginable), as because death puts an end to the possibility that *Dasein* is (even more than to its possibility to "do" this or that thing). Now, the *ego* knows a similar paradox, not, to be sure, with regard to its death, but with regard to its freedom; for possibility opens up, in Cartesian terms, with the free will, the only infinite formally in the finite *res cogitans*. This free will uncovers its impossibility when it confronts the divine omniscience and omnipotence, which annihilate the very notion of the possible; in such a meeting, the *ego cogito* does not only confront the impossibility of (free)

possibility, which nevertheless imposes itself according to theory; it also meets the possibility of impossibility, since it decides, in the practical order, to act as if it could act freely, even though it does not understand how it can. In each action, the *ego cogito* comports itself as if it were free and as if the impossible (an event not necessarily predetermined by God) again became open to the possible. The possibility of the impossible can therefore be understood of freedom as of Being-toward-death. Thus, *Dasein* confirms the ego again according to the possibility of impossibility.

Even if one admits that these convergences rest on indisputable textual bases, it would nevertheless still seem dangerous, or even specious, to pretend to draw from them as a consequence an essential homogeneity between the ego and *Dasein*. No formal similarity seems to counterbalance the critique bearing on the ontological indetermination of the *ego cogito* supposedly established in principle by Descartes: "What he left undetermined [*unbestimmt*] when he began in this 'radical' way, was the kind of Being which belongs to the *res cogitans*, or—more precisely—the *meaning of the Being of the 'sum.'*" A "complete ontological indetermination [*völlig ontologische Unbestimmtheit*]" not only gives rise to a "non-determination [*Nichtbestimmung*] of the *res cogitans*," but it even leaves "the *cogitationes* ontologically undetermined [*unbestimmt*]." If ontologically the ego and *Dasein* differ as the undetermined and the determined, is it not necessary simply to conclude that, from the strictly ontological point of view of *Sein und Zeit*, they differ absolutely?

4. But it is precisely this indetermination that, far from leading to an opposition without mediation, will suggest a fourth convergence that draws the ego near to *Dasein* at least as much as it first seemed to separate them. For *Dasein* itself—and this is precisely why the existential analytic is required—frees itself only slowly from an inevitable indetermination. Thus, when it is a matter of responding to the existential question concerning the *who* of *Dasein*, the suspicion immediately arises that "the ontological horizon for the determination of the being that is accessible in pure and simple givenness remains fundamentally undetermined [*unbestimmt*]." Even more, "the Being of *Dasein* remains [itself] ontologically undetermined [*unbestimmt*]"[55] insofar as the sole determining phenomena of anxiety and care do not intervene. Therefore, the indetermination that is denounced in the *ego cogito* concerns *Dasein* just as much—at least provisionally, until the analysis of anxiety; to escape ontological indetermination remains a formidable task, whether one is dealing with *Dasein* or the ego, to the point that the final section of *Sein und Zeit* (§ 83) could allow one to suppose that a sufficient determination of the horizon of givenness has not yet been attained.[56] But there is more: the indetermination put forward against the ego and affecting

Dasein as an insufficiency can also receive a positive phenomenological characterization at certain decisive moments within the elucidation of *Dasein.* In other words, the indetermination can sometimes become an ontological determination, when it manifests the disappearance of any determination of *Dasein* by beings. Such a reversal can be located in at least three circumstances.

1. During the experience of *anxiety, Dasein* suffers an absolutely indistinct mood, for "that before which anxiety is anxious is totally undetermined [*das Wovor der Angst ist völlig unbestimmt*]. Not only does this indetermination [*Unbestimmtheit*] leave factually undecided what intraworldly being threatens, but it signifies that in general it is not intraworldly being that is 'relevant.' " Anxiety therefore deploys a mood that is "totally undetermined" (in the very terms first put forward against the ego) whereby *Dasein* no longer confronts this or that being, but precisely the impossibility of identifying any being in face of which to flee; the fact that no determinate being can any longer come to determine anxiety as a specific fear determines the nothing as such; thus, "the peculiar indetermination of that alongside which *Dasein* finds itself in anxiety comes to expression: the nothing and the nowhere."[57] In short, through the ontic indetermination of anxiety, *Dasein* reaches its ontological determination; its transcendence with regard to being is accomplished only through radical ontic indetermination (the nothing); only thus can it be determined in its Being.

2. In Being-toward-death, the indetermination reappears in an indisputably phenomenological function. Indeed, death implies, precisely so that and because it is certain, a temporal indetermination: "Along with the certainty of death goes the indetermination [*Unbestimmtheit*] of its *when.*" It is precisely the conjunction of the certainty of death with its indetermination that opens it up as the possibility of *Dasein*: "*Death, as the end of Dasein, is Dasein's ownmost possibility—non-relational, certain and as such indeterminate [gewisse und als solche unbestimmte], not to be outstripped.*" This indetermination—of dying—"originarily opens in anxiety," because it is equivalent to the "*indetermination [Unbestimmtheit] of being-able-to-be,*" such as it characterizes and therefore determines ontologically the being that can be resolute because it exists—"the indetermination [*Unbestimmtheit*] that rules a being that exists." Not to be determined amounts, for *Dasein,* to being only in the mode of existence, through resoluteness and according to possibility—in short, it is equivalent to being determined ontologically.

3. In the analysis of conscience as call and care, the phenomenological "positivity" of indetermination is explicitly recognized: "The indetermination and indeterminability [*Unbestimmtheit und Unbestimmbarkeit*] of

the caller [*Rufer*] is not nothing, but a *positive* characteristic." In fact, it is resoluteness itself, such as it frees and sums up all the prior existentials, that imposes an essential indetermination—that of existence as such: "To resoluteness necessarily *belongs* the *indetermination* [*Unbestimmtheit*] that characterizes any factically thrown Being-able-to-be of *Dasein*. Resoluteness is sure of itself only as decision. However, existentiel *indetermination*, being determined in each case in decision alone, possesses its *existential determinateness* [*existentiale Bestimmtheit*] from resoluteness."[58] One must therefore hold as established that the ontic indetermination of *Dasein* assures it, precisely, its ontological determination, as the being that decides *itself* with nothing of beings. *Dasein* decides *itself* through its own resoluteness only inasmuch as nothing of beings determines it and inasmuch as it does not determine itself as a being. Related to the initial objection made to the ego, what does the "positive" indetermination of *Dasein* signify? At the very least it signifies that the debate is not played out between indetermination and determination, but between, on the one hand, an ontological indetermination (ego, ontically determined) and, on the other hand, an ontic indetermination (*Dasein*, ontologically determined by this very possibility). The opposition therefore concerns two indeterminations; the one, ontic, positively assures *Dasein* of determining itself in its Being, while the other, ontological, negatively leads the ego not to be determined in its Being. But does this conflict suffice to disqualify the ego definitively? Nothing is less sure, as soon as it belongs essentially to *Dasein* to give itself first as the *They* and to miss itself as such. Everything happens henceforth as if, even in its indetermination, the ego were miming *Dasein*, in the way that the *They* mimes, in the inauthentic mode, the authentic *Dasein* to which it essentially belongs.

Thus ego and *Dasein* meet according to finitude, *mineness*, the possibility of the impossible, and indetermination. That their similarities remain separated, or even opposed, according to authenticity and inauthenticity does not suffice to alienate them one from the other— since this final opposition belongs entirely to the existence of *Dasein*. It does not seem so easy to decide phenomenologically between the ego and *Dasein* as strict strangers. But what mime still unites them?

7. The Repetition of the "Ego"

What are we to deduce from these conditional confirmations? No doubt that the "destruction" of the *res cogitans* would never have shown such an urgency, already with the introduction to *Sein und Zeit*, and then throughout the whole work, if *Dasein* had not been able to recognize itself so easily therein; the ego appeared to *Dasein* like a failure, but first as its own failure, and therefore above all as a danger whose fascination imposes its norms and against which it is necessary to resist better than did Husserl. In the ceaseless struggle to mark *Dasein* off from the *ego cogito*, *Sein und Zeit* therefore had step by step to locate the *ego cogito*'s insufficiencies, highlight its decisions, and invert its orientations; such a confrontation, as warlike as it is, cannot avoid a sort of mimetic rivalry, where the victor sometimes appears, under some aspect, to be vanquished by the vanquished. In short, the *ego cogito*, precisely because *Sein und Zeit* does not cease to reject it, there appears all the more enigmatic in itself and all the more intimately tied to *Dasein*. The analytic of the one, because it advances only with the "destruction" of the other, confirms its undecided validity. This paradoxical conclusion could indeed have first been that of Heidegger:

> If the *ego cogito* is to serve as a point of departure for the existential analytic, there would have to be not only a reversal [*Umkehrung*], but even a new ontologico-phenomenologico-phenomenal confirmation (*Bewährung*) of its tenor. The first statement would then be "sum," in the sense of "I-am-in-a-world." As such a being, "I am" in the possibility of Being toward various attitudes [*cogitationes*] as [so many] modes of Being alongside intra-worldly beings. Descartes, on the contrary, says that *cogitationes* are present-at-hand [*vorhanden*] and that in them there is conjointly present-at-hand an *ego* as worldless *res cogitans*.[59]

It is amazing that at the end of the preparatory analytic of *Dasein* and after the essential part of its "destruction" of Descartes, Heidegger still outlines the possibility of a retranscription of the analytic of *Dasein* in the terms—to be sure, displaced and reinterpreted—of the Cartesian ego. Its historial figure doubtless must have exercised a powerful fascination in order that, surviving its historical avatars and its phenomenological critique, it should still be referred to. The confirmation here accorded the *cogito sum* can be justified phenomenologically only if, in a way still to be determined, the formal statement consigned by Descartes can be rendered manifest under the aspect of another phenomenon than that to which Descartes, and therefore also Kant and Husserl, limited themselves. Concerning the possibility of such a confirmation of what nevertheless has just suffered a reversal, it can be a matter only of repeating, in a non-Cartesian mode, Descartes's *ego cogito sum*. As strange as it may appear, the plan of such a repetition has nothing of the *hapax* about it, not only because *Sein und Zeit* attempted to see it through, but also because even the last seminars still formulate it: "The paragraphs dedicated to Descartes in *Sein und Zeit* constitute the first attempt to exit from the prison of consciousness, or rather no longer to reenter it. It is not at all a matter of reestablishing realism against idealism, for by limiting itself to assuring that a world exists for the subject, realism remains a tributary of Cartesianism. It is rather a matter of managing to think the Greek meaning of the ἐγώ." To overcome the ego in the direction of the ἐγώ was no doubt what Heidegger undertook topically by commenting on Protagoras and stressing his irreducibility to Descartes.[60] But had he not, beforehand, accomplished this more radically through the analytic of *Dasein*—a non-Cartesian and perhaps already more than Greek ego?

And in that case, must one not recognize definitively that in *Sein und Zeit*, in the "destruction" of the ego's Cartesian acceptation, the ego not only does not definitively disappear, but is born for the first time to its authentic phenomenological figure? Even more, would not the "new beginning" be inaugurated with the declension of the ego according to the not metaphysical, but existential, requirements of *Dasein*? It is therefore necessary to examine how the ego-hood of the ego can attain its phenomenological—that is, its non-Cartesian—legitimacy.

Given *Dasein*: How does it differ essentially from the beings that are not in its mode? In the fact that it is the being for whom its Being is an issue, that is, the being for whom Being is in each case its own. But, since "the Being which is an issue for this being in its Being is in each case mine," it is necessary to admit that "the claim of *Dasein*, in accordance with this being's characteristic *mineness*, must always speak the *personal* pronoun: 'I am,' 'you are.'" Because it brings the Being in it into play, *Dasein* can only put *itself* into play, and therefore it can express itself only in person, since it can bring itself into play only as an *I*: "I myself am in each case [*bin ich je selbst*] the being that we call *Dasein*, and I am so as a being-able-to-be for whom it is a matter of Being that being."[61] Here, the possibility of saying "I am," and therefore of declining *Being* in the first *person* results from *Dasein*'s property of bringing itself *in person* into the play of its own Being. The *I* would have neither interest nor legitimacy if, in the capacity of an "existential determination of *Dasein*," it did not have to be and could not be "interpreted existentially," that is, if "'I'-hood and ipseity were not conceived existentially." But these two terms do not remain equivalent, as if the one could be substituted for the other. On the contrary, their existential interpretation demands that "the self [*Selbst*] which the reticence of resolute existence unveils be the originary phenomenal ground for the question of the Being of the 'I.'" Only the phenomenal orientation concerning the meaning of the Being of authentic being-able-to-be-oneself [*Selbstseinkönnen*] puts the meditation in the position of being able to elucidate what ontological right might be claimed by substantiality, simplicity, and personality as characteristics of ipseity [*Selbstheit*]."⁶² Selfhood (ipseity, *Selbstheit*) alone renders possible, through its absolute coincidence with self, what might be expressed by no matter what *personal* pronoun, and it therefore assures the *I* of any possible "I am" its authentic possibility; if the Self did not determine the *I*, no being would be such that it might in itself bring itself into play in its very Being—precisely because no *same* would then be accessible. Conversely, in its position as They, *Dasein* claims to stick to the *I*, itself the mere "appearance of a Self [*scheinbare Selbst*]."⁶³ The I can therefore say "I am" with perfect existential legitimacy only if it is reduced to the essential phenomenon of the Self (*Selbst*). But the Self becomes visible and given only in the phenomenality of care (*Sorge*); indeed, "the expression 'care of self' [*Selbstsorge*] . . . would be a tautology";⁶⁴ in all care, it is indeed precisely of itself, with respect to other beings, that *Dasein* takes care: it cares only for itself, or rather all care concerns itself with other beings only by virtue of the care that the Self thus shows to take of itself. In this context, the "I am" finds a proper phenomenological site—it puts into operation the Self's care of itself, according to care as the Being of *Dasein*. The "I am" intervenes, therefore, in order to mark the mineness of *Dasein*—"I am in each case myself [*bin ich je selbst*] the being that we call *Dasein*, and I am so as a being-able-to-be for whom that Being is an issue."

Next it intervenes more precisely in order to develop the phenomenon of debt (*Schuld*): "But where will we find the criterion for the originary existential meaning of the 'in debt' [*schuldig*]? [Answer:] the essential here is that the 'in-debt' arises as the predicate of the 'I am' [*ich bin*]." In the end, it is finally the whole opening of *Dasein* that, through resoluteness, is at play with and in the "I am": "Henceforth, what is attained with resoluteness is the more originary, because authentic, truth of *Dasein*. The opening of the There co-originarily opens the Being-in-the-world that is in each case total, that is, the world, Being-in, and the Oneself that this being is as an 'I am' [*als 'ich bin'*]."⁶⁵ Not only does the "I am" not always imply the ontological indetermination of the *sum* in which Descartes founders, but it offers the most visible phenomenon for reaching the Being of *Dasein*, the care that establishes the Oneself. For the unique *I* can be developed phenomenologically in two opposite ways, which are inscribed precisely in the two postures offered to *Dasein*, authenticity and inauthenticity; thus the *I* opens itself to two statures, since "the ontological concept of the subject characterizes *not the ipseity of the I as Self* [*die Selbstheit des Ich qua Selbst*], *but the identity and the constancy* [*Selbigkeit und Beständigkeit*] *of a being that is always already present-at-hand*

[*Vorhanden*]." One could not say it more clearly: the *I* can manifest itself either as the identical constancy of substance, and therefore in the mode of a being of the world, and even of a being present-at-hand (persistent and subsistent), or, on the contrary, as and starting from the Self, and therefore from the mineness that puts *Dasein* into play in its Being.

The *I* therefore turns from the status of (subsistent) *res cogitans* to that of the "I am" according to whether it pertains to identity (*Selbigkeit*) or to the Self (*Selbstheit*). The unique *I* sustains resoluteness, in the very sense that *Dasein* does not cease to be at play in it: in order to decide on the way of Being of its Being. How does the *I* indeed reach its non-Cartesian status? By opposing to the ontological indetermination, and therefore also to the existential irresoluteness of inauthentic fallenness, "the ipseity [*Selbstheit*] . . . that is discerned existentially in authentic being-able-to-be, that is, in the authenticity of *Dasein's* Being *as care* [*Sorge*]." Taken starting from care, ipseity could not persist as a *res*; if it offers a "constancy of the Self [*Ständigkeit des Selbst*]," a "self-constancy [*Selbst-Ständigkeit*]," it does so not because the Self "is a constantly present-at-hand ground of care [*ständig vorhandene Grund*]," but because the Self does not cease to resolve itself authentically according to and on the basis of its most proper Being: "Existentially, Self-constancy [*Selbst-Ständigkeit*] signifies nothing other than anticipatory resoluteness."[66] The conclusion becomes unavoidable: the *I* can just as well have to be "destroyed" as to be able to be "confirmed," according to whether it is repeated by one or the other of the possible determinations of *Dasein*; either inauthentically, in the Cartesian way of the persistent and subsistent *res cogitans*; or authentically, in the way of anticipatory resoluteness, of the structure of care, of the mineness of *Dasein*. The "I think" therefore no longer appears as a metaphysical thesis to be refuted, among others, in order to free up the phenomenon of *Dasein*, but as the very terrain that *Dasein* must conquer, since no other terrain will ever be given to *Dasein* in which to become manifest. *Ego cogito, sum* states less a countercase of *Dasein* than a territory to occupy, a statement to reinterpret, a work to redo.

Between the ego and *Dasein*, between Descartes and Heidegger, therefore, it would be a matter, beyond the patent critique, of a struggle for the interpretation of the same phenomenon—"I think," "I am." This placement of the two interlocutors on the same level leads one first to recognize them as interpreters of one another, more essentially than as interpreter and interpreted. But it also leads one to allow a new question to arise. If the *I* is determined ontologically only in the measure of ipseity (*Selbstheit*), such as it is set into operation in care, it becomes legitimate to formulate two questions. (1) Is the *I* of "I am" in fact determined entirely by ipseity? In turn, is the latter defined sufficiently and exclusively by the structure of care? Does that same ipseity reach all beings or only the beings that are on par with *Dasein*? And in that case, what other determination takes over for it for the other beings?[67] These questions are internal to the undertaking of *Sein und Zeit*. (2) There are others that go beyond *Sein und Zeit*, like this one: Even granting that it is attested more essentially as an "I am" than as an "I think," is the *I* that is to be determined exhausted for all that in its status as the *I* of a *sum*? In other words, does the *I* attest to its ultimate ground and does it reach its final phenomenality in its function as an "I am," fulfilled phenomenologically in "*Da-sein*"? Is the putting into play of the self by itself that characterizes the *I* devoted only to Being? Or indeed, in the *I* that I undoubtedly am, is not something also, or even first, at stake other than to be? Is what is put into play in, through, and in spite of the *I* exhausted necessarily, indisputably, and exclusively in terms of Being? Is it Being that is first at issue in the *I*, or, beyond that, is a more original stake at play? Is it permitted, despite the silence of *Sein und Zeit*, to pose this very question?

4

Question of Being or Ontological Difference

1. The Breakthrough and the Difference: "Sein und Zeit"

Phenomenology is accomplished by accomplishing, with the *Logical Investigations*, a first breakthrough: that of the intuition in play with intention in order to reach the things themselves. But phenomenology accomplishes a second breakthrough when Heidegger calls intentionality to return, as concerns things, not only to beings, but to the very Being of beings. Superimposed on, if not added to, the distinction between intuition and intention is the difference between Being and beings. The ontological difference wholly defines the breakthrough carried out (if not completed) by Heidegger. It does so, first, because it displaces phenomenology from the knowledge of beings to the thought of Being, first according to fundamental ontology and then according to the *Ereignis*. It does so, secondly, because the ontological difference alone allows one to make the distinction between metaphysics—attached to Being only as the Being of beings and with a view to beings—and the thought of Being as such; that is, it alone allows one to practice a "destruction of the history of ontology" that, in fact, allows and requires one to rewrite the history of metaphysics as the history of the forgetting of Being, as an unthought history of Being. In short, the ontological difference decides on both the phenomenological thought proper to Heidegger and the site of all preceding metaphysics. It would therefore suffice that its notion be poorly attested, or that its emergence remain confused, in order that both the breakthrough proper to Heidegger and his reinterpretation of the metaphysical history of ontology be weakened. The ontological difference allows for a hermeneutic of the history of metaphysics because it alone undertakes a hermeneutic of being with a view to Being: it is this second hermeneutic, in fact, that alone renders the first possible— and not the reverse; as an indirect consequence, the phenomenological breakthrough alone allows the historical destruction—and not the reverse.¹ Thus, it is of primary importance to determine how Heidegger understood and formulated the very notion of ontological difference. The least imprecision, the least hesitation, the least ambiguity would here take on considerable importance: it would be a matter of the weakening not of this or that concept or aspect of Heidegger's thought, but of the radical phenomenological breakthrough (*Durchbruch*) on which the entire Heideggerian advance depends. Any gap between the ontological difference and the fluvial course of thought, any delay between the ontological difference and the implementation of the breakthrough, would obviously count as symptoms of a deep incoherence of the whole enterprise. Where and when does the ontological difference appear in Heidegger's work? The stakes of this question are not restricted to a specific doctrinal point but affect the whole of Heidegger's thought inasmuch as the question is decisive for whether or not that thought constitutes a breakthrough.

These almost unlimited stakes of the ontological difference are doubled again by an almost unparalleled difficulty. Indeed, the ontological difference must all the more emerge, but it can do so all the less insofar as it remains in a latent—if not lethal—state throughout the history of metaphysics. In fact, it is a characteristic proper to metaphysics to think the divergence between Being and beings only by leaving it unthought as such: "the thinking of metaphysics remains involved in the difference which as such is unthought [*die als solche ungedachte Differenz*]."² The ontological difference escapes all the more insofar as it is not absent, but indeed at work in a latent mode: the Being of *beings* is lacking precisely because it is at play only to the benefit of beings. We never think outside of or before the ontological difference, since even when we ignore it we still think within its concealment, which is covered up by its covering over. Hence, to break through to the ontological difference could not mean finally to reach it, starting from a territory or from a position absolutely foreign to it, but only to pass from its latent state to its patent state. The breakthrough breaks through from one state of the ontological difference to the other, the difference remaining in any case anterior. But it is thus a matter of nothing less than the step back from metaphysics (as the unthought of ontological difference) toward the new beginning: "We speak of the *difference* [*Differenz*] between Being and beings. The step back goes from what is unthought, from the difference as such, into what it is necessary to think, which is the *forgetting* of the difference. The forgetting here to be thought is the veiling of the difference as such, thought in terms of λήθη (concealment); this veiling has in turn withdrawn itself from the beginning. Forgetting belongs to the difference because the difference belongs to forgetting."³ The step back from metaphysics (unthought ontological difference) is exactly equivalent—in being accomplished—to the breakthrough into ontological difference. Consequently, the movement through which Heidegger tears himself away (or attempts to tear himself away) from metaphysics—namely, *Sein und Zeit*—must also by definition accomplish a breakthrough into the ontological difference, and the ontological difference thought as such. To destroy the history of ontology would not have any meaning nor the least success if there did not open up, at the same time and in the same movement, access to the explicit ontological difference. Can this requirement be satisfied by the facts? Two difficulties seem to make us have to doubt it. (1) Since the breakthrough toward the ontological difference takes its eventual point of departure in the unthought of that very difference, its entire process unfolds in the heart of latency, in the original unthought, finally in the undecided. The thrust of the breakthrough, consequently, would have to be born in the very heart of ontological indecision. Through what undecided and provisional rupture could the breakthrough emerge? Can an emergence, which is no doubt progressive, ever be suitable to a breakthrough? (2) By its very excellence, the ontological difference would have to emerge as soon as the program for a destruction of the history of ontology is imposed. Since the latter is formulated explicitly in *Sein und Zeit*, § 6, it would also be necessary that the ontological difference be explicitly formulated there. Now, precisely, does *Sein und Zeit* not ignore the ontological difference?

2. The Emergence and the Delay

Where, then, and when does the ontological difference appear? According to Heidegger himself, and this is a first paradox, it remains ignored by *Sein und Zeit*, both as unthought and as thought. Indeed, in a 1949 foreword to the third edition of the essay entitled *Vom Wesen des Grundes*, which was written in 1928 for a volume in homage to Husserl that appeared in 1929, Heidegger specifies: "The treatise *Vom Wesen des Grundes* was written in 1928, at the same time as the lecture *Was ist Metaphysik?*. The latter meditates on the Nothing, the former names the ontological difference [*jene nennt die ontologische Differenz*]."[4] At first glance, this judgment seems perfectly correct. The lecture *Was ist Metaphysik?* does in fact meditate on the Nothing, its genesis, its appearance, and its status. As for *Vom Wesen des Grundes*, it can name the difference only starting from the Nothing, since "the ontological difference is the Nothing" and the Nothing (as *nihilating not*) is "not identical, but the Same" as the "*nihilating not* of the difference." In the text itself, the ontological difference in fact appears explicitly: "Ontic truth and ontological truth each concern in different ways [*je verschieden*] *being in* its Being and the *Being* of being. They belong together essentially, by reason of their relationship to the *difference between Being and beings* (the ontological difference) [*zum Unterschied von Sein und Seienden* (*ontologische Differenz*)]. The inevitable bifurcation of the essence of truth into ontic and ontological is possible only through the opening, at the same time, of this difference [*dieses Unterschied*]."[5] Truth here leads to the ontological difference; or rather, the duality of the truth, as much that of beings as of their Being, takes its possibility from the anterior difference of Being from beings in the sole Being of beings. One will therefore conclude, on Heidegger's word, but above all on the evidence of the textual facts, that the ontological difference is named only in 1928–29, and therefore *after Sein und Zeit*, which would thus appear as the only one of Heidegger's major texts to remain unfamiliar with the ontological difference.

When examined, however, this conclusion seems extremely weak, as widely accepted as it may be. And this is so for several reasons. (1) If the text from 1929 "names [*nennt*] the ontological difference,"[6] it is necessary not to confuse nomination and meditation; it could be only a question of "the difference that is named but not yet thought."[7] In short, is naming the ontological difference here sufficient for thinking it as such, that is, for freeing the unthought that, metaphysically, characterizes it? (2) One will perhaps respond that the text of 1929 thinks the ontological difference just as much as it names it, since it establishes it on the basis of a meditation on the ontico-ontological "bifurcation" of the truth, where the unveiledness of Being is distinguished from the manifestation of beings: "*Enthülltheit des Seins ermöglicht erst Offenbarkeit des Seienden.*" This unveiledness is named, as the truth of Being, "*ontological truth.*"[8] But such an alethological origin of the difference goes back to a date prior to 1928–29. Thus the course of the 1927 summer semester establishes an almost identical distinction: "This is why we distinguish [*scheiden*] not only terminologically but also for reasons having to do with the thing itself the *uncoveredness of a being* [*Entdecktheit eines Seienden*] from the *disclosedness of its Being* [*Erschlossenheit seines Seins*]." Even more, here, the two figures of truth already go back explicitly to the ontological difference:

> In other words, we must manage to conceptualize, in its possibility and its necessity, the difference between uncoveredness and disclosedness [*den Unterschied von Entdecktheit und Erschlossenheit*], but likewise also to comprehend the possible unity of the two. This implies at the same time the possibility of grasping the difference [*Unterscheidung*] between the

being uncovered in the uncoveredness and the Being disclosed in the disclosedness, that is, of establishing the distinction between Being and beings, the ontological difference [*die Unterscheidung zwischen Sein und Seienden, die ontologische Differenz*]. In addressing the Kantian problem, we thus arrive at the question of the *ontological difference* [*der ontologischen Differenz*].[9]

Even more, *Sein und Zeit* strongly thematizes this same opposition, as far as to suggest a difference between its terms: "Being, as that which is asked about, requires its own mode of being brought to light [*Aufweisungsart*], which is essentially different [*unterscheidet*] from the uncoveredness of beings."[10] This comparative analysis thus finds its entire outcome in § 44 of *Sein und Zeit*. Consequently, if the ontological difference must emerge starting from the investigation concerning and the conquest of the dividing of the truth, it would be necessary to suppose that it appears as soon as the truth is divided up into two irreducible acceptations, which means well before *Vom Wesen des Grundes*. (3) This conclusion so little contradicts Heidegger's 1949 declaration (which, let us underline, speaks of a naming but not of a *first* naming of the ontological difference in 1928–29) that it is he himself who, in a 1929 note to his text, specifies with regard to the formula "*Unterschied von Sein und Seiendem [Ontologische Differenz]*":

> See the first public communication on this subject in the 1927 summer semester course, *Basic Problems of Phenomenology*, § 22. Its conclusion returns to the beginning, where Kant's thesis on *Being*—that it is not a real predicate—is elucidated with the intention of taking into view for the first time the ontological difference as such [*die ontologische Differenz als solche erst einmal in den Blick zu fassen*], and this on the basis of ontology, itself experienced, however, in the mode of fundamental ontology. This whole course belongs to *Sein und Zeit*, First Part, Division 3.[11]

We therefore have at our disposal an explicit declaration: the ontological difference, if it appears in the immediately published texts only in 1928–29, emerges in the public courses as early as the summer of 1927, in the *Grundprobleme der Phänomenologie*, that is, in the work that immediately follows *Sein und Zeit*. *Sein und Zeit* therefore becomes, because of this ever more clearly authorized precision, *the* text par excellence to have ignored—at least in its published part—the ontological difference. Such a clear conclusion, however, carries the marks of a twofold difficulty. First, *Sein und Zeit* does indeed distinguish and differentiate (*unterscheiden*), like the other texts, two modes of the truth;[12] how are we to understand the fact that it alone, among all these texts, does not infer from this the ontological difference? Secondly, if the 1927 summer course, the first "inventor" of the ontological difference, "belongs to *Sein und Zeit*" and to its overall project, how are we to understand the fact that its published part carries no trace of it, especially in the long introduction (§§ 1–8) that is an introduction to the whole, including the unpublished part (in particular Part 1, Division 3, "Zeit und Sein," mentioned in 1929)? Could it be that such a radical break proposed by Heidegger between *Sein und Zeit* and the ontological difference seems *too* sharp to be acceptable?

Before debating this thesis, it would be advisable to verify how, for Heidegger himself, it becomes unavoidable. This examination requires two stages.

1. Where does the 1927 course present the ontological difference and how? Answer: in § 22. In fact, after having provisionally concluded, in § 21, the analysis of the Kantian thesis on Being as a position, Heidegger underlines, in § 22 *a*, that, in common usage, "Being is taken as a being in the question concerning what being is *inasmuch as* being is." *Dasein* most certainly understands *Being* in a certain way (for otherwise it quite simply would not be in the mode of *Dasein*), but it only ever understands it confusedly, in a latent state: "The difference [*Unterschied*] between Being and being *is there* [*ist . . . da*] in a latent manner in *Dasein* itself and its existence, even if it is not expressly known. The difference [*Unterschied*] *is there*, which means that it has the mode of Being of *Dasein*, that it belongs to existence. Existence almost means 'to be in the performance of this distinction.'" But this achievement, which cannot be dismissed since it defines *Dasein* as the ontically ontological being, is in no way equivalent to an avowed thought of the difference as such. On the contrary, *Dasein* remains in the difference without knowing it. In this sense, here, "the difference [*Unterschied*] between Being and beings is there *pre-ontologically*, in other words without an explicit concept of Being, *latent in the existence of Dasein*. But as such, it can become an *explicitly understood difference*." In order to pass from the implicit to the explicit, the difference must be understood as the *da* of the two differing things, thanks to the temporality of *Dasein*. Hence a modified naming when the difference is carried out: "We therefore name the difference [*Unterschied*] between Being and beings, when it is carried out explicitly, the *ontological difference* [*die ontologische Differenz*]."[13]

This text, therefore, does indeed introduce the ontological difference, but it does so in a mode that renders the latter highly problematic. Indeed, the difference is designated first by a latency that is so deep that Heidegger finds himself compelled to use two terms, according to whether the difference is concealed [*Unterschied*] or whether, more rarely, it ends up appearing [*Differenz, ontologische Differenz*]. One can even wonder: while it is certainly named here, is the ontological difference, for all that, really established? Are we dealing with a phenomenological report of victory or rather with a program for a breakthrough that is still to be achieved? Does the first "public communication" of the ontological difference announce a conquest or a difficulty still to be overcome? The problem is confirmed with the incomplete character of the 1927 course: of its second part, which promised nothing less than to examine "The fundamental ontological question of the meaning of Being in general. The fundamental structures and the fundamental modes of Being," only a first chapter is "communicated," entitled "the problem of the ontological difference." Now, it itself contains only four paragraphs, of which only the last (§ 22) approaches, and in a single section (§ 22 a), the difference— inasmuch as proximally and for the most part it is *not* explicitly onto- logical. Such a lowering of the aim in the degree that it comes closer to its declared goal would leave one to suppose that a difficulty checks it and that an aporia impedes it, not that a breakthrough liberates thought. Everything happens as if the ontological difference were marked and named "first" during the summer of 1927 only in order to acknowledge the aporia of a question that still lacks an answer.

2. Hence the second stage: Does this text maintain a privileged relation with *Sein und Zeit*? Does it mark a continuity or a rupture? Evidently, it remains in a close continuity with the book from the winter of 1927. It does so first because the *Grundprobleme* are inscribed in § 1, presupposition 3, of *Sein und Zeit*, as is confirmed by *Vom Wesen des Grundes*[14] and the plan for the whole given in § 8.[15] It does so next because the transition from implicit difference (*Unterschied*) to explicit and truly ontological difference (*Differenz*) depends, here, on the temporality of *Dasein*: the difference (*Differenz*) is there (*da*) only if *Dasein* understands itself temporally to the point of unfolding in itself the Being of beings. Thus, not only does the analytic of *Dasein* not constitute an obstacle (to be overcome by the *Kehre*) to reaching the ontological difference, but it alone, as the exercise of temporality on the basis of the structure of care (*cura, Sorge*), allows one to think explicitly the originally temporal character of Being *überhaupt*. Hence, if *Dasein* appears as its sole temporal worker, how can one suppose that the ontological difference, in its "first public communication," overcomes or rejects *Dasein*? But then how can one not suppose that, already with *Sein und Zeit*, *Dasein* was working in its analytic at the clarification of the ontological difference, which still remains at least latent to it? Paradoxically, we are reversing the initial question—How far from *Sein und Zeit* does the ontological difference appear?—in order to ask: Is it conceivable that the analytic of *Dasein*

does not thoroughly and from the beginning serve, already with *Sein und Zeit*, the clarification of the ontological difference?

3. The Occurrences and the Notes

Two types of answers can be given to this question. On the one hand, one can simply deny that *Sein und Zeit* ever names the ontological difference, whose appearance one will attribute to *Vom Wesen des Grundes*; thus L. M. Vail: "the term *ontological difference* does not appear as such in *Sein und Zeit*," for it is "the 1928 essay that first makes use of the term *ontological difference*."[16] On the other hand, one can maintain that if the word certainly does not appear, the thing is already at work in the 1927 text; thus argue, among others, John C. Sallis: "Even the first great work of Heidegger, *Sein und Zeit*, moves already within the framework of the ontological difference";[17] and then G. Granel, who recognizes that "what is 'properly thought' by Heidegger 'already' in 1927 [is] *die Differenz*."[18] The extreme paradox of an ontological difference that is all the more at work in *Sein und Zeit* insofar as it never appears in it found its perfect expression with Jean Beaufret:

> One would therefore have to admit that *Sein und Zeit* is the form in which the difference and the participation of Being and being appear to Heidegger for the first time. As a result, *Sein und Zeit* would be the book of the difference between Being and beings. What is characteristic is that this word "difference," which Heidegger very often uses, in reality does not figure thematically in his well-known first book, namely, *Being and Time*, but that the phrase "ontological difference," and by this we mean the difference having to do with the distinction between Being and beings, this phrase of ontological difference appears in his teaching only in the months following the publication of *Sein und Zeit*, that is, in the course *Basic Problems of Phenomenology*, which he gives at the University of Marburg where he is then professor during the summer semester, *Sein und Zeit* having appeared in the month of February. One can therefore say that *Sein und Zeit* is the book of the difference between Being and beings, but in such a way that the word "difference" does not yet enter in at the forefront.[19]

Such an explication itself demands an explication: How is it to be understood that "the book of the difference between Being and beings"—which issues from it and leads back to it—is precisely that book which is completely silent as to "the phrase" and the "word"? How is it to be admitted that the (second) phenomenological breakthrough should not have known how to speak or understand its own vocabulary? This interpretation, which is paradoxical to the point of incoherence, would doubtless not have imposed itself on such a great number of readers if the authority—among others, but first—of Jean Beaufret had not supported it. Can one dispute it? No doubt, by first distinguishing two theses in it: (1) *Sein und Zeit* never employs the phrase "ontological difference" (an assertion of fact); (2) *Sein und Zeit* moves within the ontological difference thought as such (a theoretical assertion). We would like to show not only that these two assertions do not stand up to examination, but above all that they contribute to concealing the true situation of the ontological difference within *Sein und Zeit*—or rather the true situation of *Sein und Zeit* within the ontological difference.

First point: already with *Sein und Zeit*, Heidegger uses the formula "ontological difference," contrary to the opinion, to our knowledge without exception, of the commentators. Let us look at the texts. (1) § 12: "In the first instance it is enough to see the ontological difference [*den ontologischen Unterschied*] between Being-in . . . as an existential and the category of 'insideness' which beings ready-to-hand [*Vorhanden*] can have with regard to one another."[20] A similar formula (but without the adjective *ontologisch*) reappears in § 40: "With the first phenomenal indication of the fundamental constitution of *Dasein* and with the clarification of the existential sense of Being-in in its difference [*im Unterschied*] from the categorial significance of 'interiority,' we have defined *Dasein* as dwelling alongside . . . , being familiar with."[21] Between *In-Sein*, which is properly existential because it belongs to *Dasein*'s way of Being, and the "interiority" of one ready-to-hand being inside another, not only is there a difference, but that difference has an ontological status: it separates two ways of Being concerning, in the end, *Dasein*, on the one hand, and *Vorhandenheit*, on the other. No pretext allows one here to weaken either the difference or its ontological character. Therefore there is here a first occurrence, in fact, of the "ontological difference." (2) § 63: "And defining the structure of care has given us the basis of a first ontological difference [*ontologische Unterscheidung*] between existence and reality. This leads to the thesis: the substance of man is existence."[22] This second occurrence must itself also be understood as that of an "ontological difference," which, like the first, separates *Dasein*'s way of Being (existence, existential) from the way of being of beings not like *Dasein* (reality, categorial). This difference reappears very significantly on the last page of *Sein und Zeit*, where, if the adjective is lacking, the differentiated terms remain the same as in the two complete occurrences: "the difference [*Unterschied*] between the

Being of existing *Dasein* and the Being of beings that do not have the character of *Dasein* . . ."; and "the 'difference' ('*Unterschied*') between 'consciousness' and the 'thing.' "[23] A sharp and clear topic is therefore put into place: between the Being of Dasein and the Being of other beings a relation is drawn that is in fact called ontological difference.[24] We are dealing here with a textual fact, which is weakened neither by formulas that are close,[25] nor by the indetermination that still affects the adjective "ontological." The reluctance of the translators and commentators here to name the *ontologischer Unterschied* and the *ontologische Unterscheidung* with the name due to them of "ontological difference" no doubt results from a hesitation to recognize a fact whose (precisely ontological) status remains indeterminate. That reluctance can be overcome only if the factual assertion of the "ontological difference" is legitimated by the theoretical assertion that, in a certain sense, the difference here named can be thought as ontological. To attempt that legitimation, it is advisable to follow more subtly the trace of the "ontological difference" in *Sein und Zeit*; in fact, along with these occurrences that are clearly identifiable by a substantive, it appears in verbal form, more discretely, in the work of the things themselves. Two occurrences thus take on a decisive importance.

1. The first intervenes in § 2, during the inaugural and solemn construction of the question of Being. This question, strangely, calls for not two but three terms: it is a matter of that which is interrogated (*das Befragte*), which is a role held here by being, or more exactly, by that unparalleled being that *Dasein* constitutes; then it is a matter of that which one is asking for in response to the question (*das Gefragte*), in this case the Being of being; finally and especially it is a matter of what one wants to know in asking the question (*das Erfragte*) and which does not coincide with that which is asked about, namely the meaning of Being (*Sinn des Seins*), or indeed what it means to be. It is precisely in distinguishing the three terms of the question of Being that Heidegger is led to specify an important point: "Being, as what one is asking for in response to the question [*das Gefragte*], therefore requires its own way of showing itself, which differs essentially [*sich . . . wesenhaft unterscheidet*] from the uncoveredness of beings." An essential difference intervenes here, and, phenomenologically, it opposes Being in its characteristic showing to beings in common uncoveredness; unless one forgets that phenomenology alone merits the name of ontology, one must here conclude, from the difference of modes of presence, an equally essential difference between Being and beings. Even more, this essential difference is opened up in the case of and at the instigation of the construction of the *Seinsfrage* as such, in order to separate its first two terms, so that it perfectly well deserves the title "ontological": a difference established

by and for the question of Being is called, very precisely, an ontological difference. The ontological work of difference here appears all the more distinctive, insofar as it intervenes already with the first "repetition" of the question of Being, in a place (the introduction) that governs all of *Sein und Zeit*, including its unpublished or unwritten sections.

2. It is also in a particularly sensitive place that the second onto-logical occurrence of the work of difference is signaled: indeed, it is on the last page of the first division ("Preparatory Fundamental Analysis of *Dasein*"), which carries out both a recapitulation and a transition toward the second division ("*Dasein* and Temporality"). Here again, exactly as in § 2, it is a matter of the question of Being and of the relation of the three terms in it: "There 'is' Being (not being) only inasmuch as truth is. And truth *is* only inasmuch as and for as long as *Dasein* is. Being and truth 'are' co-originarily. What does it signify that Being 'is,' where Being must nevertheless be differentiated from every being [*wo es doch von allem Seienden unterscheiden sein soll*]? That can be posed concretely as a question only if the meaning of Being and the scope of the understanding of Being are in general clarified."[26] This is a fundamental declaration, since being, the Being of being, and finally the meaning of Being explicitly repeat the question of Being that was posed to begin with (§ 2); it is not yet a matter of claiming to answer the question, because its third term has not yet been understood (a task reserved for the second part, at least in principle); but the analytic of *Dasein* henceforth—almost—completed allows one to indicate with complete phenomenological ex-actitude, starting from the ontologically distinctive being, the divergence and the relation between Being and being within the Being of being. But in order to characterize this indissolubly identical divergence, Heidegger here (as in § 2) employs, precisely, the verb *differentiate, unterscheiden.*[27] If Being is differentiated from being, how can one not conclude that it is indeed a matter of an ontological difference? One ought not object that the interpreter is here forcing the letter of the text, nor that Heidegger in fact did not employ "ontological difference." For in his personal copy, he wrote down, right after the sequence, "*unterscheiden sein soll,*" this simple note: "*Ontologische Differenz.*"[28] Already with *Sein und Zeit*, therefore, the ontological difference indeed works the indissoluble divergence between Being and being—the text gives occurrences of it, and Heidegger himself confirms its meaning.

One should highlight, moreover, the frequency and the conver-gence of the notes in Heidegger's personal copy that comment on *Sein und Zeit* with the help of the phrase "ontological difference" and with a view to its concept. Beside the already mentioned § 44, four texts in particular deserve to be cited.

1. At the moment of establishing phenomenology as the only possible ontology, Heidegger repeats the triple dimension of the *Seinsfrage*: " . . . the necessity of a fundamental ontology, taking as its theme the distinctive ontologico-ontic being, *Dasein*, so as to confront the cardinal problem, the question concerning the meaning of Being in general" (§ 7). It is indeed a matter here of the three terms of the *Seinsfrage*, grouped into two couples: first the distinctive being (*Dasein*) and its Being, and then, facing the first couple, the meaning of Being. Now, Heidegger comments on this *Sinn des Seins überhaupt* by specifying in a note: "Being—not a genus, not Being for beings in general; the 'in general' = καθόλου = in totality of: *Being of* beings; meaning of the difference."[29] Thus the meaning of Being attains its radicality only inasmuch as *Being*, even in the *Being of beings*, is already accentuated in favor of Being, not of beings; and in such a way that with the couple Being-beings, it is already a matter of an ontological (and not ontic) difference. Here again, the *Seinsfrage* is indeed revealed to harbor, already in its first construction, the ontological difference (unless it is not rather harbored in that difference).

2. Stigmatizing in § 20 the exemplary insufficiency of the Cartesian determination of ontology, Heidegger indicates the ambiguity of *substantia*, which offers a signification that is sometimes ontic and sometimes ontological. And to conclude: "Behind this insignificant difference of signification, however, there lies hidden an inability to master the fundamental problem of Being." This *Unterschied* of signification must appear all the less negligible insofar as it is a matter of an "ontico-ontological signification," and therefore of the play between Being and beings. Moreover, Heidegger comments on this sentence in a note: "ontological difference [*ontologische Differenz*]." What Cartesian metaphysics (as, in fact, *all* metaphysics) leaves unthought is, through the indetermination of the concept of *substantia*, the ontological difference itself. Thus even the "destruction of the history of ontology" is carried out, in *Sein und Zeit* and in the same capacity as the construction of the *Seinsfrage*, starting from the ontological difference.[30]

3. On the threshold of the analysis and with a view to not leaving "the Being of *Dasein* undetermined" (§ 39), Heidegger recalls the opposition between Being and beings: "Beings *are* independently of experience, of knowledge and of the grasp through which they were opened, uncovered, and determined. But Being 'is' only in the understanding of it by the being to whose Being something like an understanding of Being belongs." It is a matter here, of course, of differentiating (*unterscheiden*, in the sense already raised from § 2) the unveiledness of beings from the unconcealment of Being, in accordance with the first requirements of the *Seinsfrage*; Heidegger insists on this in a note: "But this understanding

[must be understood] as a listening. This never means, however, that 'Being' is only 'subjective,' but [it means] Being (*qua* the Being of beings) *qua* difference 'in' *Da-sein* as the having-been-thrown of (the throw)."[31] Distinctive in that, as a being, it is ontologically, *Dasein* therefore plays at the hinge and the fold between Being and beings, or better it *is* in person that fold and that hinge.

4. Finally, taking up again the canonical statement that "Being can never be explained by beings," since on the contrary it shows itself only through the understanding that Dasein has of it, Heidegger comments, once again, "ontological difference."[32]

One can no doubt legitimately remark that a text should not be read on the basis of *marginalia* or of notes, especially when they are much later than that text; one can remark, again, that Heidegger's retroactive self-interpretation often gives rise to more obscurities than clarifications (we even saw that here, moreover). But, while giving due to these justified cautions, one cannot deny the evidence: in these occurrences, Heidegger did not have to overinterpret his own texts in order to read an ontological difference in them, an ontological difference that is all the more implicit in certain places (*Seinsfrage*, destruction, distinctive characteristic of Dasein) insofar as it appears explicitly in others. No *coup de force*, even perpetrated by Heidegger himself, would have been able to introduce the ontological difference into *Sein und Zeit* anachronistically if *Sein und Zeit*, of itself and from the beginning, did not move within the horizon already opened by the ontological difference. Let us conclude, therefore: the "ontological difference" appears literally in *Sein und Zeit* itself because the breakthrough of 1927 is carried out at the very heart of the ontological difference.

4. The Most Cardinal Unthought

A *certain* difference therefore traverses *Sein und Zeit*—as in its center (§ 44)—from one end (§ 2) to the other (§ 83).[33] Establishing this fact, however, does not amount to demonstrating that *Sein und Zeit* already sets into operation the later and canonical concept of *the* ontological difference. On the contrary, the whole question from this point on comes down to identifying the meaning and measuring the scope of what *Sein und Zeit* allows to appear under the title of "ontological difference," without understanding it in advance on the basis of what the same phrase will indicate after 1927. Before any interpretation, therefore, it would be advisable to find the guiding thread that could have led *Sein und Zeit* to introduce such an "ontological difference" (or better, to introduce itself into it). We propose the following hypothesis: the guiding thread through which to reach the ontological difference, such as it works *Sein und Zeit*, takes its origin in Husserl.

First, let us raise a coincidence: Husserl himself also employs the phrase "ontological difference," and he does so in 1913, in the second edition of the *Logical Investigations*. In fact, the Third Investigation, dedicated to the theory of wholes and parts, in a first chapter entitled "Difference [*Unterschied*] between Independent and Dependent Objects," on three occasions qualifies this same difference with the adjective "ontological": " . . . the universal, ontological difference [*ontologischen Unterschied*] between abstract and concrete contents"; then, " . . . the essence of the ontological difference [*des ontologischen Unterschiedes*] between *concrete* and *astract*"; and finally, " . . . to shed light on the ontological difference [*des ontologischen Unterschiedes*]."[34] These occurrences prove at least that, in 1927, Heidegger did not have to look far for a legitimacy for his own formula. One can even remark here another curious coincidence: *Sein und Zeit*, § 39, opposes beings, as "independent [*unabhängig*] of experience, of knowledge and of comprehension," to the Being that depends on the "understanding of beings" that *Dasein* is; this passage, precisely, is commented on, in a later note from the personal copy, in terms of difference: " . . . Being (*qua* Being of beings), *qua* difference 'in' *Da-sein*."[35] This double meeting does not yet prove any theoretical filiation; at least it does not render such a filiation unthinkable.

But in still another way, Husserl appears, at least just beneath the surface, as the indisputable interlocutor of one of these two occurrences of the "ontological difference" in *Sein und Zeit*. Indeed, when he sets up an "ontological difference [*ontologische Unterscheidung*] between existence and reality" (§ 63),[36] Heidegger rediscovers a distinction established canonically, in 1913 by *Ideen I* (§ 42), between consciousness and reality:

> Being as consciousness and Being as reality. The difference [*Unterschied*] in principle between the modes of intuition. . . . A fundamental and essential difference [*Unterschied*] is introduced between Being as consciousness and Being as a thing. . . . Thereby is announced also the difference in principle [*prinzipielle Unterschiedenheit*] of ways of Being, the most cardinal that is found in general, that between *consciousness* and *reality* . . . a *difference* [*Unterschied*] *in principle* of the modes of givenness.[37]

Quite obviously, if he keeps the term of reality, Heidegger substitutes for consciousness that of *Dasein*; but *Dasein* does not disqualify the Husserlian difference, precisely because, by repeating it with a slight correction, it consecrates that difference in all of its pertinence; this, moreover, is why it happens that Heidegger takes up again, as in a citation and with the reservation of quotation marks, the very terms that Husserl used in equivalence with his own; thus he evokes "the difference [*Unterschied*] between the Being of existing *Dasein* and the Being of beings that do not have the character of *Dasein* (for example reality)," but immediately and as if equivalently "the 'difference' ('*Unterschied*') between 'consciousness' and 'thing.' "[38] The Husserlian difference comes to haunt, so to speak, the Heideggerian difference all the way up to the last page of *Sein und Zeit*. Other texts from 1913 incontestably establish that Husserl indeed had sufficiently set up such a principial and most cardinal difference. *Ideen I*, § 43, locates between perception, on the one hand, and symbolic representation, on the other hand, an "unbridgeable difference of essence [*Wesensunterschied*]"; further on, § 49: "immanent or absolute Being and transcendent Being are indeed both called 'being,' an 'object,' and both certainly have their content of objective determination; but it is evident that what is here called from the two sides object and determination of object is similar only according to empty logical categories. Between consciousness and reality there opens, gaping, a real abyss of meaning [*Abgrund des Sinnes*]." But what is an abyss of meaning between two acceptations of "being" if not a difference of *ways* of Being, and therefore an already ontological difference? Finally, in order to establish the divergence between the original region (*Urregion*) of consciousness, as the original category of Being in general (*Urkategorie des Seins überhaupt*), and the other regions of Being (*Seinsregionen*), § 76 specifies: "The doctrine of the categories must therefore start entirely from this difference of Being, the most radical of all [*von dieser radikalsten aller Seinsunterscheidungen*]— Being as *consciousness* and Being as 'announcing itself' in consciousness, as 'transcendent.' "[39] Here again, how could one not consider that a difference of Being, beyond the distinction among beings (precisely, as such, logically indistinct), amounts to an ontological difference?

Let us recapitulate: between the ways of Being of two types of beings, which are named consciousness and thing (*res, Realität*), Husserl introduces a quasi-ontological difference of essence; he was therefore able to offer to Heidegger as early as 1913 not only the phrase "ontological difference" (in the second edition of the *Logical Investigations*) but above all the determination of the two beings and ways of Being that render that phrase phenomenologically effective (in the *Ideen I*); and Heidegger himself admits this origin by using, parsimoniously, to be sure, but all the more significantly insofar as we are dealing with the finale of *Sein und Zeit*, the terms that his master proposed to him. From this point on, how could one not presume that the point of departure for the ontological difference in 1927 (and therefore previously) is given by Husserl in 1913?

It would even be necessary to go further. Perhaps one could suggest that the theoretical break between Husserl and Heidegger even before 1927 was played out precisely over the interpretation of the difference (named ontological or not) between "consciousness" (or existence) and "thing" (or reality). Heidegger does not separate himself from Husserl by introducing an "ontological difference" that Husserl would have ignored, but by radically deepening as ontological a difference of essence and of ways of Being still left undetermined as such by Husserl. At least two themes confirm that this debate precedes the writing of Sein und Zeit.

1. In the 1925 course, *Prolegomena zur Geschichte des Zeitbegriffs*, after having cited the passages which we mentioned previously from *Ideen I* (§§ 49 and 76), and after having recognized that Husserl thus claimed indeed to have established a "fundamental difference" (*Grundunterschied, fundamentaler Seinsunterschied*), Heidegger observes that Husserl has in no way managed to do so:

> But now we note something astonishing: the conquest of the most radical of the differences of Being [*Seinsunterschied*] is here claimed, and yet no question is properly posed concerning the Being of being which enters into the difference [*Unterschied*]. . . . During the conquest of this fundamental difference of Being [*Seinsunterschiedes*], not once is the question posed concerning the way of Being itself of the terms of the difference [*der Unterschiedenen*], nor concerning the way of Being of consciousness, nor fundamentally concerning what in general governs the whole difference of the difference of Being [*die ganze Unterscheidung des Seinsunterschiedes*]—concerning the meaning of Being. Hence it becomes clear that *the question of Being is not just any question, only one among other possible questions, but the most pressing question* inherent in the most proper meaning of phenomenology itself—pressing in an even more radical sense than we have hitherto clarified, concerning the intentional."[40]

With the title of the essential difference between ways of Being, Husserl indeed names the difference between (intentional) consciousness and the (real) thing, but he does not go any further: he never thinks what he names; he never thinks what is meant by a difference of ways of Being, because he lacks access to the condition of possibility of that question— the meaning of Being (*Sinn des Seins*). Husserl therefore commits a double "omission" (*Versäumnis*): first with respect to the difference that he names, because he never takes seriously the fact that one is there dealing with a question concerning the different Being of different beings, to the point that one must say that Husserl stops exactly at the moment when the fundamental difficulty begins—when it is a question of thinking truly as ontological the difference of the ways of Being; next, not questioning himself ontologically concerning the way of Being of the being-consciousness, Husserl misses that of the intentional and therefore commits a strictly phenomenological error: "Is phenomenological research in fact so unphenomenological [unphänomenologisch] that it excludes its most proper domain from the phenomenological question?"[41] What does Husserl lack in order to pass from the *difference* (of ways of Being) to a properly *ontological* difference? He fails to remain phenomenological all the way to the end. How does he fail to remain phenomenological? He fails not to miss the meaning of Being (*Sinn des Seins*)—for only the meaning of Being allows one, by preceding it, to pose a question that knows how to interrogate consciousness and the intentional with a view to their Being. What prohibits Husserl from thinking the difference phenomenologically coincides with what holds him back from thinking ontologically—namely, the horizon of the meaning of Being. The break with Husserl concerns the intersection, upon the difference of the ways of Being of consciousness and of the thing, of the requirements of the phenomenological method and of the question of Being. In these two ambiguities, the difference appears then as the crossing of paths.

2. Such a confrontation was expressed, moreover, directly between Husserl and Heidegger; indeed, in his famous letter of 27 October 1927, the latter presents to the former some disagreements that concern, beyond the project of a shared article for the *Encyclopedia Britannica*, the distance that *Sein und Zeit* takes from the "unphenomenological" phenomenology of Husserl. In this context, it seems quite remarkable that Heidegger should introduce his most characteristic breakthrough by mentioning, precisely and on two occasions, difference; first with respect to the world: "the *problem* that is directly posed is that of knowing what the mode of Being is of the being in which the 'world' is constituted. Such is the central problem of *Sein und Zeit*—namely, a fundamental ontology of *Dasein*. It is a matter of showing that the mode of Being of human *Dasein* is totally different [*total verschieden*] from that of all the others and that it is precisely because of this specific mode of Being which is its own that it harbors within itself the possibility of transcendental constitution."[42] Having to do with the couple being = world / being = constituting the world, it is therefore directly a matter here of the relation between the real thing and unreal, intentional consciousness, which is also called "human" *Dasein*; their "total difference" thus opposes not only two beings, but the two "ways of Being [*Seinsarte*]" of those beings; consequently one must recognize therein an ontological difference. To establish it constitutes

the essential project of *Sein und Zeit*—which means, in fact, that *Sein und Zeit* thus accomplishes what Husserl could not and did not want to undertake. The same problematic reappears next with respect to the understandability (or not) of being: "Through a regression toward what is that understanding obtained? / What does one mean by an absolute *ego* [when it is taken into view] in its difference [*im Unterschied*] from the purely psychic? / What is that absolute *ego*'s way of Being [*Seinsart*]—in what way is it the *same* as the self that is in each case factical, in what sense is it *not* the same?"[43] By absolute ego, Heidegger here means, to be sure, *Dasein* itself, such as its way of Being differs from that of any other being, even from pure psychism, conceived as itself intra-worldly (does it correspond to the *I* in the state of falling or even to the *They*?). Thus again we are dealing with a difference (*Unterschied*) between *Dasein*'s way of Being and that of any being that does not have the character of *Dasein*, a difference comparable to that which *Sein und Zeit* describes as ontological. The confrontation with Husserl therefore bears doubly on difference (ontological or not): first mediately, through the intermediary of the 1925 course, and then immediately, face to face, so to speak, through the letter of 1927, which no doubt reflects oral discussion from the preceding days. The difference intervenes, according to whether it is deepened or not as ontological, at the crossing of paths.

The point of rupture between Husserl and Heidegger is therefore reached with the interpretation of the status of the difference between the way of Being of the being "consciousness" (become *Dasein*) and the way of Being of other beings, or real things. This can be orchestrated in three conclusions. (1) Already in 1913, Husserl indeed furnished Heidegger with the point of departure toward a veritable "ontological difference" in *Sein und Zeit*, by offering him the phrase, without the concept, in the second edition of the *Logical Investigations*, and the concept, without its ontological determination, in the *Ideen I*. (2) Heidegger takes the decisive step against Husserl by interpreting the difference of the ways of Being of the beings "consciousness" and "thing" as decidedly ontological, starting from what the *Ideen* continually miss, the meaning of Being which alone accords to *Dasein* the understanding of Being. In short, Husserl ends up at the cardinal difference without understanding it and above all without thinking it as such, namely as ontological: he stops precisely where the true difficulty opens and where the phenomenological method should have been deployed (hence *Sein und Zeit*, § 7, which undertakes to treat the Being of beings precisely as a phenomenon). Husserl literally does not understand what he says in naming "the most cardinal of the differences": Heidegger understands it by thinking it, a first time, as ontological. (3) Difference (as ontological or not) not only works *Sein und Zeit* but precedes it and renders it possible, since Husserl reveals, before anyone else, the ontological difference between two ways of Being, precisely by not thinking it as such, that is, as ontological. From 1925 at the very least, Heidegger is confronted, thanks to and against Husserl, by the ontological difference unthought as such. Only that Husserlian unthought could have provoked the Heideggerian thought effort. From the beginning, between Husserl and Heidegger it is a matter of thinking the unthought of difference—that it is characterized as ontological.

5. The Irreducibility of the "Question of Being" to the "Ontological Difference"

If *Sein und Zeit* does not so much discover the difference as undertake to interpret it for the first time as ontological, one must show concretely, leaving aside the occurrences (decisive or not) of the phrase "ontological difference," how its concept operates there. In other words, does *Sein und Zeit* already put clearly into operation, in its concept, the ontological difference that will canonically determine the whole of Heidegger's thought in or after the "turn"? At first, it seems that *Sein und Zeit* does decidedly distinguish between beings and Being with an unambiguous vigorousness that will not be surpassed by what follows. Thus " 'Being' is not something like beings"; "the Being of beings 'is' not itself a being"; "Being cannot be 'explained' on the basis of beings"; "Being cannot be explicable by beings"; "Being is not explicable by beings";[44] "that Being can never be explained by beings but is for each being already the 'transcendental.' "[45] Does this formally indisputable distinction suffice, however, to establish the ontological difference as such? Certainly not, since as formulated it leaves one to suppose that Being offers itself to be known, as accessible as beings, like another term that would count among beings, that would double or reduplicate beings at the risk of concealing what it is a matter of thinking—the difference not of beings, but of ways of *Being*. The Being of beings does not differ from being as another being would, but as the way of Being differs from what is. The way (and not itself a being) in which beings are, Being therefore remains indissolubly tied to beings, on the surface of which it must be "read." The difference between Being and beings implies both: "Being is in each case the Being of a being"; "Being means the Being of beings"; "because the phenomenon, understood phenomenologically, is always only what makes up [*ausmacht*] Being, while Being, for its part, is in each case the Being of beings . . ."; "beings *are* independently of the experience, the knowledge, and the grasp through which they are open, unveiled, and determined. But Being 'is' only in the understanding of the being to whose Being something like the understanding of Being belongs."[46] The difference between Being and beings is rightly required—as ontological in the strict sense—only precisely because, ontically, Being is confused with beings and, to begin with, is *not* distinguished from them or, what amounts to the same thing, cannot be reached as such. The ontic indifference between Being and beings constrains one to reach Being only by means of a distinction that is neither real, nor formal, nor material, nor rational, but indeed ontological. It is precisely because Being, ontically null and void, becomes accessible only through, in, and on the surface of beings that one must differentiate it ontologically from beings. To reach Being—to bring it into the light of day as a phenomenon—is possible only in the mode of the ontological difference that interprets beings with a view to their Being. In this sense, the ontological difference acts as the implementation of the phenomenological method in the—absolutely unique—case where the phenomenon to be rendered manifest in its givenness is not any being, and therefore "is" not, since it "is" Being before beings. We therefore have at our disposal in *Sein und Zeit* a working of the ontological difference between Being and beings.

However, this observation cannot be made without raising two difficulties. First: How are we to understand the fact that this working of the concept of ontological difference does not coincide with any of the occurrences of the phrase "ontological difference"? Second, and above all: How are we to understand the fact that this concept distinguishes Being from beings, while all the occurrences of the phrase themselves distinguish, in fact, two beings (*Dasein* and *thing*) or even two ways of Being for those beings (existence and reality)? It is not simply a matter here of a noncorrespondence between the phrase and the working of the concept, but indeed of the irreducibility of one differentiated pair of terms to the other: How are we to reconcile the difference between two beings with the difference between Being and a being? To answer this question requires reconstructing the topic of the ontological difference, which in 1927 Heidegger traces with a much greater complexity than subsequently. Three figures of difference here overlap at least partially. (1) The strictly ontic difference, which Husserl already marks, between "consciousness" and "reality." (2) The difference between the ways of Being of those two beings—existence for the one, reality or *Vorhandenheit* for the other—which, on the basis of an ontic difference, claims to reach a difference concerning [the way of] Being; it is this difference (and it alone) that, according to the occurrences raised previously (§ 3 above), *Sein und Zeit* names "ontological." (3) The difference, finally, between

Being, on the one hand, and beings, on the other, which Heidegger will name "ontological" after 1927, and which explicitly inaugurates *Sein und Zeit*, without the relation that it directly establishes between Being and beings receiving the qualifier of "ontological" difference. Among these three figures of difference, two present no ambiguity theoretically: the first has absolutely nothing ontological about it; the third totally fulfills its ontological function. There remains the second; it is encountered only in *Sein und Zeit* and combines, with a complex ambiguity, the two parameters that it is precisely a matter of distinguishing: the ontic and the ontological; everything happens as if, here at least, Heidegger could break through the cardinal unthought left by Husserl only by arming himself with the plan known under the title of analogy (of proportion): the relation of one being to its way of Being becomes intelligible only when compared to the relation of another being to its way of Being. Hence, first, an analogy between two ontico-ontological relations:

$$
1. \quad \frac{\text{thing}/\textit{res}}{\textit{Realität}/\textit{Vorhandenheit}} = \frac{\textit{Dasein}/I}{\text{existence}}
$$

But, by conversion, it then permits an analogy between

$$
2. \quad \frac{\text{thing}/\textit{res}}{\textit{Dasein}/I} = \frac{\text{Being as } \textit{Vorhandenheit}}{\text{Being as existence}}
$$

It is this complex play of two figures of the same analogy that *Sein und Zeit* names "ontological difference." As opposed to the later ontological difference, the relation of beings to Being is here split: it is always a matter of the Being of one of the two types of being and never of beings in general in face of Being in general; consequently, this relation of beings to Being is complicated: Does the Being involved in the one or the other type of being indeed offer Being itself, or only an indication toward Being as such, in general? In short, does the ontico-ontological analogy open beings to Being as such, or only to a difference between two ways of Being for beings? The ontic mediation of the question of Being thus characterizes *Sein und Zeit* massively; the ambiguity of its topic and of its results nevertheless leads one inevitably to ask whether it indeed breaks through toward the ontological difference or whether, on the contrary, it does not set up an obstacle for it that is all the more insurmountable insofar as it claims an irrefragable phenomenological necessity.

How, then, can one justify phenomenologically the irruption of *Dasein* within the topic of the "ontological difference," at the risk of dissimulating it? *Dasein* intervenes at the heart of the "ontological difference" because it appears, in 1927, as the worker par excellence of the question concerning Being, which marks the divergence between Being and any being. For in the period of *Sein und Zeit*, the *Seinsfrage* can be posed only inasmuch as it is first posed in its "formal structure": "The question concerning the meaning of Being must be constructed [*gestellt*]." Such a construction implies not two elements (as in a simple difference), but indeed three; the question first mobilizes that which or the one whom it questions—the interrogated, the interpellated (*das Befragte*)—namely, being; but the question questions being only in order to make it say what is, with regard to that being, in question (*das Gefragte*), to make it respond to the interrogation concerning that for which it *is* the guarantor [*répondant*], that for which, as a being, it has precisely to answer—namely the Being of that being. Let us stop this enumeration for a moment in order to underline an essential point: if *Sein und Zeit* § 2 did not take another step, we would *already* be in possession of the canonical ontological difference, such as it is put into play between being and the Being of being; the equivalence will appear even more exact if one notes that the same § 2 establishes, precisely, a *difference* between the two terms: "Being, as that which is asked for [*Gefragte*], therefore requires a mode of showing that differs essentially [*sich . . . wesenhaft unterschiedet*] from the uncoveredness of beings."[47] If the construction of the question of Being in 1927 stuck to this divergence, it would coincide literally, in its first two terms, with the ontological difference taken in its canonical acceptation; the difficulty in harmonizing them that we noticed above would not even have been able to appear. But, and this is the decisive point, the construction of the question of Being according to *Sein und Zeit* § 2 goes further: it introduces a third term which is totally foreign to the canonical ontological difference, and which by that very fact renders it impossible to reconcile these two undertakings—the one decidedly ternary, the other definitively binary. What third term is at issue here? The question interrogates the one interpellated (*Befragte*), being, concerning what is in question (*Gefragte*), the Being of being; neither being nor the Being of being exhausts the questioning; it still remains to be known what the being itself does not know, even when it answers unreservedly concerning its Being, what is divined and sought only by the one who hears, within the explicit answer to the explicit question, the real story and the final word of the question—what it wants to know (*das Erfragte*)— the meaning of Being (*Sinn von Sein*).[48] The meaning of Being marks the final aim of the question concerning Being: it is not only a matter of going back, starting from a being and as if through it, to its Being (first divergence, ontological difference), but also, thanks to the Being *of that* being, of reaching even the meaning of Being, and therefore Being in general (*schlechthin, überhaupt*), and ultimately the temporality of Being starting from the temporality of *Dasein.* This redoubling of the first two terms of the question of Being by the meaning of Being can be interpreted in two directions. On the one hand, it can be interpreted with a view to the canonical ontological difference, and in that case as an impasse; on the other hand, it can be interpreted with a view to *Dasein,* and in that case as a phenomenological breakthrough.

Related to the ontological difference in its two terms, being and Being, the question of Being offers, with its three terms, two divergences: the first between being and the Being of being, the second between the Being of being and the meaning of Being. Which of these two divergences could accommodate the canonical ontological difference? Apparently the first: it plays already between Being and being; however, what Being is thus at issue if not the Being of *that* being? How is one to avoid the fact that this first divergence does not in fact cover any ontological leap other than that from the thing to its οὐσία, or even from the thing to its status as a being (τὸ ὄν)? Obviously, by stressing that the being put into question within the divergence between Being and being has the rank of *Dasein* and, consequently, puts into play along with itself not only its own Being but Being itself. This response, however, as correct as it might appear, is valid only within the conditions established by *Sein und Zeit* for the question of Being: namely, that a single being can support a question concerning its Being as a question concerning Being itself, *Dasein*; but does not this restriction of the ontic field of the question of Being betray violently either that beingness in general has not yet been reached, or that Being still questions within overly narrow limits? In short, the first divergence, provided by the question of Being constructed in 1927, remains too limited ontically and too superficial ontologically to accommodate even the anticipation of the canonical ontological difference. In order to arrive there, then, must one resort to the second divergence, between the Being of being and the meaning of Being? No doubt, since it does indeed seem to be the final "goal" of the analytic of *Dasein*: "In explaining the tasks of ontology we found it necessary that there should be a fundamental ontology taking as its theme the being that is ontico-ontologically distinctive, *Dasein* . . ."— here it is a matter of the first divergence, with its lacunae—" . . . in such a way that it stands in face of the cardinal problem, the question concerning the meaning of Being in general [*Sinn von Sein überhaupt*]."[49] Heidegger himself indeed seems to recognize in this second divergence the canonical ontological difference, remarking here: *"Being of* being; meaning of the difference."[50] However, several arguments render such a comparison weak and disputable. First, the meaning of Being in general was not reached by *Sein und Zeit*; if, therefore, it counted in 1927 as the Being of the difference, one would have to infer that the ontological difference is itself equally missed; but it was a matter of proving the reverse. Second, can one identify the Being of the difference with the meaning of Being, and therefore with its temporality? Indeed, must Being be understood within the horizon of time? Not only will *Sein und Zeit* end up doubting so,[51] but the abandonment of the horizon of time will be pushed to the point of subjecting time itself to the *Ereignis*. Third, the second comparison—of the Being of being to the being of difference— seems pretty much unjustifiable. Thus, none of the two divergences maintained by the three terms of the question of Being as *Sein und Zeit* constructs it can accommodate the canonical ontological difference, nor even anticipate it. The topic of the *Seinsfrage*, therefore, does not lead to that of the ontological difference so much as it seems to dispense with it and take its place in advance.

This result presents a paradox. First because it excludes from *Sein und Zeit* any ontological difference, after, however, we had already brought up the phrase within the originary question: the clear relation between Being and being. But precisely, the paradox remains apparent: *Sein und Zeit* indeed evidently confronts what will be thematized a short while later under the sole title of ontological difference; only it does not confront it head on; it adds to it and gives preference to the question of Being; therefore it is subjected to the obligatory mediation of *Dasein*. However, the ontological difference does not disappear as one of the stakes; only it appears protean and deformed by the two divergences of the question of Being; under the hold of the question of Being, the ontological difference disappears only by being multiplied into two differences, which are equally inadequate to it: between *Dasein* and its Being, and between that Being and temporality. Such a multiplication of difference in *Sein und Zeit*, to the point of prohibiting it from being qualified as ontological, could be confirmed by a remark from Heidegger (to M. Müller, who relates it); in the third division of the first part of *Sein und Zeit*, entitled "Zeit und Sein," no less than three differences were supposed to intervene: "*a*) The 'transcendental' or ontological difference in the narrow sense: the difference of being from its beingness; *b*) The difference 'according to transcendence,' or ontological difference in the broad sense: the difference of being *and* beingness from Being itself. *c*) The 'transcendent' or theological difference in the narrow sense: the difference of God from being, beingness, and Being."[52] Such an enumeration, almost quantitative, indicates more a hesitation than a rigorous elaboration; it could even be that one is dealing here with an enumeration of the hesitations that we have just located: indeed, does not the difference *a*) between being and beingness not designate the first divergence (*Dasein*—the Being of that being)? Would the difference *b*) between being (including beingness) and Being itself designate the second divergence (the Being of being—the meaning of Being in general)? That in both cases one should be dealing with an ontological difference, narrow or broad, would be suitable, at the very least, to the indetermination that the question of Being, constructed in 1927, imposes on the ontological difference, which is reached but still undetermined; the ternary topic of the "question of Being" as *Sein und Zeit* constructs it, when it does not marginalize the "ontological difference," must divide it in order to make room for it. Thus, to do justice to an already attained "ontological difference," *Sein und Zeit* would lack only an excess of lack itself.

6. The Ontic Primacy of the Question of Being as an Interrogation

We were just remarking that just as the redoubling of the first two terms of the question of Being (being/Being) by a third (the meaning of Being) leads to an impasse from the point of view of the ontological difference, so, from the point of view of *Dasein*, does it make an advance. Indeed, the meaning of Being is added to the other two terms only by specifying the identity of one of them: within the constructed question of Being, the being put into question must be understood exclusively as *Dasein*, the distinctive being. No more than it ignores the phrase "ontological difference" does *Sein und Zeit* pull away from the duty of making Being differ from being. But—and its strange originality consists in this—it exercises the ontological difference phenomenologically only on the basis of a topic other than that, which is dual, of difference—on the basis of the topic, which has three terms, of the question of Being. Through this imbalance, it comes down to *Dasein* to accomplish the very difference that it disrupts and, at the same time, despite everything, renders possible. Indeed, the question of Being is constructed, in 1927, thanks to the privilege and the ontic priority that it grants *Dasein*. Consequently, if, as we are claiming, the ontological difference actually at work in 1927 is nevertheless only ever exercised within the inappropriate topic of the question of Being, it is necessary to show, by way of confirmation, that *Sein und Zeit* subjects to the same privileging of *Dasein* the oblique accomplishment of the ontological difference itself. In this way we might perhaps also understand why the occurrences of the phrase "ontological difference" do not coincide with the ontological difference that is in fact set into operation by *Sein und Zeit.*

Dasein exercises the ontological difference first inasmuch as *Dasein* is transcendent. Here again, Husserl provides the negative point of departure by having entrusted transcendence only to objects and things "exterior" to consciousness, which from that point on is confined to immanence. Heidegger radically inverts this distribution in favor not, to be sure, of consciousness, but of what eliminates consciousness in deploying it, *Dasein:* "It is not objects that transcend—things can never transcend or be transcendent—but it is 'subjects,' taken in the ontological sense of *Dasein,* that transcend [*transzendierend*], that is, that transgress and surpass [*durch- und überschreitend*] themselves."[53] *Dasein* transcends itself and by itself. But in order to transcend itself, *Dasein* on the one hand transcends beings and on the other hand transcends within the dimension of Being: "Being and the structure of Being lie well beyond each being and each possible determination of a being. *Being is the transcendens par excellence.*"[54] The transcendence of *Dasein* is established (against Husserl) only, so to speak, within the aspiration of the transcendence par excellence, that of Being itself: *Dasein* enters into transcendence only by virtue of the opening of Being by itself—transcendence of *Dasein,* but through Being, "transcendence of the Being of *Dasein.*" If "*Dasein must transcend* the thematized beings," it owes this to the fact that, first, "Being can never be explained by beings, but is in each case already for each being the 'transcendental.'" Here the formulas "transcendence of the world" or "world-time"[55] must not mislead: the world and its temporality do not themselves belong to the being of the world, but open in a dimension rendered possible only by Being-in-the-world, and therefore by *Dasein,* which, through them, alone transcends beings. The difference between beings and the Being that is irreducibly inexplicable by beings is attested phenomenologically by a gap, a gap to be traversed, and therefore a transcendence from the one to the other—or better a transcendence of the one that, for the first time, makes the other appear. That transcendence can be accomplished only in starting from being—and therefore by a being—to the point of breaking with all being—and therefore by a being that escapes beingness. A being that escapes beingness transgresses itself to perform transcendence in and outside of itself—thus is *Dasein* characterized: the worker, then, of the ontological difference that it does not name because it makes it.

But—and this is the second point—*Dasein* could not exercise the ontological difference in this way, through self-transcendence, if, more essentially, it were not itself that difference. How, indeed, might one otherwise understand its paradoxical determination: "Dasein is ontically distinctive in that it *is* ontological"?[56] The qualification of *Dasein* to transcend the being that it is toward and according to the Being that no being is or explains, does not stem from any mix up or compromise, but from the distinctive fact that it is the sole being for whom *Being* has a meaning [*sens*]. *Dasein* has the sense [*sens*] of Being like the musician has a sense of harmony, the painter a sense of colors, the athlete a sense of competition. For *Dasein* and *Dasein* alone, Being is to be understood: *this* being contains within its simple ontic definition the understanding of Being; conversely, Being consists in *nothing*—in no being—for it resides solely in the understanding that the meaning of Being allows *Dasein* to have of it: "But Being 'is' only in the understanding of the being to whose Being there belongs something like the understanding of Being."[57] *Dasein* is in such a way that it takes itself into account as a being only by understanding, through its sense of Being, Being itself. It is as a perpetual transition from the ontic to the ontological, or rather as a transition of the ontic in it through the ontological.[58] How is this transition actually accomplished? It is accomplished because *Dasein* is the being that is determined by possibility and projection, in a mode so radical (Being-toward-death, care, anticipatory resoluteness) that, in that projection, not only is an ontic determination of *Dasein* at stake, but its very Being: "Rather, it is ontically distinguished by the fact that, in its very Being, that Being is an issue for it."[59] According to projection (or according to its refusal of any possible projection), *Dasein* exists properly or improperly, that is, it determines its way of Being—the way of its Being. But there is more: the Being that *Dasein* sets into play could not be reduced to a beingness; first because Being receives no determination from any being whatsoever, and then because, from the very beginning, the question of Being aims at the meaning of Being in general, and not only the Being of beings. Also, the preceding formula reappears, at times calling into question Being itself as such: "*Dasein is* in the mode of understanding, as a being, something like Being"; "for this being it is Being that is an issue"—which one must understand in light of a later note: "Which [i.e., Being]? Being the there and thus to uphold Being in general [*das Seyn überhaupt zu bestehen*]."[60] Presenting itself as a nonspatial link, *Dasein* therefore accomplishes in itself the transition from being to Being. It *is* in the mode of the ontological difference because it is ontically the ontologically different.

However, in 1927, Heidegger does not identify *Dasein* with the ontological difference but, on the contrary, with the question of Being: "The questioning is itself a being that is given in the act of carrying out the question concerning the Being of a being, whether it is seen explicitly or not."[61] Two reasons, perhaps, allow one to conceive this. First, because here again the ontological difference (with two terms) is reinterpreted through and included in the question of Being (constructed with three terms). Second, and above all, because the question of Being adds, as a third term, to the (dual) ontological difference (of being and Being) nothing other than *Dasein* itself. The supplementary term is in fact not the meaning of Being—since that falls to Being in general—but *Dasein*, which, as opposed to the being that does not have the character of *Dasein* (and therefore of Being), puts Being itself in general into play. *Dasein*, moreover, does not introduce a third term so much as it offers the sole possible link (*Da-*) to the difference in question between Being and being. In any case, the intervention of *Dasein* as the ontically ontological being renders the (dual) ontological difference operative only by confusing it with and inscribing it in the question of Being (constructed with three terms). Thus, in *Sein und Zeit*, the ontological question had to fade behind the question of Being—had to let itself be covered over by the "ontological difference" between the way of Being of *Dasein* alone and that of other beings—precisely because the question of Being *is Dasein* itself.

7. The Failure to Understand the Ontological Difference by the "Ontological Difference"

We thus end up with a double, paradoxical conclusion. On the one hand, against the authorized interpretation, *Sein und Zeit* does know an "ontological difference." On the other hand, following the received interpretation, *Sein und Zeit* does not yet think the ontological difference due to the simple fact that it names an "ontological difference." We believed ourselves able to give a reason for this paradox: the "ontological difference" in *Sein und Zeit* obeys the ternary construction of the question of Being in such a way as to prohibit itself access to the strictly dual dimension of the future ontological difference. And the third term is introduced here with *Dasein*, which, between being and Being, gives rise to the—perhaps opaque—mediation of a Being of beings: for whatever precautions one takes to stress that *Dasein*, as a pure ecstatic *da*, opens the absolutely docile transition between being and Being more than it imposes a third instance, it remains nonetheless that what *Sein und Zeit* accomplishes publicly remains totally and explicitly devoted to *Dasein*— either directly (the analytic of *Dasein*, Division 1), or indirectly ("*Dasein* and Temporality," Division 2)—without the consideration of Being in general, absolutely and in its meaning, ever receiving more than a few strictly programmatic mentions. It therefore seems legitimate, even inevitable, to pose a question in the form of a hypothesis: if it is *Dasein* itself that, precisely because it makes it possible to construct the (ternary) question of Being, prohibits one from moving to the (binary) ontological difference, and therefore to the meaning of Being as such, would *Sein und Zeit*'s incompletion, or in other words its inability to think Being in general and absolutely, be tied to the obstacle constituted *by Dasein*? In short, would it be necessary to see *Dasein* not only as the driving force behind the appearance of the question of Being in *Sein und Zeit*, but even as that which blocks its access to the ontological difference? Or again, does not *Dasein* make possible the question of Being—through the "ontological difference" that is named—only then to prohibit answering that question—through the ontological difference that is thought? If this question could at least be found in Heidegger's text it would provide an interesting confirmation of our whole analysis up to this point. But if *Sein und Zeit* itself literally attributed its incompletion to the very function of *Dasein*, the confirmation would become an almost indisputable validation.

Now, one must note the fact that the last two published pages of *Sein und Zeit*, those of § 83, pose precisely this question; even more, they respond to it explicitly.

1. The question is posed when Heidegger first recalls what has been established: the factical totality of *Dasein* has been brought out in its ontological and existential foundation according to the double possibility of propriety and impropriety. This foundation manifested itself on the basis of its Being, care; and, in turn, care found its meaning (of Being) in temporality. But as considerable as it is, this result remains "preparatory," just like the analytic of *Dasein*.[62] One is still dealing only with a "path," a "provisional goal," for "the analysis of *Dasein* is not only incomplete, it is also provisional."[63] On the other hand, "the goal is the elaboration of the question of Being in general [*überhaupt*]," of the "idea of Being in general [*überhaupt*]," the "ecstatic projection of Being in general [*überhaupt*]."[64] The divergence thus designated opens between *Dasein* with its Being (care), on the one hand, and, on the other, the meaning of Being (in general); one is dealing, therefore, with the second divergence maintained by the ternary structure of the question of Being, which is expressly mentioned as remaining to be overcome so long as the first divergence has not been surpassed. In other words, philosophy is carried out as "*universal* phenomenological ontology" only by "exiting" (*ausgehen*) from the analytic of *Dasein*.[65] Exiting from the analytic of

Dasein obviously does not mean renouncing it, critiquing it, or forgetting it, since the phenomenological process will never cease to come from it; but that provenance still implies an equally decisive overcoming, for even with the original posing of the question, it was never a question of considering the first divergence for itself; the urgency of the transition from one divergence to the other finally grows all the more insofar as, in the end, the overcoming of the second divergence seems problematic. The distinctive character of § 83 is due, among other things, to this: instead of mentioning the second divergence only as a project not yet carried out, within the programmatic framework of the whole plan of the work, it confronts the incompletion as a current difficulty which is not yet surmounted in fact and is possibly insurmountable in principle. The difficulty is doubled: not only is it necessary to exit from the analytic of *Dasein* in order to reach Being in general, but *Dasein* might not offer the means to move from one divergence to the other. It is well, then, to pose a question: Does *Dasein* allow one to reach Being as such?

2. What response does § 83 give? Before any other consideration, we must raise a crucial point: *Dasein* (as the overcoming of the very first difference between being and the Being of being) is determined twice by the "ontological difference," or at least by the opposition that characterizes it throughout *Sein und Zeit.* In one case, the "difference between the Being of existing *Dasein* and the Being of the being that does not have the character of Dasein (reality, for example)"; in the other, "the 'difference' between 'consciousness' and 'thing.'" *Dasein* as such, that is, in its characteristic way of Being, is marked by a difference from any other way of Being—an "ontological difference." Although normal in *Sein und Zeit,* that identification appears nonetheless perfectly remarkable *here*—first because we are dealing with the last page of the work, where Heidegger undertakes to mark out the reason for its incompletion, even to diagnose an aporia; but above all because the "ontological difference" thus identified with *Dasein* appears only to be exposed to an open critique: it offers "only a point of departure [whence one must exit, *Ausgang*] for the ontological problematic, but no point of rest for philosophy"; it is even necessary to ask oneself: "does it suffice in general for an originary unfolding of the ontological problematic?" The path toward Being in general that is presented by *Dasein* and therefore also by the (restricted) "ontological difference" that it sets into play—is this path *a* path, is it even the sole and *unique* path?[66]

Of what path is it a question here? Of the "ontological difference" in the restricted sense, and therefore of Dasein, which alone can set it into operation. The question therefore bears on a single point: Can *Sein und Zeit*'s undertaking be seen to traverse the second divergence (between the Being of being and the meaning of Being) in relying solely on the selfsame *Dasein*, which, in itself, traverses the first divergence (between being and the Being of being)? Or again: Can access to Being *in general* be grounded in a being, even a distinctive one, like access to the Being *of beings?* In short, does the question of Being as such (ontological difference: Being/being) admit of an ontic foundation (*Dasein* in its Being, "ontological difference")? Heidegger declares it explicitly: the analytic of *Dasein* "is to be regarded not as a dogma, but rather as a formulation of a fundamental problem that is still 'veiled': can ontology be grounded *ontologically,* or does it also need an *ontic* foundation, and [in that case] *what* being must assume the function of the foundation?"[67] This question, which openly breaks out on what will become the last page of *Sein und Zeit,* is obviously not addressed to an undetermined or future interlocutor: it aims, retrospectively, at one of the most originary phenomenological decisions of *Sein und Zeit* itself. As soon as the formal structure of the question concerning Being is elaborated, *Sein und Zeit* already asks: "Upon *what* being must the meaning of Being be read [*abgelesen*], from what being must the disclosure of Being take its point of departure?" When the question of Being is constructed concretely, it claims and confirms its "ontic primacy" by dedicating itself to and relying on the distinctive (*ausgezeichnet*) being—which is named *Dasein. Dasein* assures the "primacy" of the question of Being by virtue of its own primacy, which is in fact triple:

> *Dasein* accordingly takes priority over all other beings in several ways. The first priority is *ontic*: this being is determined in its Being by existence. The second priority is *ontological*: *Dasein* is in itself "ontological," because existence is thus determinative for it. But with equal primordiality *Dasein* also possesses—as constitutive for its understanding of existence—an understanding of the Being of all beings that do not have the character of *Dasein. Dasein* has therefore a third priority as providing the ontico-ontological condition for the possibility of any ontologies. *Dasein* has thus shown itself, before any other being, as what must first be questioned ontologically [*das primär Befragende*].[68]

The priority of the question of Being, therefore, does indeed rest on the priority of *Dasein*; even more, the priority of *Dasein* is multiplied into ontic and ontological so as finally to set into operation the ontological difference (ontico-ontological priority). The "ontic foundation" of the question of Being that is called into question in § 83 thus corresponds exactly to the *Dasein* established in its "ontic priority," but also its ontological priority, and therefore its ontico-ontological priority, by § 4, and thus by the entire introduction of *Sein und Zeit.* Therefore, if the role of *Dasein* (ontic foundation, ontic priority) becomes questionable to the point of opposing to it a directly ontological foundation of ontology (without ontic mediation), if even the γιγαντομαχία over Being has not yet been able to break out because the eventual adversaries have not been able hitherto to arm themselves (*Zurüstung*) with only the priority of *Dasein,* if one must even ask again *"how is this disclosive understanding of Being at all possible for Dasein,"*[69] it is necessary to admit this conclusion: the last question of *Sein und Zeit* calls into question the priority of *Dasein*— and therefore its claim to mediate the terms of the question of Being, its capacity to traverse the divergence between the Being of beings and Being in general, and the legitimacy of its reduction of the ontological difference to the "ontological difference."

Several arguments would confirm that we are indeed dealing here with a self-critique and that § 83 puts radically into question the initial decisions for the construction of the *Seinsfrage.* (1) The construction of the question of Being begins by asking: "Upon *which* being must the meaning of Being be read [*abgelesen werden*]?" In a note in his personal copy, Heidegger comments and critiques: "Two different questions put together; lending to misunderstanding, above all as to the role of *Dasein.*"[70] Indeed the meaning of Being (the second divergence of the *Seinsfrage*) cannot be read directly on any being whatsoever; a being, even *Dasein,* only ever allows one to read the Being of beings (first divergence of the *Seinsfrage*); to say that *Dasein* directly manifests the meaning of Being therefore amounts, first, to confusing the two moments and divergences of the question of Being, and, then, to overestimating arbitrarily the scope of *Dasein* (as the aporia of § 83 will confirm). (2) The same construction of the question of Being is followed immediately by an interrogation concerning the priority of the exemplary being: "from *which* being must the disclosure of Being take its point of departure [*Ausgang*]? Is this point of departure [*Ausgang*] just any one, or rather does some specific being have priority [*Vorrang*] in the elaboration of the question of Being? What is that exemplary being and in what sense does it have priority?" Here Heidegger indicates in a note: "Open to misunderstanding. *Dasein* is exemplary because it sets into play in an echo the counter-play [*Bei-spiel*] that Being addresses and entrusts to it [as to a partner] in general [*überhaupt*] in its essence as *Dasein* (attending to the truth of Being)."[71] One can understand this as follows: *Dasein* has no intrinsic priority in the elaboration of the question of Being, as if it grounded that question in itself; it has only an exemplarity, which comes to it from its setting into play (*Beispiel* as *Bei-spiel*) the play of Being itself; *Dasein* does not open to the question of Being by virtue of an antecedent priority so much as it allows itself to be worked by the advent within itself of Being as such. In a word, the priority no longer characterizes *Dasein* (as a distinctive being), but Being itself, which is in play ontologically and not ontically. (3) The ontic foundation of the question of Being is thus critiqued (retrospectively) *a contrario* in the situation of *Verfallen*: "The Being which is falling [*verfallende*] . . . covers up ontically *Dasein*'s authentic Being, so that the ontology directed toward this being is denied an adequate basis."[72] Here one is dealing, negatively, with the very situation established in § 2—to read Being upon the distinctive being (priority). But Heidegger will later note: "Backwards! As if ontology could be read [*abgelesen werden könnte*] starting from [even] authentic ontics. What is an authentic ontics if it is not authentic starting from a pre-ontological project—supposing already that the whole must rest in that distinction." Several points here seem remarkable. First the explicit rejection of any reading (*ablesen*) of Being starting from being, even from authentic *Dasein*, in literal contradiction to the intitial construction of the *Seinsfrage*.[73] Next, the affirmation that ontology (in the most radical sense) does not depend on ontics, but that ontics depends on the priority of ontology, or even, before it, on a more originary sending. Finally, the ontico-ontological difference [*Unterscheidung*] becomes the horizon—perhaps, it is true, provisional—of the question of Being.

These three self-critiques (which are no doubt not the only ones in the margins of *Sein und Zeit*) confirm that Heidegger was, after the fact, perfectly aware that the incompletion of the "breakthrough" attempted in 1927 depended intimately on the unquestioned primacy in it of the priority accorded to *Dasein* in the construction of the question of Being.[74] But that primacy, because it introduces a mediating term, prohibits the question of Being from bringing out straightaway the canonical ontological difference (Being-being) and substitutes for it the "ontological difference" between two beings and their ways of Being. It therefore seems legitimate to conclude that *Sein und Zeit* owes its incompletion only to the concealment within it of the ontological difference by the "ontological difference"—namely by *Dasein* itself. Which does indeed add, in it, "enigma upon enigma."[75]

5

Being and Region

1. The Possibility of Ontology

Is it suitable that the phenomenologist take the question of Being into view? If such seemed to be the case, would it be a matter of one object among other possible objects, or would it require a special treatment, and—in that case—which one? Would it be suitable that phenomenology restore then the old title, at once envied and disdained, of ontology?

As soon as we pose this question to Husserl, we note that in fact we can already no longer address it to him directly. Between him and our question, imperceptibly but unstoppably, a sort of third has always already interfered which stands as a screen. That third screen prohibits us from hearing Husserl's eventual answer directly, because it immediately predetermines, or even deforms, the answer. The screen's name is Heidegger. We read Husserl in general on the basis of what Heidegger designates to us as his greatness and his weaknesses; and even when we resist, it is still most often in relation to that pre-understanding that we are guided. As soon as it is a matter of the question of Being or even simply of an ontology within phenomenological terrain, our dependence deepens even more, insofar as Heidegger imposed upon phenomenology a radical ontological deepening. At least for a while, then, let us follow this inevitable constraint, for we can free ourselves from it only after having made it visible. What do we learn by allowing Heidegger to pose the question of Being in phenomenological terms?

If one sticks to the essential, two radical theses come to the fore.

1. "With regard to its subject matter, phenomenology is the science of the Being of beings—ontology."[1] This proposition in fact sums up several successive, indissociable theses. Having the function of making the phenomenon manifest, phenomenology culminates in bringing to light what, in the phenomenon, proximally and for the most part conceals itself and therefore tacitly awaits its ascent into the light of day. Now,

proximally and for the most part, what gives itself to be seen as an evident phenomenon is only being and not Being, which is essentially unreal, imperceptible, invisible. Consequently—far from having to induce from that invisibility the de facto and de jure impossibility of a phenomenon of Being as such, which would be different from being—it is suitable, on the contrary, to posit that only a phenomenology strictly understood, that is, taken in its essence, will manage to open up the visibility of Being itself. Only phenomenology as the bringing to light of what does not show itself immediately as a phenomenon can bridge the gap that differentiates beings, which are always already visible, from Being, which is always already invisible. Thus, "*ontology is possible only as phenomenology.*"[2] Indeed, only phenomenology, as "the method of scientific philosophy in general,"[3] can fix upon a being—in fact the only privileged being, *Dasein*—in order to attempt, proceeding on the basis of its ontic evidence, to force into visibility the invisible phenomenon par excellence, "the Being of beings, its meaning, modifications and derivatives."[4] Phenomenology therefore does not only offer a method for making evident all the phenomena— which are proximally and for the most part visible; but it offers itself above all as the sole method that might make visible one phenomenon, the phenomenon par excellence because the least visible, the Being of beings. Consequently, it does not in this way extend its field of operation to include one more object, but it is itself dedicated, in principle and by predilection, to this nonobject that it alone can make accessible. Not to recognize in phenomenology the sole appropriate method for ontology, in short, to ordain it to other objects—or quite simply to *objects*—amounts essentially to misunderstanding its essence. Consequently, then, the second thesis becomes intelligible.

2. From the point of view of *Sein und Zeit*, Husserl's use of phenomenology betrays a double misunderstanding of its essence. First because its uniform and undifferentiated application to all fields of objects (even if, as such, it remains legitimate) cannot not mask its exceptional privilege—that of constituting the sole adequate method for ontology. Everything happens as if Husserl, fascinated by his ceaselessly confirmed discovery of the operative power of the reduction within ever richer and more diverse objective fields, yielded to an intoxication with constitutions that were all the more programmatic insofar as they were promising, and, imprisoned by that charm, remained blind to the ultimate destination of phenomenology. Hence the amazing paradox of Husserl: he discovered a mode of thought that absolutely revolutionizes metaphysics without, however, understanding its final scope. The second misunderstanding, moreover, confirms the first: the frenetic and programmatic conquest of new objective fields distracts Husserl from

the task of clarifying phenomenologically the ways of Being of the two original regions: that of "consciousness," such as it is excepted from the reduction in carrying it out, and then that of the general objectivity of what falls under the reduction. In short, Husserl does not return to the things themselves, or at least to the two things that are most instantly presupposed by the reduction and constitution: the always privileged exercise of the phenomenological act distracts him from thinking it, and therefore from measuring its exceptional scope and destination. As Husserl deploys it, "phenomenology is, in the basic task of determining its ownmost field *un-phenomenological!*—that is, *phenomenological only in intention!*"[5] Thus, according to the third screen that Heidegger's polemic erects between Husserl and us, we cannot avoid a twofold conclusion: Husserl misses the essence of phenomenology itself precisely because he claims to exercise it without concentrating it on its ownmost destination— that of giving ontology its sole method.

2. Phenomenology as "Universal and Authentic Ontology"

That it is not legitimate to finish so quickly with the relation established by Husserl between phenomenology and ontology, that Heidegger thus answered the question all the less insofar as he in a sense did not truly pose it—this is indicated unambiguously by several texts from the final period. The conclusion of the *Cartesian Meditations* clearly indicates that "as developed systematically and fully, transcendental phenomenology would be *ipso facto* the true and *genuine universal ontology* [*die wahre und echte universale Ontologie*]." This statement already appeared literally in the *Pariser Vorträge* and finds its confirmation when the Second *Cartesian Meditation* posits that even "the phenomenological *epoché* lays open (to me, the meditating philosopher) an infinite and entirely new sphere of Being [*Seinsphäre*]."[6] Can one relativize the importance of these declarations by claiming that they suffer the counterblow of the position taken by Heidegger himself in 1927 (and in fact, since at least 1925)? It is not even useful to enter into this classic and uncertain debate in order to give a clear answer to such a question. Indeed, the declarations of the *Cartesian Meditations* resonate precisely with much earlier and equally clear positions. (1) Thus, already in 1912, *Ideen III,* a decisive text on this point and a text whose difficult doctrine will occupy us later, states that "the part effectively swallows up [*verschlingt*] the whole, and rational phenomenology in the end embraces [*umschlingt*] not only the rest of rational psychology but even all rational ontologies," in such a way that the *mathesis universalis* counts as the "mother of all ontologies . . . , swallows up [*verschlingt*] all ontologies step by step."[7] Such a swallowing up no doubt remains extremely ambiguous and could indicate just as much a suppression as an assumption; at least even such a suppression could still accomplish, maternally, so to speak, a begetting; and phenomenology does not assume the role of Medea: it allows its children—ontologies—to live. (2) This is what is confirmed by a group of texts issuing from the 1924 classes dedicated to first philosophy. Ontologies there are maintained even in a phenomenological situation: "It is further necessary to signal that all new disciplines, which rationalism elaborated through an *a priori* method, and more specifically ontologies, had to assume a significant function at the moment [*in dem Momente*] when the task of a phenomenology as immanent transcendental philosophy was correctly posed and understood." Here, however, the relation between ontology and phenomenology cannot be summed up as a simple absorption of the first by the second; indeed, if on the one hand "every ontology projected within a naive evidence or, what amounts to the same thing, every rational discipline is to be taken up in phenomenology," on the other hand ontology remains necessary to the deployment of phenomenology itself: "In the language of my *Ideas for a Pure Phenomenology*, I said that the fundamental concepts and principles [*Grundbegriffe und Grundsätze*] of ontologies are the necessary 'guiding threads' for a universal phenomenology at its highest level, that of a phenomenology of reason, that is, for the systematic project of the constitutive problematic."[8] Two short texts, one from 1924 and the other from 1923, boldly establish the definitive function of an ontology within the fulfillment of phenomenology as a constitution. *The Idea of a Complete Ontology* opens by positing that "ontology constructs the *logos* of a possible world in general, or it is the science of possible forms, of the disjunctively necessary forms of possible worlds, such as they must finally be able to be;" consequently, "the factually given [*faktisch gegebene*] world requires an ontology as an ontology of *this* world." A philosophy could therefore be completed only by carrying out the program of ontology so understood, for "*completely concrete ontology is ipso* facto nothing other than *authentic transcendental philosophy*, and in its poorly clarified historical effort to develop itself, no transcendental philosophy ever had anything other in view, finally, than that ontology." Or again: "All 'philosophy' is preceded by *logic as first philosophy*—not *formal*, relatively poor logic, nor even *Mathesis universalis*, which from certain systematic points of view is itself relatively limited—but indeed by *transcendental ontology*." This position is summed up clearly, though not without giving rise to some questions, in two theses from a note to *The Path towards Transcendental Phenomenology as Absolute and Universal Ontology*.

First, it is "a universal ontology—as a universal *a priori* science of the world, of a world in general." Secondly, "being is a being of knowledge."[9] We have to admit the textual facts—that is, we have to conclude that at least as early as 1912 and without any later retraction, Husserl recognized that phenomenology, as a transcendental science of the constitution of the world, and therefore of all the rational possibilities of the world in general, had finally to lead to an ontology, itself universal and absolute. It therefore does not seem in any way legitimate to follow the critique that Heidegger addresses to Husserlian phenomenology—that of having missed the question of Being, of having ignored that phenomenology can be fulfilled only as the methodical and dedicated worker of ontology. For Husserl maintained this thesis before Heidegger himself.

To be sure, the fact that Husserl maintained the ontological destination of phenomenology before Heidegger in no way signifies that he thought it in the same sense as *Sein und Zeit*. But from this point on the question must at the very least be displaced: it is no longer a matter of determining, within the conflict between Husserl and Heidegger, whether and in what measure the first missed the phenomenological approach to ontology, but rather, since in fact it is Husserl first who attempted to establish ontology, it is a matter of deciding in what measure the two treated ontology in the same sense according to the phenomenological method. This means that the question is essentially displaced: it is played out on phenomenological terrain, to be sure, as Heidegger wished; but it is played out also within the field of the question of Being, since, contrary to what Heidegger claimed, Husserl already occupied that terrain, and solidly so.

3. The Anonymous Concept of an Ontology

There is more. Not only does Husserl claim to have attempted to rethink the question of an ontology by means of phenomenology used as the method, or even as the matrix of any possible ontology, but he claims above all that such an aim goes back to the *Logical Investigations*, that is, to the Husserlian text that Heidegger privileges, contrary to the later developments (in particular those of 1910 and 1913). Thus, far from Husserl having misunderstood the ontological scope of his first works in order then to privilege the scientific figure of transcendental phenomenology, he himself brings out the imbrication between phenomenology and ontology, such as it appears explicitly, however, only in 1912, in the sole text that Heidegger recognizes as carrying an ontological charge. Before pursuing an examination of this new restriction of the debate, it would be suitable to list the texts that make it necessary. (1) In 1929, in the § 27 entitled "The introduction of the idea of formal ontology in the *Logical Investigations*," *Formal and Transcendental Logic* specifies that

> to my knowledge, the idea of a formal ontology is presented for the first time in philosophical literature in Volume I of my *Logical Investigations,* and it does so in the essay on the systematic development of the idea of a pure logic. . . . Moreover, the *Logical Investigations* and especially the *Investigations* of Volume II dared again to take up under a new form the old idea—so forbidden [*versponte Idee*] because of Kantianism and empiricism—of an *a priori* ontology, and they attempted to ground it as necessary for philosophy in some fragments of concretely developed studies.

Husserl therefore claims to have broken first, and a quarter century before Heidegger, with the prohibition decreed against what Kant branded with "the proud name of ontology" (KrV, A 247, B875). This reversal nevertheless remains subject to caution, since, as Husserl honestly acknowledges, this reappearance does not yet show up "under the *name* of formal ontology."[10] However, the simple fact that Husserl here claims to reestablish ontology when its name is nevertheless lacking leaves one to suppose that, in his writing from 1900, he directly acknowledges its *concept.* Anonymity never weakens a concept; Aristotle showed that it often strengthens it.[11] The main argument against the self-interpretation that Husserl hazards here no doubt comes from elsewhere: he claims to have raised the name of ontology as early as 1900, but he does so, here, only in 1929; can one not imagine, then, that the reestablishment of the "word" owes a bit of its audacity to the far more explicit and imposing effort of *Sein und Zeit* two years previous?

It is here that we must cite other texts, dated from 1913. (2) First, *Ideen I,* § 10: "At that time [that of the *Logical Investigations*] I did not venture to take over the expression 'ontology,' which was shocking [*anstossigen*] for historical reasons; rather I designated this investigation . . . as part of an 'a priori *theory of objects as such.*' . . . . With the changing times, however, I consider it more correct to reestablish in its validity the old expression of 'ontology.' "[12] Once again, Husserl admits to having remained half-way in the reestablishment of ontology: the word was not at all there even if the concept did enter in; on the other hand, he specifies precisely what in 1900 was the quasiconcept of ontology: it was a question of the formal objective categories such as they are established in § 67 of the *Prolegomena* by pure logic and then in the Third Investigation by the theory of the pure forms of whole and of parts. These references, moreover, confirm those of *Formal and Transcendental Logic*, whose § 27 also referred back to the *Prolegomena*. Finally, a last text again furnishes similar references: (3) the preface written in 1913 for the second edition of the *Investigations*. Husserl there repeats first that it is "in [his] *Investigations* [that] the idea of ontology was revived in a proper way, without resting on any historical support and also in being thereby exempt from the fundamental obscurities and errors that affected the old ontologies and that justified the resistance that was opposed to them"; and he adds (parenthetically, of course) that "only the word was avoided in the first edition." As for the concept, it is always a matter of "ontology or the theory of the object" such as it is developed not only by "*pure mathesis* (that would include the entire first volume and Investigations III and IV from the second) but also the entire first volume of the work," inasmuch as it opposes psychologism with a "pure *a priori analysis of essences.*" Without confusing a phenomenological a priori and an ontological a priori, it was nevertheless a matter of freeing up an "authentic ontological analytic."[13]

Two conclusions here become unavoidable. First, it is at least as early as 1913 that Husserl entrusts the responsibility of ontology to phenomenology, first explicitly in *Ideen I* and *III*, and then through the retrospective interpretation of the *Investigations*. This date, which could no doubt be moved back earlier, proves two points: that Husserl did not await the backlash of *Sein und Zeit* upon his own thought in order to tie phenomenology to ontology; and that he affirms this tie at the very moment when Heidegger (in this, following Ingarden) believes himself able to condemn its undoing. Hence the second result: if, like Heidegger, Husserl recognizes in the *Logical Investigations* the privileged meeting place of the two instances, he nevertheless never refers back, as Heidegger always will exclusively, to the Sixth Investigation, but only to the *Prolegomena* and to the Second, Third, and Fourth Investigations; for a second time (for his self-interpretation) not only does Husserl not depend on Heidegger, but he formally contradicts him. Consequently, one must hold as established that the conflict between Heidegger and Husserl is played out not only in the terrain of phenomenology but also fundamentally in the terrain of ontology—because both of them occupied that terrain, Husserl as much as Heidegger. Even more, for both of them the debate bears upon the ontological scope and center of gravity of the *Logical Investigations*. If Husserl missed the ontological approach to the *Seinsfrage*, as Heidegger claimed, one must acknowledge that at the very least it was not by default, since for him also (and no doubt first) "phenomenology . . . would be *ipso facto* the *true and authentic universal ontology.*"[14] From this point on, therefore, it is no longer a question of understanding why Husserl would have missed the question of Being, but indeed of understanding how he thought it—without and against Heidegger.

4. The Formality of Objectity

Husserl therefore ignores ontology no more than he regionalizes it, since he establishes a universal ontology as one of the accomplishments of phenomenology. Once one has done justice to Husserl on this point, one must still determine how he arrives at such a universal ontology, that is, one must assess what universality is at issue in that ontology, and especially in what sense it answers the question of Being.

A reading of two strategic texts will allow us to outline an answer to this twofold question. The first of them comes from *Ideen I*, §§ 8–10. Hierarchizing the sciences in order to indicate the dependence of the factual sciences on the eidetic sciences and, in turn, the independence of the latter, § 8 establishes the conditions of possibility for any experimental science: it must of course follow the principles established by formal logic and manage its "*material* essential fund," but above all it must, "like all sciences oriented toward objects, closely follow the laws that belong to the essence of *objectity* [*Gegenständlichkeit*] *in general*." What must be understood by such an objectity in general? Husserl immediately specifies that it is a matter of a "formal-ontological complex" of different but connected "disciplines": first formal logic "in the narrow sense," and next and especially "formal '*mathesis universalis*,'" which groups together arithmetic, pure analysis, and the theory of multiplicity. A bit later Husserl will stress its universal validity: ". . . *formal mathesis*, which is related in one and the same manner to all sciences taken universally."[15] This schema remains relatively confused because it brings together four heterogeneous terms: the material essential fund, formal logic in the narrow sense, *mathesis universalis*, and finally objectivity in general. As early as § 9, the *Ideen* render the schema more coherent. In fact, in this context it is a matter of specifying the givenness of essences and the conditions of a pure eidetics; in this sense a "regional ontology" amounts to a "regional eidetic science," or, equally, an "eidetic ontology"; thus understood, such an eidetic ontology assures, within a region that it opens and defines, the possibility of factual knowledge. Now, "this knowledge depends on the empty form of objectity [*Gegenständlichkeit*] in general, on the one hand, and, on the other, on the *eidos* of the region, which, as it were, represents a *necessary material form* of all the objects of the region." Thus, the four terms are reduced to two: on the one side regional ontology and the material fund, on the other formal logic and objectity in general. Formal ontology therefore takes on the function of an absolutely universal form—but as a form established by objectity in general. Now, if the first equivalence can be understood so easily, since the regional ontology is suitable to the material fund as its formal structure, the same is not the case when it comes to leading formal logic (abstracted absolutely from any concrete position of existence) back to objectity in general. Even more, the latter has not yet received any determination, nor has it justified its claim to the title of ontology. Could it be that the rapprochement between ontology and formality—"formal ontology"— only presents a clearer contradiction between them?[16]

This difficulty precisely occupies *Ideen I*, § 10. It is a matter of considering any eidetic science whatever, and thus a regional ontology; in order to know its objects it uses categories (for it is a question here, materially, not of essences but of the objects of essences); those categories, however (thing, property, relation, state of affairs, etc.), "refer back each time to a type of objectity that, so to speak, has the privilege of *originary objectity [Urgegenständlichkeit]*." Indeed, a region is determined not only by a material fund, or by the formal properties of the region; it is determined also according to the "*form of the region in general*," the "*empty form of the region in general*"; the region in general does not offer a new region, still material although wider; nor does it open a first region, but the region itself as first form; an empty region, it therefore remains absolutely formal; a region in general, it makes possible any entrance into a region, and therefore any entrance into objectity of any object whatever; in the mode of the objectity that it renders accessible to any object, the formality of the region therefore exercises an ontological function: "*Formal ontology at the same time* [zugleich] *harbors in itself the forms of all possible ontologies in general (of all the ontologies that are, 'properly speaking,' 'material')*." Formality shoulders an ontological responsibility because objectivity itself can be formalized as the region in general. "Let us start from formal ontology (always as pure logic in its full extent as *mathesis universalis*), which, as we know, is the eidetic science of any object whatever." We see it here clearly: in order to raise formal logic to the rank of ontology despite the contradiction in terms, Husserl must "extend" the first to *mathesis universalis* and understand the second as pure objectity. We will have to ask later about this second operation, but for now, it is necessary to clarify the first.

With or without the title of *mathesis universalis*, how could formal logic formally attain objectity in general? Answer: it is necessary to divide, or rather redouble the categories. (1) The categories of signification concern "the essence of the proposition," whether they determine it as such (subject, predicate, plurality, etc.) or whether they govern the relations between propositions (conjunction, disjunction, hypothesis, etc.); these categories constitute apophantics, whose formality does not bear directly on objects as such; remarkably, Husserl nevertheless does not call them logical categories, no doubt in order to indicate that true logic must, on the contrary, attain to the objectity of objects; with the categories of signification, therefore, it is a matter only of what § 8 calls "formal logic in the narrow sense." (2) The logical categories must therefore intervene as Husserl's original and decisive initiative which aims at rendering ontology formal: "Henceforth we define as *logical categories* or *categories of the logical region, object-in-general, the purely logical fundamental concepts* [*Grundbegriffe*]—concepts through which the logical essence of object-in-general is determined within the whole of the system of axioms or which express the constitutive and unconditionally necessary determinations of an object as such, of any something whatever [*eines irgend Etwas*]—inasmuch as [such] a something must in general be able to be." The categories are logical precisely because the objectity of any object in general constitutes the first form, which is a pure form since it precedes and determines all regions, their eidetic essences and their respective material funds. In giving as examples the categories of object, of unity, of relation, of state of affairs, of identity, of collection, of whole and part, of genus and of species, etc., Husserl does not limit himself to completing the list of the categories; he thinks the very objectity of the object, posited as an object pure and simple, as the sole originary form; ontology does not contradict the movement of formal abstraction, but carries it out beyond what formal logic in the narrow sense allows. This thesis therefore implies that Husserl might justify that objectity pure and simple indeed opens access not only to one "logical region" among others, but to the most originary region—to the point that it becomes, more than a region, the "empty form of a region in general."[17] But then it would be necessary to wonder less about the logical legitimacy of assigning categories to objectity than about the ontological possibility of establishing objectity in general at the level of first form.

The scope and the fragility of the objectity that is privileged in this way are clearly indicated in *Formal and Transcendental Logic*. There it is a matter of unifying different disciplines within formal logic taken in its most complete meaning. Can the theory of judgment, also known as formal apophantics, merge with formal mathematics? In the capacity of pure syllogistics and analytics, it limits itself to respecting the principle of noncontradiction, such as it defines possibility.[18] Now, since it proceeds through formal judgment, it is enough that mathematics be formalized in order that the one might agree with the other. But does the same hold for nonapophantic mathematics, which neither calculate nor predicate (set theory, theory of cardinal numbers, of permutations and combinations, etc.)? It is nevertheless necessary to respond positively, for just as formal apophantics requires a "concept of the most general object (that of a substratum in general)," so a "*formal mathematics taken in all its fullness*" requires a "universal domain," defined "as the extension of the supreme concept of *object in general* [*Gegenstand überhaupt*] or as the extension of the something thought in its emptiest generality." Consequently, formal (even nonapophantic) mathematics agrees with formal logic in the unique assumption of the most empty objectity; taken in this acceptation, "one is not far from considering all mathematics as an *ontology* (an *a priori* theory of the object), but as a *formal* ontology, relating to the pure modes of the something in general."[19] Mathematics and logic can be founded in an ontology only inasmuch as they accede to a single formality—the most empty and abstract objectity of any something whatever. Conversely, ontology becomes possible only on condition of its absolute abstraction. Mathematics and logic are surpassed in an ontology only under the sign of formality, and therefore in forcing that ontology to empty itself without remainder of any determination other than undetermined objectity. But then should one still speak of an ontology?

Husserl seems to acknowledge that one is dealing here with a difficulty of the first order when he experiences, after the fact, the need to distinguish clearly the apophantic[20] and the ontological attitudes. Why is it necessary to return to this point? Because empty objectivity has achieved such an extension that it characterizes indifferently the ontological attitude and, equally, the apophantic attitude; even more, objectity falls first to apophantics: "It is also true that nowhere but in the judgment does the empty concept Something [*Leerbegriff Etwas*] make its appearance, the concept in which all objects are thought by logic."[21] Would it be necessary, then, by consequence, finally to reduce ontology (even formal) to apophantics, as if there were no radical "difference [*Unterschied*]" between "*orienting oneself thematically toward judgments*" and orienting oneself toward objects? In principle, one is dealing here with a "separation" that is fundamental, since it alone allows one to pass beyond simple formal logic "in the narrow sense" in order to reach, through and beyond it, formal ontology; but Husserl must acknowledge that, since apophantics *already* has at its disposal the empty concept of objectity, it cannot easily be distinguished from ontology, to the point, he admits, that their "distinction, however, is at the same time an equivalence [*eine Scheidung, die zugleich doch Äquivalenz ist*)]' and that "*for this reason* they have to function [*gelten*] as one and the same science."[22]

Husserl no doubt puts forward some arguments in order to distinguish ontology from simple apophantic logic. (1) Judgment itself always refers finally to an object, and not to the consciousness of the object, since intentionality forces apophantics itself also to pass beyond the judgment toward the object of the judgment: "In judging, we are directed, not toward the judgment, but toward the *'objects about which'* we make a judgment (the substratum objects)."[23] (2) The variation of syntactical operations, which permits one to say equally of object S, "S is *p*," or "this, that 'S is *p*,' " etc., always refers in the end to a final substratum, the object. (3) The syntactical forms always derive from the object, as "*derivative forms* of the something, of the fundamental formal category, 'object,' " which thus plays the role of a first category, οὐσία πρώτη.[24] Moreover (4), the syntactical operations create new forms only in order to aim, through the latter, at the same *object*: "*The one who judges is directed toward the object, and being thus directed he never has anything to do with the object otherwise than in some categorial forms . . . which are therefore ontological forms.*"[25] In fact these four arguments all return to the first, the intentionality that even ordains the judgment to the object; it is solely in that measure that objectity, although already used by the judgment, will be able also to be transcended toward the object. Therefore, the argumentation rests entirely upon the single thesis that "*categorially formed objectity* [Gegenständlichkeit] *is not an apophantic concept but an ontological concept.*"[26] Now, the difficulty here is of a piece with the answer that one brings to it: even if apophantics and formal logic (in the narrow sense) use the object in general and the empty form of the something, the passage from the judgment to the object of the judgment, to the ontic, or even to the ontological, cannot be decided by pure and simple reference to objectity; the concept of objectity helps in no way to transcend the representation of the object, since it secures representation just as much as it designates the object. As for the recourse to intentionality, it offers no new discriminant between the judgment and the object, since it undertakes only to traverse every concept, including that of the object in general, without producing any new one; as such the intentional aim remains invisible, unformulatable, and unrepresentable, since it has the intention only of rendering visible, formulatable, and presentable an other than itself; its very irreality renders it conceptually indiscernible.[27] The passage from the formal to the ontological can therefore be carried out only through a new treatment—in fact intentional—of the concept (and of the judgment) of objectity. Only intentionality can carry out this new treatment; but by definition, it will carry it out without introducing any new concepts other than those already used by the judgment. Formal ontology, therefore, while remaining in the domain of the objectity already established through apophantics, will have to make use of it ontologically, thanks to the intentional transgression—it being understood that, since it shows the object, intentionality never shows itself, like a new concept fit to discriminate the ontological attitude from the formal attitude. The supposedly strict separation between logic and ontology is summed up in a nonconceptualizable transgression, without an objective *discrimen* in a common field. The Husserlian conquest of a domain proper to ontology finds an insoluble limit in the undecidable ambivalence of objectity.

Husserl had anticipated a strict separation, but one and the same science; he should rather have said: one and the same objectity and, in principle but without any real distinction, two sciences. It is in this sense and in this sense alone that Husserl can claim that "*as a formal doctrine of science, analytics* has like the sciences themselves an *ontic* direction and, truth be told, thanks to its *a priori* generality, an *ontological* direction."28

5. The First Insufficiency: According to Universality

One therefore should not object to Husserl for having deserted or misunderstood ontology, since in fact he elaborated with great conceptual care a "formal ontology" that claims to be "authentic." One should no longer suspect him of having conceded only a regional function to "formal ontology," since in fact he grants it a validity all the more universal insofar as it would have for its object only the pure "something, whatever it might be," according to objectity in general. Authentic and universal, does Husserlian ontology resist for all that the objection of Heidegger—namely that such a "formal ontology" responds all the less to the question of Being insofar as the very conditions that preside over its elaboration prohibit one from hearing the question that is posed, silently to be sure, by Being? But, against Heidegger, it will no doubt be necessary to show that Husserl does not miss the question of Being because he would have failed by default to define an ontology, but to the contrary because he only too perfectly succeeded in constructing it.

The paradox that failure before the question of Being is directly proportional to the success of "formal ontology" can be proved through an examination of three characteristics of the latter: the logical status of being, the primacy of the objectity of the object, and finally the originarity of possibility.

1. In accordance with the indistinction—if not through the unreal intentionality—between apophantics and formal ontology, it becomes possible to consider the latter as a science: "the formal laws of mere

non-contradiction become conditions for the possibility of truth and can be stated as such. Pure mathematical analytics then becomes . . . an authentic and analytic doctrine of science, or, what is equivalent, a 'formal ontology.' "[29] How can one accept such an "equivalence" between mathematics (even in a developed sense) and ontology (even formal), if not by admitting that the being that claims to aim at ontology remains always and first an object of predication, and therefore eventually an object for an analytics? Beings are and continue to be only in the measure that a judgment persists in determining them: "Being [*das Seiende*] is for the one who judges a being 'that has some future [*hinfort*]'—as long as the one who judges does not give up his 'conviction' and does not cancel the validity [of the being], which is also a *validity for the future* [*Fortgeltung*]."[30] Thus the permanence and perdurance of being strictly depends on a judgment, on a predication. Husserl maintains that being is spoken, at least first, according to logical authority and within predication. Ontology does not break through beyond logical space but is limited to making use of it in an intentional mode, aiming at being as through a screen that it nevertheless never transgresses. Far from undertaking the destruction of the history of logic that Heidegger will carry out, in order to regain direct access to being in its Being, far even from taking up again (or even from citing a single time) the results of the Sixth *Logical Investigation*, Husserl sticks obstinately to the equivalence between logic and ontology, leaving unquestioned the position of Being as such, admitting the object only as the substratum of a judgment. A text from 1923 established it with an amazing conviction:

> The doctrine of the something or of the something in general, that is to say of objects in general as substrata of possible predicative meanings, having to be able to be judged [*urteilbar*] coherently in the course of a predication, such is *formal ontology*. It is only a correlative manner of considering the doctrine of coherent judgments in general and of the forms in which they are united in systems of coherent and consistent judgments. An apophantic logic conceived in its *whole* scope is by itself a formal ontology, and conversely a formal ontology that is *wholly* developed is by itself a formal apophantics.[31]

Formal ontology therefore operates more as a form, as a formality— aiming at the form of the general substratum of predication—than as a science of being as being. Designating only a pure formality, formal ontology remains only a pure formality of ontology.

2. The second characteristic of formal ontology has to do with the primacy of objectity. "If we call an *a priori* science of any objects whatever *formal ontology*, that means nothing more than [that it bears

on] *possible objects [taken] purely as such.*" Or: "In conclusion, let us note further that *the task of formal ontology can be undertaken directly from the very beginning, without starting from the idea of a science.* In that case the question of formal ontology is: what can one state within the limits of the empty region of object-in-general?"[32] Thus, in order to elaborate formal ontology no presupposition is required, not even the model of science (contrary to Heidegger's critique); it is enough to admit objectity. One must be more precise: object and objectity here indicate that ontology requires nothing more than to be able first to predicate a substratum (like apophantics), and then to aim at this substratum as both the logical and the ontic point of attribution of any statement; it therefore is not (yet) a matter of the scientific ideal of objectivity, but of the originary requirement of a point of reference, the sole valid interlocutor of predication and of intention; in short, it is already less a matter of an object than first of an objective in relation to which to speak and aim, as an a priori condition, or even as a need of reason. We will therefore say henceforth that formal ontology presupposes objectity.[33] Now another question arises: Can and must being exhaust itself adequately in the objectity of the object? Does the subsistence of a permanent substratum (even in contingency that which demands permanence) reach the sole and final meaning of the Being of beings? To be sure, Husserl sometimes imagines "broadening" the concept of formal ontology to "values," but that is still in ordaining them to the "object in general."[34] He does not seem to imagine any other mode of Being than the subsistence of the substratum, in the sense that Heidegger during that same period attempts to break through toward the existence of *Dasein.* The fact that Husserl had not even glimpsed that ontology could pass beyond logic (and thus predication) confirms precisely his inability to see that the objectity of the substratum (of predication) had to be put into question. This twofold and consistent blindness does not result, however, from a privation of sight but much rather from a bedazzlement in face of the evidence, supposedly unquestionable, of an ontology of the subsistence of objectity. Husserl misses the question of Being because he sticks only too well to his own formal ontology, whose sole objective consists in objectity itself.

3. Formal ontology is characterized, finally, by the originarity of possibility. Indeed, because it needs only objectity, and therefore an object in general, an "any something whatever," Husserlian phenomenology can be satisfied with possibilities as well as, or even more than, with actualities; thus it first refers to the possible as to the object in general: "Though it seemed obvious that a science relating with this universality to anything and everything [*auf alles und jedes*]—to everything possible and everything thinkable—deserves to be called a formal *ontology*, still, if it is to be one actually, then the *possibility* of objectities belonging in

its sphere must be founded by intuition."[35] According to this remarkable text, not only does formal ontology accept the possible as the first figure of objectity, but above all even the recourse to intuition, that is, to the proper contribution of phenomenology, does not pass beyond that possibility (for example, as one would have expected, toward objectivity), but reinforces it by "founding" it as possibility. "An *a priori* science *of possible objects [taken] purely as such*," it aims at the "something-in general, to which also belong all the forms, not only those where one judges with certitude, but also those [where one judges] according to possibility."[36] It is even necessary to go to the point of concluding that actual objects properly come back to regional ontologies, whereas only possible objects, or better possibility as radically originary objectity, are suitable to the unconditioned universality of formal ontology. The latter, therefore, neither first nor especially concerns this actual world, but possible worlds: "Ontology constructs the *logos* of a possible world in general, or again it is the science of possible forms, of disjunctively necessary forms of possible worlds, such as they must end up being able to be."[37] How then is one to understand the solemn declaration of the *Cartesian Meditations*: " . . . a new ontology, fundamentally and essentially [*grundwesentlich*] different from that of the 18th century which proceeded by way of logical concepts removed from all intuition"?[38] For intuition does not do away with the privilege of possibility but on the contrary "founds" it; therefore, formal ontology sticks to possibility as the radical origin of beings more and not less decidedly than Leibniz and Wolff manage to. Possibility here surpasses, or rather precedes actuality only in order to secure objectity more originarily. Possibility opens to Husserlian ontology no other possibility than that of founding the impossibility of transgressing the determination of being as object. Does Husserl do justice to ontology? The answer is affirmative. Does he give to it only a regional status? The answer is twofold: first negative, because he grants it a universal domain, the form of any region, namely the object in general as the pure possibility of objectity; then affirmative, because ontology is thus precisely confined within the horizon of objectity as the first and last possibility. In this sense, formal ontology is regionalized with respect to the question of Being because it leaves unquestioned objectity's way of Being.

6. The Second Insufficiency: According to Reduction

The unquestioned privilege of objectity does not prohibit but much rather requires that one subordinate that very objectity to the instance of the transcendental I, in accordance with the idealist principle that *"subjectivity* [Subjectivität] *comes into the dignity of Being before* [vorher] *objectivity* [Objektivität] and that all objectivity (all worldly Being) is Being only starting from the passive and active sources of subjectivity."[39] One should not see any contradiction here: the objectivity of any being remains first only by virtue of its sole condition of possibility, the subjectivity that, moreover, "comes before" it. Indeed, "every region of objectivity [*gegenständliche*] is constituted according to the measure of consciousness [*bewußtseinsmässig*]"; therefore, following the supposedly most radical difference between the regions of consciousness (immanent Being) and world (transcendent Being), the objectivity of the world receives only a "Being for the I," or is only "for the I."[40] The world has only an "entirely relative Being [*durchaus relatives Sein*]." Pure consciousness has "absolute priority" in relation to which all Being is the a posteriori. The immanence of consciousness not only renders it "unrelative" in itself,[41] but above all confers upon it the extraordinary power of relativizing all transcendent Being. Is consciousness, then, that is, the *I*, limited to being in a radically different way than the Being of the objects of the world, of which it would constitute only a particular, although primordial, ontological region— the "region of 'absolute Being' "?[42] But what does "Being" signify if it must be spoken at one and the same time of two regions that are otherwise abysmally different? What determination of "Being" allows one to maintain that, in spite of the border that separates the absolute from the relative, nevertheless "immanent or absolute Being and transcendental Being both mean, of course [*heisst zwar beides*], 'being,' 'object,' and both possess their [own] content of objectity determinations [*gegenständliche Bestimmungsgehalt*]"? Is it not better to see in this common denomination only the effect of "empty logical categories," which neither conceal nor reduce "a veritable abyss of meaning" between the two terms?[43] But then, if "being" is suitable to the two terms only in an empty fashion, why maintain its real validity with regard to consciousness—insofar as it is self-evident that one must give up attributing to it the title of "object"? Even if one wants to speak, with respect to the *I*, of the *"Urkategorie des Seins,"*[44] what retreat short of Being accomplishes therein the originary anteriority of such a category? Could the originary category, from which Being would issue, itself still belong to the domain of Being, or indeed does "pure subjectivity-consciousness" not "assume in the new ('transcendental') attitude the essentially and fundamentally new sense of a region of an absolutely peculiar [*eigenständig*] type, whose experiential givens are pure, and therefore also unworldly, unreal [*unweltlich, unreal*]"?[45]

But then, if on the one hand the *I* precedes objectity, the world, and reality, and if on the other hand ontology treats exclusively of the objectity of objects, must one not necessarily conclude that the *I* is excepted from Being and that a phenomenology that would recognize it would precede any ontology? It is a fact that Husserl drew this consequence: "Thus one comes to a first philosophy that is prior even to ontology and which consists in an analysis of the necessary structure of a subjectivity."[46] Phenomenology alone can rise in this way above ontology, because it alone "makes of the *a priori* an *a posteriori* and itself in turn presupposes the *a priori*."[47] The *I*, the sole a priori, comes before ontology; a consequence therefore becomes unavoidable: "the task of an *apriori* ontology of the real world . . . is inevitable, but on the other hand it remains one-sided and not in the full sense philosophical [*einseitig und nicht im Endsinne philosophische*]." With fewer precautions, Husserl elsewhere says that "in itself . . . *ontology is not phenomenology*," that "*phenomenology . . . is in no way an ontology [überhaupt keine Ontologie]*."[48]

The anteriority of the *I* over any object and of subjectivity over objectity designates a space beyond ontology; phenomenology occupies that space; it therefore presents itself in the strictest sense as the instance of what does not have to be in order to exert itself. What exactly is signified here by "not having to be"? We cannot even sketch an answer before having better understood how phenomenology establishes its divergence from ontology and how, despite that divergence, it remains its "mother." First, two remarks. (1) The elaboration of regional ontologies and especially of formal ontology intervenes, in *Ideen I*, before and without the criterion of phenomenological givenness ("the principle of all principles" in § 24) and without the operation that sets it to work, the phenomenological reduction (in §§ 31ff.). Thus ontology has received only a conditional legitimacy; it must next appear before the tribunal of reason. "We can thus relate formal logic and the whole of *Mathesis* in general to the explicitly reductive [*ausschaltende*] *epoché*," in short "we carry out *explicitly a broadening of the originary reduction* to all transcendental eidetic domains and to the *ontologies* belonging to them."[49] The very singularity of the *I* is attested only through the exercise of the reduction, which therefore guided by anticipation all of the preceding analysis of its nonrelative absoluteness. (2) As such the reduction brackets not only ontology—"for all ontologies . . . fall under the blow of the reduction"— but even what one must already call the question of Being: it is a matter of a "universal ἐποχή with respect to the Being or non-Being of the world."[50] These declarations must be understood exactly as they give themselves, as indicating "the suspension of actual Being." Before the object, the first question precisely no longer asks whether it is, or how it is, for "the science of the onta . . . 'dissolves into the phenomenological.' "[51] What then does phenomenology look for when it approaches the object that it claims above all not to recognize as a being?

The paradox is reinforced by the fact that, while bracketing ontology, phenomenology still claims "to harbor within itself all ontologies," for which it secures a *"maternal ground [Mutterboden]."*[52] Thus the phenomenologist indeed has the idea of a possible thing "just as the ontologist does" and operates upon the "same propositions [*dieselben Sätze*]" as he. The difficulty no longer consists in distinguishing two materials, but two modes of consideration of the "same" material, and therefore it consists in understanding what "same" means here, "how 'the same' according to concepts and propositions functions in ontological research and [in] phenomenological [research] . . . , if it is actually the same," or if it shows up "in a totally different way."[53] The response offers no ambiguity, if not full light. "In the phenomenology of the consciousness of the thing [*Dingbewußtsein*], the question is not [to know] how things in general *are,* nor what in truth belongs to them as such, but how the consciousness of things is made, what types of thing-consciousness are to be distinguished, in what way and with what correlates a thing gives itself to be seen [*sich darstellt*] and announces itself as such in the manner peculiar to consciousness." Thing-consciousness is not equivalent to the consciousness of the thing itself; thing-consciousness is accented according to the consciousness and envisages the thing only between quotation marks, as an "object of research"; but to seek the "correlate" "does not mean seeking things, things as such. A 'thing' as a correlate is not a thing."[54] Whereas in ontology it is a matter of positing theses "oriented toward the objects absolutely [*schlechthin*]," the phenomenologist, for his part, does *not* orient himself toward objects (as things by full right) but "exclusively toward lived experiences and the correlates of lived experiences." Thus appear some "cardinal differences," elsewhere brought together in "a cardinal difference [*ein kardinaler Unterschied*] between the mode of psychic constitution and that of the constitution of the thing."[55] The cardinal difference between ontology and phenomenology separates two objectives: on the one hand the objective of the object itself, as a thing, and on the other hand the objective of the consciousness of the "object," as opposed to the thing.

Such a reduction of all ontology to the reduction calls for two conclusions and recalls a question evoked above. 1. In the reduction situation, ontology undergoes a regionalization. In fact, the reduction sets into operation and makes appear a "cardinal difference" between the consciousness region and the region of the world,[56] but especially between the thing (or the object) as such, on the one hand, and the "thing" as a lived experience or consciousness of an object, on the other;

now, this difference intervenes between what pertains to being (and therefore indirectly to Being) and what does not pertain to it, but frees itself from it; therefore, this difference between the ontico-ontological and the nonontic does not have an ontological status. The "radical difference" operates like a nonontological difference. The ontological difference is not cardinal, and the cardinal difference is not ontological. The nonontological difference therefore can accord only a regional site to ontology, even formal ontology, which, although it is supposed to open the form of *any* region, is nevertheless limited to occupying *one* among others. It is therefore necessary to grant Heidegger's critique: the question concerning the mode of Being of objects yields for Husserl to the question of the mode of access to their cognition. It is even necessary to push this further: the reduction does not only distract from the question concerning the Being of beings, either of "consciousness" or of the world, but above all it annuls that question's claim to primacy: before knowing how what is can be, it is necessary to know how I can know it; "first philosophy" unfolds outside of ontology, even "gray" ontology. The reduction of ontology to the reduction therefore calls for a censure of the point of view of ontology. 2. The reduction of ontology also calls for a censure of the point of phenomenology itself. There is no paradox here. For when in order to distinguish the ontological approach from the phenomenological approach concerning the "same" givens, Husserl opposes the "consciousness of things" in a strict sense to "thing-consciousness," which concerns only the state of consciousness and its correlate, he must finally admit that "a 'thing' as correlate is not a thing," that "to make the thing-intention as such, namely the correlate . . . , into the object of research . . . does not mean researching things [*Gegenstand der Forschung/Dinge erforschen*]."[57] We ask: Is the principle of the return to the thing in question (*zur Sachen selbst*) satisfied when the research of the "thing" placed in quotation marks (*"Ding"*) also brackets the research of the thing as such? In other words, is it phenomenologically self-evident that, as concerns the ultimately given *Sache*, the reduction leads one back to the "thing" and distracts one from the thing (*Ding*)? Would not the whole phenomenological enterprise consist rather in exercising the intentional aim radically enough so that, through the lived experiences and not in them, the thing (*Ding*) should hold the rank of *Sache*, instead and in place of the "thing"? Privileging the "thing" as the objective correlate of consciousness against the thing itself could, far from respecting the methods and rights of phenomenology, misunderstand their aim—namely, the intentional aim itself—and sacrifice the return to the things themselves to a regression toward the psychologism most classically closed to givenness, even more so if it is a matter of the ultimate givenness—that of beings. Here again, it would be necessary to admit the legitimacy of the Heideggerian critique: at the very moment when it misunderstands the question of Being, Husserlian phenomenology misunderstands first its own phenomenological method.

These two remarks come together to raise anew the fundamental question: If phenomenology is separated from ontology by a "cardinal difference," where then *is* it? If the *I* is excepted from the reduction (because it carries it out) and if, as well, "all ontology falls under the blow of the reduction," if therefore the *I* is excepted from all ontology, where then *is* it? Formally, only two paths open here: either to weaken the "cardinal difference" in order to suppose that the *I* also is, even if its mode of Being—left entirely indeterminate by Husserl—no longer has anything in common with the other modes of Being for "things"; or else to admit the most difficult but the most obvious consequence: the *I*, and therefore the phenomenological reduction with it, *is* not.

7. "I" Outside of Being

We will therefore attempt to determine whether this last position can actually be thought. Such an attempt in fact implies two assumptions, equally bold. (1) To admit that Husserl himself might have been the first to imagine that the *I*, which exercises the reduction of all ontology because it is freed up in that very reduction, in fact and in principle transcends the reign of ontology in general, in short that the *I* is expressed outside of Being. (2) To admit that the critique addressed by Heidegger to Husserl might be reversed: just as it remains established that Husserlian phenomenology misses the *Seinsfrage* and that it thus contradicts its own principle of returning to the things themselves, so the interpretation of this remains open: it is a matter of a failure only if the Being of beings indeed offers, in itself as much as for Husserl, the ultimate and irrevocable *Sache selbst*; if not, then by not returning, as concerns the thing itself, to the Being of beings, Husserl would in no way have failed but would have attempted an unprecedented and at first glance unthinkable leap: a leap from the region of beings in general (conceived according to objectity) to a phenomenological horizon not determined by Being, properly outside of Being, in traversing without stopping in or trying to satisfy the domain of the question of Being, where Heidegger attempted to lodge—and to block—phenomenology. In other words, Heidegger's slogan against Husserl—that the possibility of phenomenology surpasses its actuality—could be turned back against the undertaking of *Sein und Zeit*: the *ultimate* possibility of phenomenology would consist in the question of Being no more than it is exhausted in the objectity of the constituted object; beyond the one and the other equally, a final possibility could still open to it— that of positing the *I* as transcendent to reduced objectity, but also to the Being of beings, that of positing itself, by virtue of the reduction carried out to its final consequences, outside of Being. Outside of Being?

Of course, it is necessary to acknowledge straightaway that Husserl did not thematize as such this horizon outside of Being. At least two reasons explain this: his intoxication with the constitution of objects according to the innumerable regional ontologies, and then his inability to recognize the ontological difference and therefore to see clearly what it is a question of transgressing. We will therefore have to outline the thesis of a horizon outside of Being starting from the internal references and requirements of Husserlian phenomenology, even if, inevitably, it will be necessary sometimes to continue without, or even beyond Husserl. For the sole way of justifying, against Heidegger, the apparent (or real) aporias of his phenomenological ontology could consist in pushing it to the extreme consequences of the reduction—which he himself does not explicitly admit any more than Heidegger. Why, indeed, would the *Seinsfrage* constitute an exception to the reduction more than all the other ontologies? In other words: Why within the elaboration of a phenomenological ontology would Heidegger not come upon the unprecedented hypothesis that Husserl glimpsed, without being able or daring to think it all the way through—namely, the bracketing of the *Seinsglaube* through a suspension of the faith in Being? If "all ontologies fall under the blow of the reduction," why would "fundamental ontology" not risk succumbing to it also, indeed *especially*, since it alone brings the ontological enterprise precisely to its peak? This question assumes all the more force insofar as Husserl himself, in a limited way, to be sure, subjected to the reduction not only regional ontologies but indeed an "authentic and universal ontology"; for him already, the reduction disqualifies even a rebuilt, restored and radicalized ontology—in short an ontology that is in its own way already fundamental.[58] Thus, if Heidegger elaborates the true "fundamental ontology," he would at least have to present the phenomenological reasons for which the latter could resist the disqualification of a reduction; but he never responds to this question; even more: he claims, at least in *Sein und Zeit*, to take up the phenomenological method without ever doing justice to the reduction.[59] Does not this massive silence mark an evasion or fear before what Husserl had liberated—the unlimited power of the reduction? In supposing (as we did above) that Heidegger attempts to carry out the reduction in the very name of the question of Being, why not have thematized this audacious identification, why not have established its possibility and its viability—if not because the power of the reduction could not easily be mastered? Heidegger presupposes that the question of Being might reduce the reduction: he never demonstrates it.

It is therefore necessary to turn to the crisis between Husserl and Heidegger concerning the reduction (or not) of the question of Being. It becomes crystallized through the comparison of two statements. In the 1943 postscript to *What Is Metaphysics?*, Heidegger states in principle that "Among all beings, only man, called by the voice of Being, experiences the wonder of all wonders: *that* being is [dass *Seiendes ist*]." In other words, when through anxiety or any other fundamental affective mood, the world of beings recedes and vanishes, what still speaks has a name— the fact of being, *that* being is, hence nothing of beings and nothing less than the nothing, hence the Being assigning man to this fact.[60] Now, it was Husserl who first risked designating an ultimate "wonder" appearing in the situation of the *epoché* of the world, as early as *Ideen III* in 1912:

> The wonder of all wonders is the pure I and pure consciousness: but even that wonder is shaded off as soon as the light of phenomenology falls upon it and as soon as it is subjected to the analysis of essence. The wonder is shaded off [*verschwindet*] in that it is transformed into an entire science full of difficult scientific problems. The wonder is ungraspable, whereas the problematical [as soon as it is grasped] in the form of a scientific problem is something graspable, it is the non-conceptualized that is elaborated for reason in the resolution of problems as conceptualizable and conceptualized.[61]

Thus two determinations of the "wonder of all wonders" meet, and in them the two greatest phenomenologists oppose one another head on. What stakes are at play here? The "wonder of all wonders." What does this formula designate? That before which the gaze cannot turn away so as to move on to another spectacle, but where it remains fixed, as attached; it is a matter of the θαῦμα par excellence, which provokes the θαυμάζειν, and hence philosophy; in phenomenological terrain, it is therefore a matter of the phenomenon par excellence, such as it gives the first givenness, and therefore opens the horizon of all future evidence. Husserl and Heidegger thus oppose one another concerning the determination of the phenomenon par excellence. Husserl recognizes it in the *I*, whose pure consciousness defines an original region that is absolutely distinct from the region of the world and from its objects precisely because it constitutes them. For the *I* that is defined by its consciousness Heidegger substitutes the *Dasein* that is determined by being in taken as a fact, and therefore by Being. Transcendence of the I or transcendence of Being—in this way two phenomena par excellence are distinguished. Or at least this is the interpretive scheme of his dilemma with Husserl that Heidegger always imposed; does it remain possible to understand it differently? No doubt, if we read Husserl's text all the way to the end. Husserl in fact establishes a "wonder of all wonders"—the *I*— only in order immediately to modulate it: for even the phenomenon par excellence "is shaded off," or better "vanishes" (*verschwindet*), as soon as the light of phenomenology inundates it; under that light, it acquires the intelligible form of the conceptualized: even the *I* must pass from the wonder to the concept in order to keep its originary phenomenological role. Thus Husserl does not only nonsuit (in advance or through ignorance matters little) the ontological fact of being of its claim to the rank of phenomenon par excellence, and he does not only oppose to it the *I* and pure consciousness; he rejects straightaway and definitively any claim of anything whatever to the rank of a "wonder" that, by bedazzling the gaze of the phenomenologist, could escape the status of the common law phenomena: that is, escape the reduction and constitution. Now, the following page will indicate: "All ontologies fall under the blow of the reduction."[62] The phenomenological method never stumbles upon the slightest limit or border—not even the Being of beings, nor even (contrary to what Heidegger leaves one to suppose) the *I*. No "wonder of wonders" will ever require the gaze, which is indissolubly reductive and constituting, to renounce clear placing-in-evidence. No phenomenon par excellence will bedazzle the pure phenomenological gaze—henceforth without idol.

To be sure, one will be able to object to this interpretation that such a disqualification of bedazzlement especially allows Husserl to remove in advance the obstacles to his scientific project of constituting the objects of regional ontologies; and it is of course necessary to concede this. It remains the case, however, that one could attempt to think a phenomenology that makes no exception to the reduction. Such a possibility of phenomenology calls for several remarks. First, if the reduction passes beyond all ontologies, then it itself absolutely does not have to be conceived in the terms of ontology. This unstoppable consequence can receive two interpretations; either, according to Heidegger, it is a matter only of a failure before the *Seinsfrage*, occasioned by and for the reestablishment of the scientific project of objectivity; or else it is a matter of a transgression beyond the question of Being as such. This latter interpretation suffers from a notable weakness: Husserl never defined, even in outline, a new realm where, beyond and otherwise than Being, the reduction would be exercised; on the contrary, he often pushed his own advance back toward objectity, and hence the least critical objectivity. It nevertheless remains that the question can and even must be posed: According to what nonontological rigor does the reduction operate? Whence does the reduction reduce? In its historical figures, metaphysics carried out reductions, but each time starting from an identified instance; the reduction of sensible or intelligible diversity to eidetic unity is produced on the basis of the τόπος ἐιδῶν; the reduction of essences to the rank of the ὄν ᾗ ὄν is produced on the basis of ontology; the reduction of beings to the rank of *cogitata* is produced on the basis of a privileged being, in whatever sense one understands that privilege (ego, transcendental *I*, even *Dasein*). The case is not the same here: reducing all ontology, the reduction no longer maintains any ontological ground on which to situate itself: it is no longer a matter of scorched earth, since the scorching has devoured all earth, to the point that, along with Being, nothingness would also be shaded off. Whence, then, does the reduction reduce? It presides over formal (or even fundamental) ontology only by remaining "outside of Being": we cannot think this place, but Husserlian phenomenology nevertheless requires nothing less, since it designates it.

Hence another remark. If the *I* exercises the reduction, its being taken up conceptually by the light of phenomenology nevertheless does not signify its dissolution in objectity. That the "wonder of wonders" itself must also reach intelligibility implies in no way that it loses its privilege; Husserl asks only that one think it correctly as the "cardinal difference" that tears the *I* away from the mode of Being of things. The question can therefore be summed up in one point: Does that difference remain irreducible to the ontological difference through lack (following Heidegger's critique) or through excess—because it anticipates, without measuring or thematizing it, a nonontological determination of the *I*? "Indescribable in and by itself: pure I and nothing other."[63] Could not the indetermination in which Husserl—indisputably—leaves it also indicate that the *I* does not have first nor especially to be determined according to Being? And, just as there are with the reduction more and better things to say of the *I* than to reestablish in it the Cartesian *inconcussum quid*, so with the transcendence of the *I* could there be more and better things to think than to consecrate that transcendence without remainder to the Being of beings. Placed outside of Being (in the sense that a ship placed out of water is protected from water damage, even though it remains exposed, or that a liquor that is "beyond age" [*hors d'age*] is not rescued from the years but accumulates them to the point of transmuting them into its spirit), the *I* can offer itself through other transcendences, or even offer itself to other transcendences which the reduction, ceaselessly radicalized, like a new apophantics, will free up for it.[64] We cannot yet express these transcendences, but phenomenology nevertheless requires nothing less.

The greatness of phenomenology stems from the fact that in it possibility always surpasses actuality. The current possibility of phenomenology no longer consists in reestablishing the scientific objective of objectivity, but nor does it consist for all that in passing beyond that objective with a view to the *Seinsfrage*. This possibility could consist in attempting to determine how and in what measure the *I*, which reduces even ontologies, does not itself have first to be. This possibility was glimpsed straightaway by Husserl, even if he did not explicitly or clearly develop it. For often, what Husserl opens in the way of possibility he does not see, whereas what he thinks he sees best, sometimes, closes possibility. But it is for this very reason that he remains for us a nourishing ground.

6

The Nothing and the Claim

1. Access to the "Phenomenon of Being"

If the enigma of *Sein und Zeit* stems from the concealment in it of the ontological difference by an "ontological difference" limited to the analytic of *Dasein*, its aporia comes down entirely to the impossibility of acceding directly to the "phenomenon of Being."[1] In privileging an indirect path—through *Dasein*—toward Being, the enterprise of 1927 was not able to stage Being directly as a phenomenon, and thus to free the ontological difference as such. Indeed, here the question of Being is always confused, in principle, with the question of the Being of *Dasein* alone: "Does our present approach *via* the existential analytic provide us an avenue for arriving at this Being [*dieses Sein*, that of *Dasein*] phenomenally?"[2] If one admits that such an ambiguity gives rise to the aporia of *Sein und Zeit*, is it immediately necessary to conclude that all access to the "phenomenon of Being" is closed off? Not at all, and for two reasons. (1) *Sein und Zeit* envisages "constructing the question of Being" as such, that is, posing the question of Being as such and in general, in a radicality of which *Dasein* appears to be the workman, but not the goal, nor the master; it is therefore necessary to attempt to examine whether the 1927 essay does not also attempt, as it were obliquely and along the margins of the existential analytic, to accede directly to the "phenomenon of Being." (2) In strict phenomenology, the ultimate instance of decision remains "the principle of all principles," namely the givenness that is justified unconditionally by intuited presence; it is before this latter instance that it might be decided whether a "phenomenon of Being" eventually gives itself. In short, it is necessary to examine *Sein und Zeit* according to a strict phenomenological criterion: Does the "return to the things themselves in question" lead to the "phenomenon of Being," does Being give itself as a phenomenon, even as the most radical of phenomena according to the most radical of givennesses?

There is nothing easy about responding to this multiform question. For does *Sein und Zeit* ever exhibit Being in general as the phenomenon par excellence, or even simply as a phenomenon? Under the requirement of givenness in person to intuition, does Being ever appear, according to phenomenological actuality, as the thing itself? A positive response is not self-evident, either because the reduction can remain at the level of objectivity and so fail,[3] or else on the contrary because it can free up the *I* outside of Being,[4] or finally because the difference of the mode of Being of *Dasein* does not coincide with the ontological difference.[5] These difficulties force one to pose clearly two questions: First, does Being give itself as a phenomenon by satisfying even once the requirements of givenness formulated by the "principle of all principles"? Next, is *Dasein* finally defined by its being destined toward Being? These two questions, moreover, come together in one: Does Being appear as the phenomenon par excellence or should we (we—the *I*, *Dasein*, or whatever one wants to say) expect another?

It is therefore necessary to re-pose the question of the "phenomenon of Being," without letting oneself be limited by the aporia of *Sein und Zeit*, and without giving up what it attained either. This tricky step appears nevertheless feasible, since it is Heidegger himself who first attempted it. Indeed, two years after the appearance of *Sein und Zeit*, the lecture *Was ist Metaphysik?* undertook to repeat the phenomenological clarification of Being—without keeping anything from the analytic of *Dasein*, however, except the analysis of anxiety. That one is dealing in this reprise of *Sein und Zeit* with the possibility of a direct access to Being is indicated by a complex textual fact. In 1927, the point of departure for a "phenomenon of Being" is defined by two propositions: Being is never without a being, even though it is never a being;[6] it is therefore suitable to analyze the being that, since it is toward Being, leads to it rather than obfuscating it, namely *Dasein*. In 1929, or rather in the 1943 *Nachwort* added by Heidegger to the fourth edition of the lecture, a new formula corrects the position of 1927: "it belongs to the truth of Being that Being 'sists' [*siste*] fully without being, but that being is never without Being [*das Sein wohl west ohne das Seiende, dass niemals aber ein Seiendes ist ohne das Sein*]."[7] We are dealing here with a decisive advance and a new ambition: if, as in 1927, being always remains the being of Being, here, contrary to 1927, Being no longer displays itself only on the occasion of a being—"Being is in each case the Being of a being"[8]—but "fully without being." Heidegger's attempt to bring forth (or let appear) the phenomenality of Being as such was perhaps never more bold than with this reversal.[9] The obstacle that was constituted, paradoxically, by the very analytic of *Dasein*—namely, the primacy of a being in the manifestation of Being in person—seems to be removed: Being would display itself without any ontic precondition, absolutely and as such. No doubt, this variation does not intervene at all in the 1929 lecture, but in the 1943 commentary; we will nevertheless privilege its reference, precisely because it concerns that lecture and because the repentance that annuls it a few years later marks its palpable difficulty. It is a palpable difficulty, indeed, to decide whether Being always depends on a singular being in order to manifest itself phenomenally, or whether it displays itself "fully" on its own and "without being," in short whether it satisfies the "principle of all principles" as a "thing itself." More sharply: if ontology completes phenomenology and if phenomenology alone renders ontology possible, it is necessary that a "phenomenon of Being" manifest itself; now, *Sein und Zeit* in 1927 does not reach that point; it is therefore suitable to repeat its undertaking by a more direct path, as *Was ist Metaphysik?* attempts in 1929; if that repetition does not arrive at the "phenomenon of Being," it will be necessary either to give up the latter, or to envisage an entirely different determination of the completion of phenomenology. Or else the one *and* the other.

2. The Moods of "Dasein"

How to pose and construct the question of the "phenomenon of Being"? In order not to repeat the aporia in which the 1927 analytic of *Dasein* ends up, we will henceforth follow the path traced by the lecture of 1929. It attempts, indeed, to accede directly (without the mediation of the Being of the being Dasein) to Being; even more, it claims to reach it on the terrain of the positive sciences, which do not cease to deny any legitimacy and any possibility of any "phenomenon of Being" whatever. The positive sciences, indeed, do not have to know Being, which never appears under their scalpel; only being, because it can be constituted as an object through methods that are in each case constituting, appears in their horizon; outside of objectivizable beings, they have nothing to study, admit, or tolerate. "That to which the worldly relation goes is being itself—and nothing other [*und sonst nichts*]. That from which every attitude receives its direction is being itself—and nothing other [*und sonst nichts*]. That with which investigative analysis occurs in its irruption is being itself—and nothing other [*und sonst nichts*]."[10] Hence a threefold paradox: the worldly relation (*Weltbezug*), the attitude (*Haltung*) and the irruption (*Einbruch*) through which the positive sciences establish their objects without reference to Being, or to anything other than that objectivity alone, is the very thing that introduces, without recognizing it explicitly and almost clandestinely, another term—a term other than any object: the "nothing other," and thus the nothing as other than the object and other than objectivized being. Such a nothing (*nichts*) undoubtedly does not say very much; strictly speaking it says and shows nothing; but that nothing of nothing nevertheless already says too much; already, we can no longer eliminate it or ignore it, since in order to abolish it one would have to repeat it, duplicate it, in short reinforce it. For if science does not mean to occupy itself with the nothing, it must, for that very reason, admit that it can say or wants to say (the difference matters little) nothing of the nothing; but to say nothing of the nothing ("Science wishes to know nothing of the nothing")[11] does not amount to nothing; nothing of nothing does not annul the nothing but doubles it, elevates it to power, in short, precisely, consecrates its power. Are we dealing here with a sophistic quibbling, producing the appearance of something where, in fact, there is nothing? One would like to think so, but then, once again, in order to say it one must name what, precisely, one is claiming to be silent about—nothing. Are we dealing, on the contrary, with the sign of an irreducible phenomenon, all the more given insofar as one believes oneself to be denying its givenness? In short, are we dealing with a major Nothing, accessible only through a "bifid essence"?[12]

The double essence of the Nothing distracts us; it tricks us [*nous double*] because it betrays our sound understanding and compels us to suspect some kind of double-dealing. In being born of the "almost nothing" of denial, the Nothing leaves one to suppose, under its appearance as "less than nothing," that it is owed the rank of a full phenomenon. But before accepting this, the sound understanding can attempt to follow one last escape route: the question concerning the Nothing leads to an absurdity, since it supposes the Nothing itself to be endowed with properties, and therefore with reality, in such a way as to liken it to an object—one that is ignored or unconscious, but still an object. In short, the question concerning the Nothing begins by likening it tacitly to a being.[13] The principle of noncontradiction would suffice, then, to disqualify a question that is in the strict sense without an object. In addressing this objection— the objection of objectity—to himself, Heidegger very lucidly anticipated the critique that Carnap will address to him from 1932 on: the approach to the Nothing starting from the ". . . and nothing other" betrays only "crude logical errors," since "the combination of the words 'only' and 'outside of it, nothing [*und sonst nichts*]' here has the usual sense of a logical particle that serves to express a negative existential statement."[14] Such a reduction of the Nothing to "a logical particle," however, does not characterize one particular philosophical school (here logical positivism) more than another; it is in a sense a need of all modern metaphysics—

that, precisely, of nihilism—to steal away from the thought of the Nothing and to take refuge in its reduction to the simple "not."

Thus Bergson, opposed to Carnap on almost everything, criticizes Heidegger's approach in advance. He does so first in stressing that, since "representing nothingness to oneself consists in imagining it or in conceiving it," it is a matter of an "idea that destroys itself," of "a pseudo-idea"; consequently, one must renounce "absolute nothingness" and limit oneself to "relative nothingnesses."[15] Henceforth, the question of the Nothing/nothingness can be reduced to negation, or rather to an exercise of negation gone astray; for we say "nothingness" only before the nonrealization of a possibility; " 'Nothing' designates the absence of what we seek, of what we desire, of what we expect," "we thus indicate that it pleases us to direct our attention toward the object that has left, and to turn our attention away from the object that replaces it."[16] In fact, in order to pass to nothingness, we attribute to negation an excessive power which in truth it does not exercise. The negation actually at work remains partial (it bears on only *a* possibility) and weak (it concerns only a *possibility*, not an actuality); moreover, no negation intervenes, since it is not a matter here of the nonactualization of some foreseen possibility, but indeed of the actualization of an unforeseen possibility. It is in this way that, from the substitution of one possibility for another, we pass to a suppression (only of the foreseen possibility), and then to the absolute abolition of that possibility, and finally to the abolition of all possibilities— baptized as an "absolute nothingness."[17] Bergson's analysis has the merit of attempting concretely the derivation of the "idea of nothingness" starting from negation, and even of distinguishing "suppression" from "substitution," where Carnap will limit himself to confirming (or even imposing) the divergence between the two terms. However, that probity makes evident the principal weakness of his critique: if "it is indeed from this supposed power inherent to negation that all the difficulties and all the errors here come,"[18] how are we to understand the fact that nothing less than the Nothing issues from a power—negation—that is in fact reputed to be in large part illusory? That one errs in giving to negation the power of engendering the Nothing itself is one assessment, as acceptable as others; but it is a fact, admitted even and above all by the critics of the Nothing, *that* we recognize the power of the Nothing starting from negation, which is supposed to be simple and intelligible; it is a fact that we produce the Nothing (at least as an "idea of nothingness") only through the help of negation; whether or not it is a matter of delirium matters little, since this delirium of negation does indeed engender the Nothing. But Bergson, having thus already admitted one fact irreducible to his critique, allows a second contradiction to his argument to appear:

If negation exercises only a "supposed power," in fact less a power than a confusion (between the substitution of one possibility for another and its suppression pure and simple), how are we to understand the fact that it might engender nothing less than "the idea of nothingness"? Does it engender that idea through the nothingness of its power? But then nothingness itself would have a power—which it was a matter precisely of *not* demonstrating. Or else would "the idea of nothingness" precede, like a regulative idea, the "supposed power" of a negation, which of itself would be incapable of reaching that idea? In short, either negation attests to the power of nothingness through its own deficiency, or else it presupposes that power as its horizon. In both cases, the Nothing escapes its logical reduction by negation.[19]

Involuntarily and at the very heart of his reduction of "the idea of nothingness" Bergson allows the real question to appear: Does the logical impossibility of the Nothing suffice to disqualify its actual givenness? This question divides into two. (1) Does negation produce the Nothing, or does the Nothing originally make negation itself possible? Without yet being able to justify it, Heidegger posits a thesis: "We assert: the Nothing is more original than the not and negation."[20] But this reversal of the problem demands that one prove that such a Nothing can intervene alone, without negation, face to face, in short as a phenomenon. (2) Hence the second question: Supposing that it precedes negation, can the Nothing be given? "If the Nothing, whatever may be the case with it, is still to be enquired into—the Nothing itself [in person, *es selbst*]—, it follows that it must be given in advance. We must be able to encounter it."[21] The Nothing will establish its primacy only by preceding negation, and therefore logic, which is possible only in its giving itself in person, originarily and intuitively, and therefore—according to the "principle of all principles"—in legitimating itself in principle. But *what* phenomenon should we expect? Since negation must no longer trace the horizon of the Nothing, it is necessary to give it, by way of preunderstanding, a new definition: "The Nothing is the negation of the totality of beings: the absolutely not-being," "The Nothing is the integral negation of the totality of beings."[22] It is important here that negation, which to be sure is maintained, concerns beings, and beings in their totality, with a view to ending up at non-being as such; we are not dealing with a negation of the phenomenon, nor even with a negative phenomenon, but with a phenomenon of the negative as such, and therefore with non-being, with the né-*ens*. The question is therefore clearly formulated: Can the Nothing give itself in person as an originary phenomenon, in a "fundamental experience of the Nothing"? And since this Nothing is defined as the negation of the totality of beings, "the totality of beings must be given beforehand [*zuvor gegeben sein*]."23 The givenness of the totality of beings appears as logically impossible to a finite essence as it seems logically impossible to reach the Nothing in person, and not only in thought. However, these formal quibbles of the understanding will fade if we actually reach a "fundamental experience of the Nothing," that is, if we actually approach beings in their totality. Now, such a totality does not remain inaccessible, provided that one not confuse "apprehending the whole of beings in itself and finding oneself at the heart of beings as a whole"; for the second possibility, as opposed to the first, is realized "constantly."24 Here Heidegger privileges two (affective) moods (*Stimmungen*) of *Dasein*: boredom and joy; in fact, joy itself divides in two, since it is a matter of the "joy felt in the presence of the *Dasein* . . . of a loved human being [*eines geliebten Menschen*]";25 to boredom and joy, therefore, it is necessary to add love. It is a matter, therefore, of understanding how each of these moods allows *Dasein* to "find itself at the heart of beings as a whole." Let us note here an essential point: in 1927, *Sein und Zeit* did not mention any of these three moods when it was a matter of gaining access to the Nothing; anxiety was sufficient to allow such an access, which, moreover, was direct. It will be necessary, later, to account for this difference.

How, then, does boredom throw us amidst beings in their totality? In the quotidian manipulation of beings, I always address myself to certain particular beings, particularized through their usage, and never to beings as a whole. Nevertheless, sometimes the being that is particularized in its manipulation comes to lose its privilege: boredom marks with indifference an until then privileged being, in order to mix all beings together through the undifferentiation of beings as a whole, such as they bore me. The 1929 lecture distinguishes, very allusively, to be sure, between boredom with such and such a being (a play, an occupation, even an idleness) and "profound boredom, stretching out like a silent fog in the abysses of *Dasein*, [which] confuses all things, all men and ourselves along with them, within a strange indifference."26 In fact, this distinction is developed much more explicitly in a contemporaneous course, *Die Grundbegriffe der Metaphysik* (winter 1929–30), which analyses two types of boredom before itself reaching "profound boredom." The first consists in being bored by something, and therefore also for something: according to the corresponding temporality, boredom regrets losing time for what does not deserve it; it therefore contests here the privilege accorded, through utilitarian manipulation, to some particular being. The second consists in being oneself bored by oneself with regard to something: according to the corresponding temporality, boredom assigns us to a present state devoid of any future; it exposes us therefore to receiving, head on and indistinctly, all beings, all beings as a whole. Finally, "profound boredom" calls into question the "self" in person: one is bored with oneself in oneself, in such a way that all beings as such enter into suspension: "Beings as a whole have become indifferent."[27] Here, access to the totality of beings results directly from indifference: it is precisely because boredom drowns in the mist of indifference not only beings, but above all the differences among beings and even *the* difference between intra-worldly beings and *Dasein*—". . . all men and ourselves along with them"—that the quantity of beings actually approached matters little: indifference renders them all undifferentiated, in such a way that a few suffice already to experience them all. By confusing all beings in undifferentiation, boredom opens one to the totality of beings, and therefore to the world: "We shall designate the expanse [*Weite*] of this 'as a whole' ['*im Ganze*'], which manifests itself in profound boredom, as world."[28] Thus, through the mood of boredom, *Dasein* gains access to beings as a whole as to a phenomenon given in person, without reserve or condition; being as a totality is given to be seen, precisely because boredom renders indifferent all the qualitative and quantitative differences among beings. *Dasein* therefore indeed finds itself thrown as such amidst beings as a whole.

This phenomenological outcome, however, gives rise to a twofold remark, to be developed later. (1) Heidegger does not even take the precaution of proving that boredom has an ontic, or even an ontological scope; but that assumption could be contested in two ways. On the one hand, one could say that boredom does not have the power to render beings indifferent, and therefore to open access to beings as a whole: Can we not imagine that a particular, absolutely exceptional being might by the mere fact of its appearing dissipate the most profound boredom? Does boredom always triumph over the splendor of the beautiful, of the sublime, or of the good? Doesn't its power exert itself especially over the resolutely common being? On the other hand, on the contrary, one could say that boredom, precisely because it could suspend even the splendor of the good and the prestige of the beautiful, is not exhausted in the ontico-ontological field, or, in short, that it deploys an authority that remains irreducible to the "question of Being." Through lack or through excess, couldn't boredom therefore escape the thematization of the "phenomenon of Being"? These questions find reinforcement in the second remark. (2) The mood of boredom is privileged in 1929 as much by the lecture as by the course. The lecture, however, makes allusion to two other moods, which moreover are related: joy before the *Dasein* of the beloved. If joy and love also permit one access to beings as a whole, why do they never receive as extensive an analysis as boredom?[29] If they are mentioned without any further consideration, is it necessary to infer therefrom that they would not have allowed one to end up at as certain a result as boredom? But then why even have mentioned them? If they do not suit the "phenomenon of Being" precisely, is it through lack (as simple intentionalities of consciousness) or through excess (as instances irreducible to philosophy)?[30] Their mention, which thus says too much and too little about them, cannot fail to provoke these questions.

At least one point seems established: boredom gives access to beings as a whole because it reduces every being to its pure and simple, undifferentiated permanence. However, once beings in their totality have become a phenomenon, the essential still remains to be achieved: the phenomenological staging of the Nothing (with a view to the "phenomenon of Being"). The "fundamental phenomenon" demands a new "fundamental (affective) mood [*Grundstimmung*]"; beyond boredom, which shows the totality of beings, anxiety inclines one toward their Nothing.[31] Boredom therefore receives only a provisional and transitional role on a route that leads from beings to their Nothing through the intermediary of their totalization. Whence the superiority of anxiety? How does it yet take over what was established by boredom? In fact, it repeats boredom's undifferentiation, but in reversing it. Like boredom, anxiety does not fix itself on any particular being; fear, on the contrary, always fears a being, which it knows as menacing, which it can identify, and which it eventually knows how to fight face to face. Anxiety does not know who or what threatens; it does not even know with certitude whether a threat actually threatens or whether it is only a matter of the imagination; but precisely because nothing is certainly threatening, everything can become so and therefore is so; no being is distinguished as threatening, and therefore the threat can come from everywhere. The indetermination of that before which I have anxiety does not indicate a lack of information, but indeed the specific definition of anxiety: anxiety assails me not despite its indetermination but indeed because of it. What gives me anxiety is not a definite being, but any being, and therefore all beings in the very measure that they remain indistinct— as in boredom. But here everything is reversed in relation to boredom. Whereas in boredom, even profound boredom, beings in their totality plunge into indifference and therefore withdraw, fade as in a fog of uninterest and leave me absolutely free to myself, in anxiety beings as a whole slip and recede into undifferentiation only in order to threaten me through that very undifferentiation: beings in their totality come back to seize me, to choke me—literally to give me anxiety—in the very movement of their withdrawal, in the indetermination that constitutes the whole threat. Far from remaining the intact spectator of the ontic shipwreck, as in boredom, here, anxious, I endure the siege of the very indetermination of beings. Henceforth, the indetermination does not make beings disappear so much as it makes me also disappear with them: indeed, beings threaten me only inasmuch as they disappear in indetermination itself. I am anxious therefore over no being, but over the very movement of the withdrawal, of the absence, of the Nothing of beings. Anxiety, to be sure, fears nothing, but that is because it is anxious over *the* Nothing. And when the "anxiety attack" ceases, I am right to say that "it was nothing," since in fact it was the Nothing in person.

The fundamental phenomenon has therefore been attained: as fundamental mood, "anxiety manifests the Nothing"; therefore, during the anxiety attack, "the Nothing itself—as such—was there."[32] From this point on, "the question concerning the Nothing remains constructed [*gestellt bleibt*]."[33] But what does the Nothing, which is there, manifest to the Being-there?

3. The Hermeneutic of the Nothing as Being

As a fundamental mood, anxiety allows one access to the Nothing as a fundamental phenomenon. However, this indisputable phenomenological advance gives rise to a new difficulty, which is more formidable than the first. Indeed, anxiety remains ambiguous, marked by a "bifid essence," in the sense that it is necessary to recognize "the enigmatic plurivocity of the Nothing."[34] Therefore, neither anxiety nor the Nothing will allow one to identify the phenomenon that they nevertheless present: the ambiguity of the mood increases the equivocation of the Nothing. The entrance of the Nothing into phenomenality is in no way sufficient for the manifestation of the "phenomenon of Being," since the Nothing itself still remains equivocal.

There is nothing accidental or superficial about this equivocation; it goes back to the most essential determination of the Nothing. Indeed, the Nothing is not defined by simple opposition to beings, precisely because it does not deny them or annihilate them; "the Nothing is encountered in anxiety only together with beings as a whole." Far from appearing only by making beings disappear, "the Nothing properly announces itself with beings and in holding on to them."[35] Neither a new being, nor an annihilating negation of beings, the Nothing is designated with and at the very surface of beings. Therefore, beings do not allow one to identify the Nothing, neither directly through identification, nor indirectly through opposition. The indetermination of the Nothing against beings is designated, moreover, not only in its definition, but also in its sudden appearance. Indeed, when anxiety displays its "fascinated rest," *Dasein's* movement of retreat issues from the Nothing and characterizes it; that retreat expels and "dismisses" [*renvoie*] beings, dispatches them and "shows them the door," in such a way that no being in particular any longer threatens, but in such a way that, because of their undifferentiation in the retreat, all instill anxiety. Therefore the retreat that "dismisses" (in the sense of expelling) at the same time signals toward the undifferentiation of beings that are engulfed and refers [*renvoie*] (in the sense this time of signaling toward) to beings as a whole. A dismissal (expulsion) that refers (signals toward, assigns to), "*abweisende Verweisung*," the Nothing therefore plays doubly with beings: it expels them in particular in order to refer to them as a whole and, in that absent whole, to designate that which instills anxiety inasmuch as it is swallowed up, inasmuch, therefore, as it is in the process of not being. The ambiguity of this reference/dismissal [*renvoi/"renvoi"*], whose dividing into two contraries is betrayed only by the silent quotation marks, does not only confirm the essential indetermination of the phenomenon of the Nothing; above all it indicates that the Nothing is born of an expulsion of . . . (every being) that refers to . . . (the fact of beings as a whole). Now, it happens that, since *Sein und Zeit*, the reference has received a phenomenological status: it is characterized by the " 'with-a-view-to' structure," which, in the case of the tool, for example, addresses one being to another, according to a recurrent phenomenality.[36] Such a structure of reference defines also and to begin with the phenomenon understood as appearance (*Erscheinung*): "*Appearance* designates on the contrary a reference relation [*Verweisungsbezug*], which is in the being itself, in such a way that what *refers* [*das Verweisende*] (*Meldende*, the one who announces) can fulfill its possible function only by showing itself in itself, only in being a 'phenomenon.' "[37] Reference [*renvoi*] characterizes a type of phenomenon, appearance (*Erscheinung*), which must still show itself in itself in order to give itself as an absolute phenomenon (*Phänomen*). Since the Nothing appears according to a reference (*abweisende Verweisung*, a "dismissal" that refers), it appears only as an *Erscheinung*, not as a phenomenon in the absolute sense; it will therefore remain phenomenologically indeterminate inasmuch as it will not at all refer to an absolute phenomenon capable of bringing it also to light in turn. The Nothing therefore does not offer the ultimate phenomenon. It must still carry out the reference that defines it alone as a phenomenon—showing itself in and of itself starting from itself.

To what must one refer the appearance of the Nothing, itself defined as a pure reference? This question has become unavoidable for our investigation due to a pure conceptual necessity; but it nevertheless encounters a gaping textual difficulty. Indeed, *Was ist Metaphysik?* most often refers anxiety back to the Nothing—"Being-there means standing in the nothing," "Anxiety manifests the Nothing," "the Nothing itself reduces to nothing [*Das Nichts selbst nichtet*]."[38] As for the Nothing, it appears as the index of the transcendence of *Dasein*: "*Dasein*'s standing into [*Hineingehaltenheit*] the Nothing on the basis of hidden anxiety is the overcoming of beings as a whole: transcendence."[39] But these references (putting aside the fact that one would have to establish their equivalence) do not coincide with two other references.

1. In *Sein und Zeit*, the same analysis of anxiety as a fundamental (affective) mood referred the anxious appearance of the Nothing to Being-in-the-world: "That before which anxiety is anxious is *In-der-Welt-sein* itself"; here one is not dealing with a "Total Nothing" but only with *a* nothing, with the "nothing of intraworldly being-ready-to-hand [*dieses Nichts von Zuhandenen*]"; anxiety disqualifies every manipulable being (as well, moreover, as every being-present-at-hand) in such a way that this strictly ontic Nothing (nothing of beings) opens access toward and gives rise to the retreat before the world as such; the disappearance of every being confronts *Dasein* with "the *possibility* of being-ready-to-hand in general, that is, with the world itself." It is no doubt legitimate to speak here of the Nothing, but on the condition that one understand it as the ontic Nothing, which refers to the phenomenon of the world: ". . . the Nothing, that is, the world," "the world as world." The "Nothing of the world" does not annihilate the world but on the contrary belongs to it, leads back to it, confronts it directly: ". . . the understanding is carried through anxiety toward Being-in-the-world as such."[40] In 1927, *Sein und Zeit* never refers the appearance of the Nothing in anxiety back to the "phenomenon of Being," at least not explicitly and directly, but only to the world, to Being-in-the-world and to *Dasein*.[41] How, then, are we to explain that the same existential analysis might in 1929 refer the same appearance to the phenomenon of Being in its difference from beings?

2. But moreover, this indecision of the reference does not result only from the disagreement between 1927 and 1929; it is clearly inscribed in the 1929 text itself. For *Was ist Metaphysik?* indicates only twice and with reservation the reference of the appearance of the Nothing in anxiety to the "phenomenon of Being" (and no longer only to Being-in-the-world). First with the formula "*Im Sein des Seienden geschieht das Nichten des Nichts* [in the Being of beings occurs the reduction to nothing of the Nothing]";[42] but the turn of phrase here is surprising: one would rather expect that the Nothing, in nihilating, should manifest the Being of beings, so to speak, without beings; in short, that the Nothing be in Being, and not the reverse; it matters little, moreover, since Being is here not explicitly equated with the Nothing. Next a double formulation: "The Nothing does

not remain the indeterminate counterpart of beings, but unveils itself as belonging [*zugehörig*] to the Being of beings. . . . Being and the Nothing are in a reciprocal belonging [*gehören zusammen*] . . . , because Being itself is finite in its essence and manifests itself only in the transcendence of *Dasein* in its standing ecstatically into the Nothing."[43] This declaration, however, is not equivalent to a reference of the appearance of the Nothing to the "phenomenon of Being," and for several reasons; first, the Hegelian context, which weighs on the comparison without, however, justifying it; next, the recourse to a mutual "belonging" of the Nothing and of Being, which is never specified as a strict identity; finally, the intervention of a mediator between the two terms: *Dasein*, whose transcendence on the one hand passes from beings to Being and on the other hand "stands out" (*hinausgehaltenen*) into the Nothing. The reference and therefore the equivalence do not yet seem established in 1929.[44]

In fact, it falls to the *Nachwort* of 1943 to carry out the reference of the Nothing to Being, and therefore to lead the simple appearance (the Nothing awaiting a reference) to the "phenomenon of Being." It is still a matter of "the radical other [*schlechthin Andere*]—in face of beings," such as it is set apart by the lecture of 1927; and, henceforth, "this radical other [*schlechthin Andere*] of every being is non-being. But this nothingness [of beings] 'sists' [*siste*] as Being [*dieses Nichts west als das Sein*]." Henceforth, in the Nothing to which anxiety gives it access, *Dasein* no longer experiences its own transcendence but, directly and as such, Being: ". . . it learns to experience in the Nothing Being."[45] It is therefore necessary to advance a thesis: inasmuch as the passage from the fundamental mood of anxiety to the appearance of the Nothing suffers neither variation nor questioning from 1925 to 1929, so the reference of the appearance of the Nothing to the "phenomenon of Being" seems problematic, since that very same appearance first and simultaneously referred, in 1925 and 1927, to the transcendence of *Dasein*, then to the world, and finally to Being-in-the-world. Hence a question in the form of a suspicion: If several references enter into competition with regard to the single appearance of the same Nothing, which one is suitable, supposing that one is more suitable than the others? In short, by what right would the Nothing admit a reference to Being rather than to another instance?

Before approaching the central difficulty head on, it is necessary to clarify a preliminary issue: How does Heidegger end up himself recognizing the reference of the Nothing to Being, which the 1929 lecture had not established any more than *Sein und Zeit* in 1927? This amounts, inseparably, to testing the phenomenological validity of the later and laborious procedures through which, after the fact, Heidegger believes himself able to refer the appearance of the Nothing to the "phenomenon of Being," and thus to postulate the full givenness of the latter. The work of interpretation that Heidegger undertakes after and upon *Was ist Metaphysik?* can be divided up into three operations: accentuations, substitutions, and an addition.

1. The accentuations aim at interpreting the Nothing as the Being that, in 1929, it nevertheless does not give to be seen. Thus "the bifid essence [*zwiespältiges Wesen*]" of the Nothing receives this commentary in a note: "Nothing as 'Being' " (1949).[46] The necessity of transcendence, and therefore of standing into the Nothing, for comporting oneself toward beings receives (in 1949) this gloss: "this means that Nothing and Being [are] the same [*das Selbe*]."[47] The reference of the Nothing to the "phenomenon of Being," left hanging by the lecture, is therefore accomplished only by the later accentuations.

2. The substitutions all end up introducing "Being" where the original text had omitted it or had preferred "being." Thus the " 'expulsion of . . .' [*renvoi de . . .*] that refers to . . . [*renvoie à*]" or the "assigning expulsion" (*abweisende Verweisung*) is explained clearly by a note from 1949: "expulsion of: being for itself; reference: toward the Being of being [*abweisen: das Seiende für sich; ver-weisen: in das Sein des Seienden*]". On the same page, " . . . what renders the manifestation of beings in general possible to begin with" is identified by "that is, Being" (1949). A few words lower, the *Da-sein* placed "before beings as such" finds itself, through a 1949 substitution, "properly facing the Being of beings, facing the difference."[48] Similarly, the thesis that "the Nothing . . . belongs originally to essence itself, zum Wesen selbst," changes its sense in 1949 through the substitution of "Being" for "essence" ("Wesen: verbal; Wesen des Seins").[49] Of course, the formula closest to a phenomenological reference of the Nothing to Being receives special attention: a note from 1949 there attempts to substitute, through an appropriate complement, the missing Being for the being nevertheless maintained in 1929; hence the sequence, "It—the Nothing in its reduction to Nothing [*in seinem Nichten*]—refers us precisely to beings [*verweist uns gerade an das Seiende*]" is prolonged with " . . . because *in* the Being of beings."[50] The tactic of the commentaries is clear: the statements concerning beings (sometimes beings in general) in 1929 are in 1949 bluntly referred through overinterpretation and substitution, to Being (or the Being of beings).

3. Above all, the additions introduce so to speak into the body of the 1929 lecture, and therefore into the spaces of the appearance of the Nothing, the ontological difference in its canonical meaning, which the transcendental analytic was no doubt unable to formulate. Thus the "bifid essence" of the Nothing becomes directly, in 1931, the "ontological difference." Likewise, when the Nothing is encountered

"together with [*in eins mit*] beings," a note from 1949 does not hesitate to find there "the difference [*der Unterschied*]." Finally, we saw also, to set *Dasein* in face of beings signifies in 1949 setting it not only "specifically in face of the Being of beings," but, the same note undisturbedly continues, "facing the difference [*vor den* Unterschied]."[51] Here, more than in the other two operations, Heidegger's effort can be divined: since the 1929 lecture does not manage to refer the Nothing opened up by anxiety to the "phenomenon of Being," it is necessary, in an a posteriori reprise that is all the more frantic in the measure that the initial failure is serious, not only to frame the weak text with a preface and a postscript, but to reinforce it through accentuations, substitutions, and additions. This work, never interrupted over the course of at least twenty years (from 1929 to 1949), would not have made any sense if Heidegger had not himself admitted that, with the appearance of the Nothing, the "phenomenon of Being" was nevertheless not attained. Between the one and the other a hermeneutic has to intervene.

But how will that hermeneutic be guided, since, far from being able to regulate itself according to the "phenomenon of Being," it is precisely up to it finally to allow that phenomenon to appear?

4. On Last Appeal: The Claim

It is a constant from this point on that anxiety does *not* give access as such to the "phenomenon of Being," but only to the Nothing, and that the Nothing still demands an interpretation in order to let Being appear in it—in order that "this Nothing 'sists' [*west*] as Being."[52] The fundamental difficulty with the staging of the "phenomenon of Being" here shines forth: even after the radicalization in 1929 of the 1927 approach, first through the abandonment of the problematic of the "question of Being" in the narrow sense, and then through the substitution of the Nothing for Being-in-the-world as the end point of anxiety, there still remains a step to be made. It is the most perilous step: that which will allow one to pass from the Nothing to Being itself.[53] The accomplishment of this step can be thought only by clarifying at least three points. (1) For what phenomenological reasons does this last interpretation become unavoidable? (2) According to what leading thread must one guide it? (3) Must it inevitably succeed?

The phenomenological necessity of this interpretation results clearly from the last point to which anxiety leads: "All things and we ourselves founder in an indifference [*Gleichgültigkeit*]." Anxiety renders all beings indistinct from one another through an indistinction that engulfs even *Dasein*; if, therefore, the Nothing must appear, it could do so only in the form of indistinction, since it is precisely the indistinction of beings as a whole that produces it; a note from 1949 specifies this without beating around the bush: "*das Seiende spricht nicht mehr an*"; we would translate this first, at the familiar level, by "beings no longer say anything [to us]"; we could also understand it without contradiction at a more conceptual level to mean "beings no longer claim [us]."[54] In anxiety, beings in effect no longer speak, since they retreat and fade as in a fog; they steal away from any speech that they would receive and, even more, any claim that they would exercise; the indistinction that confuses them with beings as a whole smothers above all the sound of the slightest word; henceforth there is nothing to say about beings as a whole, precisely because no beings any longer present themselves, but only a vague whole; the nothingness of anxiety leaves me speechless, because with nothingness there are no longer any grounds for speaking, nor any place for speech—even that which it addressed to me. The Nothing says nothing (to me), not even itself, because it simply does not say. As a fog smothers sounds, the Nothing renders beings silent by dissolving them within being in general, then it silences that being in general by passing it over in silence, and finally it is silent concerning itself. The silence of the Nothing, then, which says nothing and asks nothing of anyone, can refer to nothing but itself. The gap whose difficult crossing we have already indicated between the Nothing and Being thus becomes phenomenologically problematic: the autistic silence of the Nothing can say nothing other than its undifferentiation, can say nothing other than the Nothing; or more exactly, it cannot even say the Nothing, since it can say nothing; it can say itself as Nothing only by not saying.

How, then, could the Nothing introduce, refer or incline one to any other instance than itself—since in it all possible instances meld in the same noninsistent indistinction? Two texts directly confirm the pertinence of this question. (1) The penultimate paragraph of the Postscript (1943) claims to express such a reference [*renvoi*]: "One of the essential places of speechlessness [*Sprachlosigkeit*] is anxiety in the sense of dread, such as the abyss of the Nothing attunes [*stimmt*] man to it. The Nothing as the other of beings is the veil of Being."[55] But read literally, this statement becomes phenomenologically untenable, even contradictory: anxiety does not only take speech away (*Sprachlosigkeit*) from the man who can no longer say anything about beings in general; it indissolubly and undoubtedly takes speech away first from beings themselves, which "no longer say anything (to me)" (*spricht nicht mehr an*). How, then, is one to pass, within such a suspension of speech, from the Nothing to Being?

How is one to identify the Nothing as Being when the Nothing is silent—when it silences everything including itself? Moreover, with a remarkable prudence that contradicts other bolder identifications, Heidegger does not, here at least, lead the Nothing back to Being; on the contrary, he maintains the gap between them: the Nothing is not equivalent to Being but remains its "veil." Veil? It is necessary to admit that before eventually being lifted to unveil, a veil *veils.* The Nothing obfuscates Being more than it stages it; it masks the "phenomenon of Being" before leading one to it; its indistinction, which keeps silent, cannot, as such, open upon the least other—and even less name it as Being. In this sense the Postscript (and with it the whole) closes with the announcement of an aporia that has not yet been traversed: of Being, the phenomenon remains yet to come.

(2) The gap, which opens like a silent abyss between Nothing and Being, is betrayed even more clearly in the incoherence of a second sequence: "Alone among all beings, man, called by the voice of Being, experiences the wonder of all wonders: *that* being *is.*"[56] The fact, or rather the givenness *that* being is here passes beyond being itself, as its Being; man, alone among beings, would reach Being through his transcendence of beings, to the point of seeing the visible among visibles, the wonder of the "phenomenon of Being"; it alone accomplishes that transcendence, because it hears the call of the voice of Being ("... *angerufen* von der Stimme des Seins"). Here arises the difficulty: For where is the man who passes beyond beings in response to the call and to the voice of Being? In the state of anxiety, as the immediately preceding sentence stresses: "Being ready for anxiety is the *yes* (given) to the instance of fulfilling the highest claim [*Anspruch*], by which alone the essence of man is touched."[57] But anxiety "leaves one speechless" (*Sprachlosigkeit*) at the very moment when the Nothing, by setting all in equivalence (*Gleichgültigkeit*), annuls any call and any decision. How, then, could any call still resound in the state of anxiety? Do not anxiety and the Nothing, by suspending, respectively, speech and distinction, immediately and necessarily bracket the very possibility of the claim (*An-spruch*)—of the least speech (*Sprache*) of a differentiating (*An-*) call? Even supposing that the least claim might still resound in the state of anxiety, the aporia would remain; for how can one determine that that claim indeed issues from Being? The interpretative difficulty of these two texts thus attests to the difficulty of interpreting, at the end of the existential analysis of anxiety, the Nothing then reached as Being.

Moreover, even in the Postscript, Heidegger seems to admit the irremediable gap between them, precisely by trying so hard to reduce it: "But this too [*sc.*, the privation of Being, *Seinslosigkeit*], as an abandonment of Being, is not in its turn a nugatory Nothing [*nichtiges Nichts*], since it belongs to the truth of Being that Being never 'sists' [*siste*] without beings, that beings never are without Being." This declaration gives rise to three comments. First, Heidegger fully well envisages the hypothesis that the Nothing would not open upon Being, remaining a "nugatory Nothing," definitively imprisoned by the "privation of Being," prohibiting every interpretation and call. Next, Heidegger sets this hypothesis aside only by relying on the reciprocal and indissoluble belonging of Being and beings: never (*nie, niemals*) the one without the other; but in a state of "essential anxiety," when Being remains a "not yet developed essence,"[58] that reciprocal belonging remains, precisely, concealed, and it steals away from any phenomenal attestation. The argument therefore presupposes what is necessary to establish, but it does not allow one to reach it: from the point of view of the fold between beings and Being, "essential anxiety" certainly does not amount to a "nugatory Nothing"— but from the foundation of "essential anxiety" the Nothing still does not open upon any Being of beings; now, we other phenomenologists (to talk like Husserl) still remain, here, in "essential anxiety" and its Nothing, with neither doors nor windows. In 1949, Heidegger finally corrected his text from 1943: the unequal relation between Being and beings—"that Being indeed [*wohl*] 'sists' [*siste*] without beings, that on the contrary beings never [*niemals aber*] are without Being"—becomes an equal and reversible relation: "that Being never [*nie*] 'sists' [*siste*] without beings, that beings never are without Being."[59] What is this modification trying to do? Obviously to reinforce the tie between Being and beings, in passing from a subordination to a reciprocal implication; obviously also, this reinforcement claims to make up for an insufficiency—that of the interpretation of the nothing (of beings) as Being itself. These references suffice to establish the first conclusion: an interpretation is, as such, required in order to reach Being starting from the Nothing, which could, otherwise, constitute the last phenomenon.

The second point therefore becomes unavoidable: According to what guiding thread must the interpretation of the Nothing as Being be developed? But what instance could carry that interpretation out, since, in the state of anxiety, nothing any longer intervenes or claims (*spricht nicht mehr an*)? Thus, Heidegger introduces, in the Postscript, a new instance, which provides a guiding thread for interpreting the Nothing as Being: the *Anspruch des Seins*. Not known in 1929,[60] it alone can pull the lecture out of its aporia. The claim exerted by Being over *Dasein* must here accomplish what the faltering claim of beings fails to do: to unveil the Nothing as Being; since the call of beings is lost, it is necessary, as a last appeal, to take recourse to the call of Being. Since the transition remains unfeasible starting from the Nothing and from beings, it is necessary to attempt it starting from the ultimate term, Being itself; the gap between the Nothing and Being could thus be traversed only starting from its far end, Being, and not at all starting from its proximate beginning, the Nothing; the traverse begins at the end—the call from afar, Being—and not at its beginning—the proximate Nothing, where we are. The addition, which alone allows the transition, is carried out precisely starting from its most unknown term: *Dasein* no longer passes from itself to Being as a phenomenon so much as it suffers the insistent summons of a phenomenon that it has not yet seen or known; and, consequently, since the claim of Being alone allows one to experience Being, the existential analysis of anxiety henceforth becomes at the very least insufficient, or even superfluous, for manifesting the "phenomenon of Being." In a word, the passage from the Nothing to Being arises from Being, and in no way from the Nothing or from beings; only Being can call one to Being. The texts indicate this unambiguously. (1) " . . . the voice of Being [*die Stimme des Seins*] . . . which takes man in his essence into the claim [*in den Anspruch nimmt*] in order that he learn to experience Being in the Nothing"; the experience of Being, even in the Nothing, does not result from an existential analysis of the one in anxiety, nor from a hermeneutic of the phenomenon of the Nothing, but, in a complete break, from the irruption of Being itself, whose "voice" summons man directly. (2) "The thinking whose thoughts not only do not calculate but are absolutely determined by the other of beings, is called essential thinking. Instead of calculating with regard to beings and with the help of beings, it expends itself in Being for the truth of Being. This thinking responds to the claim of Being [*antwortet dem Anspruch des Seins*] inasmuch as man gives over in response [*überantwortet*] his historial essence to the simplicity of the unique necessity that does not necessitate by constraining, but creates the urgency that is consummated in the freedom of sacrifice." With an admirable clarity, the claim is displayed: the one who claims is indeed Being, the claim bears on the (noncalculating) thinking of man; far from man claiming Being on the basis of anxiety or of the Nothing, it is Being that claims man on the basis of Being; this reversal is indicated by the thematization of a response to Being required of man: to hand-over-in-response (*überantworten*) his essence to the simple, as a sacrifice responding to the prior favor of Being. (3) "Sacrifice is rooted in the essence of the event [*Ereignis*] through which Being claims [*in den Anspruch nimmt*] man for the truth of Being." What here appears remarkable is the intervention of the *Ereignis* to accomplish the claim of Being; moreover, Heidegger comments in 1949 on the 1943 sequence, " . . . Being claims [*in den Anspruch nimmt*]": "*er-eignet, braucht,* to appropriate, to use";[61] thus the call of Being befalls man through the *Ereignis* itself, namely, the last name of

Being, or even the name of what, for Heidegger, comes after Being. With the intervention of the *Ereignis*, the center of gravity shifts: the existential analytic, which claimed to go from beings back to Being, decidedly yields to the event of Being, which alone initiates its phenomenon—if there still is a phenomenon when the "there is" appears. The sole guiding thread for the interpretation of the Nothing as Being issues directly from Being, demands a response before Being, and is accomplished in the *Ereignis*. The passage to Being depends solely on the Being that claims. In the final instance, it is not a matter of Being but of the claim that it exerts and thanks to which it befalls man; or, if one refuses to separate Being abstractly from its claim, one would have to say that in the final instance Being intervenes as claim. In every case, only attention to the claim opens the phenomenality of Being; or better: opens phenomenality to Being (phenomenality)—according to the double meaning of the expression [i.e., of *ouvre la phénoménalité à l'être*—TRANS.]. Being expresses itself only by claiming, and it therefore gives itself only to a response. To hear that claim as that of Being, to give it a response according to the measure of Being, would therefore decide, finally, the "phenomenon of Being."

5. Boredom of the Depths

We thus end up at the most violent, but least avoidable, question: Supported from here on by the *Ereignis* that claims in the name of Being, does the interpretation of the Nothing as Being finally manage to stage the "phenomenon of Being"?

We should doubt so for several strictly phenomenological reasons.

1. While it is supposed to speak directly, Being nevertheless never states anything, like the Nothing, nor does it ever speak except with a "soundless voice";[62] with that blank voice, can Being still claim otherwise than with blanks, can it still identify the unique one, can it, in short, show what is speaking? If one retorts that such a silence precisely designates Being itself, beyond any ontic specification, it remains to be discerned how the supposedly ontological silence is distinguished from simply ontic silence; for the Nothing, the other of beings, does not yet speak directly in the name of Being. Does that blank voice that claims claim starting from and with a view to Being? In what way does it bear the seal of Being rather than that of the lack of beings?

2. This question seems all the more legitimate insofar as in 1927 *Sein und Zeit* had already analyzed a call (*Ruf*)—that which conscience issues to *Dasein*; but precisely that call, far from calling to and in the

name of Being, referred only to nothing, or even the Nothing: "What does conscience call to the one called [*Angerufenen*]? Strictly speaking— nothing. The call states nothing, gives no information concerning events, has nothing to recount." In allowing itself to be called and claimed by that call, *Dasein* hears, strictly speaking, nothing, since it finds itself called only to itself: "*Dasein* is both the one who calls and the one called."[63] Far from the call of conscience leading *Dasein* from the Nothing to Being, it blocks it in pure indetermination. *Sein und Zeit* seems to agree, moreover, concluding that analysis as it does by admitting that "the *ontological meaning of the notness* [*Nichtheit*] of this existential nullity [*Nichtigkeit*] is still obscure."[64] A claim can indeed still remain anonymous in 1929 and 1943, since a call had in fact already done so in 1927.

3. Even supposing that this silent call suffers no ambiguity and properly says what is proper to Being, the claim would nevertheless not be accomplished. The Postscript in effect insists on this: to the claim there must respond a response, to the "favor of Being [*Gunst des Seins*]" there must respond, "in echo," the "sacrifice [*Opfer*] in which there occurs the concealed gratitude [*verborgene Dank*]" of thought. Consequently, there where the claim of Being silently resounds, and precisely because it is a matter of offering a sign of gratitude "which no necessity requires," the response can be lacking. In fact, in 1941, Heidegger explicitly evoked this hypothesis: "There are claims [*Ansprüche*] that claim man in his essence and that need and desire [*verlangen*] his response." Thus the initial (Greece): "a claim [*Anspruch*] issues therefrom to which the opinion of the individual as well as of the masses is condemned to remaining deaf. . . . We can remain deaf to the call [*Anspruch*] of the initial. . . . In fact, we can not only remain deaf to the call of the initial [*Anspruch des Anfänglichen*], but even lull ourselves with the illusion that it would not be hard to lend our ear to it since we already have a 'knowledge' of it." In face of a claim, and especially that of Being, it is a matter first of a "choice," even before the response: "Only meditation and inner choice [*innere Wahl*] save [*rettet*] us here: do we want to be exposed to the claim of the essential [*Anspruch des Wesenhaften*] in us, or not?"[65] If, therefore, the claim offers a true question and opens a true choice, it essentially includes the possibility of deaf and abrupt refusal; if *Dasein* does not have ears to hear, then Being itself will not be able to make itself audible, nor its "phenomenon" manifest.

4. Not only does this impossibility threaten the Postscript in its attempt to lift the aporias of the lecture, but the Postscript itself seems to succumb to them. In effect it minimizes the primacy of gratitude (*Danken*) over thought (*Denken*); in at least one case, the corrections from 1949, contrary to the text from 1943, subordinate gratitude to thought: "The

response of thought [1943: the silent response of gratitude in sacrifice] is the origin of the human word. . . . If a thought [*Denken*; 1943: *Danken*] were not so well hidden in the essential foundation of historial man, then it would never be capable of gratitude [*Danken*; 1943: *Denken*], supposing that in any thinking about something [*Bedenken*] and in any giving thanks [*Bedanken*; 1943: *Andenken*] there must be a thought that originally thinks the truth of Being."[66] There is little importance, in fact, in the motives for these corrections, which could simply appear as so many of Heidegger's misinterpretations of himself. All that matters is that he himself did not always do full justice to gratitude (*Danken*), whose unconditional anteriority alone was supposed to respond fittingly to the claim of Being.

If Being makes itself accessible only through the claim that it exerts, if that claim can demand a response only by exposing itself to a deaf denial of "gratitude," then the ontological hermeneutic of the Nothing *can* fail, since in order to be carried out it *must* be able to fail. We already know about beings that, in anxiety, they no longer either say anything (to us) or make any claim ("Das Seiende spricht nicht mehr an"). Henceforth there arises the possibility that Being itself no longer make a claim (upon us) except in vain, since it also could no longer say anything (to us). This situation must be envisaged phenomenologically as the setting into operation of a new existential of *Dasein*; or rather, it is a question here of a counterexistential, which suspends the destining of *Dasein* to Being by giving to it the possibility of refusing the call that is nevertheless heard. Above all, more than of a new moment in the existential analytic, it is a matter here of an overall suspension of its possibility: the Nothing to which *Dasein* ultimately gains access can not lead *Dasein* to Being itself, such that this *Dasein* is uncovered there, but not necessarily for and by Being, but as for and by a more originary indistinction than any ontic indetermination: indecision in face of "anticipatory resoluteness" itself ensues from the indecision of Being to give itself immediately in a phenomenon. In other words: Does the blank voice with which Being makes a claim make that claim in the name of Being, or, through its indistinct silence, could it not allow to appear a new abyss that is anterior, or at least irreducible, to Being?

Such a possibility will find an authentic phenomenological legitimacy only if we can manifestly produce this counterexistential. We suggest recognizing it as boredom: Heidegger had invoked it, cursorily, in order to make beings as a whole accessible, *before* taking recourse to anxiety in order to reach the Nothing. In spite of this essential role, he nevertheless confined it within the limits of a strictly ontological function: precisely, to set *Dasein* in face of the whole of beings; the long and remarkable expositions dedicated to it in the course given a few months after the 1929 lecture do not remove these limits: it is a matter of liberating *Dasein* with a view to confronting it with the world as such,[67] and therefore still and only of progressing toward the "phenomenon of Being." But is boredom limited to the ancillary function of freeing us from a being, in order to put us face to face with beings as a whole? Could not boredom also—or even first—intervene in order to free us from the call through which Being claims us? Contrary to Heidegger, but in accordance with the things themselves, could boredom not repeat ontologically, and with an incommensurably greater power, what it already effects ontically according to Heidegger and in accordance with the things themselves? In short, in its most formidable exercise, does boredom not manage to place *Dasein* in a situation where Being, and not only beings, no longer says anything (to us)—where *das Sein*, and therefore *der Anspruch des Seins, spricht nicht mehr an*? That boredom might make us disinterested with regard to the claim of Being over us, that it might render us deaf to its call and thankless for its grace, is what we must now, in outline, show.

Another boredom, or a boredom liberated from its ancillary condition, can indeed come to light, a mood even more fundamental than the "fundamental mood" of anxiety, a boredom of the depths even more disarming than "profound boredom." One need only go back to Pascal to see it appear: "Man's condition. Inconstancy, boredom, restlessness," "man is so unhappy that he would be bored even if he had no cause for boredom, by the very nature of his temperament." Boredom does not, among other fundamental moods, affect man; it originarily determines his worldly condition; man is bored in the very measure that he is, or rather that he endures his condition as a being; just as no other being apprehends itself purely as a being, likewise no being must or can confront its beingness according to the distance of boredom; *divertissement* engenders the inconstancy of distractions in order to mask the restlessness of the being that knows itself to be a being—or rather of the being that, precisely because it knows itself to be a being, can distance itself from its condition—disqualify itself from being as that being. The "condition" coincides fairly closely here with facticity: "man," according to Pascal, finds himself already here and there imprisoned by that fact that has already made him what he is, like *Dasein*. But no doubt contrary to *Dasein*, which ever oscillates only between the two postulations of its mode of being a distinctive being (namely, authenticity or inauthenticity), "man" directly recognizes it as his "condition" to keep his distance from everything in the world that will ever be able to determine him as the being that, nevertheless, he alone purely is. "Man" inhabits, by the fact of boredom, the divergence from himself that is created by the distance of his beingness. Thus arises the final power of boredom: "without the hunger for spiritual things, one becomes bored."[68] Between "spiritual things," that is to say the imperceptible, the incalculable, and the invisible (hence the only real thing), and "man" it opens a distance that is uncrossable, at least if some "hunger" does not provoke the desire to traverse it. Pascal therefore thinks here, at least by allusion, the necessity of an end, and therefore the possibility of a disgust not toward what inspires and merits disgust but, precisely, toward what should provoke desire—"the spiritual realities" themselves. Nothing, not even the beatitude of justice, nor anyone (since even "Jesus [finds himself] in boredom")[69] escapes the disgust provoked by boredom.

Before pursuing the determination of such a boredom of the depths, one must be careful not to misunderstand it. It is not to be confused with nihilism, whose "for what?" exerts itself over "values" and with a view to giving rise to "new values"; but "values" always name beings, interpreted in their very essence through the will to power; the latter disqualifies some as unavowed ("will to truth"), unavowable (the "other world"), or condemnable ("twilight of the idols"), only in order to affirm others and, finally, establish the unity of Being with becoming. In the end, nihilism affirms, or even has a great love for, the world such as it *is*; it greets being in its totality with a "great Amen." But boredom does not evaluate, does not affirm, does not love. Nor can it be confused with negation. First because negation always presupposes, even within its apparently most adventurous advances, predication and therefore, at least as a copula, Being, and therefore, at least as a substratum, substance. Next because negation, even though "it always denies," thus avows a passion, a desire, an interest: the elimination of beings remains for it a "hunger" that feeds on itself, from which it does not cease to be reborn as from a fire. Negation, moreover, always supposes an other, whose human or quasihuman face tears from it at least the recognition of a denial of justice: even murder betrays an avowal of alterity, which it contradicts through a putting to death only by honoring it still as an interpellation. Boredom does not deny because it is not reached by any antagonist, by any combat, by any other. Boredom, finally, cannot be confused with anxiety, since in anxiety it falls to beings to be lacking; indeed, when *Dasein* is in anxiety, all beings slip into indeterminacy, such that there return, like a trap closes, beings in their mass, beings in their absent totality, and therefore the Nothing in its authority. But in boredom, beings do not lack by slipping into the indeterminate, since on the contrary beings do not cease to arise in all their brilliance, to offer themselves to distraction, to surround restlessness, in short, to live it up; the lack comes from the one who is bored, since he takes his distance from beings, flees their assiduity, never takes up their invitations, in short, is absent in the very heart of the presence bound by facticity. In this way boredom distinguishes itself just as much from nihilism and negation as from anxiety: it does not value, nor depreciate; it does not fight, nor predicate; it does not lack beings, nor suffer the assault of the Nothing.

How, then, does the power of boredom exert itself? Do we not end up at an impasse, where nothing happens, not even the Nothing? To be sure, boredom leads us to an impasse; but it is precisely in that very aporia that boredom holds sway. Boredom leaves beings in place, without denying them, depreciating them, or suffering their absent assault. It leaves beings in place, without affecting them, above all without being affected by them; it peaceably and serenely abandons beings to themselves, as if nothing were the matter [*comme si de rien n'était*]. But that very abandonment defines it: considering the mute interpellation of beings, of the other, even of Being, it removes itself from them with an equally mute constancy; no wonder ever sets it into ecstasy; boredom defuses the explosion of any call, whatever it might be; it covers itself, refuses to expose itself, defuses the conflict by deserting the field. Absent to beings, to the other, even to Being, it is not there for anyone, to the point that in a sense the one who yields to boredom no longer is. He no longer is for what is, because he hates what is. Boredom hates—it even takes its French name from that hate: *ennui* comes from *est mihi in odio,* to me it is in hate, through the substantive *inodium,* which assimilates every object to the object of hate.[70] One obviously should not understand this hate as a passion or an intention, since, precisely, it suspends all passion and all intention. One should much rather understand it as a radical uninterest: the one who yields to boredom and henceforth proceeds from it hates (*est mihi in odio*) because nothing makes any difference for him (*nihil interest mihi*); indifference to things provokes their undifferentiation; nothing distinguishes them, since between them and the one who is bored there is nothing; there is nothing among them because there is nothing between them and whoever is bored. The suspension of the world does not manifest any Being-in-the-world but the dissolution of worldhood itself. The bracketing of worldly things does not reduce to the region of consciousness, but discovers that all consciousness absents itself. *I* desert, a desert rises over the things of the world.

Boredom therefore provokes a double undoing. (1) The *I* that is bored abandons itself to boredom, but above all it quite simply abandons itself. For in not letting itself ever be called, or rather in never letting itself respond, not even to a call that comes from itself with a view to itself alone, it abandons that through which it could still say "I"; it becomes impersonal: I no longer am, *I* is, who regresses from the level of actor to that of a spectator disengaged from a rejected world. The *I* that abandons itself in boredom cannot and does not want to hear the least call; paralyzed by a boredom that is insurmountable because without reason or motive, it can yield to no request, nor offer prayer, " . . . *nullo accedente extrinsecus provocatione.*"[71] In this silence of every interpellation, the impersonal *I* allows to be lost even its own inscription in being: "I perceived my existence only through a profound feeling of boredom."[72] In short, boredom relieves the *I* of its character as a being in whose Being Being in general is an issue. (2) Boredom, engulfing first and foremost the *I*, dissolves also the things, the beings of the world. Not that it destroys them, since it leaves them to themselves; but precisely, it leaves them because it abandons them; in neither hearing them nor calling them, it abandons and deserts them; it deprives them of their whole denomination as beings by ceasing from its function of being the being in whose Being the Being of all other beings is an issue. No doubt, beings still are before the *I*, but henceforth "everything exists in vain before it, it lives alone, it is absent within all the living world."[73] Bereft of the *I* in charge of their Being, beings remain, to be sure, but silently struck with vanity: nothing changes, nothing moves, nothing disappears, but all is as if it were not. The bored *I* abandons beings as if nothing were the matter [*comme si de rien n'était*]. *As if nothing were the matter*—a wonderful phrase, which places beings in equivalence with the Nothing, to which they nevertheless do not in fact return, by virtue of the strange power of the "as if": the world indeed keeps its beingness, its splendor, and all its prestiges; but it is as if it were not. From where does the "as if" draw its power to undo what it nevertheless does not destroy? From where does there rise the indistinct and sticky cloud that dismisses without killing, that leaves intact in annulling? From boredom alone.[74]

If boredom deploys a power such that boredom hates what is, if it makes the *I* abandon itself, and if it strikes beings with vanity, would it not in principle disqualify *every* call? But then why would the claim of Being form an exception? But if the claim of Being finally allows only a hermeneutic of the Nothing as Being, does not the disqualification of every call prohibit one from reaching Being from the Nothing? Does boredom not therefore obfuscate the "phenomenon of Being" that anxiety claimed to uncover?

6. The Third Reduction

Boredom suspends the claim that Being exerts over *Dasein*. In other words, if *Dasein* is defined as *Dasein* by its openness to (and by the fact of) Being, and therefore because it "stands ecstatically into the truth of Being,"[75] if boredom provokes the desertion of the *I* in opposition to all that is precisely because it hates all that is, one must therefore conclude first that the *I* can elude the destiny of *Dasein*, and next that it can suspend every claim, hence also and above all that of Being. Such conclusions could not fail to give rise to some reservations, inasmuch as they contradict the explicit intention of the Heideggerian enterprise. But the fact of advancing such a contradiction, however, does not suffice to disqualify it; in principle, only a strictly phenomenological objection would seem acceptable, an objection that would ask whether the renewed analysis of boredom can affect the claim of Being in the same way as any other claim concerning a being. In short, does boredom suspend ontologically like it disqualifies ontically? Legitimizing phenomenologically the application of boredom to the claim of Being requires the establishment of two theses: (1) that Being offers itself to phenomenality in such a way that the fundamental mood of boredom might apply to it as such; (2) that *Dasein* might endure the affective mood of boredom precisely inasmuch as it is the being that is characterized ontologically, that is, that *Dasein* might find itself affected ontologically and not only ontically. It therefore remains to establish these two theses if we intend to make manifest the possibility of a suspension of Being.

Is Being exposed to boredom? A formal, and therefore radical, response could suffice: if Being makes a claim, its claim is exposed, like every other claim, to the indifference of the boredom that deserts. But a second, more precise response comes to complete the first; for Being itself offers itself to boredom for an essential ontological reason: it provokes and demands wonder. Indeed, in defining "the wonder of wonders *that* being is," Heidegger repeats something instituted by Aristotle, but above all by Plato: μάλα γὰρ φιλοσόφου τουτο τὸ πάθος, τὸ θαυμάζειν·οὐ γὰρ ἄλλη ἀρχὴ φιλοσοφίας ἢ αὕτη[76]—the *I* does not even reach the question that asks "what is that?" unless it is subjected to the affection (πάθος) of astoundment. Indeed, the question bearing on what is could not be posed, and therefore the *that which* or the *that* could not appear as worthy of question, if wonder did not assure them an open attention; it matters little whether that wonder precedes the question or results from it, provided that one recognize that the *that* or the *that which* of being occurs only in the affective mood of astounded amazement. This wonder, to be sure, presides over the encounter with the being to be objectified; thus, for Descartes: "When our first encounter with some object surprises us and we find it novel . . . this causes us to wonder and to be astonished at it. Since all this may happen before we know whether or not the object is beneficial to us, I regard wonder as the first of all the passions."[77]

But it presides as well over the arrival of Being as claim: "Alone among all beings, man, claimed by the voice of Being [*angerufen von der Stimme des Seins*] experiences the wonder of wonders: *that* being is."[78] Here the wonder both demands and provokes a wonderment that is guaranteed, on another level, by the claiming call of Being; Being claims, through its call, the attention in order that the wonder of the fact of Being (of beings) receive the amazement that it deserves. The call of amazement fulfills one unique role—to grant *Dasein* to that which is destined to it and which, without amazement, could not manifest itself, the "phenomenon of Being." The transition of Being toward its own phenomenality requires that *Dasein* lend it attention, and therefore lend itself to what gives itself. In a strictly phenomenological sense, wonder becomes the condition of the unveiling of Being, precisely as the hearing of its claim; the claim on hearing is doubled by a claim on the attention. Consequently, boredom can exert itself ontologically on the "phenomenon of Being" no longer for one but indeed for two reasons. First, as a desertion that hates what is, boredom can render *Dasein* deaf to the call through which Being claims it—a boredom of the ear, so to speak. Next, as a blindness that wants to see nothing, boredom can render *Dasein* indifferent to all wonders, even to the "wonder of wonders *that* being is"—a boredom of the eye, so to speak. Call and wonder are exposed to a double boredom that, by suspending them, suspends along with them what they make visible and audible, the "phenomenon of Being."

In what sense could *Dasein* exercise boredom as an ontological determination? This is a matter not only, as imagined by *An Introduction to Metaphysics*, of the hypothesis that "we might say no to our Being,"[79] but of the possibility that our *Dasein* itself might say no to its Being, in such a way as either to make itself the there for something other than that Being, or to eclipse any *there* in it. But what precisely would it mean for *Dasein* to refuse (itself to) its Being? Doesn't that possibility simply contradict the very definition of *Dasein* as Being-there, which it cannot not be? In evoking it don't we condemn ourselves to seeking a pure and simple chimera, phenomenologically nonattested and nonattestable? It could be, quite to the contrary, that one of the most essential characteristics of *Dasein* gives the means for thinking how that same *Dasein* could here, through boredom, refuse itself to its Being. Indeed, "Dasein is ontically distinctive in that it *is* ontological," which signifies that *Dasein* "is that being in whose Being that Being itself is an issue," or even that, in the mode of Being of existence, *Dasein* puts into play not only its ontic subsistence, but its way of Being, that is, the way of its Being; or even more, in that play it makes the way of its Being visible; in short, the play of *Dasein* with itself makes manifest the play of Being with itself. Now, this ontological dignity of the distinctive being *Dasein* offers two points where the exercise of boredom might be anchored.

On the one hand, *Dasein*'s characteristic way of Being—existence as possibility—implies resoluteness, and therefore also "a possibility of itself: to be itself or not itself";[80] now, since it is this whole alternative that defines possibility, inauthenticity defines *Dasein* just as essentially as authenticity. But as soon as being oneself is equivalent to the putting into play of Being in one's Being, doesn't the possibility of not being oneself amount to revoking the call of Being itself? Without undertaking here—as it might be tempting to do—to celebrate inauthenticity, mustn't we envisage the possibility that it designates another essential relation to Being—the refusal not only to put it into play in one's existence, but above all to put oneself into play solely for what is at stake in Being? Inauthenticity does not, to be sure, negate the instance of *Dasein*, since it still exemplifies it; but it does already suspend *Dasein*'s essential characteristic: it denies that the reference to Being itself constitutes the final possibility of what I am. Inauthenticity is not interested in its being put into play in the play of Being; it thus claims to play a game that owes nothing to Being, or, if that game still has to do with Being, inauthenticity acts *as if* Being played no part in it. Carefully undecided everydayness steals away from its destiny as *Dasein* and hence through a busy and *bon vivant* boredom removes *Dasein* from its essence as that being in whose Being that Being is an issue.

On the other hand, as an existence in which this being puts itself at stake in its Being, *Dasein*'s way of Being implies that "in each case it has its Being to be, and has it as its own."[81] *Dasein* is not simply what it is; it falls to *Dasein* as a distinctive character of its way of Being to have to be (*zu sein hat*); it is itself only in claiming that the Being at stake is its own, only in taking upon and for itself the Being that is at play, only in lending itself, and therefore in giving itself to the game whose stakes are Being; the *I* plays truly as *Dasein* only in associating in person with Being, in making it its own without remainder, or rather in abandoning itself without reserve to its game. Moreover, without this condition, the enterprise of reading (*ablesen*) Being on the surface of the play of this being would immediately become impossible; *Dasein* renders its Being manifest, and in that Being Being itself, only by presupposing that in its ownmost game, it immediately plays that of Being. Now, such a duty to be (or such a having to be Being as one's own) marks a second weak link in the chain, which must tie back to the "phenomenon of Being": the existential analytic can be deployed as the phenomenology of Being only if *Dasein* receives in its innermost liturgy and as a surtax on it the ontological cosmogony; it can do so only by assuming the destiny of Being as that of its Being, and hence finally as its own as a being. Here precisely the point of rupture appears. For if *Dasein* has to be its Being, instead of being it through obscure and factual necessity, it can also very well not be it—in this precise sense, it can not play the Being of beings as its own Being, or rather as its ownmost affair; because it is in the privileged mode of having to be, *Dasein* can not take as its ownmost the Being that it would have to be. Boredom can then intervene: boredom, which hates what is and hence also Being, by exerting itself at the heart of *Dasein*, turns it away from the obligation of having to be the Being of beings; it weighs on the joint where *Dasein* is articulated with Being; it attacks the fold where being is subjected to Being, that is, *Dasein* itself. But this time, boredom could work in the name of and in favor of authenticity; for in separating *Dasein* from the Being that it has to be, boredom tends only to free it so that it might devote itself to a more essential property—in order to let it eventually establish itself as (the) *there* for another instance than the Being of beings. Thus, in suspending the claim by Being over *Dasein*, boredom would not only be inscribed strictly within the moments of the existential analytic, but above all it would re-open the entire case of *Dasein*, by insinuating the possibility that another, more proper precisely insofar as removed from the claim of Being, would maintain the *there*, or better maintain itself there.

The one who does not have to be—because boredom frees it from responding to the claim of Being as to its own proper stake—nevertheless does not break totally with *Dasein*. It attempts to succeed *Dasein* in the possession, and therefore the identification of the *there*: For why does the *there*, which I am, stand there? When the *there* is defined as a *Dasein*, a *Being-there*, it stands *there* in order to be, and hence more essentially for Being; indeed, Being claims it, and the claim of Being destines the *there* to (being there for) that Being, to standing there inasmuch as *Being-there*. If boredom liberates the *there* from the call of Being, it sets it free only in order better to expose it to the wind of every other possible call; thus, the liberated *there* is exposed to the nonontological possibility of another claim, which would qualify it to stand there in favor of another— of another favor. That the claim might exert itself under another name than that of Being, in the name of an other than Being, Heidegger, moreover, admitted, by opposing to the *Anspruch des Seins* the *Anspruch des Vaters*: "The Christian sees the humanity of man, the *humanitas* of the *homo*, in contradistinction to *Deitas*. He is the man of the history of redemption who as a 'child of God' hears and accepts the claim of the Father in Christ."[82] Quite obviously, Heidegger rejects the priority of this other call over the *Anspruch des Seins*; but by that very fact he admits its possibility (if not its legitimacy). We might add that E. Lévinas will not fail to take up a call related to the one that Heidegger disqualifies: the "*in face* of the face in its expression—in its mortality—assigns me, demands me, claims me"; even more, from now on "the wonder of wonders" no longer issues from the fact that being is, and hence from the claim of Being, but rather from "the wonder of the self [*moi*] claimed by God in the face of the neighbor."[83] If it is important to maintain the difference between these two calls (one Christian, the other Jewish), it is even more important to hear in them the unique word from which they both issue: "Listen, Israel, Jahweh our God, Jahweh alone" (Deuteronomy 6:4). It is obviously not a question here of invoking revealed authority in order to broaden the field of phenomenology, but of confirming that another call—no doubt the call of the other—might dismiss or submerge the first call issued by the claim of Being. In fact, the call that demands "Listen!" does not pronounce *one* call among other possibilities to the benefit of a particular authority so much as it performs *the* call as such—the call to render oneself to the call itself, with the sole intention of holding to it by exposing oneself to it. The call itself intervenes as such, without or before any other "message" than to surprise the one who hears it, to grab even the one who does not expect it. The model of the call exerts itself before the simple claim of Being, and more fully. Before Being has claimed, the call as pure call claims. Such a transgression of the claim of Being and of *Dasein*, supposing that it might be accomplished, raises above all a question of principle: Does it still lead to an authentically phenomenological situation or does it not rather renounce the elementary requirements of a "strict science"? A fundamental principle allows for a response: the transgression of the claim of Being by the pure form of the call belongs to the phenomenological field for precisely the same reason that would allow the *Dasein*-analytic to replace the constitution of the transcendental *I*: the Husserlian "breakthrough" and the Heideggerian "new beginning" alike proceed according to the reduction, in two figures that are different, to be sure, but equally phenomenological.[84] Now, the reconduction of the claim of Being back to the pure form of the call, which, moreover, alone renders it possible, again repeats the reduction: more essential than the reduction of objects to the consciousness of an *I*, there intervened their reduction to the rank of beings, and hence the reduction of beings to *Dasein* as the sole ontological being; even more essential again, there was affirmed the reduction of all beings to Being, which claimed the putting into play of *Dasein*; more essential, in the end, than this (reduction by the) claim there finally appeared the reduction of every claim to the pure form of the call. After the transcendental reduction and the existential reduction there intervenes the reduction to and of this call. That which gives itself gives itself only to the one who gives himself over to the call and only in the pure form of a confirmation of the call, which is repeated because received. The claim of Being itself can call only in putting on this pure form—which Heidegger, however, persists in silencing. The transcendental reduction could not give any object to the *I* if the latter did not admit the givenness given to it as a perfect actuality—according to the "principle of all principles." The call thus appears as the originary scheme of the two previous reductions, precisely because it alone allows one to reconduct to . . . , in that it demands that one give oneself over to the deal [*donne*] of the call as such—to render oneself to the call in the double sense of abandoning oneself to it and of moving toward it. As a pure reduction—because a perfect reconduction to . . . —the call that claims for itself belongs eminently to the domain of phenomenology.

7. "There" Outside of Being

Boredom makes the call as such appear. In the pure form of the call a reduction is carried out: nothing manages to give itself as a phenomenon if a response does not give itself over to it as to an originary claim. Beings and the Being of beings constitute no exception: Being comes down to giving, and therefore requires that one give oneself over to it. In suspending the *Anspruch des Seins*, boredom confirms that the *Anspruch* precedes Being and alone renders it possible. The pure form of the call plays before any specification, even of Being. It would therefore remain to determine what, before or without Being, deploys the call: we will not decide here whether this claim requires immediate passage to another order or whether Being gives rise to the very conditions of its reception. It would already be enough to specify what, before or without *Dasein*, receives or rejects the call, or simply hears it. Neither constituting *I*, nor *Dasein*, who is—if, precisely, this one can still "be"—the one who gives oneself over to the call that gives?

The claim calls *me*. I have not even been able to say *I* before the claim has already hailed me, and therefore has taken and comprehended me, because it has summoned and named me as a *me*. Indeed, what can I answer to a claim, if not "Here I am [*Me voici*]! Speak!", such that I no longer have to speak (myself) in the name of *I*? The claim alone first speaks and therefore exempts me from the *I* and establishes me as a *me*. Contrary to appearances, it is not a matter here of repeating the classic critique of the empirical and objective *I/me* by and on behalf of the transcendental *I*, in the manner either of Kant or of the first Husserl and of Sartre; for the more it stigmatizes the transcendent *I* as objective (constituted, empirical), the more radically the objection (critical or phenomenological) reestablishes a transcendental *I*, which is not objectivated but objectivating, not constituted because constituting, safe from the reduction because reducing, free of transcendance because immanent to itself. Here, in a metaphysical system, the relativity of the empirical *I* underscores all the more the absolute priority of the constituting and, in this sense, autonomous *I*. On the contrary, when the claim—whatever it may be—interpellates *me*, the self [*moi*] that it imparts to *me* does not designate any transcendental, autarchic and unconditioned *I*, but refers back only to the interpellation itself. The trial of the *me* that I hear *myself* say [*que je* m'*entends dire*] offers no proof of any transcendental *I*; it entrusts me to a new name, which is improper because spoken beforehand from elsewhere, in assigning me to the claim. This pole of reference of the (I/) *me* neither returns nor refers to any ulterior-*I* of the world beyond—invisible because always already there, the unique pole of a by definition determinate phenomenological horizon; it designates an inconceivable, unnameable, and unforeseeable instance which is comprehended less than it surprises, namely the claim itself. No doubt, when I hear *myself* interpellated, I experience *myself* interpellated; but *I* do not ever thus acquire the lived experience of the (empirical) *I* or of the (transcendental) *I*, but only of the (I/) *me*, and therefore only and always of a constituted (*me*); I experience *myself* and oppose to the point of divorce the *I* to the *me*, or else abolish the first in the second, in order to refer it to the claim which, originarily, assigns the *I* as a *me*. Thus I experience—or: the I is experienced—as claimed, assigned, and convoked in the accusative, deprived of its right to the nominative that names every thing in the manner of an accused; interpellated in the accusative, dispossessed of the nominative by the appeal lodged against it, the *me* manifests phenomenally the absence of any *I*. Under the in this sense absolute hold of the claim, the *me* that it provokes attests to the relegation of any transcendental or constituting *I*.

We saw above that a similar analysis can be carried out concerning *Dasein*: before putting itself and in order to put itself into play in its Being according to the stakes of Being itself, *Dasein* must hear the *Anspruch des Seins* and render itself thereto. It thus exposes itself as the *there* offered to Being; but it appears also that such a *there* offers itself to Being only inasmuch as Being exerts a claim, such that the claim alone can give rise to a *there*, in order that Being might render itself thereto; the claim—more than Being—assigns *Dasein* to Being and, within this plan, convokes man to this *there* where Being takes position in him. In recognizing himself to be determined as a *Dasein*, man nevertheless does not admit depending on Being, but only on the claim that assigns him as a *there* for Being. In short, to read it literally, *Dasein* itself contradicts the strictly ontological definition of man by which Heidegger means to privilege it: for the *there* here precedes and always determines Being—*da sein*—and not at all the reverse. Indeed, the site must first expose itself to Being in order to give it to be seen as the stake of its own game; now, the opening of this exposed site results itself from a claim; that, with regard to *Dasein*, the claim issues from Being in order to return to it confirms rather that even Being accedes to a site (a *there*) only through the instance of a claim. *Dasein* exposes itself to Being so as to become its site only inasmuch as it renders itself to the call that convokes it—in the name of Being. The irreducibility of the claim to each of its specifications (Being, the other, the Father, etc.) establishes the legitimacy of *Dasein* only in requiring that one think it starting from the *there* in it, rather than from its *Being* (or from any other instance): it will be necessary to learn to read *Dasein* more as *Da(sein)* than as *(da)Sein*, as the *there* of Being more than as Being in its *there*; Being does not stand in *Dasein* like a master on his land, but like a wanderer received in the home of a host—because he claimed him. Such a precedence of the *there* forces one to think *Dasein* in its totality starting from the instance that claims it and therefore gives it to itself as a *there*; convoked by the call, instituted in the locative, the *there* renounces any other usage of the nominative than that of rendering itself in person to the convocation; but this nominative, reduced to appearing by name and nominatively, without default, to the audience, remains thoroughly determined by the call, since it serves only to respond thereto. Between the locative of *Da(sein)* and the accusative of the *me*, a similarity comes out on its own: the claim determines these two instances of the *I* in such a way that it must renounce any autarchy, and hence admit itself essentially altered.

Does the scale of this alteration—which affects the two principal figures of the phenomenological subject—authorize one still to speak even of a trace of the *I*? Does underscoring the privilege of the claim over Being and over beings lead finally to dissolving every interlocutor of the call? But precisely the question designates the response—namely, that the sought interlocutor is identical with the respondent to the question. We therefore name it as such the *interloqué* (*der Angesprochene*). It is defined by at least four traits.

1. The *interloqué* is characterized by the fact that it receives a convocation from the claim; it admits itself *interloqué* in the very measure that it does not steal away from the convocation; this assumed blow does not prejudge the response (adhesion or desertion) to come, but registers the fact of the claim. Consequently, in admitting the blow of the claim, the *interloqué* acknowledges first and definitively having renounced the autistic autarchy of an absolute subjectivity. This compulsion to alterity

(whatever it may be) precedes even any form of intentionality or of Being-in-the-world; indeed it disqualifies them. In classical terms, one will say that the derived and secondary category of relation, which in principle should not apply to the first category, substance, not only applies to it but subverts it; the *interloqué* discovers itself as a subject always already derived starting from a relation, a subject without subecti(vi)ty. Only the one convoked remains, the one *interloqué* by the claim.

2. The *interloqué* suffers a surprise. One should here understand surprise less as an amazement or an astonishment than as the antagonist of every ecstasy—as much that of intentionality as that of "anticipatory resoluteness"; for if ecstasy no doubt institutes the subject outside of itself, it never exteriorizes the subject except starting from the subject alone and in order to dispose it to return upon itself; such an ecstasy confirms the subject in its function as originary pole and even presupposes it in the excess of overcoming. On the contrary, surprise grabs hold of the *interloqué* starting from an absolutely foreign place and event, in such a way as to annul any pretension of a subject to constitute, reconstitute, or decide on what surprises it; surprise takes [*prend*] the *interloqué* in that it detaches [*déprend*] it from any subjecti(vi)ty, challenges [*s'en prend à*] any self-constituting polarity in it, and finally comprehends [*comprend*] it starting from and in an event that the *interloqué* itself does not in any way comprehend (comprehending indeed supposes a taking possession, which simple knowledge does not impose). Literally, surprise prohibits the *interloqué* from comprehending the convocation that it nevertheless receives.

3. The *interloqué*, deposed from any autarchy and taken by surprise, nevertheless does not dissolve in indifference, nor disappear in indistinction: as much as an accusative *me* as a (locative) *there*, it works, in the vocative, to respond to the vocation that the convocation silently expresses: "Listen!" Consequently, precisely because it renounces exercising (itself as) an *I* only by virtue of a convocation that surprises it, the *interloqué* can be identified with itself all the more insofar as another—the claim—provokes it to decide. "Mineness"—the characteristic according to which I am at issue, in person and without any possible substitution—can then be accomplished without self-determination or "anticipatory resoluteness," provided that a claim imposes a choice on me; or better: that a claim poses *me* as the *there* where one might recognize oneself. The proper name can be proclaimed only when called—by the call of the other. In short, the claim does not destroy the irreducible identity-with-self by dismissing any *I* in me, but, inversely, underscores it and provokes it.

4. The *interloqué* must finally be understood on the basis of what ancient juridical language defined as an interlocutory judgment: "To order that a thing be proved or verified before one gives a final decision

on the case."[85] For the *interloqué* finds itself exposed to an interlocutory judgment: before any question of principle (concerning what it is, concerning its transcendental subjectivity and concerning what it constitutes, etc.), it is necessary to answer a question of fact: What claim originarily surprises it? The fact of that claim, in the paradoxical manner of an a priori that is essentially after the fact, decides the horizon where any theory of the *interloqué* will become legitimately thinkable. A facticity therefore precedes the theory, but it is no longer a matter of my facticity as *Dasein*; it is a matter of the absolutely other and antecedent facticity of the claim convoking me by surprise.

Thus, the four characteristics of the claim—convocation, surprise, identification, and facticity—institute the *interloqué* as such, without any other presupposition than the pure form of the call. The call that convokes suffices to give rise to the *interloqué*, which thus originates in the first passion, wonder.

However, the thesis of the priority of the *interloqué* draws an objection: Who or what claims the *interloqué*? To evoke here God, the other, self-affection, and all the figures of difference allows one only to name the difficulty, not to resolve it; for the *interloqué* would become in each case a derived, regional, and secondary phenomenon—a simple variation of the subject, taken in relation to an other and thus specified instance. This objection rests, however, on the illusory presupposition that it is necessary to name the instance that claims in order to suffer its convocation. Now, following the order of a strict phenomenological description, the reverse happens: I recognize myself as *interloqué* well *before* having consciousness or knowledge not only of my eventual subjectivity, but especially of what leaves me *interloqué*. The imprecision, the indecision, and indeed the confusion of the claiming instance attests much rather that in the beginning is found the pure form of the call, as such. The surprise surprises precisely because it surprises the one who knows neither its name nor its wish; I discover myself *interloqué* precisely because I know, in the instant of the claim, neither who nor what. In fact, the indetermination of the claiming instance alone renders possible a claim which otherwise would not surprise and which therefore would provoke no *interloqué*. This a priori exerts itself all the more insofar as it is not identified, since it consists only in its pure recognition by the *interloqué*. The claim itself is attested in the recognition by the *interloqué* that it incurs a claim. The *interloqué* itself decides the beginning—the poorest determination, and hence also the first. The autarchy of the subject discovers itself initially wounded by the fact that a call has already struck and undone it. Without knowing either by whom or by what, I know *myself* from the beginning already *interloqué*.

Conclusion:
The Figures of Givenness

"So much appearance, so much Being"—this thesis, common to Husserl and Heidegger, marks by its paradoxical equivalence the attainment peculiar to phenomenology: before any discrimination between illusion and reality, apparition intervenes as what, already, is (even if it is nothing more than that apparition). This thesis, however, presupposes yet another principle: apparition could reach the full status of phenomenon only inasmuch as appearing is sufficient for the accomplishment of Being. Apparition is sufficient for Being only inasmuch as, in appearing, it already perfectly *gives* itself; but it thus gives itself perfectly by the sole fact that it appears only inasmuch as it is *reduced* to its givenness for consciousness. Thus, givenness is deployed according to the direct measure of the reduction: the more the reduction is radicalized, the more givenness is deployed. Or rather, they progress in inverse proportion, for the reduction is radicalized in reducing (itself) to a point of reference that is all the more original and unconditioned insofar as it is more restricted, whereas the givenness that ensues is broadened to a field that is all the more vast insofar as it imposes fewer conditions. The more the reduction reduces (itself), the more it extends givenness. The less the reduction brackets what is in question, the less givenness will be able to render it accessible. The preceding rule—"so much appearance, so much Being"— is therefore doubled by a more essential statement: so much reduction, so much givenness.

In other words, the conditions of the reduction fix the dimensions of givenness. The more that that which or the one who reduces reduces radically, the more things give themselves amply to it or him. But likewise, that which or the one who reduces lets itself or himself be measured by the dimension of what gives itself and be identified with and by the identity of that givenness in such a way that the amplitude of what gives (itself) always

203

also anticipates the determination of that which or the one who reduces. Thus, the rule that ties reduction to givenness demands in each case that one designate, if only in outline, the constellation of (1) that which or the one who reduces—to which it is an issue of leading back the things in question (to whom?); (2) that which it is thus a matter, by reduction and reconduction, of giving as such (which given?); (3) the mode of that givenness, hence its horizon (given how?); (4) or, to formulate it by negation, that which that givenness excludes from givenness (how far?).

The investigations pursued previously allow one to reconstitute this constellation three times, and hence to establish three cases where reduction and givenness overlap with one another, in conformity with the four accepted criteria. The first reduction, which is transcendental ("Cartesian," "Kantian," "phenomenological," it matters little here), amounts to a constitution of objects. (1) It is deployed for the intentional and constituting *I*. (2) It gives to the *I* constituted objects (3) taken within regional ontologies which, through formal ontology, are in full conformity with the horizon of objectity. (4) It thus excludes from givenness everything that does not let itself be led back to objectity, namely the principial differences of ways of Being (of consciousness, of equipmentality, of the world).

The second reduction declares itself to be existential, in that it sets itself into operation through the existing being, or else ontological, in that it works the question of Being. (1) It reduces to *Dasein*, understood according to an intentionality that is broadened to Being-in-the-world, and led back through anxiety to its transcendence with regard to beings as a whole. (2) It gives (or claims to give) the different ways of Being, and hence the ontological difference in person, in short, the "phenomenon of Being"; (3) according to the horizon of time, and hence especially according to Being itself as original and ultimate phenomenon. (4) It excludes therefore that which does not have to be, in particular the preliminary conditions of the "phenomenon of Being" (boredom, claim, etc.).

The third reduction—our entire enterprise has tended toward nothing other than to render the recognition of it inevitable—properly speaking *is* not, because the call that exercises it nevertheless rigorously no longer issues from the horizon of Being (nor of objectity), but from the pure form of the call. (1) It reduces to the *interloqué*, by leading every *I* or even *Dasein* back to its pure and simple figure as an auditor preceded and instituted by the call which is still absolute because indeterminate. (2) It gives the gift itself: the gift of rendering oneself to *or* of eluding the claim of the call. (3) According to no other horizon than that of the absolutely unconditional call and of the absolutely unconstrained response. (4) The originary absence of conditions and determinations of the claim allow it to appeal, without any limit, as much to what is not objectivated as to what is objectivated, as much to what does not have to be as to what must be. The last reduction reduces to the *interloqué*, and hence gives all that can call and be called.

It remains to be understood precisely and conceptually how the pure fact of the call can allow the most strict reduction—hence immediately the most ample givenness, before and outside of objectity and the question of Being. But to think givenness as such—as originarily unconditional—it will be necessary to elaborate new and rigorous paradoxes.

Notes

Introduction: Phenomenology as Such

1. *Die Ziele und Aufg~be der Metaphysik*, 24 October, 1887, Halle (see K. Schuhmann, *Husserl-Chronik: Denk-und Lebensweg Edmund Husserls* [The Hague, 1977], 22).

2. *Ideen I*, § 62 *Hua*, III, 148 [Eng. trans., 142]. On these points see our foreword to *Phénoménologie et métaphysique*, ed. J.-L. Marion and G. Planty-Bonjour (Paris: Presses Universitaires de France, 1984), 7–14.

3. Heidegger, *Sein und Zeit*, § 83, 437, lines 37–41.

4. The distinction between *l'étant* and *l'être*, corresponding to the distinction between the German *Seiendes* and *Sein*, will be indicated throughout the translation by being or beings and Being, respectively.—TRANS.

5. Heidegger, *Sein und Zeit*, § 7, 38, lines 29–31.

1. The Breakthrough and the Broadening

1. *Logische Untersuchungen*, vol. 2, viii, see xiv [Eng. trans., vol. 1, 43; mod.] (from here on we will refer to this work according to the pagination and the volume numbering of the second edition of 1913, reprinted in 1968 [Tübingen; Niemeyer], since the excellent translation of H. Elie, A. L. Kelkel and R. Schérer [Paris; Presses Universitaires de France, 1961–64], keeps it in its margins). See: "Die *Logische Untersuchungen* als ein Durchbruchswerk," *Entwurf einer Vorrede zu den "Logische Untersuchungen"* (1913), published by E. Fink, in *Tijdschrift voor Philosophie* (1939), 127 [English translation, *Introduction to the Logical Investigations: A Draft of a Preface to The Logical Investigations* (1913), ed. Eugen Fink (The Hague; Martinus Nijhoff, 1975), 34] (with, however, some reservation concerning the completion of the break, 117, 124) [Eng. trans., 24, 32]. On this prefatory project, see K. Schuhmann, "Forschungsnotizen über Husserls 'Entwurf' einer 'Vorrede' zu den *Logischen Untersuchungen*," *Tijdschrift voor Filosofie* (1972). The expression reappears even in the *Krisis*, § 48, *Hua*, VI, 169, 169 n. 1 [Eng. trans., 166]. Heidegger maintains the expression, in 1925, during his presentation on the "fundamental discoveries of phenomenology," at the beginning of the *Prolegomena zur Geschichte des Zeitbegriffs*, GA, 20 (Frankfurt, 1979), 30, 103 [Eng. trans., 24, 75].

2. See, among others, R. Ingarden, "Bemerkungen zum Problem 'Idealismus-Realismus,' " *Jahrbuch für Philosophie und phänomenologische Forschung*,

Ergänzungsband (Halle, 1929), and *On the Motives Which Led Husserl to Transcendental Idealism* (The Hague, 1975) (Eng. translation of a Polish original, Warsaw, 1963).

3. Above all R. Schérer, *La phénoménologie des "Recherches logiques" de Husserl* (Paris: Presses Universitaires de France, 1967).

4. Heidegger, *Questions IV* (Paris, 1976), 315. See also the "Summary of a Seminar on the Lecture 'Time and Being,' " in *Zur Sache des Denkens* (Pfullingen, 1976), 47.

5. J. Derrida, *La voix et le phénomène* (Paris: Presses Universitaires de France, 1st edition 1967; 4th edition 1983) respectively, 57, 27 [Eng. trans., 51, 26] (see 8, 37, 111, 114ff.). On principle we will confine ourselves to this work, which is exemplary and decisive for the whole of Derrida's later itinerary.

6. *LU*, vol. 2, *Introduction*, § 3, 9, 11 [Eng. trans., vol. 1, 254, 256; mod.].

7. *Ibid.*, § 2, 5, 6 [Eng. trans., vol. 1, 251, 252]. See *LU*, V, § 8, 362, and § 12, 367.

8. *Phänomenologische Psychologie* (summer course, 1925), § 4, *Hua*, XI, 46–47 [see Eng. trans., 33–34]. See § 3: "More accurately speaking, the particular investigations of the second volume involved a return of the intuition [Rückwendung der Intuition] back toward the logical lived experiences that take place in us whenever we think, but which we absolutely do not see, which our gaze does not take into consideration, whenever we carry out the activity of thinking in the originally natural mode" (ibid., 20–21) [Eng. trans., 14; mod.].

9. *LU*, vol. 2, Introduction, § 2, 6 [Eng. trans., vol. 1, 252].

10. *LU*, II, § 23, vol. 2, 163 [Eng. trans., vol. 1, 384].

11. *Entwurf einer Vorrede*, 333; French translation, 399–400.

12. *Selbstanzeige* of the *LU*, published in *Vierteljahrsschrift für wissenschaftliche Philosophie* 25 (1901), 260, reprinted in *LU*, II, 2, *Hua*, XIX/2, ed. U. Panzer, 782 and translated by J. English, in *Articles sur la logique* (Paris: Presses Universitaires de France, 1975), 208–9.

13. *LU*, vol. 2, Introduction, § 7, 22 [Eng. trans., vol. 1, 266] and *LU*, VI, Appendix 2, vol. 3, 227 [Eng. trans., vol. 2, 856].

14. *Entwurf einer Vorrede*, 116, 131, then 117 [Eng. trans., 23, 39, 24; mod.]. In the same style, see 120, 334 [Eng. trans., 27, 55–56].

15. *Ideen I*, § 24, *Hua*, III, 52 [Eng. trans., 44; mod.] (see § 19, 44 and § 20, 46; § 78, 185; § 140, 347). To this *Rechtsquelle* corresponds, in 1901, "an adequate phenomenological justification [*eine . . . Rechtfertigung*], and therefore a replacement by evidence" (vol. 2, 22); in 1913, in the *Entwurf einer Vorrede*, "the right of what is seen clearly" "*dem klar Gesehen sein Recht lassen*" (117) [see Eng. trans., 24]; in 1936, in the *Krisis*, and precisely in order to underscore the novelty of the *Investigations*, "the right" that, "for the first time, the *cogitata qua cogitata*, as essential moments of each lived experience of consciousness" (§ 68, *Hua*, VI, 237) [Eng. trans., 234; mod.] be recognized.

16. *LU*, V, § 8, vol. 2, 362 [Eng. trans., vol. 2, 550; mod.]. See all of § 27, 438ff. [Eng. trans., vol. 2, 606ff.].

17. *LU*, vol. 2, Introduction, § 7, 19, 21 [Eng. trans., vol. 1, 263–64, 265].

Aristotle, *Second Analytics*, II, 19, 100b, pp. 10–11, 13–14 (see *Prolegomena*, § 66, *LU*, vol. 1, 242, which, as it were, cites Aristotle implicitly but literally).

18. *LU*, II, § 26, vol. 2, 173ff. [Eng. trans., 393].

19. Respectively, *Selbstanzeige* (*Hua*, XIX–12, 782, Fr. trans. *Articles*, 208) and the *Entwurf einer Vorrede*, 333 [see Eng. trans., 54].

20. *LU*, VI, Introduction, vol. 3, 5–6 [Eng. trans., vol. 2, 670; mod.], which moreover repeats the announcement of the Sixth Investigation made by the Second, § 26, vol. 2, 173–74. Husserl's italics.

21. Respectively, *LU*, VI, § 37, vol. 3, 120, and § 45, 142, 143 [Eng. trans., vol. 2, 763–64, 785; mod.]. See § 53, 165, " . . . broadening [*Erweiterung*] of the concept of Intuition" [Eng. trans., vol. 2, 803; mod.]; and § 66, which identifies, on the one hand, sensible intuition and intuition according to the narrow acceptation, and, on the other, categorial intuition and "intuition in the broadened sense [*erweiterten Sinne*]" (vol. 3, 202) [Eng. trans., vol. 2, 832; mod.].

22. Respectively, *Selbstanzeige*, *Hua*, XIX–2, 779, 782, 781 (Fr. trans. *Articles*, 205, 209, 207). See also *Entwurf einer Vorrede*: "the general sense and style of the solution . . . manages to be recognized in *Investigation VI* " (118) [Eng. trans., 25; mod.], "the . . . *most important* investigations—*viz.*, the fifth and, above all, the sixth" (323) [Eng. trans., 45], and above all an attitude that curiously seems to define Heidegger's attitude in advance: "some careful readers of the work (and especially those of the younger generation) have . . . understood its full meaning by taking their cue from the sixth investigation" (330) [Eng. trans., 52]. Such a subordination of the First Investigation to the Sixth indeed seems to contradict the decision (essential for his whole interpretation) of Jacques Derrida, "pointing out in the first of the *Investigations* those roots which will remain undisturbed in Husserl's subsequent discourse" (*La voix et le phénomène*, 8; Eng. trans., 9).

23. *LU*, vol. 2, Introduction, § 6, 17 [Eng. trans., vol. 1, 260–61]. The precept of such a zig-zag remains operative in the *Krisis*, § 9, I, *Hua*, VI, 59 [Eng. trans., 55].

24. *Entwurf einer Vorrede*, respectively, 118, 119 [Eng. trans., 25, 26; mod.]. One should consult the illuminating note by J. English [in *Articles*, 366–67].

25. *LU*, II, § 8, vol. 2, 124, and *LU*, I, § 31, vol. 2, 101 [Eng. trans., vol. 1, 352, 330; mod.].

26. *LU*, II, vol. 2, Introduction, § 3, 9–10 [Eng. trans., vol. 1, 255; mod.].

27. *LU*, I, § 9, vol. 2, 38 n. 1 [Eng. trans., vol. 1, 281; mod.].

28. *Phänomenologische Psychologie*, § 3, *Hua*, XI, 24 [Eng. trans., 17; mod.].

29. *Critique of Pure Reason*, A 51/B 75 [Eng. trans., Norman Kemp Smith (New York: St. Martin's Press, 1929), 93].

30. *Krisis*, § 30, *Hua*, VI, 118 [see Eng. trans., 116]. *LU*, VI, § 66 already explicitly reproaches Kant for having missed the "fundamental broadening [*Erweiterung*]" (vol. 3, 202ff.). On this point see I. Kern, *Husserl und Kant* (The Hague, 1964), §§ 9, 11.

31. *LU*, II, § 25, vol. 2, 168 [Eng. trans., vol. 1, 388; mod.], which is better understood according to Heidegger's commentary on it: "concrete intuition expressly *giving* its object is never an isolated, single-layered sense perception,

but is always a multi-layered [*gestufte*] intuition, that is, a categorially specified intuition" (*Prolegomena*, § 6, *GA*, 20, 93) [Eng. trans., 68].

32. *LU*, II, respectively, § 15, vol. 2, 145; then § 10, 131; finally § 4, 114 [Eng. trans., vol. 1, 369, 357, 344]. See likewise § 1, 109 and § 25, 171, but also, as early as *LU*, I, § 10, vol. 2, 41 and § 23, 76.

33. *LU*, II, § 1, vol. 2, 109 [Eng. trans., vol. 1, 340]. To be compared with §§ 8 and 15, as well as the *Prolegomena*, § 39, vol. I, 128–29.

34. *LU*, II, § 8, vol. 2, 124–25 [Eng. trans., vol. 1, 352; mod.]. See *Phänomenologische Psychologie*, § 9, *Hua*, IX, 86–87, and Heidegger: "The categorial 'forms' are not constructs of acts but objects which manifest themselves in these acts" (*GA*, 20, 96) [Eng. trans., 70].

35. See *LU*, II, § 1, vol. 2, 109 and § 22, 162; or *LU*, I, § 13, vol. 2, 50.

36. Respectively, *LU*, II, § 1, vol. 2, 109 [Eng. trans., vol. 1, 340]; § 22, 162 [Eng. trans., vol. 1, 383]; *LU*, I, § 11, vol. 2, 44 [Eng. trans., vol. 1, 285], and finally § 13, 49–50 [Eng. trans., vol. 1, 289; mod.].

37. *Prolegomena*, § 6, *GA*, 20, 90–91 (see 93, 96) [Eng. trans., 66–67, mod. See Eng. trans., 68–69, 70–71]. The interpretation developed in *Speech and Phenomena* always presupposes the self-sufficiency of the First Investigation, and therefore in principle underestimates the Sixth (cited only once, in a note, French, 67) [Eng. trans., 60]; this separation leads to a complete misunderstanding of the intervention of the categorial in the First Investigation itself, which could not but warp any approach to signification as such. Moreover, Husserl later subordinated the First Investigation to the last two, for example in the *Vorlesungen über Bedeutungslehre, Sommersemester 1908, Hua*, XXVI, 6, 17, etc.

38. *LU*, VI, § 45, vol. 3, 142–43 [Eng. trans., vol. 2, 785; mod.].

39. *LU*, VI, § 45, vol. 3, 143 (*wirklich*, vol. 3, 156, 146, etc.) [Eng. trans., vol. 2, 785].

40. On the analogical character of categorial intuition, see below notes 92 and 98.

41. *LU*, VI, § 52, vol. 3, 162 [Eng. trans., vol. 2, 800].

42. *Idee der Phänomenologie, Hua*, II, 74 [see Eng. trans., 59]: Word for word: "Everywhere givenness . . . is a givenness in the *phenomenon of cognition*, in the phenomenon of a thought in the broadest sense." To be sure, it is a matter here of givenness, not simply of intuition. But the decisive importance of this gap will only become visible later. For now, we can receive from givenness only the intuited or the intuitable. See below, note 82. A significant repetition of this situation can be found in J. N. Mohanty's essay, "Modes of Givenness," in his work *Phenomenology and Ontology* (The Hague, 1970), chap. 1.

43. *LU*, II, § 24, vol. 2, 168 [see Eng. trans., vol. 1, 388].

44. *Phänomenologische Psychologie*, § 10, *Hua*, IX, 88 [Eng. trans., 66; mod.]. Likewise: "If we were to deny that the world as world is experienceable [*erfahrbar*], then we would have to deny exactly the same for every single thing" (ibid., § 11, 97) [Eng. trans., 73].

45. Nietzsche, *Fragment*, 16 [32], *Werke*, VIII/3, 288 (*Wille zur Macht*, § 1041) [Eng. trans., W. Kaufmann (New York: Random House, 1967), 536]. The question

of the relation between Nietzsche and Husserl, although sometimes pointed out (as in *La voix et le phénomène*, 27 n. 1 [Eng. trans., 25 n. 5]) has hardly been posed. R. Boehm's essay "Deux points de vue: Husserl et Nietzsche," *Archivio di Filosofia* (1963), reprinted in *Vom Gesichtspunkt der Phänomenologie* (The Hague, 1968), is not yet sufficient to pull it off.

46. *Ideen I*, § 62, *Hua*, III, 148 [Eng. trans., 142], confirmed by the *Krisis*, § 14, 55, 57, *Hua*, VI, 71, 193, 202ff.

47. *Thus Spoke Zarathustra*, III, § 4, "Before Sunrise" [Eng. trans., W. Kaufmann, in *The Portable Nietzsche* (New York: Perguin, 1982), 277].

48. *Ideen I*, § 24, *Hua*, III, 52, lines 9–13 [Eng. trans., 44; mod.]. Or again: "One must . . . take the phenomena as they are given" (*Philosophie als strenge Wissenschaft*, § 52 = *Aufsätze und Vorträge* [1911–21], *Hua*, XXV, 33).

49. Nietzsche, *Fragment*, 7 [54], *Werke*, VIII/1, 320 (*Wille zur Macht*, § 617).

50. Husserl, *Ideen III*, § 13–14, *Hua*, V, 76–77 [see Eng. trans., 65–66]. Likewise *Philosophie als strenge Wissenschaft*, § 48: "no difference between the phenomenon [*Erscheinung*] and Being" (*Hua*, XXV, 29) [see Eng. trans., 106]; or *Krisis*, § 71: "Through the reduction, this world—and he [*sc.* the psychologist] has no other which is valid for him (another one would have no meaning at all for him)—becomes a mere phenomenon [*zum blossen Phänomen*] for him" (*Hua*, VI, 257) [Eng. trans., 254].

51. Except in outline, *La voix et le phénomène*, 27, note; 68; 83 note, and 93. [Eng. trans., 25–26, 61, 74, and 83].

52. *La voix et le phénomène*, respectively, 109, 100, 104 [Eng. trans., 97, 90, 93]. See: "What is structurally original about meaning would be the *Gegenstandslosigkeit*, the absence of any object given to intuition" (ibid., 107) [Eng. trans., 92]; and: "The possibility of this nonintuition constitutes the *Bedeutung* as such, the *normal Bedeutung* as such" (ibid., 107) [Eng. trans., 96].

53. *LU*, I, § 2, vol. 2, 25. The Husserlian definition of signification, if it begins with the distinction of types of signs, very quickly reaches, as early as the First Investigation, the status of an "ideal unity" (§ 28, 91; § 29, 92); hence the possibility of granting it an *ideal* "content," without intuition, which assigns it apart from the sign. See below, note 71.

54. *La voix et le phénomène*, respectively, 76, 109 [Eng. trans., 68, 97].

55. Respectively, *LU*, VI, § 26: "*einen phänomenologisch irreduktibeln Unterschied*" (vol. 3, 93) [see Eng. trans., vol. 2, 742]; then § 5, 21 [see Eng. trans., vol. 2, 685] and § 66, 201 [Eng. trans., vol. 2, 832].

56. The full development of *LU*, VI, § 23, vol. 3, 79ff. [Eng. trans., vol. 2, 731ff.].

57. *LU*, I, respectively, § 6, vol. 2, 32 [Eng. trans., vol. 1, 276; mod.], then § 10, 41 [Eng. trans., vol. 1, 283]. See also *LU*, VI, § 13: "Our analyses have been lightly sketched rather than thoroughly executed, but they lead to the result that *both signification-intentions and acts of signification-fulfillment, acts of 'thought' and acts of intuition, belong to a single class of objectifying acts*" (vol. 3, 52) [Eng. trans., vol. 2, 709].

58. *LU*, I, § 10: "without need of a fulfilling or illustrative intuition" (vol. 2, 41) [Eng. trans., vol. 1, 283]; likewise *LU*, VI, § 63, vol. 3, 191. *Eventuell: LU*, I, § 9, vol. 2, 37; § 10, 39. Other texts: *LU*, VI, § 4, 15 (*ohne*); § 5, vol. 3, 15, 18–19, 20 (*ohne*), etc.

59. *LU*, I, § 11, vol. 2, 45 [Eng. trans., vol. 1, 286; mod.]. See § 13, 49; § 18, 66. These are confirmed by *LU*, VI, § 46, vol. 3, 144ff. and § 70, 220.

60. *LU*, I, § 18, vol. 2, 65 [Eng. trans., vol. 1, 302; mod.].

61. *LU*, I, § 31, vol. 2, 100 [Eng. trans., vol. 1, 329–30; mod.], which one can compare with § 11, 45.

62. *LU*, I, § 15, vol. 2, 57 [Eng. trans., vol. 1, 295; mod.] could certainly serve as an anticipated response to *La voix et le phénomène*, 109 [Eng. trans., 97]. We should take this occasion to stress that our own precise subject (the status of signification in the breakthrough of the Investigations) only concerns chap. 7 of Derrida's work. We do not have to examine here the whole of his resumption of diverse Husserlian themes any more than we have to discuss the whole of Heidegger's relation to Husserl (see below, chaps. 3–4).

63. *LU*, I, § 11, vol. 2, 44 [Eng. trans., vol. 1, 285–86], cited in *La voix et le phénomène*, 109 [Eng. trans., 97].

64. Ibid., 44–45 [Eng. trans., 285–86; mod.]. We should note that the phrase "as one says [*zu sagen pflegt*]" finds an echo on the following page: "the fundamental ambiguity of the word 'judgment' habitually leads one [*zu treiben pflegt*] to confuse [*vermengen*] the evidently grasped ideal unity with the real act of judging"—habit here again confuses an evidence, far from defining its nature. § 15 will stigmatize as a typical misinterpretation the "confusion [*Vermengung*] of signification with fulfilling intuition" (vol. 2, 57) [Eng. trans., vol. 1, 295], or again "the tendency . . . to treat *fulfilling intuitions* as [being] significations (in this case one habitually [*man pflegt*] neglects the acts that give them a categorial form)" (ibid., 56ff.) [Eng. trans., vol. 1, 295; mod.]. When § 16 uses quotation marks— exactly like the passage cited from § 11—to evoke J. S. Mill's use of the "name that is meaningful in a 'genuine' and 'strict' sense," it is in order immediately to denounce a confusion and an error therein. Such a confusion must be denounced all the more in that it is common and leads to an "insoluble enigma" (§ 19, 67) [Eng. trans., 303]. The formula "*Man pflegt zu sagen*" elsewhere characterizes natural consciousness, e.g., in *LU*, VI, § 40, vol. 3, 130.

65. *LU*, I, § 26, vol. 2, 82 [Eng. trans., vol. 1, 315; mod.], cited in *La voix et le phénomène*, 107 [Eng. trans., 96].

66. *LU*, I, § 13, vol. 2, 49 [Eng. trans., vol. 1, 289]. See: "signification is nevertheless nothing other than what we mean [*meinen*] by an expression" (*LU*, II, § 15, vol. 2, 143ff.) [Eng. trans., vol. 1, 368; mod.]. For Hegel, see *Phänomenologie des Geistes*, II, *GW*, 9, eds. Bonsiepen, Hedde (Hamburg, 1980), 71ff.

67. Respectively, *LU*, V, § 14, vol. 2, 386 and § 12, 376 [see Eng. trans., vol. 2, 568, 561]—" . . . nothing to remark"—which speaks of consciousness as a simple "bundle of experiences." Here *I* says the expression but never expresses itself as such therein.

68. *LU*, VI, § 5, addendum, vol. 3, 22–23 [Eng. trans., vol. 2, 686]. See § 60, 184 [Eng. trans., 819], where S and P, as *Anzeigen* in the mathematical formula

(notation), refer, in their global signification, to categorial elements that are significant because given. In light of these texts, the lack of "*Gestaltqualität*" which characterizes the *Anzeige* at the beginning of the journey (*LU*, I, § 2, vol. 2, 25) [Eng. trans., vol. 1, 270], can seem destined to be reduced, at least tangentially. At least it is not self-evident that it constitutes a structure that is insurmountable and immediately exclusive of *any* signification.

69. *LU*, I, § 26, vol. 2, 82 [Eng. trans., vol. 1, 315].

70. Respectively, *LU*, I, § 11, "... we ... find them there [*darin*]" (vol. 2, 44) [see Eng. trans., vol. 1, 285], and *LU*, VI, § 26, vol. 3, 92 [Eng. trans., vol. 2, 741] (see § 4, 14ff.).

71. Respectively, *LU*, I, § 11, vol. 2, 44 [Eng. trans., vol. 1, 285]; § 14, 52 [Eng. trans., vol. 1, 291] (intentional sense as one of the possible contents, on the same level as fulfilling sense and the object itself); § 29, 92 [Eng. trans., vol. 1, 323; mod.] (*Gehalt*); § 31, 99 [Eng. trans., vol. 1, 329; mod.] (*logischer Gehalt*); and § 30, 96–97 [Eng. trans., vol. 1, 327; mod.]. See note 53, above.

72. *LU*, VI, § 63, vol. 3, 191 [Eng. trans., vol. 2, 824; mod.], then § 4, 14 [Eng. trans., vol. 2, 680].

73. *LU*, I, § 21, vol. 2, 71 [Eng. trans., vol. 1, 306], then *LU*, VI, § 8, vol. 3, 33 [Eng. trans., vol. 2, 695; mod.].

74. *LU*, I, § 35, vol. 2, 105 [Eng. trans., vol. 1, 333; mod.]. Such are the last words, indeed *the* last word of the First Investigation: the excess of signification and not its lack. One must not, therefore, privilege § 28, 91 [Eng. trans., 321–22] (as does *La voix et le phénomène*, 113) [Eng. trans., 100–101]. This holds inasmuch as this text itself, in its last paragraph (omitted by Derrida), ends with the reminder of having to understand "signification as ideal unities."

75. *LU*, I, § 31, vol. 2, 100 [Eng. trans., vol. 1, 329; mod.]; § 11, 45 [Eng. trans., vol. 1, 286] (see § 29, 94–95).

76. *LU*, IV, § 12, vol. 2, 327 [see Eng. trans., vol. 2, 517]: "... *aber die Bedeutung selbst existiert*" (and the combinations of signification also, § 13, 332) [Eng. trans., 521]; § 13, 330 [see Eng. trans., 519]: "... *die* ... *wirklich seiende Bedeutungen—seiend als Bedeutungen*" (see 326, 329, 333, etc.). Likewise already *LU*, II, § 8, vol. 2, 124.

77. *LU*, VI, § 63, vol. 3, 192 [Eng. trans., vol. 2, 824]. Here there must intervene as a response to the "broadening of intuition," the 1925 text that proposes, with and beyond the *mathesis universalis* reached by the *Investigations*, to push "the broadening from a priori and formal logic and mathematics to the idea of a total system [*Gesamtsystem*] of a priori sciences" (*Phänomenologische Psychologie*, § 3f., *Hua*, IX, 43) [Eng. trans., 31]. The *Gesamtsystem* corresponds, in the "broadening" of signification, to the *Gesamtanschauung* in the "broadening" of intuition." It is here again that the *Überschuss* of signification is at play (*LU*, VI, § 40, vol. 3, 131, taken up by Heidegger, *GA*, 20, 77).

78. According to the excellent diagnostic formulated by Derrida, *La voix et le phénomène*, 16 [Eng. trans., 16].

79. *Krisis*, § 68, *Hua*, VI, 237 [Eng. trans., 234].

80. *Krisis*, § 46 and n. 1, *Hua*, VI, 168–169 [Eng. trans., 165; mod.]. On this correlation, see *Die Idee der Phänomenologie*: "The word 'phenomenon' is

ambiguous in virtue of the essential correlation between *appearance and that which appears.*" (*Hua*, II, 14) [Eng. trans., 11].

81. *Selbstgegebenheit* in fact demands a double translation of *selbst. Gegebenheitsweisen*, ibid., *Hua*, VI, 169. To be compared with *LU*, VI, § 39, I, vol. 3, 122.

82. *Die Idee der Phänomenologie, Hua*, II, respectively, 61 and 50 (where, following A. Lowit, we correct the German punctuation); see above, note 42 [Eng. trans., 49, 39–40; mod.].

83. *Ideen I,* § 24, *Hua*, III, 52, lines 14–16 [Eng. trans., 44; mod.]; see § 19: "Immediate 'seeing' (noein), not merely sensuous, experiential seeing, but *seeing in the universal sense as an originarily giving* [*originär gebendes*] *consciousness of any kind whatever,* is the ultimate legitimizing source of all rational assertions" (44) [Eng. trans., 36; mod.]; § 79, 191, etc. For Heidegger also, intuition is originary only inasmuch as it gives: *GA*, 20, 64, 67.

84. *LU*, V, § 11, vol. 2, 373 [see Eng. trans., vol. 2, 559]; see Introduction, § 2, 5.

85. *LU*, I, § 14, vol. 2, 50–51 [see Eng. trans., vol. 1, 290].

86. Ibid. [Eng. trans., 291], then § 29, 92 [see Eng. trans., 323].

87. "*Zunächst ist dabei die Bedeutungsintention und zwar für sich gegeben; dann erst tritt entsprechende Anschauung hinzu*" (*LU*, VI, § 8, vol. 3, 33) [Eng. trans., vol. 2, 695], then *LU*, I, § 35, vol. 2, 105 [see Eng. trans., vol. 1, 333]; see § 9, 37 and *LU*, II, § 31, 183. Conversely, "The act of signifying cannot be fulfilled only by means of intuition" (*LU*, I, § 21, vol. 2, 71) [see Eng. trans., vol. 1, 306].

88. *LU*, VI, § 37, vol. 3, 117, and § 23, 83; see § 38, 121: "*Selbsterscheinung des Gegenstandes.*"

89. *LU*, VI, respectively, § 46, vol. 3, 146, and § 48, 154. See §§ 45, 47 and 52, vol. 3, 142, 151, and 162.

90. Respectively, *GA*, 20, 97 [see Eng. trans., 71] and *Questions IV*, 315.

91. The attribution, without discontinuity, of categorial intuition as Heidegger's point of departure constitutes the paradoxical meeting point between J. Beaufret, *Dialogue avec Heidegger,* vol. 3 (Paris: Editions de Minuit, 1974), 129, and T. Adorno, *Negative Dialektik,* (Frankfurt, 1966), 75, without citing commentators of lesser rank. It is moreover clear that J. Derrida could not ask if "Heidegger's thought does not sometimes raise the same questions as the metaphysics of presence" (*La voix et le phénomène,* 83, note) [Eng. trans., 74] if he did not himself also accept such a continuity.

92. *Questions IV,* 131, 315, respectively. The italics are, of course, from the editors of the seminar held by Heidegger.

93. *Prolegomena, GA,* 20, respectively § 4, 30 (103); § 6, 64; § 5, 54; § 6, 80 [Eng. trans., 24, 47, 41, 60]. See *leibhafte Gegebenheit,* 81 and *leibhafte Selbigkeit,* p. 83.

94. Ibid., respectively, § 6, 85; then 87 and 98 [Eng. trans., 63, 64, 72].

95. Ibid., § 6, 89 [Eng. trans., 66; mod.].

96. Ibid., § 8, 104 [see Eng trans. 76: "the demand to lay the foundation"].

97. Respectively, *LU*, VI, § 39, vol. 3, 123; Introduction, 5; finally § 44, 140 and § 45, 143 [see Eng. trans., vol. 2, 766, 670, 782, 785].

98. *LU*, VI, § 44, vol. 3, 141 [Eng. trans., vol. 2, 784]. See a similar deduction in § 46, 146; § 47, 152; § 52, 163, 164.

2. Beings and the Phenomenon

1. Respectively, *Prolegomena zur Geschichte des Zeitbegriffs*, GA 20, 98 [Eng. trans., 72; mod.], and *Ideen III, Beilage* 1, § 6, *Hua*, V, 129 [Eng. trans., 117].

2. Respectively, *Cartesianische Meditationen*, § 41, *Hua*, I, 118; then § 62, 176 [Eng. trans., 86, 150; mod.]; then the *Nachwort*, § 5, 152.

3. *LU*, VI, vol. 2, 236 [Eng. trans., vol. 2, 863; mod.].

4. *Ideen I*, § 153, *Hua*, III, 379 [Eng. trans., 369; mod.].

5. *Cartesianische Meditationen*, § 59, 164 [Eng. trans., 137]. One can also understand the sequence: " . . . *eine einseitige und nicht im Endsinne philosophische*" in the sense of: " . . . non-philosophical in the full sense of the term."

6. *Die Idee der Phänomenologie, Hua*, II, 22–23 [see Eng. trans., 18]. Ontology appears in *this* sense in the article for the *Encyclopaedia Britannica*: "In ihrer [transcendental phenomenology] *systematischer Durchführung verwirklicht sie die leibnizsche Idee einer universalen Ontologie*" (in *Phänomenologische Psychologie, Hua*, IX, 296).

7. *Die Idee der Phänomenologie*, 31 [see Eng. trans., 24].

8. "*den allgemeinsten Satz* . . . : *die Gegebenheit eines reduzierten Phänomens überhaupt ist eine absolute und zweifellose*," (ibid., 50) [Eng. trans., 40; mod.].

9. Respectively, *Ideen III*, § 13, *Hua*, V, 76 [Eng. trans., 65]; then the *Nachwort*, § 3, 145. See Heidegger: "The term 'phenomenon,' however, says nothing about the Being of the being that is encountered, but only characterizes the *mode of access* to it" (*GA*, 20, 118; see 157) [see Eng. trans., 86]. Obviously, it is a question of much more than a simple reinterpretation, as James R. Mensch claims in *The Question of Being in Husserl's Logical Investigations* (The Hague, 1981), 182ff. One would need only to read Husserl's marginal annotations in Heidegger's *Kant und der Problem der Metaphysik*, such as they are related by I. Kern, *Husserl und Kant* (The Hague, 1964), 188–91.

10. Respectively, *Ideen III*, § 14, *Hua*, V, 77 (our emphasis), 78 [Eng. trans., 66–67]. See *Cartesianische Meditationen*, § 64: "Wieder dasselbe besagt, die systematisch voll entwickelte transzendentale Phänomenologie wäre *eo ipso* die wahre und echte universale Ontologie; aber nicht bloss eine leer formale, sondern zugleich eine solche, die alle regionalen Seinsmöglichkeiten in sich schlösse, und nach allen zu ihnen gehörigen Korrelationen" (181); and also *Ideen I*, § 62, *Hua*, III, 147–49; likewise *Erste Philosophie*, II, *Beilage* 30, *Hua*, VIII, 482. Good clarification by E. Fink in *Studien zur Phänomenologie*, French trans. *De la phénoménologie*, trans. D. Franck (Paris, 1974), 233–34.

11. Respectively, *Sein und Zeit*, § 7, 35 [Eng. trans., 60]—"Only as phenomenology is ontology possible"—and 37 [Eng. trans., 61; mod.]—"Taken in its reality, phenomenology is the science of the Being of beings."

12. *Grundprobleme der Phänomenologie, GA*, 24, respectively, 24, 16 [Eng. trans., 20, 12]. Hence the methodological primacy of phenomenology: "phenomenology is accordingly a '*methodological*' term," concerning not the thing or being but "the *how*, the way in which something is and has to be thematic in this research" (*Prolegomena, GA*, 20, 117) [Eng. trans., 85].

13. *Sein und Zeit*, § 7, 38 [Eng. trans., 62], a formula that is found at the end of the work, to attest to its inchoate character, § 83, 436 [Eng. trans., 487].

14. *Ideen I*, § 62, *Hua*, III, 118 [Eng. trans., 142].

15. *Prolegomena*, § 32, *GA*, 20, 423 [Eng. trans., 306; mod.].

16. Ibid.; in the formula "Das Sein am Seienden soll abgelesen werden, d. h. was phänomenologische Interpretation in die Vorsicht stellt, ist das Sein," *ablesen* anticipates the question through which *Sein und Zeit* begins to privilege *Dasein* among all legible beings: "An *welchem* Seienden soll der Sinn von Sein abgelesen werden?" Heidegger will add in the margin of his copy: "Aber nicht wird an diesem Seienden der Sinn von Sein abgelesen" (*Sein und Zeit*, § 2, 7).

17. Respectively, *Sein und Zeit*, § 7, 37; and "Ein Vorwort. Brief an P. William J. Richardson," in W. Richardson, *Through Phenomenology to Thought* (The Hague, M. Nijhoff, 1963), xvii. A similar passage of phenomenology beyond itself, and therefore for the first time to what provokes it, can be discerned as early as 1925 (*Prolegomena*, § 6 *"durch sie hindurch . . . ," GA*, 20, 63, and 183–84).

18. *Prolegomena*, § 8: " . . . Apriori als eines Charakters des Seins des Seienden, nicht des Seienden selbst" (*GA*, 20, 102–3) [Eng. trans., 75; mod.].

19. *Prolegomena*, § 9, *GA*, 118 [Eng. trans., 86; mod.], from which also this declaration: "Phänomenologie als Wissenschaft von den apriorischen Phänomenen der Intentionalität hat es also nie und nimmer mit Erscheinungen oder gar blossen Erscheinungen zu tun." The criterion of phenomenality is also formulated explicitly in 1927, but only under its positive aspect, and therefore less brutally: "Now that we have delimited our preliminary conception of phenomenology, the terms '*phenomenal*' and '*phenomenological*' can also be fixed in their signification. That which is given and explicable in the way the phenomenon is encountered is called 'phenomenal'; this is what we have in mind when we talk about 'phenomenal structures.' Everything which belongs to the mode of showing [*Art der Aufweisung*] and of explication and which goes to make up the way of conceiving demanded by this research, is called 'phenomenological' " (*Sein und Zeit*, § 7, 37) [Eng. trans., 61; mod.]. The reverse of the phenomenological so defined remains at work perhaps under the name, then used, of the "vulgar concept of the phenomenon."

20. *Prolegomena*, § 13: "*die Seinsart der Akte bleibt unbestimmt*" (*GA*, 20, 172, see 157, 177, 178, etc.) [Eng. trans., 124].

21. *Prolegomena*, § 11, *GA*, 20, 147 [Eng. trans., 107]; see 153–54.

22. "Es bedarf wohl kaum des Geständnisses, dass ich mich auch heute noch Husserl gegenüber als Lernender nehme" (*Prolegomena* § 13, *GA*, 20, 168). Whence the famous note 1 from *Sein und Zeit* § 7, 38, and the remark in *Hegels Phänomenologie des Geistes* (1930–31), *GA*, 32, 40.

23. *Prolegomena*, *GA*, 20, 173 [Eng. trans., 125].

24. "Ein unüberbrückbarer Wesensunterschied," *Ideen I*, § 43, *Hua*, III, 99 [Eng. trans., 93]. See § 42, 96: "die prinzipielle Unterschiedenheit der Seinsweisen, die kardinalste, die es überhaupt gibt . . . ein prinzipieller Unterschied der Gegebenheitsart"; § 49, 117: "Zwischen Bewußtsein und Realität gähnt ein wahrer Abgrund des Sinnes"; § 76, 174: "dieser radikalsten aller Seinsunterscheidungen—Sein als *Bewußtsein* und Sein als sich im Bewußtsein '*bekundendes*,' 'tran-

szendentes' Sein." This last text is quoted and commented on, with a view to underlining the "fundamental failure," by Heidegger in *Prolegomena*, § 13, *GA*, 20, 157–59. See below, chap. 3, § 2, chap. 4, § 4, and chap. 6, § 1.

25. *Ideen I*, § 46, which reaches the "high-point" of the meditation (*Hua*, III, 109, "*Höhepunkt*"), indeed defines the immanent sphere of consciousness as "*eine Sphäre absoluter Position*," even as "*absolute Wirklichkeit*" (108). Consciousness' mode of Being is separated radically from the mode of Being of the transcendence of the world only by miming it, through a reciprocal reference that inscribes them equally in an actual and present position.

26. *Prolegomena*, § 13, *GA*, 20, 178 [Eng. trans., 128; mod.]. See § 9, 118; § 11, 147; § 13, 159; § 14, 183.

27. *Sein und Zeit*, § 7, 27, 34, but also *Zur Sache des Denkens*, 48, and "Ein Vorwort: Brief an P. William Richardson," xiiiff. But, for Heidegger, Husserl does *not* respect his own watchword: *Prolegomena*, §§ 13 and 14, *GA*, 20, 158–59, 184–85.

28. Respectively, *Ideen I*, § 24, *Hua*, III, 52 and § 59, 142 [See Eng. trans., 44, 136].

29. *Zur Sache des Denkens*, 69–70 [Eng. trans., 62–63; mod.]. It is clear that the collection of 1969, in opening up the "matter of thinking" through the ultimate explicitly phenomenological recentering of the *Seinsfrage* on Being as Being and on the *Ereignis*, answers in its very title to the Husserlian requirement of the return *zur Sache selbst*—with an answer that also accomplishes the task only at the price of a new decisive break with Husserl. *Zur Sache des Denkens* attempts, with and therefore against Husserl, to carry out for the first time the return to the "thing" in question, as the matter of thinking according to the *Ereignis*. In this sense, the continuing allusions to his phenomenological past are not to be taken as a genealogy rewritten after the fact, but as the indication of his finally becoming fully conscious of the ambivalence of his relation to Husserl and to his "breakthrough."

30. *Philosophie als strenge Wissenschaft*, Hua, XXV, 31 [Eng. trans., 108].

31. *LU*, VI, *Beilage*, § 2, vol. 2, 227 [Eng. trans., vol. 2, 856; mod.]. See the Introduction, § 2, which brings together in the same pages the two principles: "Wir wollen auf die 'Sachen selbst' zurückgehen. An vollentwickelten Anschauungen wollen wir uns zur Evidenz bringen, dies hier in aktuell vollzogener Abstraktion Gegebene sei wahrhaft und wirklich das, was die Wortbedeutungen im Gesetzesausdruck meinen; . . . durch Rückgang auf die analytisch durchforschten Wesenzusammenhänge zwischen Bedeutungsintention und Bedeutungserfüllung" (vol. 2, 6). For Husserl, there is no doubt that the return to the things themselves does not lead beyond the "principle of principles" and that the distinction of two principles does not even make any sense: at the very most it is a matter of two formulations of the same requirement. Thus it is only from a point of view that is *already* Heideggerian that we managed to remark a scission between two statements.

32. Respectively, *Ideen I*, § 45 and § 46, *Hua*, III, 104 and 107 [See Eng. trans., 98, 101].

33. *LU*, V, § 8, vol. 2, 362 [Eng. trans., 550; mod.]. § 20 very clearly declares: "Für die reell phänomenologische Betrachtung ist die Gegenständlichkeit selbst nichts: sie ist ja, allgemein zu reden, dem Akte transzendent. . . . Der Gegenstand ist ein intentionaler, das heisst ein Akt mit einer bestimmt charakterisierten

Intention, die in dieser Bestimmtheit eben das ausmacht, was wir die Intention auf diesen Gegenstand nennen" (vol. 2, 412–13). Nothing indicates better that the objectivity of the object depends on the intentional act than the expression *Akterlebnis*, lived experience of the act (vol. 2, 344, 376, 377).

34. Respectively, *Ideen I*, § 19, *Hua*, III, 44 and § 79, 190 [see Eng. trans., 36, 186–87]. See other comparable formulas: "Wir lassen uns in der Tat durch *keine* Autorität das Recht verkümmern, alle Anschauungsarten als gleichwertige Rechtsquellen der Erkenntnis anzuerkennen" (§ 20, 46); "Argumente . . . die bei aller formalen Präzision jede Anmessung an die Urquellen der Geltung, an die der reinen Intuition, vermissen lassen" (§ 78, 185). The "principle of all principles" is qualified, moreover, by the title of *"absoluter Anfang . . . principium"* (§ 24, 52).

35. *LU*, respectively, V, § 2, vol. 2, 349 [Eng. trans., 538; mod.]; then VI, Beilage, § 5, vol. 3, 233–34 [Eng. trans., 860–61; mod.]. One might compare these also with *LU* III, § 3: ". . . hinsichtlich der Erscheinungen im Sinne der erscheinenden Objekte als solcher, als auch hinsichtlich der Erscheinungen als der *Erlebnisse*, in denen die phänomenalen Dinge erscheinen" (vol. 2, 231); and again, *LU* V, § 2: "Als dem Bewusstseinszusammenhang zugehörig, erleben wir die Erscheinungen, als der phänomenalen Welt zugehörig, erscheinen uns die Dinge. Die Erscheinungen selbst erscheinen nicht, sie werden erlebt. . . . Sprechen wir von dieser letzteren Beziehung (i.e., die Beziehung zwischen *der Dingerscheinung als Erlebnis und dem erscheinenden Ding*), so bringen wir uns nur zur Klarheit, dass das Erlebnis nicht selbst das ist, was 'in' ihm intentional gegenwärtig ist" (vol. 2, 350); or again, *LU* VI, *Beilage*, § 8: "Die Äquivokation des Wortes Phänomen, die es gestatten, bald die erscheinenden Gegenstände und Eigenschaften, bald die den Erscheinungsakt konstituierenden Erlebnisse (zumal die Inhalt im Sinne von Empfindungen) und schlisslich alle Erlebnisse überhaupt als Phänomene zu bezeichnen, erklären die nicht geringe Versuchung, *zwei wesentlich verschiedene psychologische Einteilungsarten der 'Phänomene'* durcheinander zu mengen: 1. Einteilung der *Erlebnisse*. . . . 2. Enteilung der *phänomenalen Gegenstände*" (vol. 3, 242–43). The lectures of 1907 on *The Idea of Phenomenology* relied explicitly on this duality:

> Die Phänomenologie der Erkentniss ist Wissenschaft von den Erkenntnisphänomenen in dem doppelten Sinn, von den Erkenntnissen als Erscheinungen, Darstellungen, Bewußtseinsakten, in denen sich diese und jene Gegenständlichkeiten darstellen . . . und anderseits von diesen Gegenständlichkeiten selbst als sich darstellenden. Das Wort Phänomen ist doppelsinnig vermöge der wesentlichen Korrelation zwischen *Erscheinen* und *Erscheinenden*. Faino/menon heisst eigentlich das Erscheinende und ist aber doch vorzugsweise gebraucht für das Erscheinen selbst, das subjektive Phänomen. (*Hua*, II, 14; see 20)

The warning of the Introduction to *Ideen I*—"Nicht eine Wesenslehre realer, sondern transzendental reduzierter Phänomene soll unsere Phänomenologie sein" (*Hua*, III, 6)—must be understood on the basis of such a fundamental ambiguity.

36. *LU*, V, § 14, vol. 2, 385 [Eng. trans., 567; mod.].

37. *LU*, VI, *Beilage*, § 5, vol. 3, 235, 235–36 [Eng. trans., 862; mod.]. See, however, *Hua*, X, 336.

38. *LU*, VI, § 39, vol. 3, 128 [Eng. trans., 766; mod.]. See *Prolegomena*, § 51: "Evidenz ist vielmehr nichts anderes als das 'Erlebnis' der Wahrheit" (vol. 1, 190).

39. *Ideen I*, § 147, *Hua*, III, 360 [Eng. trans., 352; mod.].

40. " . . . *das reine Phänomen, das reduzierte*," *Die Idee der Phänomenologie, Hua*, II, 7 [see Eng. trans., 5] (see, 50, 56, 58, etc.).

41. *Die Idee der Phänomenologie, Hua* II, 59 [Eng. trans., 47; mod.]; see 32, 35, 60, 80.

42. *Ideen I*, § 111, *Hua*, 268 [see Eng. trans., 261].

43. "*Absolute Gegebenheit ist ein Letztes*," *Die Idee der Phänomenologie, Hua*, II, 61 [See Eng. trans., 49]. See " . . . *die Wesensserschauung [ist] der letztbegründende Akt*," *Ideen* I, § 7, *Hua*, III, 21.

44. *Ideen I*, § 46, *Hua*, III, 109 [Eng. trans., 102; mod.]. See D. Franck's penetrating commentary, *Chair et corps: Sur la phénoménologie de Husserl* (Paris, 1981), 24ff. Indeed, the transcendent itself belongs to the domain of corporal presence in person: "Das Raumding, das wir sehen, ist bei all seiner Transzendenz Wahrgenommenes, in seiner *Leibhaftigkeit* bewußtseinsmässig Gegebenes" (*Ideen I*, § 43, *Hua* III, 98).

45. *Ideen I*, § 45, *Hua*, III, 104 [Eng. trans., 98; mod.]. See the role assigned to the originary present throughout § 46.

46. *Ideen I*, § 49, *Hua*, III, 115, intentionally citing and modifying Descartes, *Principia Philosophiae*, I, § 51. Heidegger raises and criticizes this submission to the whole most strictly metaphysical tradition in *Prolegomena*, § 11, *GA*, 20, 143–45. See below, chap. 3, § 2.

47. *Ideen I*, § 49, *Hua*, III, 116 [Eng. trans., 111; mod.].

48. *Ideen I*, § 43, *Hua*, III, 99–100 [Eng. trans., 93; mod.].

49. *Sein und Zeit*, § 7, respectively, 28, 31, 36 [Eng. trans., 51, 54, 60] (to be compared with *Prolegomena*, § 9, *GA*, 20, 119). Although illuminating, the comparison with *LU*, VI, §§ 11 and 14 must not be overestimated: the same point of departure leads only to a more clear final opposition. " . . . on the basis of itself": we understand it thus, following J. Hyppolite, "Ontologie et métaphysique chez Martin Heidegger," in *Figures de la pensée philosophique*, vol. 2 (Paris, 1971), 615ff. (and M. Haar, *Le chant de la terre* [Paris, 1985], 37).

50. *Sein und Zeit*, § 7, 35 [Eng. trans., 59]. One should take into account the note of the French translators and even more the note of Heidegger who, in his rereading, specifies that, in the final analysis, what "remains hidden" is called the "*Wahrheit des Seins*" (*GA*, 2, 47). That which in the phenomenon requires the phenomenological work of unveiling, precisely because of itself it remains concealed, is nothing less than the (always veiled) unveiling of the truth.

51. Respectively, *Prolegomena*, § 9, *GA*, 20, 119 [Eng. trans., 86–87]; § 14, 188–89 [Eng. trans., 139; mod.]; and § 9, 111 [Eng. trans., 81; mod.]. Finally, *Grundprobleme*, § 21: "*Das Phänomen erwies sich aber als rätselhaft*" (*GA*, 24, 446).

52. *Sein und Zeit*, § 7, 36 [Eng. trans., 60].

53. *Prolegomena*, § 14, *GA*, 20, 189 [Eng. trans., 139; mod.]. See *"Aber wieviel, Schein-soviel Sein"* (*Prolegomena*, § 9, *GA*, 20), 119, and *"Wieviel Schein jedoch, soviel Sein" Sein und Zeit*, § 7, 36). This formula appeared already in Husserl, *Cartesianische Meditationen*, § 46, *Hua*, I, 133.

54. *Sein und Zeit*, § 7, 35 [Eng. trans., 59; mod.].

55. *Prolegomena*, § 32, *GA*, 20, 423 [Eng. trans., 95]. The same problematic is applied to the *"Phänomen der Zeit,"* § 14, 191, 192.

56. *Questions IV*, 339. With which one might compare the expression *Phänomenologie des Unscheinbaren*, used in a letter to R. Munier, 16 April 1973 (in *Martin Heidegger* [Paris, L'Herne, 1983], 112).

57. Respectively, *Prolegomena*, § 6: "Dieses 'Sein' hier . . . ist nicht wahrnehmbar" (*GA*, 20, 78) [Eng. trans., 58; mod.]; *Grundprobleme*, § 10, *GA*, 24, 109 [Eng. trans., 78; mod.] (see 58, 77, 443); and finally *Sein und Zeit*, § 7: "Das Sein des Seienden 'ist' nicht ein Seiendes" (6 [Eng. trans., 26], and again 35); or again: " . . . so gewiss das Sein nicht aus Seiendem 'erklärt' werden kann" (§ 41, 196; see § 43, 207). One must nevertheless recognize the anteriority of Husserl's formula: "Sein sei schlechthin nichts Wahrnehmbares" (*LU*, VI, § 43, vol. 3, 138). But there it is only a question of a Kantian theme.

58. *Grundprobleme*, § 22, *GA*, 24, 461–62 [Eng. trans., 324].

59. See below, chap. 6, § 3.

60. *Grundprobleme*, § 9, *GA*, 24, 102 [Eng. trans., 72; mod.].

61. *Prolegomena*, § 32, *GA*, 20, 423 [Eng. trans., 306; mod.] (see 424 and 427, as well as *Sein und Zeit*, § 2, 7).

62. *Prolegomena*, respectively, § 17, *GA*, 20, 201; and § 32, 423 [Eng. trans., 149, 306; mod.].

63. *Prolegomena*, § 14, *GA*, 20, 186 [Eng. trans., 137; mod.].

64. *Sein und Zeit*, § 7, 38. See the explication of *Grundprobleme*, § 4: "Wir übersteigen das Seiende, um zu Sein zu gelangen. Bei diesem Überstieg versteigen wir uns nicht wiederum zu einem Seiendem, da etwa hinter dem bekannten Seienden läge als irgendeine Hinterwelt" (*GA*, 24, 23). Because in the strict sense the act of transcending reaches *nothing* (no being), it consists concretely in a self-transcendence, and therefore in the transcendence of *Dasein* by itself. Hence the necessity of understanding the transcendence of Being as a transcendence of *Dasein*, since only the latter excludes the danger of falling back into the expectation of another being. There is therefore nothing less surprising than the following declarations: "Ebenso hängt mit dem ekstatisch-horizontalen Charakter die Wesensbestimmung des Daseins zusammen, dass es in sich selbst *transzendiert*" (*Grundprobleme*, § 19, *GA*, 24, 379); "Das Dasein selbst ist in seinem Sein überschreitend und somit gerade *nicht das Immanente. Das Transzendierende sind nicht die Objekte*—Dinge können nie transzendieren und transzendent sein—sondern transzendierend, d. h. sich selbst durch- und überschreitend sind die 'Subjekte' im ontologisch recht verstandenen Sinne des Daseins. Nur Seiendes von der Seinsart des Daseins transzendiert, so zwar, dass gerade die Transzendenz das Sein wesenthaft charakterisiert" (*Grundprobleme*, § 20, *GA*, 24, 425). Or again: "Das Dasein ist selbst das Transzendente. Es überschreitet sich, d. h. ermöglicht

allererst das Existieren im Sinne des Sichverhaltens zu sich selbst als Seiendem, zu Anderen als Seienden und zu Seiendem im Sinne des Zuhandenen bzw. Vorhandenen" (*Grundprobleme*, § 22, *GA*, 20, 460).

65. *Grundprobleme*, § 5, *GA*, 29 [Eng. trans., 21; mod.]. For, the text continues, "Wie jede wissenschaftliche Methode wächst und wandelt sich auch die phänomenologische Methode aufgrund des mit ihrer Hilfe gerade vollzogenen Vordringens zu den Sachen. Wissenschaftliche Methode ist nie eine Technik. Sobald sie das wird, ist sie von ihrem eigenen Wesen abgefallen." Would one not have to conclude from this that Heidegger distances himself from Husserl through a concern for *greater* rigor in the exercise of the phenomenological method—through a *more* methodical attention to the things themselves?

66. *Prolegomena*, § 10, *GA*, 20, 136 [Eng. trans., 99; mod.]; see § 12, 150, etc. On this point, see W. Biemel, "Husserls *Encyclopaedia-Britannica*-Artikel und Heideggers Anmerkung dazu," *Tijdschrift voor Philosophie* 12 (1950), reprinted in *Husserl/Wege der Forschung*, ed. N. Noack (Darmstadt, 1973). A part of this dossier (published in *Hua*, IX, 237–99) was translated and given a commentary by J.-F. Courtine, in *Martin Heidegger*, 38–46.

67. Respectively, Husserl to Ingarden, 26 December 1927, in *Briefe an Roman Ingarden*, ed. R. Ingarden (The Hague, 1968), 43 (see the parallel of the letter of 2 December 1929, 56); and *Nachwort*, in *Ideen III*, *Hua*, V, 140. In the same direction, *Cartesianische Meditationen*, § 41, *Hua*, I, 119, "Phänomenologie und Anthropologie," in *Philosophy and Phenomenological Research* 2 (1941–42); reprinted in *Aufsätze und Vorträge (1922–1937)*, *Hua*, XXVII (The Hague, 1989). The classic thesis of an abandonment of the reduction by Heidegger is repeated by, among others, E. Tugendhat, *Der Wahrheitsbegriff bei Husserl und Heidegger* (Berlin, 1967), 62. On the contrary, G. Granel, "Remarques sur le rapport de *Sein und Zeit* et de la phénoménologie husserlienne," in *Traditionis Traditio* (Paris, 1972); and J.-F. Courtine, "L'idée de la phénoménologie et la problématique de la réduction," in *Phénoménologie et métaphysique*, ed. J.-L. Marion and G. Planty-Bonjour (Paris, 1984), 211–45; or "Le préconcept de la phénoménologie et de la problématique de la vérité dans *Sein und Zeit*," in *Heidegger et l'idée de la phénoménologie*, ed. F. Volpi (Dordrecht, 1988).

68. *Prolegomena*, § 15, *GA*, 20, 193 [Eng. trans., 143; mod.]. See *Sein und Zeit*, § 2: "Die Frage nach dem Sinn von Sein soll *gestellt* werden" (5).

69. *Sein und Zeit*, § 2, 5 [Eng. trans., 24; mod.]. See below, chap. 4, § 5.

70. *Prolegomena*, § 16, *GA*, 20, 195 [Eng. trans., 144–45; mod.]; the whole of § 16 of this course should be consulted. In 1935, the same ternary argument will remain at work in *Einführung in die Metaphysik*, *GA*, 40, 24–25. See, as counterproof, the metaphysical diversion of a question concerning Being by a response concerning, in fact, being (here, Thales provides the example in *Grundprobleme*, § 22, *GA*, 24, 453–54).

71. *Zeit und Sein*, in *Zur Sache des Denkens*, 68 [Eng. trans., 24]. See J. Beaufret, *Entretiens* (Paris, 1984), 40–41, 103.

72. *Prolegomena*, § 17, respectively, *GA*, 20, 199–200 [Eng. trans., 148, 147; mod.]. One should here consult all of § 17.

73. Respectively, *Prolegomena*, § 17, *GA*, 20, 200 [Eng. trans., 148]; and *Sein und Zeit*, § 4, 12 [Eng trans., 32]; hence the opposite view that "*das Seiende, dass wir je selbst sind, ist ontologisch das Fernste*" (*Sein und Zeit*, § 63, 311).

74. *Grundprobleme*, § 19 and § 9, respectively, *GA* 24, 379 and 91 [Eng. trans., 268, 65]; see 425ff., cited above, note 64.

75. *Sein und Zeit*, § 4, 12 [see Eng. trans., 32] (see § 9, 42; § 41, 191; and § 45, 231).

76. Respectively, in 1927, *Grundprobleme*, *GA*, 322, then 444 (see 453) [Eng. trans., 227, 312]; and in 1928, *Vom Wesen des Grundes*, in *Wegmarken*, *GA*, 9, 134 [Eng. trans., 27; mod.]. In the 1928 course, *Metaphysische Anfangsgründe der Logik im Ausgang von Leibniz*, one reads the definition: "Das menschliche Dasein ist ein solches Seiendes, zu dessen Seinsart selbst es wesenhaft gehört, dergleichen wie Sein zu verstehen. Das nennen wir die Transzendenz des Daseins, die Urtranszendenz" (*GA*, 26, 20). We should note, however, that *Sein und Zeit* sometimes lifts the ambiguity; for example in § 9: "Das Sein ist es, darum es diesem Seienden je selbst geht" (42), and the manuscript note indeed adds: ". . . das Seyn; überhaupt" (*GA*, 2, 56).

77. Respectively, *Prolegomena*, § 15, *GA*, 20, 193 [Eng. trans., 143; mod.], and *Wegmarken*, *GA*, 9, 106 [see Eng. trans., 245].

78. *Wegmarken*, *GA*, 9, 112 [Eng. trans., 245; mod.]. In *Heidegger and Modern Philosophy: Critical Essays* (New Haven, 1979), S. Rosen already considers the analysis of anxiety as "Heidegger's existential version of the phenomenological epoche" (132).

79. *Sein und Zeit*, § 40, 184ff.; see *Wegmarken*, *GA*, 9, 111, and already *Prolegomena*, § 30 *b*, *GA*, 20, 400ff.

80. *Wegmarken*, *GA*, 9, 110 [Eng. trans., 247; mod.].

81. *Wegmarken*, *GA*, 9, 114. See below, chap. 6, § 3.

82. Respectively, *Prolegomena*, § 9, *GA*, 20, 113 [Eng. trans., 82; mod.]; and *Sein und Zeit*, § 7, 31 [Eng. trans., 54; mod.]. One should note that the 1929 lecture maintains the eminent role of the concept of transcendence (*GA*, 9, 115, 120), just as that of the first redoubled reduction.

83. *Wegmarken*, *GA*, 9, 115 [Eng. trans., 251; mod.]: "Im Sein des Seienden geschieht das Nichten des Nichts"; then: "Das Nichts bleibt nicht das unbestimmte Gegenüber für das Seiende, sondern es enthüllt sich als zugehörig zum Sein des Seienden" (120) [see Eng. trans., 255].

84. *Wegmarken*, *GA*, 9, 134 (and the note referring to *Grundprobleme*, § 22).

85. Respectively, *Wegmarken*, *GA*, 9, 106 (addition from 1931); 107 (from 1949); 113 (from 1949); and 114 (from 1949). On the legitimacy of these additions, see below, chap. 6, § 3, notes 43–48.

86. *Einführung in die Metaphysik* (from 1935), *GA*, 40, 108 [Eng. trans., 101; mod.].

87. For the first redoubled reduction (through *Dasein*), see chap. 3: "The Ego and Dasein"; for the second (through the Nothing), see chap. 6: "The Nothing and the Claim"; finally, for the relation between these two redoublings of the reduction, see chap. 4: "Question of Being or Ontological Difference."

88. *Sein und Zeit*, § 7, 38 [Eng. trans., 62–63]. A famous text that will not be deprived of more explicit commentary: "The greatness of the discovery of phenomenology lies not in factually obtained results, which can be evaluated and criticized . . . , but rather in this: it is the *discovery of the possibility of research in philosophy*" (*Prolegomena*, § 14, *GA*, 20, 184) [Eng. trans., 135–36; mod.]. Practically at the end of his path of thinking, Heidegger will maintain this assessment:

> The age of phenomenological philosophy seems to be over. It is already taken as something past which is only recorded historically along with other schools of philosophy. But in what is most its own, phenomenology is not a school. It is the possibility of thinking, at times changing and only thus persisting, of corresponding to the claim of what is to be thought [*die zu Zeiten sich wandelnde und nur dadurch bleibende Möglichkeit des Denkens, dem Anspruch des zu Denkenden zu entsprechen*]. If phenomenology is thus experienced and retained, it can disappear as a designation in favor of the matter of thinking [*Sache des Denkens*] whose manifestness remains a secret. (*Zur Sache des Denkens*, "Mein Weg in die Phänomenologie," from 1963, 90) [Eng. trans., 82; mod.]

3. The Ego and Dasein

1. *Phänomenologische Interpretationen zu Aristoteles: Einführung in die phänomenologische Forschung*, *GA*, 61, *Anhang* 1, respectively, 173, 172. In the prior texts, mentions of Descartes are, to our knowledge, quite discrete (e.g., *Frühe Schriften*, *GA*, 1, 43).

2. *Aus letzten Marburger Vorlesung*, in *Wegmarken*, *GA*, 9, respectively, 79, 89–90.

3. *Questions IV*, respectively, 263, 282; the original here is in French. See 122, 220, 245, 289, 320. On the relation of Descartes to Fichte and Hegel, one should consult the recent investigations of A. Philonenko, "Sur Descartes et Fichte," and B. Bourgeois, "Hegel et Descartes" (in both cases more reserved than Heidegger), *Les Etudes philosophiques* (1985), 205ff., 221ff.

4. *Questions IV*, 319–20.

5. *Aus Erfahrung des Denkens*, *GA*, 13, 233.

6. *Erste Philosophie*, II, I, I, § 28, *Hua*, VIII, 4.

7. When does Husserl enter into conversation with Descartes? The latter is mentioned already in the First Logical Investigation, 64 (concerning the distinction between imagination and understanding), *LU*, vol. 2, § 18, and he is discussed at length in the appendix, "External and Internal Perception. Physical and Psychic Phenomena," added as a complement to the Sixth Investigation, *LU*, vol. 3, 223, 225, 240, 241; but then it is a question only of an adversary. On the reversal and its limits, see F.-W. von Herrmann, *Husserl und die Meditationen des Descartes* (Frankfurt, 1971), and "Husserl et Descartes," *Revue de Métaphysique et de Morale* (1987). Very early, this encounter became an obligatory theme, e.g., in O. Becker, "Husserl und Descartes," in *Dem gedächtnis an René Descartes (300 Jahre*

Discours de la Méthode), ed. C. A. Emge (Berlin, 1937); and then A. de Waehlens, "Descartes et la pensée phénoménologique," *Revue néo-scolastique de Philosophie* 41 (1938) (reprinted in *Husserl, Wege der Forschung*, ed. H. Noack [Darmstadt, 1973]).

8. *Prolegomena zur Geschichte des Zeitbegriffs*, § 11, *GA*, 20, 140–41 [Eng. trans., 102; mod.].

9. *Ideen I*, respectively, § 43, § 49, § 42, *Hua*, III, 99, 117, 96 [Eng. trans., 93, 111, 90; mod.]. See above, chap. 2, § 2, n. 24; and below chap. 4, § 4.

10. *Ideen I*, § 49, 115 [Eng. trans., 110; mod.].

11. *The Philosophical Writings of Descartes*, vol. 1, trans. John Cottingham, et al. (Cambridge: Cambridge University Press, 1985), 210.

12. Ibid.

13. We cannot here follow (either phenomenologically or historically) the restrictive and vague interpretation of *res* that R. Boehm wants to see here in order to defend Husserl against Heidegger (R. Boehm, *Vom Gesichtpunkt der Phänomenologie* [The Hague, 1968], 82–83). On the importance of the difference between finite substance and infinite substance, which Heidegger agrees with Husserl to pass over in silence, see von Herrmann, *Husserl und die Meditationen des Descartes*, 17ff., and, from Descartes's point of view, my study *Sur le prisme métaphysique de Descartes* (Paris, 1986), chap. 3, § 13, 161ff.

14. *Prolegomena*, § 11, *GA*, 20, 145 [Eng. trans., 105–6; mod.].

15. Ibid., 147 [Eng. trans., 107; mod.].

16. Ibid., 178 [Eng. trans., 128]. On the scope of this critique, see chap. 2, § 2.

17. *Regulae ad directionem ingenii*, respectively, IV, AT, X, 378, 8, and I, AT, X, 360, 19–20. [AT refers to *Oeuvres de Descartes*, ed. C. Adam, P. Tannery (Paris: Vrin, 1964–76)—TRANS.] On the textual establishment of the *universalissima Sapientia*, see my edition of the *Règles utiles et claires pour la direction de l'esprit en la recherche de la vérité* (The Hague, 1977), 96.

18.

> Already here we can detect an affinity [*Verwandtschaft*] with Descartes. What is here elaborated at a higher level of phenomenological analysis as pure consciousness is the field which Descartes confusedly foresaw under the heading of *res cogitans*, the entire field of *cogitationes*, while the transcendent world, whose exemplary index for Husserl as well is to be found in the basic stratum of the world of material things, is what Descartes characterizes as *res extensa*. This affinity is not only contingently factual [*faktisch*]. Husserl explicitly assumes a relation to Descartes at the point where he observes that the reflection has reached its climax." (*Prolegomena*, *GA*, 20, 139) [Eng. trans., 101; mod.]

A note by Heidegger in his personal copy of *Sein und Zeit* confirms the constancy of his judgment concerning this "affinity": criticizing the *Cartesian* reduction of the phenomenon of the world to material nature, he adds "Critique of Husserl's construction of 'ontologies'!" (*Sein und* Zeit, § 21, *GA*, 2, 132 n. 2).

19. *Sein und Zeit*, § 18, respectively, 88, line 37; 89, lines 5–7; 89, line 27; 89, line 28 [see Eng. trans., 122, 123].

20. This analysis should be completed and confirmed by the parallel from *Prolegomena*, § 22, "Das traditionnelle Überspringen der Frage nach der Weltlichkeit der Welt am Beispiel Descartes" (*GA*, 20, 231ff.).

21. *Sein und Zeit*, § 6, respectively, 22, lines 14–18; 24, lines 16–29 [Eng. trans., 44, 46]. See also § 6, 24, lines 30–31 ("*völlig ontologischen Unbestimmtheit der res cogitans*"), and § 10, 49, line 28 ("*auch die cogitationes ontologisch unbestimmt bleiben . . .*").

22. Ibid., respectively, § 6, 24, lines 31–32; and § 10, 45, line 39–46, line 4 [Eng. trans., 46, 71; mod.].

23. IIIe *Responsiones*, AT, VII, 194, 12 ["The distinction between essence and existence is known to everyone"; Eng. trans., *The Philosophical Writings of Descartes*, vol. 2, trans. John Cottingham, Robert Stoothoff, and Dugald Murdoch (Cambridge: Cambridge University Press, 1984), 136].

24. *Sein und Zeit*, respectively, § 5, 16, line 1; § 6, 21, line 11 [Eng. trans., 37, 42; mod.]; see § 12, note c, "*Eine Rückdeutung*, an interpretation in return," *GA*, 2, 78.

25. On its posterity in the later work, see H. L. Dreyfus, "De la *technè* à la technique: le statut ambigu de l'ustensilité dans *L'Etre et le temps*," in *Martin Heidegger* (Paris: L'Herne, 1983), 292ff.

26. *Sein und Zeit*, § 21, respectively, 95, line 36–96, line 12; and 99, line 15 [see Eng. trans., 128, 132]. Likewise: "*die grundsätzlich ontologische Orientierung am Sein als ständiger Vorhandenheit*" (96, lines 15–16); "*Die Idee von Sein als beständige Vorhandenheit*" (98, line 1); ". . . ein Sein . . . —*ständige Dingvorhandenheit*" (99, line 15).

27. According to *Meditatio* II, AT, VII, 30, 19ff. "*Remanetne adhuc eadem cera? Remanere fatendum est*" ["But does the wax remain? It must be admitted that it does"; Eng. trans., *Philosophical Writings*, vol. 2, 20], and *Principia Philosophiae*, II, § 4, cited by *Sein und Zeit*, §§ 19, 21.

28. AT, VII, 25, 22–24 ["so that what remains at the end may be exactly and only what is certain and unshakeable"; Eng. trans., *Philosophical Writings*, vol. 2, 17; mod.]. On this omission and the whole of *Sein und Zeit*'s thesis on Descartes, see *Sur le prisme métaphysique de Descartes*, § 14, 184–86.

29. *Sein und Zeit*, § 8, 40, lines 4–6.

30. *Principia Philosophiae* I, § 52, cited in *Sein und Zeit*, § 20, 94, lines 4–6 ["we cannot initially become aware of a substance merely through its being an existing thing, since this alone does not of itself have any affect on us"; Eng. trans., *Philosophical Writings*, vol. 1, 210].

31. *Sein und Zeit*, § 20, 94, line 27 = § 19, 90, line 2. See § 21, 100, lines 7–14. The Cartesian aporia of the doctrine of substance cannot be underestimated (*Sur le prisme métaphysique de Descartes*, §§ 13–14).

32. *Sein und Zeit*, § 20, 94, lines 29–30 [see Eng. trans., 127], and then *GA*, 2, 127. Concerning the Cartesian failure to recognize the ontological difference, see before, chap. 4, § 3.

33. *Meditatio* III, AT, VII, 42, 22 [". . . that I am not alone in the world"; Eng. trans., *Philosophical Writings*, vol. 2, 29].

34. On this point, see our outline, "L'unique *ego* et l'altération de l'autre," in *Archivio di Filosofia* 54 nos. 1–3 (Rome, 1986).

35. *Sein und Zeit*, § 43 *a*, 202–8, which follows, here at least, Husserl, *LU*, V, *Beilage*, vol. 2, 421ff., and *Cartesianische Meditationen*, §§ 40–41. On the equivalence between Descartes and Kant in 1927, in addition to § 43, 204, lines 9 and 25, see § 21, 101, lines 10–12; and § 64, 320, line 1.

36. *Sein und Zeit*, respectively, § 21, 98, lines 8–10; § 43 *a*, 203, lines 25–28 [Eng. trans., 131, 247; mod.]. See *Prolegomena*, § 22, GA, 20, 239.

37. *Sein und Zeit*, § 43, 208, lines 3–4 [Eng. trans., 251; mod.]. This formula, which is the usual one, that "Being can never be explained by beings" (208, lines 3–4 = 207, lines 30, 34; § 2, 6, line 18; § 41, 196, line 17, etc.) receives, in a note from the personal copy of Heidegger, a decisive commentary: "*Ontologische Differenz*" (*GA*, 2, 275). It is thus explicitly confirmed that the indetermination of the meaning of Being entails (or results from) Descartes's failure to recognize the ontological difference. See below, chap. 4, § 3.

38. *Sein und Zeit*, respectively, § 64, 320, line 1, and § 43 *a*, 208, lines 6–11 [Eng. trans., 497, 251–52; mod.].

39. Ibid., § 14, 66, lines 27–28 [Eng. trans., 95].

40. Ibid., § 44, 230, lines 18–20 [see Eng. trans., 273].

41. Respectively, *Discours de la méthode*, AT, VI, 11, 8, 9–10 [Eng. trans., *Philosophical Writings*, vol. 1, 116]; *Meditationes*, AT, VII, 17, 13–18 ["I have expressly rid my mind of all worries"; Eng. trans., *Philosophical Writings*, vol. 2, 17]; and *Sein und Zeit*, respectively § 4, 11, lines 35–36; § 13, 61, lines 26–28 [Eng. trans., 32, 88; mod.].

42. *Sein und Zeit*, § 23, 104, line 33; § 24, 111, lines 33–34 [Eng. trans., 138, 146; mod.] (and this notwithstanding the difficulties with the temporalization of space, raised by D. Franck, *Heidegger et le problème de l'espace* [Paris, 1986]).

43. *Sein und Zeit*, respectively, § 4, 12, lines 11–12; § 4, 12, lines 4–12 [Eng. trans., 32; mod.] (see § 9, 41, lines 28–42, etc.).

44. Respectively, *Sein und Zeit*, § 6, 24, lines 34–35; *Meditationes*, AT, VII, 144, 24–25 [". . . the basis on which it seems to me that all human certainty can be founded"; Eng. trans., *Philosophical Writings*, vol. 2, 103]; *Discours*, AT, VI, 31, 18–19 [see Eng. trans., *Philosophical Writings*, vol. 1, 127]; *Meditationes*, AT, VII, 24, 12–13 [". . . just one thing . . . certain and unshakeable"; Eng. trans., *Philosophical Writings*, vol. 2, 16] and 17, 7 [". . . anything . . . stable and likely to last"; Eng. trans., 12], and finally *Discours*, AT, VI, 15, 6 [see Eng. trans., *Philosophical Writings*, vol. 1, 118].

45. Respectively, *Sein und Zeit*, § 4, 12, lines 25–26 [Eng. trans., 33; mod.]; and *Meditationes*, AT, VII, 25, 12 ["*I am, I exist*"; Eng. trans., *Philosophical Writings*, vol. 2, 17] (= 27, 28 according to a formula specific only to the text of 1641; see *Sur la théologie blanche de Descartes* [Paris, 1981], § 16, 378ff.). Heidegger does not give any privileged attention to this nevertheless remarkable formula, since it could be for the ego directly a matter of its Being (as existence) without the intermediary of representation. On this hypothesis, see M. Henry, *Généalogie de la psychanalyse: Le commencement perdu* (Paris, 1985), and my discussion, "Générosité et

phénoménologie: Remarques sur l'interprétation du *cogito* cartésien par Michel Henry," *Les Etudes philosophiques* (1988).

46. Respectively, *Sein und Zeit*, § 9, 42, lines 8–12 [Eng. trans., 67; mod.]; *Recherche de la vérité*, AT, X, 524, 10–13 ["I would never have believed that there has ever existed anyone so dull that he had to be told what existence is before being able to conclude and assert that he exists"; Eng. trans., *Philosophical Writings*, vol. 2, 417].

47. AT, VI, 33, 4–7.

48. Respectively, *Sein und Zeit*, § 4, 13, lines 12–13 [Eng. trans., 33; mod.]; *Discours*, AT, VI, 33, 4–7 [Eng. trans., *Philosophical Writings*, vol. 1, 127]; *Sein und Zeit*, § 63, 316, line 1; § 75, 388, line 23 [Eng. trans., 363, 440]. The Cartesian formula " . . . *non me solum esse in mundo*" [" . . . that I am not alone in the world"] (AT, VII, 42, 22), far from weakening, in fact confirms the absence of any *In-der-Welt-sein*, since it presupposes a simple relation of inclusion of the *ego* in the world, which thus presupposes its interpretation according to simple *Vorhanden-heit*.

49. Respectively, *Sein und Zeit*, § 65, 329, lines 37–38 [Eng. trans., 379]; *Meditatio*, III, AT, VII, 45, 21 ["when I am finite . . ."; Eng. trans., *Philosophical Writings*, vol. 2, 31].

50. *Sein und Zeit*, § 10, 48, line 27 [Eng. trans., 74]. See § 60, 24, lines 30ff.; § 20, 92, lines 6ff.; § 21, 95, lines 5–25; § 44, 289, lines 36–40. The *rapprochement* of the ego with *Dasein* according to finitude was precisely underlined by von Herrmann, "Husserl et Descartes," 16–17.

51. *Sein und Zeit*, respectively, § 4, 12, lines 22–23; § 9, 42, lines 23–29 [Eng. trans., 32–33, 67–68].

52. *Mediationes*, AT, VII, respectively, 25, 12 (= 27, 9); then *Discours*, AT, VI, 32, 19; and finally *Mediationes*, AT, VII, 25, 11–12 ["this proposition, *I* . . ."; Eng. trans., *Philosophical Writings*, vol. 2, 17].

53. That the Cartesian "ego-hood" anticipates the Heideggerian "mineness" could find confirmation in the similarity of the reproach of "injustice" addressed to them, respectively, by Pascal (*Pensées*, 397, 597) and E. Levinas (*Totalité et infini* [The Hague, 1962], 61, etc.) For other positive acceptations of "*Ich bin*," see § 58, 281, lines 25–27; § 60, 297, lines 15–17; § 63, 313, lines 28–30; § 64, 317, lines 27–28, etc.

54. *Sein und Zeit*, § 50, 250, lines 39–40 [Eng. trans., 294; mod.]. For an interpretation of Cartesian freedom in these terms, see *Sur le prisme métaphysique de Descartes*, chap. 3, § 15, 203–16.

55. *Sein und Zeit*, respectively, § 6, 24, lines 21, 31; § 6, 25, line 11; § 10, 49, line 28; § 25, 116, line 6; § 39, 183, lines 21–22 [Eng. trans., 46, 75, 150, 228; mod.].

56. See below, chap. 4, § 7.

57. *Sein und Zeit*, § 40, respectively, 186, lines 18–10, 188, lines 28–30 [Eng. trans., 231, 233; mod.].

58. Ibid., respectively, § 52, 258, lines 23–24, and 258, lines 39–259, line 1 (see § 53, 265, lines 22ff.); § 62, 308, lines 34–35, then 22–23, then 24–25; § 57,

275, lines 2–3; and finally, § 60, 298, lines 30–35 [Eng. trans., 302, 303, 356, 319, 345; mod.].

59. Ibid., § 43, 211, lines 13–20 [Eng. trans., 254; mod.].

60. Respectively, "Séminaire du Thor" (1968), in *Questions IV*, 222 (on the false opposition of realism and idealism, see *Sein und Zeit*, § 43, 208, lines 3–11); and *Nietzsche*, vol. 2, 135ff. (Descartes and Protagoras).

61. *Sein und Zeit*, respectively, § 9, 42, line 23, and lines 27–30; § 63, 313, lines 28–30 [Eng. trans., 67, 68, 361; mod.]. This formula is already established in 1924: "Das Dasein ist ein Seiendes, das sich bestimmt als 'Ich bin.' Für das Dasein ist die Jeweiligkeit des 'Ich bin,' konstitutiv," (*Begriff der Zeit*, unpublished in *GA*; French translation by M. Haar and M. de Launay, in *Martin Heidegger*, Paris, L'Herne, 30).

62. *Sein und Zeit*, respectively, § 25, 117, lines 6–7; § 64, 318, lines 3–4 (see § 64, 317; § 68, 348, line 5); § 65, 323, lines 3–9 [Eng. trans., 152, 364, 370; mod.].

63. Ibid., § 64, note to 317, line 35, *GA*, 2, 420.

64. Ibid., respectively, § 41, 193, line 10; § 64, 318, line 10 [Eng. trans., 237, 366; mod.].

65. Ibid., respectively, § 63, 313, lines 28–30 (see § 9, 42, lines 23–29); § 58, 281, lines 25–26; § 60, 297, lines 13–17 [Eng. trans., 361, 326, 343; mod.].

66. Ibid., § 64, respectively, 320, line 35; 322, lines 23–25, 22, 31–32 [Eng. trans., 367, 369; mod.].

67. See the curious limitation placed upon ipseity in Heidegger, *Grundbegriffe der Metaphysik*, § 56, *GA*, 29–30, 340, along with the reflections of D. Franck, "L'être et le vivant," *Philosophie* 16 (Paris 1987).

4. Question of Being

1. This, moreover, is why the destruction as Heidegger exercises it proves to be not very negative or deconstructive: it places (to be sure, sometimes forcefully) under the light of Being the discourses that metaphysics has held concerning being: "But this destruction is just as far from having the *negative* sense of shaking off ontological tradition. We must, on the contrary, stake out the positive possibilities of that tradition, and this always means keeping it within its *limits*. . . . But to bury the past in nullity [*Nichtigkeit*] is not the purpose of this destruction; its aim is *positive*; its negative function remains unexpressed and indirect" (*Sein und Zeit*, § 6, 22, line 35–23, line 5) [Eng. trans., 44].

2. *Identität und Differenz* (Pfullingen, 1957), 69 [Eng. trans., 71].

3. Ibid., 46–47 [Eng. trans., 50]. Likewise: " . . . a thinking that is on its way, a thinking which accomplishes the step back, back out of metaphysics into the essence of metaphysics, back out of the forgetting of the difference as such into the sending that veils to us, by withdrawing itself, the conciliation" (71) [Eng. trans., 72; mod.].

4. *Wegmarken*, *GA*, 9, 123 [Eng. trans., 3; mod.].

5. Ibid., 134 [Eng. trans., 27; mod.].

6. Ibid., 123 [Eng. trans., 3; mod.].

7. *Identität und Differenz*, 52 [Eng. trans., 61; mod.].

8. *Wegmarken, GA,* 9, 131 [Eng. trans., 23].

9. *Grundprobleme der Phänomenologie,* § 9, *GA,* 24, 102 [Eng. trans., 72; mod.]. One could also compare the *Prolegomena zur Geschichte des Zeitbegriffs,* § 20 a, *GA,* 20, 348–49 (but without any return toward the ontological difference), as P. Jaeger stresses, *GA,* 20, 349, 444 (concerning variations in the terms of the opposition). Note also *ontologische Differenz* in *GA,* 24, 22, 102, 106, 109, 170, 321ff.

10. *Sein und Zeit,* § 2, 6, lines 23–25 [Eng. trans., 26; mod.].

11. *Wegmarken, GA* 9, 134, n. b.

12. *Sein und Zeit,* § 2, 6, line 25.

13. *Grundprobleme,* § 22, 454 [Eng. trans., 319; mod.].

14. *Wegmarken, GA,* 9, 134.

15. *Sein und Zeit,* § 8, 39, line 39.

16. Ley M. Vail, *Heidegger and the Ontological Difference* (Pennsylvania State University, 1972), 5, 47. This dating, attenuated, to be sure, by the consideration of the *Grundprobleme,* is maintained by J. Grondin, "Réflexions sur la différence ontologique," *Les Etudes philosophiques* (1984), 338 n. 5, and by J. Greisch: "If the ontological difference subtends all the analyses of *Sein und Zeit,* it is nevertheless not designated there as such, nor is it identified as a central theme of ontological thought" (*La parole heureuse,* [Paris, 1987], 68).

17. John C. Sallis, "La différence ontologique et l'unité de la pensée de Heidegger," *Revue philosophique de Louvain* (1967), 194. But what is one supposed to understand by such a "framework," which would remain nameless at the very instant that it frames? Does the location of the "ontic pole of the difference" (195) suffice, precisely, truly to locate an ontological difference?

18. G. Granel, "Remarques sur le rapport de *Sein und Zeit* et de la phéno-ménologie husserlienne," *Durchblicke, Martin Heidegger zum 80. Geburtstag* (Frankfurt, 1972), reprinted in *Traductionis traditio* (Paris, 1972). Why introduce these quotation marks, if not to introduce a (correct) thesis despite its (apparent) absence of literal justification? One finds the same ambiguity in the accurate but textually unargued judgment of T. Langan: ". . . that ontic-ontological distinction, so strongly emphasized in *Sein und* Zeit, which will play an important role throughout Heidegger's works" (*The Meaning of Heidegger* [1959], 74). J. Grondin, even if he goes back to the 1927 course, even if he recognizes it "without being named" in 1925, still admits as norm "the first public appearance in 1929" ("Réflexions," 338). A. Rosales also remains in the same ambiguity: "Da das Problem der Differenz z.B. in *Sein und Zeit,* wenn auch nicht ausdrücklich, *entfaltet* wird . . ." (*Transzendenz und Differenz: Ein Beitrag zum Problem der ontologischen Differenz beim frühen Heidegger* [The Hague, 1970], xii; see 246. And again C. Esposito, *Il Fenomeno dell'essere: Fenomenologia e ontologia in Heidegger,* (Bari, 1984) § 16, 184–95.

19. J. Beaufret, *Entretiens* (Paris, 1984), 11–12. One finds the same loose and implicit attribution, without textual justification, of the ontological difference to *Sein und Zeit* in F.-W. von Herrmann, *Subjekt und Dasein—Interpretationen zu "Sein und Zeit"* (Frankfurt, 1974; 2d ed, 1985), 28.

20. *Sein und Zeit*, § 12, 56, lines 12–14 [Eng. trans., 82; mod.]. E. Martineau indeed translates this (63) by *différence ontologique*; likewise, R. Boehm and A. de Waelhens, *L'Etre et le temps* (Paris, 1964), whose note unhappily and without discussion joins the common opinion: "The 'ontological difference' of which this sentence speaks is not to be confused with the famous difference between Being and beings which, moreover, will be distinguished for the first time as 'ontological difference' only in *Vom Wesen des Grundes*, 1929" (287). The whole question is precisely whether the same formula can change its meaning in such a short time and why, for it is a not a matter here, as for example in § 20, 92, lines 28ff., of a purely ontic *Unterschied ihres Seins*, nor, as in § 5, 18, line 9, of a "*naive Unterscheidung der verschiedenen Regionen des Seienden.*" F. Vezin commits an error in translating by "*distinction ontologique*" (*Etre et temps* [Paris, 1986], 90). Curiously, A. Rosales paraphrases this text without citing it or seeing that it contradicts the common thesis (*Transzendenz und Differenz*, 3).

21. *Sein und Zeit*, § 40, 188, lines 30–34 [Eng. trans., 233; mod.]. Martineau here says *opposition* (147), as does F. Vezin (*Etre et Temps*, 239); this choice is justified all the less insofar as it is Heidegger himself who refers here, in a note, to the precise passage from § 12 that introduces the ontological difference as such (note 20). R. Boehm and A. de Waelhens (*L'Etre et le temps*, 231) use *différencier*, which is better but still insufficient.

22. *Sein und Zeit*, § 63, 314, lines 5–7 [Eng. trans., 362; mod.]. Martineau here translates *Unterscheidung* by *différenciation* (223) (followed, moreover, by D. Franck, *Heidegger et le problème de l'espace* [Paris: Minuit, 1986] 29). That seems to us untenable for several reasons: (1) A few lines lower (314, line 13), Martineau himself translates "*Die Unterscheidung zwischen Existenz und Realität*" by "*La distinction entre existence et réalité*"; why not have used *distinction* to begin with? And then why not *différence*? (2) The difference between *Unterscheidung* and *Unterschied* is not pertinent in the texts of Heidegger: the translator therefore does not respect his own choice; thus, in this same § 63, 313, lines 33ff., the second term replaces the first in order to distinguish the same terms as it: "Mag der Unterschied von Existenz und Realität noch so weit von einem ontologischen Begriff entfern sein . . ." (Martineau here translates *différence*, 222). The equivalence of the German terms at times becomes a complete identity: "die Unterscheidung innerhalb des Seienden zu gewinnen, den Fundamentalunterschied innerhalb des Seienden zu fixieren, das heisst, im Grunde, die Seinsfrage zu beantworten" (*GA*, 20, 157); or again: "die Möglichkeit, den Unterschied zwischen dem in der Entdeckteit entdeckten Seienden und dem in der Erschlossenheit erschlossen Sein zu fassen, d. h. die Unterscheidung zwischen Sein und Seienden, die ontologische Differenz zu fixieren" (*GA*, 24, 102). While Heidegger thematizes the divergence, sometimes, between *Unterschied* and *Differenz*, he does not essentially distinguish between *Unterschied* and *Unterscheidung*. Therefore it is indeed a matter here of a *difference* (despite the attenuation of Martineau) and of an *ontological* difference (despite F. Vezin, who entirely omits translating the adjective, *Etre et temps*, 374). J. Macquarrie and E. Robinson also avoid the complete formula: " . . . to distinguish ontologically between existence and Reality" (*Being and Time* [Oxford, 1967], 362).

23. *Sein und Zeit,* § 83, respectively, 436, lines 36–37; 437, line 11 [Eng. trans., 487; mod.].

24. This topic is confirmed (by the verb *unterscheiden* only) in § 26, 118, lines 15–17; § 31, 143, lines 31–34; § 57, 276, lines 12–13: "Die Faktizität des Daseins aber unterscheidet sich wesenhaft von der Tatsächlichkeit eines Vorhandenen"; § 58, 283, lines 21–24; § 69, 364, lines 6–9.

25. Likewise the "ontological indifference [*ontologische Indifferenz*]" of life in Dilthey (§ 43, 209, line 33), which by extension affects the "difference between the ontic and the historical" that Yorck disputes in him. But this difference, besides the fact that it is criticized and assumed, does not concern, precisely, the ways of Being of beings and does not approach the question of Being. See § 77, 399, line 31; 400, lines 8–9; 403, lines 15, 19 (*Unterschied*); 403, lines 35–36. Even the *Unterschied* between reality and existence can also be found " . . . weit von einem ontologischen Begriff entfernt" (§ 63, 313, lines 33–34).

26. *Sein und Zeit,* respectively, § 2, 6, lines 23–25; and § 44, 230, lines 5–10 [Eng. trans., 26, 272; mod.].

27. Ibid., 230, line 8. Martineau, usually irreproachable, seems here to make an error by introducing a reservation ("provided that it has to be distinguished from every being . . ."), where the German indicates a counteraffirmation (*doch, soll*); moreover, *to distinguish* weakens, here as often elsewhere, *unterscheiden* (169). R. Boehm and A. de Waelhens keep *to distinguish,* but miss the affirmation ("although having to . . .") (*L'Etre et le temps,* 275ff.). F. Vezin mistranslates the whole sentence (*Etre et temps,* 281). J. MacQuarrie and E. Robinson correctly give "What does it signify that Being 'is,' where Being is to be distinguished from every entity?" (*Being and Time,* 272).

28. *Sein und Zeit,* § 44, *GA,* 2, 304.

29. *Sein und Zeit,* § 7, 37, lines 23–27 [Eng. trans., 61; mod.]; and then the additional note, ibid., *GA,* 2, 50.

30. *Sein und Zeit,* § 20, respectively, 94, lines 31–33; 94, line 31 [Eng. trans., 127; mod.]; and the note, *GA,* 2, 127. In the same § 20 one should take into account, as convergent signs, occurrences of the phrase "*Unterschied des Seins*" (93, lines 12–13), and similar ones (92, line 28; 93, line 18). For an approach to the interpretation of Descartes, see above, chap. 3, § 4.

31. *Sein und Zeit,* § 39, respectively, 183, lines 21–22; 183, lines 28–31; § 2, 6, line 25 [Eng. trans., 228, 26; mod.]; and *GA,* 2, 244.

32. *Sein und Zeit,* § 43, respectively, 208, lines 4–5 [Eng. trans., 251; mod.] (see, among other parallels, § 2, 6, lines 18–23; § 7, 35, lines 26–29; § 41, 196, lines 15–18; § 43, 207, line 34, etc.); and *GA,* 2, 275.

33. Respectively, § 44, 230, line 8; § 2, 6, line 25; § 83, 436, line 38; § 83, 437, 11.

34. *Logische Untersuchungen,* vol. 2; *Untersuchungen zur Phänomenologie und Theorie der Erkenntnis,* § 9, 248–49 [Eng. trans., 452–53; mod.]. As signaled by the French translation (by H. Elie, A. L. Kelkel and R. Schérer [Paris, Presses Universitaires de France, 1961–64], vol. 2, 30–31), the first edition of 1901 never used *ontologisch,* but, respectively, "fundamental *objektiv,*" "difference" without an adjective, and "objective" (327, 328). For what reason, or even under what

influence, did Husserl in 1913 correct these first formulations with *ontologisch?* We don't know.

35. *Sein und Zeit,* § 39, respectively, 183, lines 28–31 [Eng. trans., 228; mod.]; and *GA,* 2, 244.

36. *Sein und Zeit,* § 63, 314, line 6 [see Eng. trans., 362]. Let us remark that in the other occurrence, "the ontological difference [*ontologischen Unterschied*] between Being-in . . . as an existential and the category of 'insideness' which subsisting beings can have with regard to one another" (§ 12, 56, lines 12–14) [Eng. trans., 82; mod.] can easily be led back to that between *Dasein* and beings that are not like *Dasein,* and therefore to the *Unterschied* between existence and reality that ensues therefrom.

37. *Ideen I, Hua,* III, 95, lines 16–18; 95, lines 25–27; 96, lines 18–21; 96, lines 24–25 [see Eng. trans., 89, 90]. This last usage of *kardinalste* should be compared with Heidegger's: "das Kardinal-Problem, die Frage nach dem Sinn von Sein überhaupt" (*Sein und Zeit,* § 7, 37, lines 25–26). See above, chap. 2, § 2; chap. 3, § 2; and below, chap. 5, § 6.

38. *Sein und Zeit,* § 83, respectively, 436, line 39–437, line 1; and 437, line 11 [Eng. trans., 487; mod.].

39. *Ideen I,* respectively, § 43, 99, lines 6–7; § 49, 116, line 37–117, line 2; and finally § 76, 174, lines 9–12 [Eng. trans., 93, 111, 171; mod.].

40. *Prolegomena,* § 13, *GA,* 20, 158 [Eng. trans., 114–15; mod.].

41. *Prolegomena,* § 13, 159 [Eng. trans., 115]. The same accusation (*unphänomenologisch*) appears on 118, 178, and 183 (*widerphänomenologisch*); see chap. 2, above.

42. Letter from Heidegger to Husserl, 27 October 1927, in E. Husserl, *Phänomenologische Psychologie, Hua,* IX, 601. To be compared with *Sein und Zeit,* § 61, 303, lines 28–29: "*Das Dasein ist ontologisch grundsätzlich von allem Vorhandenen und Realen verschieden,*" or even with § 59, 294, lines 24–25 (*völlig anderes sein*).

43. Letter from Heidegger to Husserl, *Hua,* IX, 602. We would make J.-F. Courtine's conclusion our own: "these texts testify not only to a brief collaboration and an open debate with Husserl, but also to the debate in which Heidegger himself is involved *with phenomenology*" (*Martin Heidegger* [Paris: L'Herne, 1983], 43). Here we meet up again with J. Grondin's judgment: "Everything leads one to believe that the ontological difference can . . . be read as a response to Husserl" ("Réflexions," 338).

44. *Sein und Zeit,* respectively, § 1, 4, line 9; § 2, 6, lines 18–19; § 41, 196, lines 17–18; § 43, 207, line 34 (see line 30) [Eng. trans., 23, 26, 241, 251; mod.].

45. *Sein und Zeit,* § 43, 208, line 4 [Eng. trans., 251]. This last fragment precisely is commented on in a note with the remark "ontological difference" (*GA,* 2, 275, cited above, § 3). This equivalence, of course, is shared by all the parallels: in this ontic inexplicability one is indeed dealing with the canonical ontological difference. This sentence would be confirmed by, among others, some sequences from the 1927 summer course: "Being itself is not a being"; "Being is nothing of a being"; "Being itself is not a being" (*Grundprobleme, GA,* 24, respectively, 58, 77, 109).

46. *Sein und Zeit*, respectively, § 2, 7, line 4 (*ablesen*); § 3, 9, line 7; § 2, 6, lines 29–30; § 7, 37, lines 12–13; § 39, 183, lines 29–32 [Eng. trans., 29, 26, 61, 228; mod.]. This will be complemented by an illuminating development from 1928: "Being is, as such, always the Being of beings. . . . Being is, as such and in its every meaning, the Being of beings. Being is different [*unterscheiden*] than beings, and only this difference [*Unterschied*] in general, this possibility of difference, insures an understanding-of-Being. Put another way: in the understanding-of-Being resides the accomplishment of the differing [*des Unterscheidens*] of Being and beings" (*Metaphysische Anfangsgründe der Logik im Ausgang von Leibniz, GA*, 26, 193) [Eng. trans., 152; mod.]. See: "We always know only beings, but never Being [as if it were a] being" (ibid., 195) [Eng. trans., 153].

47. *Sein und Zeit*, § 2, respectively, 5, line 2; 6, line 30; 6, line 15; 6, lines 23–25 [Eng. trans., 24, 26; mod.]. See above, chap. 2, § 6.

48. *Sein und Zeit*, § 2, 6, line 25 [Eng. trans., 26]. On the irreducible triplicity of a constructed *Seinsfrage*, see, besides *Sein und Zeit*, § 2, in particular 7, lines 37–40, and § 7, 37, lines 22–26, the *Prolegomena*, § 15 (*GA*, 20, 193ff.; § 16, 195ff.); there one is indeed dealing with a triplicity, *das Dreifache* (195, 197). For the most part, that triplicity will disappear after 1927. Concerning the specificity of the meaning of Being, there are some good references in J. Beaufret, *Entretiens*, 40–41, 103.

49. *Sein und Zeit*, respectively, § 2, 5, line 17; § 7, 37, lines 22–27 [Eng. trans., 24, 61; mod.].

50. *Sein und Zeit, GA* 2, 50. See, *a contrario*, the same redoubling of the divergences: "One can determine beings in their Being without necessarily having the explicit concept of the meaning of Being at one's disposal" (*Sein und Zeit*, § 2, 7, lines 37–41) [Eng. trans., 27; mod.].

51. *Sein und Zeit*, § 83, 437, lines 40–41.

52. Quoted by Max Müller, in *Existenz philosophie im geistigen Leben der Gegenwart* (Heidelberg, 1949, 1964), 66–67: "a. die 'transzendentale' oder ontologische Differenz im engeren Sinne: Den Unterschied des Seienden von seiner Seiendheit. b. die 'transzendenzhafte' oder ontologische im weiteren Sinn: Den Unterschied des Seienden *und* seiner Seiendheit vom Sein selbst. c. die 'transzendente' oder theologische Differenz im strengen Sinne: Den Unterschied des Gottes vom Seienden, von der Seiendheit und vom Sein." Quoting this remark, O. Pöggeler wonders whether Heidegger did not renounce "die Aufgliederung der Differenz und die Gründung einer in der anderen, wie er sie im dritten Abschnitt von *Sein und Zeit* durchführen wollte," because it was a matter there of a doctrine that was "not proven but only speculatively constructed" (O. Pöggeler, *Der Denkweg Martin Heideggers* [Pfullingen, 1963, 1983], 92). There remains another hypothesis: that the distinction of the differences insufficiently or wrongly formalizes what was already at bottom proven. Then there would be a *withdrawal* and not an excess of this formulation with respect to the proof already made. A. Rosales gives a useful commentary on this text (*Transzendenz und Differenz*, 175 n. 5).

53. *Grundprobleme*, § 20, *GA*, 25, 425 [Eng. trans., 299; mod.]. See the remark-

ably clear development of this theme given in 1928 in *Metaphysische Anfangsgründe*, § 11 (*GA*, 26, 203–53), which attributes to *Dasein* an *Urtranszendenz* (*GA*, 26, 20).

54. *Sein und Zeit*, § 7, 38, lines 10–12 [Eng. trans., 62; mod.].

55. Ibid., respectively, § 7, 38, line 12; § 69, 363, lines 29–30; § 43, 208, lines 3–5; § 69, 364, line 20 (= 366, line 2); and § 80, 419, lines 5–6 [Eng. trans., 62, 415, 251, 415, 471; mod.].

56. Ibid., § 4, 12, lines 11–12 [Eng. trans., 32].

57. Ibid., § 39, 183, lines 30–32 [Eng. trans., 228; mod.].

58. See ibid., § 63, 311, *passim,* and *Prolegomena,* § 17: "The actual elaboration of the position of the question is thus a *phenomenology of Dasein,* but it already finds the answer truly and finds it as an answer for the investigation only inasmuch as that elaboration of the question concerns the being that contains in itself a distinctive understanding of Being. *Dasein* is decisive here not only ontically but, at the same time, for us phenomenologists, ontologically" (*GA*, 20, 200) [see Eng. trans., 148]. *Dasein* is in the mode of the understanding of Being (§ 4, 12, lines 11–12. "The understanding of Being is itself a determination of the Being of *Dasein*") [Eng. trans., 32; mod.]. See *GA*, 9, 134; *GA*, 24, 322–23, 444, 453; *GA*, 26, 20, etc.

59. *Sein und Zeit*, § 4, 12, lines 4–5 [Eng. trans., 32]. See the same formula in § 9, 42, lines 23–24; § 30, 141, lines 19–30; § 41, 191, lines 28–29; § 45, 231, lines 13–14, etc.

60. *Sein und Zeit*, respectively, § 5, 17, lines 30–31; § 9, 42, lines 1–2 [Eng. trans., 39, 67; mod.]; and the note in *GA* 2, 56. See, in this sense, § 12, 56, lines 8–11 (just before the occurrence of *ontologischer Unterschied*); § 4, 12, lines 4–5 (with the explanatory note: "But here Being not only in the sense of the Being of man [existence])" (*GA*, 2, 16); § 28, 133, lines 1–14, etc.

61. *Prolegomena,* § 17, *GA*, 20, 199 [see Eng. trans., 147].

62. *Sein und Zeit*, § 83, 436, line 18; § 45, 231, lines 3 and 6, etc. (see 41, lines 6, 8, 26, etc.).

63. Ibid., respectively, § 83, 436, line 24 (= 437, line 19 [*ein Weg*]); 1, line 16 (*vorläufiger Ziel*); and § 5, 17, lines 14–15 (*vorläufig*) [Eng. trans., 487, 19, 38; mod.].

64. Ibid., § 83, respectively, 436, lines 24–25 (*überhaupt*); 436, line 27 (*überhaupt* = 437, line 16); 437, line 38 [Eng. trans., 487, 488; mod.].

65. Ibid., respectively, § 83, 436, lines 29–30 (= § 7, 38, line 21); and 436, line 30 or 437, line 1 [Eng. trans., 487; mod.].

66. Ibid., § 83, respectively, 436, line 38; 437, line 1; 437, lines 10–11; 437, lines 1–3; 437, lines 10–12; 437, line 19 [Eng. trans., 487; mod.]. See the note in *GA*, 2, 576: "and not 'the' only one."

67. *Sein und Zeit*, § 83, 436, lines 35–37 [Eng. trans., 487; mod.].

68. Ibid., respectively, § 2, 7, lines 3–5; § 4, 11, lines 29, 37; § 4, 13, line 23 [Eng. trans., 26, 32, 34; mod.].

69. Ibid., § 83, 437, line 25, and then lines 32–33 [Eng. trans., 488].

70. Ibid., respectively, § 2, 7, lines 3–4 [see Eng. trans., 26]; and note *b* in *GA*, 2, 9.

71. *Sein und Zeit,* respectively, § 2, 7, lines 4–8 [see Eng. trans., 26]; and note *c* in *GA,* 2, 9. This text is practically untranslatable, since *Beispiel* here resonates with *Spiel, spielen, zuspielen,* etc. Even the subtle translation of *Bei-spiel* by *al-lusion* (*ad-lusio, ludere*), which F. Vézin proposes (*Etre et Temps,* 30), does not allow one to overcome the difficulty of rendering the other harmonics of *spielen.*

72. *Sein und Zeit,* § 63, 311, lines 12–16 [Eng. trans., 359; mod.].

73. Ibid., respectively, § 63, *GA,* 2, 412, note *a*; and § 2, 7, line 4.

74. To which one should compare this later and magnificently lucid diagnostic concerning § 83: "Whether the realm of the truth of Being is an impasse [*Sackgasse,* a dead-end] or whether it is the free horizon where freedom conserves its essence is something each one may judge after he himself has tried to take the designated path, or even better, after he has blazed a better one, that is, one more befitting the question" (*Brief über den Humanismus, GA,* 9, 344) [Eng. trans., 223; mod.]. It is therefore Heidegger himself who envisages the hypothesis of a "dead-end" for *Sein und Zeit.* Moreover, it is not certain that, within its own unfolding, *Sein und Zeit* did not pave the way for a "running aground," or even a "shipwreck" (*scheitern*): § 31, 148, lines 9–12; § 45, 233, lines 22–26; § 64, 317, lines 6–10. But at least it could be a matter of an "authentic running aground" (§ 37, 174, line 15).

75. *Sein und Zeit,* § 71, 371, line 20 [Eng. trans., 423].

5. Being and Region

1. *Sein und Zeit,* § 7, 37, lines 21–22 [Eng. trans., 61; mod.].

2, Ibid., § 7, 35, lines 36–37 [Eng. trans., 60; mod.].

3. *Grundprobleme der Phänomenologie,* § 1, *GA,* 24, 3 [Eng. trans., 3]. See § 5, 27; § 22, 466.

4. *Sein und Zeit,* § 7, 35, lines 38–39 [Eng. trans., 60; mod.].

5. *Prolegomena zur Geschichte des Zeitbegriffs,* § 6, *GA,* 20, 178 [Eng. trans., 128; mod.]. See above, chap. 2, § 2.

6. Respectively, *Cartesianische Meditationen,* § 64, *Hua,* I, 181 [Eng. trans., 155]; *Pariser Vorträge, Hua,* I, 38; *Cartesiansiche Meditationen,* § 12, *Hua,* I, 66 [Eng. trans., 27; mod.].

7. *Ideen III,* § 12, *Hua,* V, 72 [see Eng. trans., 61–62].

8. *Erste Philosophie,* I, § 26, *Hua,* VII, 187 (and note 1).

9. *Erste Philosophie,* II *Idee der vollen Ontologie* (1924), and *Weg in die transzendentale Phänomenologie als absolute und universale Ontologie durch die positiven Ontologien und die positive erste Philosophie* (1923), in *Hua,* VIII, respectively, 213, 215, 217, 219.

10. *Formale und Transzendentale Logik,* § 27, *Hua,* XVII, 90 (my emphasis) [Eng. trans., 86].

11. On the legitimacy of an anonymous concept according to Aristotle, see *Metaphysics* Z, 7, 1033a14, Z, 8; 1034 a I; I, 5, 1056a25; and *Categories* 7, 7a19; etc.

12. *Ideen I,* § 10 n. 3, *Hua,* 28 [Eng. trans., 22; mod.].

13. *Entwurf einer Vorrede zu den "Logischen Untersuchungen"* (1913), in *Tijdschrift voor Philosophie* 1, 320–22 [Eng. trans., 41–43; mod.].

14. See n. 6, above.

15. *Ideen I*, § 8, *Hua*, 23 [see Eng. trans., 18], and § 9, 25 [Eng. trans., 19]. On the translation of *"Gegenständlichkeit"* by *"objectity,"* see below, note 33.

16. *Ideen I*, § 9, *Hua*, III, respectively, 23–24, 25, 24 [Eng. trans., 18; mod.].

17. *Ideen I*, § 10, *Hua*, III, respectively, 26, 27, 27–28, 27 [Eng. trans., 20, 21; mod.].

18. On the principle of contradiction, see *Formale und transzendentale Logik*, § 18.

19. *Formale und transzendentale Logik*, § 23, *Hua*, XVII, 77, and § 24, 81–82 [see Eng. trans., 73, 76–78]. Aristotle's ontology is put aside because it is "real," not yet formal (§§ 26–27). This is surprising since Aristotle ties the Being of being directly to its form (*eidos*).

20. For a definition of the apophantic: " . . . the *apophantic sphere*—that of assertions (of 'judgments' in the traditional logical sense)" *Formale und transzendentale Logik*, § 12, 53 [see Eng. trans., 48]; see the parallels in § 13, 56; § 14, 60; § 17, 67, etc.

21. Ibid., § 41, 115 [Eng. trans., 110].

22. Ibid., § 42 *a*, 116 [Eng. trans., 111; mod.].

23. Ibid., § 42 *a*, 117 [Eng. trans., 112; mod.].

24. Ibid., § 42 *c*, 119 [Eng. trans., 114; mod.].

25. Ibid., § 42 *d*, 120 [Eng. trans., 115; mod.].

26. Ibid., § 54 *b*, 151 [Eng. trans., 145; mod.].

27. The unreal character of intentionality was established as early as its first thematization, in the Fifth Logical Investigation: *"die Unterscheidung zwischen dem reellen Inhalt eines Aktes und seinem intentionalen Inhalt"* (*LU*, V, § 16, vol. 2, 397, see the note, and 399). It remains established up to the *Cartesian Meditations*. For example: "Also *dasselbe* besagt hier wie überall: identischer intentionaler Gegenstand getrennter Erlebnisse, ihren also nur als Irreelles immanent" (§ 55, *Hua*, I, 155). On the unreality of intentionality, see J. N. Mohanty, *The Concept of Intentionality* (Saint Louis, 1972), part 2, chaps. 1 and 2; J. R. Mensch, *The Question of Being in Husserl's "Logical Investigations"* (The Hague, 1981), 77–78.

28. *Formale und transzendentale Logik*, § 43, 125 [see Eng. trans., 120] (and previously, § 42 *a*, 116). See the pertinent analyses of D. Souche-Dagues, *Le développement de l'intentionalité dans la phénoménologie husserlienne* (The Hague, 1972), in particular, 212ff.

29. *Formale und transzendentale Logik*, § 76, 199 [Eng. trans., 191; mod.].

30. Ibid., § 42, 123 [Eng. trans., 118; mod.]. It would be necessary to relate (in order to oppose it) this mode of duration of the object (which persists through its repetition "for me," or even "though me") to the mode of duration of the Cartesian *ego*, which persists in being only "as long, *quamdiu*" and only "as often, *quoties*" as it is thought by itself (AT, VII, 25, 9, and 27, 9, etc.).

31. *Erste Philosophie*, I, 3, *Hua*, VII, 28. See *Ideen I*: "Jedes formal-logische Gesetz ist äquivalent umzuwenden in ein formal-ontologisches. Statt über Urteile

wird jetzt über Sachverhalte, statt über Prädikatbedeutungen . . . über Gegenstände . . . geurteilt wird" (*Hua*, III, 362). Not only does the equivalence between judgment and state of affairs remain unjustified, but it is itself again fully at play within the judgment.

32. *Formale und transzendentale Logik*, § 54, respectively, 149, 153 [Eng. trans., 144, 148; mod.].

33. *Objectité* is used by S. Bachelard to translate *Gegenständlichkeit*, e.g., in the Introduction, *Hua*, XVII, 16 (French translation [Paris, 1984], 18 and note) and § 27, 91. We have always done the same in order not to confuse scientific objectivity—which in 1900 Husserl still held to be essential: " . . . the central question of the theory of knowledge, which concerns the objectivity (*Objectivität*) of knowledge" (Introduction to the *Prolegomena*, § 3, *LU*, vol. 1, 8)—with what more essentially renders it possible: the construction in general of an object, presupposing in its turn a mode of Being specific to what is called an "object"—precisely objectity.

34. *Ideen I*, § 148, *Hua*, III, 363 [see Eng. trans., 354]; see: "hier eine ganz ausserordentliche Erweiterung der Idee des *on* vorgenommen ist" (in fact embracing under the term *Seiende* "norms," power," etc.), *Idee der vollen Ontologie*, *Hua*, VIII, 217.

35. *Formale und transzendentale Logik*, Introduction, 16 [Eng. trans., 12; mod.].

36. Ibid., § 54, 149, and § 35 n. 105 [Eng. trans., 144, 101; mod.]. See *Ideen I*, § 10, *Hua*, III, 27.

37. *Idee der vollen Ontologie*, *Hua*, VIII, 213. In what measure would the undisputed ontological primacy of objectity justify one in speaking of a Scotism in Husserl? We should remark that Heidegger is mentioned, as an author, only once in *Formale und transzendentale Logik*: in a note from § 12, precisely for his work on the pseudo–Duns Scotus, *Die Kategorien- und Bedeutungslehre des Duns Scotus* (1915, *GA*, 1, 189ff.), cited on 54 n. 2.

38. *Cartesianische Meditationen*, § 64, *Hua*, I, 181.

39. *Idee der vollen Ontologie*, *Hua*, VIII, 215.

40. Respectively, *Ideen I*, § 148, *Hua*, III, 364, § 44, 101; § 45, 105 [Eng. trans., 355, 95, 99; mod.].

41. Respectively, *Ideen III*, § 12, *Hua*, V, 74–75 and 75 [Eng. trans., 64]; then *Nachwort*, ibid., 153. Likewise *Formale und transzendentale Logik*, § 102: "A *formal ontology of any possible world*, as a world constituted in transcendental subjectivity, is a non–self-sufficient moment [*unselbständiges Moment*] of *another 'formal ontology'*" (*Hua*, XVII, 276) [Eng. trans., 271; mod.]; and again in § 103: "*Every being* [*alles Seiende*] (as opposed to the false ideal of an absolute being and its absolute truth) is finally relative [*relativ*], and, along with everything that is relative in the usual sense and in whatever way that might be, it is *relative to transcendental subjectivity*" (ibid., 279) [Eng. trans., 273; mod.].

42. *Ideen I*, Beilage 10, *Hua*, III, 394. "*Sein als Bewußtsein*" or "*Sein des Bewußtsein*": § 42 and § 49, respectively, 95, 115; "*eine prinzipiell einartige Seinsregion*"; § 32, 72.

43. *Ideen I*, § 49, *Hua*, III, 116, 117 [Eng. trans., 111; mod.].

44. *Ideen I*, § 76, *Hua*, III, 174 [see Eng. trans., 171].

45. *Ideen I*, *Beilage* 9, *Hua*, III, 394.

46. Reported by D. Cairns, *Conversations with Husserl and Fink*, ed. Husserl-Archiv (The Hague, 1976), 76 (conversation dated 19 May 1932).

47. *Ideen III*, § 12, *Hua*, V, 75 [Eng. trans., 64].

48. Respectively, *Cartesianische Meditationen*, § 59, *Hua*, I, 164 [Eng. trans., 137; mod.]; *Ideen III*, *Beilage* 1, § 6, *Hua*, V, 129 [Eng. trans., 117]; and finally, *Apriorische Ontologie und Phänomenologie* (1906–07), *Hua*, XXIV, 422.

49. *Ideen I*, § 59 and § 60, *Hua*, III, respectively, 142, 143 [Eng. trans., 136, 138; mod.].

50. Respectively, *Ideen III*, § 13, *Hua*, V, 76 [see Eng. trans., 65]; then *Cartesianische Meditationen*, § 15, *Hua*, I, 72 [Eng. trans., 34]. See: "diese Epoché, was das Ausser-Vollzug-Setzen des Seinsglauben hinsichtlich der Erfahrungswelt bedeutet," *Nachwort*, *Hua*, III, 145.

51. *Ideen III*, § 13 and § 14, *Hua*, V, respectively, 76, 78 [see Eng. trans., 65, 66–67]. See *Ideen I*, § 153 and § 59, *Hua*, III, respectively, 379–80, 142.

52. *Ideen III*, § 14 and § 20, *Hua*, V, respectively, 77, 105 [Eng. trans., 66, 90; mod.]. See § 12, 72, 73, and "Mutterboden aller philosophischen Methode": § 15, 80.

53. *Ideen III*, § 15, *Hua*, V, 79, 80, 84 [Eng. trans., 68, 72; mod.]. See "das Identische von uns soeben mit Grund in Anführungszeichen gesetzt wurde" (§ 16, 85).

54. *Ideen III*, § 15, *Hua*, V, 84, 85 [Eng. trans., 72; mod.]. On the nonconfusion of ontic concepts with the intuition of noemata, see § 16, 83, 86. The quotation marks (see note 53, above) here play a real conceptual role, starting from the "dasselbe" (§ 15, 80, line 12; see 84, line 4); thus § 16, 85, lines 1–2 and 26–28; 88, lines 32–37, etc.; in fact their thematic use goes back, at least with regard to what concerns us, to *Ideen I*, § 10, *Hua*, III, 26. In a strict sense, all the ambiguity of the Husserlian undertaking of a phenomenological ontology is at play in the placement in quotation marks of the "object," since it is thus exposed to a second placement in parenthesis, reducing it to the status of a simple noematic correlate.

55. *Ideen III*, respectively, § 16 and § 11, *Hua*, V, 88, 67 [Eng. trans., 76, 58; mod.].

56. *Ideen I*, § 42, *Hua*, V, 96 [see Eng. trans., 90]: "*die kardinalste Unterschiedenheit*"; likewise § 43, 99: "*unüberbrückbarer Wesensunterschied*"; and again § 49, 119. See above, chap. 2, § 2; chap. 3, § 2.

57. *Ideen III*, § 15, *Hua*, 84ff. [see Eng. trans., 72ff.].

58. As for the objection according to which the meanings of *ontology* would remain so perfectly equivocal from Husserl to Heidegger that no solid conclusion could result from their confrontation, it sets up as a solution the very statement of the problem: the ambiguity of the use of *ontology* designates precisely the indecision of the different possible relations between ontology and phenomenology; the Husserlian sense remains limited, in appearance at

least, only inasmuch as Husserl undertook to reduce ontology, even "universal" ontology. Moreover, Heidegger maintains the Husserlian usage of "region" with respect to the ontology of *Dasein*, thus tacitly admitting the legitimacy of the uses of "ontology" by Husserl (D. Sinha, *Studies in Phenomenology* [The Hague, 1981], 110ff.).

59. At least explicitly. See above, chap. 2, §§ 5–7. Does the absence of the reduction imply its radicalization by Heidegger, as have held E. Tugendhat, *Der Wahrheitsbegriff bei Husserl und Heidegger* (Berlin, 1967), 263ff., and M. Sukale, *Comparative Studies in Phenomenology* (The Hague, 1976), chap. 3, 100–120? It still remains the case that, radicalized or abandoned, the reduction is never exercised over the *Seinsfrage* and never contests its primacy.

60. *Nachwort zu "Was ist Metaphysik?"* (1949), *GA*, 9, 307 (see 310) [see Eng. trans., 261]. One could compare to this the determination of *Dasein* as "das nackte 'Dass' im Nichts," the naked "that" in nothingness, according to *Sein und Zeit*, § 57, 276, line 40.

61. *Ideen III*, § 12, *Hua*, V, 75 [Eng. trans., 64; mod.]; see the description of this "wonder": "Aber welches Wunder! Der Erlebnisstrom birgt nach idealer Möglichkeit . . . das *cogito* mit Ich und *cogitatum*" (71, line 25). The formula would issue from P. Natorp: "Wunder aller Wunder . . . das überhaupt etwas für uns ist" (*Philosophische Systematik: Aus dem Nachlaß*, ed. H. Natorp [Hamburg, 1958], 22)—according to W. Röd, "*Phaenomenôn omnium mirabilissimum*, Die Frage nach der Erscheinung als Grundfrage der neuzeitlichen Metaphysik," in *Sinngestalten: Festschrift für E. Coreth*, ed. D. Muck (Vienna, 1989). See below, chap. 6, § 6.

62. *Ideen III*, § 13, *Hua*, V, 76 [see Eng. trans., 65].

63. *Ideen I*, § 80, *Hua*, III, 195 [see Eng. trans., 191].

64. The paradox of this thesis will appear less untenable if one considers that the development of phenomenology, with the massive exception of Heidegger, to be sure, has aimed only at constructing a doctrine without the Being of the I: thus Merleau-Ponty and the flesh, Levinas and exposure to the other, Michel Henry and self-affection as life, even J. Derrida. Concerning the possibility of subjecting the *Seinsfrage* to the rule of the reduction, the interpreters diverge. Some unambiguously exclude it: "the *epoché does not disqualify [preisgeben] the Being of the world but retains it* . . . , it does not simply turn away from Being but reaches the lived experience of Being [*Zugang zum Erleben von Sein*]" (E. Ströcker, "Das Problem der *Epoche* in der Philosophie Husserls," *Analecta Husserliana* [1971], reprinted in *Phänomenologische Studien* [Frankfurt, 1987], 44). Others envisage it, but in order to exclude it: "It would seem rather improbable that such a principle [*sc.* subjectivity] taken into consideration in this way should itself be—unless by a *tour de force* [in French in the text]—divorced from Being" (Sinha, *Studies in Phenomenology*, 114; see all of chap. 6, "Is Phenomenology Ontologically Committed?"). E. Fink, whose faithfulness to Husserl could not be questioned, nevertheless goes much further, speaking not only of "escaping as a thinker from the universal belief in Being [*universellen Seinsglauben*]," or of "inhibiting the belief in Being," but above all of "suspending the one who inhibits, the subject who puts out of operation its own belonging to the world, and therefore its own belief," in short, of suspending not

only the correlate of the thesis but above all the " 'Being of the thesis' and of the one who posits it" ("Reflexionen zu Husserls phänomenologischer Reduktion," *Tijdschrift voor Filosofie* [1971]; reprinted in *Nähe und Distanz: Phänomenologische Vorträge und Aufsätze*, ed. F.-A. Schwartz [Freiburg, 1976], respectively, 310, 312, 313, 321).

6. The Nothing and the Claim

1. See above, chap. 2, § 4; and chap. 4.
2. *Sein und Zeit*, § 39, 181, lines 24–26. [Eng. trans., 226].
3. See above, chap. 2, § 3; chap. 3, §§ 3–5; and chap. 5, §§ 4–5.
4. See above, chap. 5, § 7.
5. See above, chap. 4, §§ 5–7.
6. See above, chap. 4, § 5.
7. *Wegmarken*, GA, 9, 306 [see Eng. trans., 260]. We take the translation of *"west"* by *"siste"* from P. Secretan (concerning this text in his translation of J. B. Lotz, *Martin Heidegger und Thomas von Aquin* [Pfullingen, 1975], *L'être selon Heidegger et Thomas d'Aquin* [Paris, 1988], 30, 89, etc.). [The neologism "sists," following Secretan's *"siste,"* translates the third person singular of the German *"wesen"* and derives from the Latin *sisto, sistere*: to stand, appear, endure, remain, etc. The Latin verb, of course, persists in such English verbs as "persist."—TRANS.].
8. *Sein und Zeit*, § 3, 9, line 7 [Eng. trans., 29; mod.].
9. That it is indeed a matter of boldness is proved by the fact that in 1949, in the fifth edition of the lecture (enlarged with a preface), Heidegger will correct and return to the position of *Sein und Zeit*, where Being is always the Being of a being: " . . . that Being never sists [*siste*] without being [. . . *dass Sein nie west ohne Seiende*], that a being never is without Being" (*Wegmarken*, 306).
10. *Wegmarken*, GA, 9, 105 [see Eng. trans., 244]. Heidegger stresses in a note that these formulas issue directly from Taine, but he does not give any specific references. One might consider, among others, certain themes developed by *De l'intelligence* (Paris, 1870): "It is necessary to remark finally that the names of force and substance, of self [*moi*] and matter designate only metaphysical entities, that there is nothing real in nature except tissues of events tied to one another and to others, that there is nothing more in ourselves nor in anything else" (II, I, I, I vol. 2, ed. 1878, 5); the power of the self receives a privileged critique: "It is a constant particularity for my resolution to be followed across ten indispensable intermediaries by the displacement of my arm. Nothing more.—Sadly, of this particularity which is a relation, we make . . . a substance . . . in itself, it is nothing. . . . the Being in question being a pure nothingness." Likewise its substance: "If one considers it (the self) at any given moment, it is nothing other than a section intercepted within the tissue. . . . At every moment the section is analogous; it is therefore nothing other, or more" (I, IV, III, vol. 1, 341 and 345).
11. *Wegmarken*, GA, 9, 106 [Eng. trans., 244].
12. "Welch zwiespältiges Wesen enthüllt sich da?" (*Wegmarken*), 106. On these points, one should refer to J. Beaufret, "La pensée du rien dans l'oeuvre de

Heidegger," *La Table Ronde* 183 (Paris, 1963); reprinted successively in *Introduction aux philosophies de l'existence* (Paris, 1971), and *De l'existentialisme à Heidegger* (Paris, 1986).

13. ". . . das Nichts überhaupt zum Gegenstand zu machen," "In diesem Fragen setzen wir im vorhinein . . . das Nichts als etwas an, das so und so 'ist'—als ein Seiendes" (*Wegmarken*, 107).

14. R. Carnap, "Uberwindung der Metaphysik durch logische Analyze der Sprache," *Erkenntnis* 2 (Vienna, 1932). Carnap's critique offers the exceptional interest of thrusting forward as an evident refutation what, for Heidegger, constitutes precisely the whole difficulty: Does logical negation eliminate the nothing? Might it not, on the contrary, issue from it and thus attest to it? The candid assurance of the objector reinforces the question.

15. H. Bergson, "L'idée de néant," *Revue philosophique* (1906), reprinted in *L'évolution créatrice* (Paris, 1907), cited according to *Oeuvres: Edition du Centenaire*, ed. H. Gouhier and A. Robinet (Paris, 1963); here, respectively, 730, 734, 745, 731. These themes reappear in "Le possible et le réel" (speech given at Oxford in September 1920, published in Sweden in 1930 in *Nordisk Tidskrift*, reprinted in *La pensée et le mouvant* [Paris, 1934], cited according to *Oeuvres*).

16. *Oeuvres*, respectively, 1337 (twice), 745.

17. Ibid.

18. Ibid., 737.

19. The strange consensus that already brings together Bergson and Carnap welcomes Sartre also: "Without any doubt, Heidegger is right to insist on the fact that negation draws its foundation from nothingness. But if nothingness founds negation, it is because it contains within itself as its essential structure the *no*. In other words, it is not as undifferentiated void or as an alterity that would not posit itself as alterity that nothingness founds negation. It founds negation as an *act* because it is negation as *Being*" (*L'Etre et le néant* [Paris, 1943], 46). Even more surprising seems to be E. Tugendhat's critique: *nicht* does not lead to *Nichtsein*, but only to the *Nichts* as "die universale *Bedingung* des Verstehens von Sein und Nichtsein"; indeed, "Sich an nichts halten zu können, ist eine echte Erfahrungsmöglichkeit, sich an das Nichts halten zu können, hingegen kaum"; it is necessary to renounce the Nothing and return to the logical ("Das Sein und das Nichts," in *Durchblicke: Martin Heidegger zum 80. Geburtstag* [Frankfurt, 1970], 159, 155, 160).

20. *Wegmarken*, 108 [Eng. trans., 246].

21. Ibid., [Eng. trans., 246; mod.].

22. Ibid., 107, 109 [Eng. trans., 245, 246; mod.].

23. Ibid., 109 [Eng. trans., 246; mod.].

24. Ibid., 110 [Eng. trans., 247; mod.].

25. Ibid., 110 [Eng. trans., 248; mod.]. On the concept of *Stimmung*, see the good analysis of J.-P. Charcosset, " 'Y / Notes sur la *Stimmung*," in *Exercices de la patience*, vols. 3–4 (Paris, 1982). A pertinent description of profound boredom's encounter with beings in their totality can be found, e.g., in Senancour, describing the "disorder of boredoms" in these terms:

> There I am in the world, wandering, solitary in the middle of the crowd which is nothing to me; like the man struck long ago with an accidental deafness, whose avid eye fixes itself on all those mute beings that pass and move about before him. He sees everything and everything is refused to him: he divines the sounds that he loves, he looks for them and does not hear them: he suffers the silence of all things amidst the noise of the world. Everything shows itself to him, and he would be able to seize nothing: the universal harmony is in exterior things, it is in his imagination, it is no longer in his heart: he is separated from the whole of beings, there is no more contact. (*Oberman*, Letters published by M. Senancour, ed. B. Arthaud [Paris, 1947], Lettre XXII, vol. 2, 101)

Similarly, Flaubert: "I have in myself, in my depths, a *boredom* [*embêtement*] that is radical, intimate, acrid and incessant, which impedes me from tasting anything and which fills my soul to the point of bursting. It reappears with regard to everything, like the bloated carcasses of dogs that return to water's surface, despite the rocks one attached to their necks in order to drown them" (*A Louise Colet*, 20 December 1846, *Oeuvres complètes*, vol. 12 [Paris, 1974], 574). In both cases, it is a matter of "everything," of "all things," of "the whole of beings," with "nothing" being an exception to a paradoxical and inverted totalization. See other references in G. Sagnes, *L'ennui dans la littérature française de Flaubert à Laforgue (1848–84)* (Paris, 1969).

26. "Das Seiende im Ganzen ist gleichgültig geworden" (*Wegmarken*, 110) [Eng. trans., 247; mod.].

27. *Die Grundbegriffe der Metaphysik: Welt—Endlichkeit—Einsamkeit*, GA, 29–30, § 31, 212 [Eng. trans., 141]. An analysis of this analysis of boredom has been provided by M. Haar, "Le temps vide et l'indifférence à l'être," in *Exercices de la patience*, vol. 7 (1986).

28. *Die Grundbegriffe der Metaphysik*, GA, 29–30, § 39, 251 [Eng. trans., 169].

29. The study of Heidegger's statements concerning love (and joy) remains to be done. Let us mention a few texts. (1) *Prolegomena zur Geschichte des Zeitbegriffs* (summer 1925), § 20: "Das, was wir hier als In-Sein des Daseins herausstellten und noch näher charakterisierten, ist das ontologische Fundament dafür, was Augustinus und vor allem dann Pascal kannten. Sie nannten das, was eigentlich erkennt, nicht das Erkennen, sondern Liebe und Hass" (*GA*, 20, 222): the reduction of love to the "question of Being" is violent enough here that Heidegger does not attempt to justify it (even "later" as promised by the remainder of the text). (2) Moreover, this same course started by treating love on the basis of intentionality, in the mode of merely one noesis among others: "Jedes Sich-richten-auf, Furcht, Hoffnung, Liebe hat den Charakter des Sich-richtens-auf, den Husserl als Noesis bezeichnet" (ibid., 61). (3) *Hölderlins Hymnen "Andenken"* (1941–42) in its own way maintains this reduction: "Liebe und Taten sind das Dichterische des Zeit-Raumes, in dem die Sterblichen eigentlich 'da' sind" (§ 54, GA, 52, p. 161). (4) *Brief über den Humanismus* (1946): "Sich einer 'Sache' oder einer 'Person' in ihrem Wesen annehmen, das Heisst: sie lieben: sie mögen" (*Wegmarken*, GA, 9, 316): here it is incontestably a matter of leading love back to the "question of Being."

(5) Other texts only repeat the reduction, characteristic of metaphysics, of love to the will: thus *Hölderlins Hymnen "Germanien" und "Das Rhein"* (1934–35), *GA*, 39, 82, 94; *Nietzsche*, vol. 1 (1935), 470 (see *Nietzsche metaphysiche Grundstellung im abendländischen Denken: Die ewige Wiederkehr des Gleichen* (summer 1937), § 22, *GA*, 44, 232). One could add to this the irrevocable judgment brought upon (against) Christian charity by *Nietzsches Wort "Gott ist tot"* (1943): "Christlicher Glaube wird da und dort sein. Aber die in solcher Welt waltende Liebe ist nicht das wirkendwirksame Prinzip dessen, was jetzt geschieht" (*Holzwege*, *GA*, 5, 254). As for joy, it does not receive a better treatment. To be sure, *Einführung in die Metaphysik* (summer 1935) opposes to boredom the "Jubel des Herzens" (*GA*, 40, 3), but without any other explanation. Nor could one consider the texts from *Nietzsche*, vol. 1 (56, 65) or from *Überwindung der Metaphysik*, § 28 (1936–46, in *Vorträge und Aufsätze*, vol. 1 [Pfullingen, 1954], 91) as sufficient phenomenological references.

30. As I outlined in *Prolégomènes à la charité* (Paris, 1986), chap. 4 in particular.

31. *Sein und Zeit*, § 39, 182, line 31. See also "Grundbefindlichkeit des Daseins," § 29, 140, line 6; § 39, 182, line 22, and 184, line 2; § 40, 184, line 9, 188, line 24, 189, line 30, 190, line 20; § 50, 251, line 21; § 53, 266, line 7; § 62, 310, line 17; § 68, 342, line 32, etc. Likewise, *Kant und das Problem der Metaphysik* proposes to elaborate—in the same period—"die 'Angst' als eine 'entscheidende Grundbefindlichkeit,' " since that Grundbefindlichkeit is supposed " . . . vor das Nichts [stellen]" (§ 43, Bonn, 1929, 228). The 1929 lecture speaks of the "Grundstimmung der Angst" (*GA*, 9, 111). We will understand *Grundstimmung* (fundamental affective mood) according to this remark from 1934–35: "By fundamental mood we mean not some sentimental mood that floats and disappears, and accompanies only speaking, but the fundamental mood [*Grundstimmunng*] opens the world, such as it receives the mark of Being [*Seyn*] in poetic speaking" (*Hölderlins Hymnen "Germanien" und "Der Rhein," GA*, 39, 79). It is therefore in two ways that the world opens in anxiety: because it is a matter of anxiety, but also because it is a matter of a fundamental mood.

32. *Was ist Metaphysik?*, *GA*, 9, 112 [Eng. trans., 249; mod.].

33. Ibid., 113 [see Eng. trans., 250]. On this construction of the question, see above, chap. 2.

34. Respectively, "zwiespältiges Wesen" (*Was ist Metaphysik?*, 106), and "die rätselhafte Mehrdeutigkeit des Nichts" (*Nachwort*, 1943, *GA*, 9, 306) [see Eng. trans., 244, 260]. Such an ambiguity of the Nothing rendered manifest to and through anxious *Dasein* will find an equally trivial and illuminating confirmation in the accusation of "nihilism" addressed to the 1929 lecture by readers who, precisely, did not know how to identify what is at play under the name of this Nothing.

35. *Was ist Metaphysik?*, 113 [see Eng. trans., 250]. The correct understanding of this formula, "together with" (*in eins mit*) as a "belonging" of the Nothing to the Being of beings ("Das Nichts bleibt nicht das unbestimmte Gegenüber für das Seiende, sondern es enthüllt sich als zugehörig zum Sein des Seienden" [*GA*, 9, 120]) marks the ultimate advance of the 1929 lecture, but it thus only augments

the lecture's ambiguity: Is the belonging equivalent to an identification or does it establish a difference?

36. *Sein und Zeit,* § 15, 68, line 28 [see Eng. trans., 97, which offers a helpful note on the English translation of *Verweisung*]. It is remarkable that the reference of a tool immediately implies a "multiplicity of references," and therefore an indetermination (69, lines 24–25). On the translation and understanding of this *abweisende Verweisung* ("dismissal" [*renvoi*] that refers, or an assigning expulsion), see above, chap. 2, § 7.

37. *Sein und Zeit,* § 7, 31, lines 4–7 [Eng. trans., 54; mod.]. One should note that, more than any other phenomenon, it is the dissimulated phenomenon, and particularly the (dissimulated) Being of (manifest) beings, that needs an "*explicit* exhibition [*ausdrückliche* Aufweisung]" (§ 7, 35, line 21); now, in the *Aufweisung* there resonates something of the *Verweisung*.

38. *Was ist Metaphysik?,* respectively, 115, 112, 114 [see Eng. trans., 252, 249, 250]. As for the at first surprising expression "Es—das Nichts in seinem Nichten—verweist uns gerade an das Seiende [it—the Nothing in its reduction to nothing—refers us, precisely, to beings]" (116), we understand it as follows: the Nothing refers us to beings in the fact of their beingness, to "die ursprüngliche Offenheit des Seienden als eines solchen: *dass* es Seiende ist [to the fact *that* it is being]" (114).

39. Ibid., 118 [see Eng. trans., 254]. See also: ". . . the transcendence of *Dasein* standing out [*hinausgehaltenen*] into the Nothing" (120) [see Eng. trans., 255] and: "Human *Dasein* can relate to beings only if it holds itself [*hineinhält*] into the Nothing" (121) [see Eng trans., 256].

40. *Sein und Zeit,* § 40, respectively, 187, lines 20, 15, 14, 19, 8–9, 25 (= 188, line 15); then § 68, 343, lines 17–19 [see Eng. trans., 231–33; 393]. This thematic goes back to the *Prolegomena* (summer, 1925), § 30: ". . . *das Wovor der Angst ist das Nichts,* d.h. nichts in der Welt Vorkommendes, Bestimmtes, nichts Weltliches . . . nämlich die *Welt in ihrer Weltlichkeit,*" or *In-der-Welt-sein as solches* (*GA,* 401, 402).

41. Thus, § 40, 188, lines 4ff. leads to Being-in-the-world (confirmed by § 50, 251, lines 16ff.) in order to found in it the Being-free and the possibility of *Dasein.* See § 62, 308, lines 17ff.

42. *Was ist Metaphysik?,* 115 [see Eng. trans., 251]. Despite the heaviness of the formulation, we prefer *reduce to nothing* rather than *annihilate* [*néantir*] to translate *nichten.*

43. *Was ist Metaphysik?,* 120 [see Eng. trans., 255]. There is a similar formulation in the 1929 book on Kant: "But the Being of beings is understandable—and in this resides the very finitude of transcendence—only if *Dasein,* by its very nature, stands in the Nothing" (*Kant und das Problem der Metaphysik,* § 43). That the Nothing, especially approached in its Hegelian equivalence with Being, offers more difficulty than assistance, is recognized explicitly in *Grundprobleme der Phänomenologie,* § 24, *GA,* 24, 443: "In the end, Hegel is on the track of a fundamental truth when he says that Being and nothing are identical, that is, that they belong together. Of course, the more radical question is: What makes such

a most originary co-belonging possible? / We are not yet sufficiently prepared to delve into this obscurity" [Eng. trans., 311–12; mod.].

44. The identity of Being and the nothing is explicitly established as early as (at least) 1935: "To go in the *question* of Being expressly to the border of the Nothing and to include the latter in the question of Being [*dieses in die Seinsfrage einbeziehen*] is *conversely* the first and only fruitful step for a true overcoming of nihilism" (*Einführung in die Metaphysik*, § 58, *GA*, 40, 212; see also § 10, 38ff., § 29, 90) [see Eng. trans., 203]. It is a matter here of a supplementary argument to consider the *Einführung* of 1935 as a repetition, a critique and a reversal of the 1929 *Was ist Metaphysik?* During the summer of 1941, that identification is not only held as self-evident ("*The Nothing does not need beings. But on the contrary the Nothing most certainly does need Being* . . . because the Nothing 'is' not an other than Being, but the latter itself [*sondern dieses selbst*]"), but it is, more curiously, attributed to *Was ist Metaphysik?* (*Grundbegriffe*, *GA*, 51, respectively, 54, 71, 72–73).

45. Respectively, *Was ist Metaphysik?*, 114 (we reestablish in brackets the "of beings" suppressed by Heidegger in 1949), and *Nachwort*, *GA*, 9, 306, and 307 [see Eng. trans., 251, 260].

46. *Was ist Metaphysik?*, 106. As above (chap. 2, § 7), we cite here and below the variants of different editions of the 1929 lecture, as well as the annotations made by Heidegger in his own personal copies, such as they were reprinted in *Wegmarken*, *GA*, 9, "Unveränderter Text mit Randbemerkungen des Autors. Herausgegeben von Friedrich-Wilhelm von Hermann" (Frankfurt, 1976).

47. *Was ist Metaphysik?*, 115.

48. Ibid., 114.

49. Ibid., 115.

50. Ibid., 116.

51. Ibid., respectively, 106, 113, 114. In fact the absence of the ontological difference in the very body of *Was ist Metaphysik?* is recognized, at least indirectly, by Heidegger: in 1949, the very year when he adds mentions of the ontological difference in the margins of the 1929 lecture, he puts forward, in the foreword to the third edition of *Vom Wesen des Grundes* (written also in 1929), that the one (*Was ist Metaphysik?*) "thinks the nothing," while the other (*Vom Wesen des Grundes*) "names the ontological difference" (*GA*, 9, 123; see above, chap. 4, § 1) [see Eng. trans., 3]. This implies, in turn, that *Was ist Metaphysik?* therefore does not name the ontological difference; the additions of 1949, which introduce it there, must therefore be read for what they are: additions, adding to the original text that which it ignored.

52. *Nachwort*, 306 [see Eng. trans., 260].

53. This last step was denied by J. Beaufret, who places *Sein und Zeit* ahead of *Was ist Metaphysik?*, while maintaining that "already with *Sein und Zeit*, therefore, everything is already in place for the development of a question that *Sein und Zeit* limits itself to raising" (*De l'existentialisme à Heidegger*, 109); J.-B. Lotz, on the contrary, remarks that "actually the existential analytic does not go beyond Nothingness," and that only "the *Nachwort* offers some indications that lead further" ("Heidegger et L'Etre," *Archives de Philosophie* 19, no. 2 [1956], 10).

Or again: "Starting from there, Heidegger's thought presents two phases: the first leaves Being veiled in nothingness; the second unveils Being or allows it to emerge as such from nothingness. The first phase, which is concretized above all in *Sein und Zeit*, carries the analyses only up to Being, which is still *veiled* in nothingness, whereas the second phase, which becomes explicit especially in the later writings, traverses nothingness toward Being" (*Martin Heidegger und Thomas von Aquin*; French translation *Martin Heidegger et Thomas d'Aquin*, 20; see 53, 78—"the intermediary of nothingness"—and 89). In fact, *Sein und Zeit* does not even carry out the first phase, which is reached only by the 1929 lecture; the second phase is accomplished with the additions of 1943 and 1949. One finds the same distinction, only half admitted, made by R. Regvald: on the one hand, in 1927, "anxiety confirms what makes one anxious . . . that with a view to which anxiety is anxious: Being-in-the-world," while on the other hand, in 1929, the Nothing "in a certain measure is Being itself," but it would be "especially in the *Postscript*" that "the hypothesis of a co-belonging of Being and nothingness begins to take form" (*Heidegger et le problème du néant* [Dordrecht, 1987], 11, 94). The distinction is much more straightforward in W. Schulz, who stresses that "the second step from the Nothing to Being is more difficult than the first, toward the Nothing" ("Über den philosophiegeschichtlichen Ort Martin Heideggers," *Philosophische Rundschau* [1953], reprinted in *Heidegger: Perspektiven zur Deutung seines Werkes*, ed. O. Pöggeler [Berlin, 1970], 116). Likewise A. Naber, "Von der Philosophie des 'Nichts' zur Philosophie des 'Seins-selbst': Zur grossen 'Wende' im Philosophieren M. Heideggers," *Gregorianum* (1947). On the abandonment of the "question of Being" in the narrow sense in 1927, see above, chap. 4, §§ 4–5; on the irruption of the Nothing as the term of anxiety, see chap. 6, § 3.

54. *Was ist Metaphysik?*, 111 [see Eng. trans., 248].

55. *Nachwort*, 312 [Eng. trans., 264; mod.]: "Schleir des Seins"; the beginning of the text poses the alternative perfectly: Does the Nothing exhaust itself in the negation of beings as a whole, or "does it unveil itself [*sich entschleiert*] as what-differentiates-itself from all beings, what we call Being"? (305) [see Eng. trans., 259].

56. Ibid., 307 [see Eng. trans., 261] (see 310 [Eng. trans., 263]: "Original thought is the echo of the favor of Being, in which is illuminated and allowed to occur the unique: *that* being is"). On the Husserlian treatment of the "wonder of wonders," see above, chap. 5, § 7.

57. "Silent voice" (add. of 1949: *lautlose Stimme*)—how to decide that it issues from Being? (*Nachwort*, 306; see 311).

58. Ibid., 306 [see Eng. trans., 260].

59. Ibid., [see Eng. trans., 260]. The unequal relation (Being without beings, but beings always with Being) marked a decisive advance over *Sein und Zeit*, which recognized Being only in its tie to a being ("Sein ist jeweils das Sein eines Seienden," § 3, 9, line 7; see § 2, 6, lines 29–30, etc.); the ultimate position of the *Nachwort* therefore goes backward. Why this turn if not, perhaps, because the advance rendered even more problematic the transition from beings to Being?

60. The lecture uses the term only once, without relating it to Being: "What it [science] rejects, it claims [*nimmt sie in Anspruch*]" (*GA*, 9, 106). The formulation, "das Seiende spricht nicht mehr an" comes from a remark from 1949 (*GA*, 9, 111).

61. *Nachwort*, respectively, 307 (which two lines lower considers the mood of preparing oneself for anxiety only as the meaning of "fulfilling the highest claim": anxiety no longer has the value of *Grundstimmung*, *Grundbefindlichkeit*), 309, 311 [Eng. trans., 260, 262, 263; mod.].

62. Ibid., respectively, 306 (with the gloss, "*Stimme der Stille* [voice of silence]"), 310, 311 [Eng. trans., 260, 263, 264].

63. *Sein und Zeit*, respectively, § 56, 273, lines 25–28; § 57, 277, line 31 (= 279, lines 31–32) [Eng. trans., 318, 322 = 324; mod.]. The call claims *Dasein* only for itself: "*In conscience Dasein calls itself* [*ruft sich selbst*]" (§ 57, 275, lines 12–13) [Eng. trans., 320].

64. Ibid., § 58, 285, lines 35–36 [Eng. trans., 331]. With regard to this last concession—". . . *dunkel*"—Husserl pertinently notes in the margin of his personal copy, "Yes!" (*Bemerkungen und Notizen Husserls zu Heideggers "Sein und Zeit*,*"* which is unpublished and for access to which we thank S. Ijsseling and R. Bernet of the Husserl Archiv de Leuven. For a first interpretation of these remarks, see D. Souche-Dagues, "La lecture husserlienne de *Sein und Zeit*," *Philosophie* 21 [Paris, 1989]).

65. Respectively, *Nachwort*, 310 [Eng. trans., 263; mod.], and *Grundbegriffe*, *GA*, 51, 5, 8, 14 [see Eng. trans., 5, 6–7, 12] (see 83 and 84).

66. *Nachwort*, 310 [see Eng. trans., 263]. How are we to understand these corrections? We suggest a hypothesis: Heidegger minimizes gratitude (*Danken*) in subjecting it again to thought (*Denken*) out of fear of the specifically liturgical and spiritual resonances of the term; but this fear itself would say more than a little.

67. *Die Grundbegriffe der Metaphysik*: "We shall designate the expanse [*die Weite*] of this 'as a whole,' which manifests itself in profound boredom, as *world*. Concerning the meaning of that before which this fundamental mood places us, we must ask: *what is the world?*" (251 [Eng. trans., 169; mod.]; see 248, 255, the "liberation of *Dasein*").

68. Pascal, *Pensées*, in *Oeuvres complètes*, ed. L. Lafuma (Paris, 1963), respectively, §§ 24, 136, 941 [Eng. trans. by A. J. Krailsheimer; mod.].

69. Ibid., § 919.

70. E. Littré, *Dictionnaire de la langue française*, vol. 2 (Paris, 1874), 1406ff.

71. Cassien, *Collationes*, V, P. L., 49, col. 369 [". . . with no provocation coming from without."]. Saint Thomas, analyzing ἀκηδία, stresses that its boredom ". . . *deprimit animum hominis, ut nihil ei agere libeat*" [". . . so weighs upon man's soul, that he wants to do nothing," trans. Fathers of the English Dominican Province (New York: Benziger Brothers, 1947); mod.] (*Summa Theologiae*, IIa IIae, q. 35, a. I, resp.): the soul is not free to will or to do as it pleases, precisely because it is no longer free for anything at all to please it. On acedia, see the article by G. Bardy, in *Dictionnaire de spiritualité*, vol. 1, col. 166–69; S. Wenzel, *The Sin of*

Sloth: Acedia in Mediaeval Thought and Literature (Chapel Hill, 1967); and C. Flüler, "Acedia und Melancholie in Spätmittelalter," *Freiburger Zeitschrift für Philosophie und Theologie* 34 no. 3, (1987); on the concept itself, see H. Tellenbach, *Melancolie: Problemgeschichte, Endogenität, Typologie, Pathogenese, Klinik* (Berlin, 1961; 3d ed., 1976); and R. Brague, "L'image et l'acédie: Remarque sur le premier 'Apophtegme,'" *Revue thomiste* 85, no. 2 (1975).

72. Chateaubriand, *René*, ed. Armand Weil (Genève, 1935), 47–48 (or *Oeuvres complètes*, vol. 3 [Paris, 1861], 84).

73. Senancour, *Oberman*, Letter 22, 101. Likewise, Rousseau's Julie: "This pain is bizarre, I agree; but it is not any less real for all that. My friend, I am too happy; my happiness bores me" (J.-J. Rousseau, *Julie ou la Nouvelle Héloïse*, VI, 8, ed. B. Gagnebin-M. Raymond, "Pléiade," vol. 2 [Paris, 1969], 694).

74. On these analyses, see *God Without Being* (Chicago, 1991), chap. 4: "The Reverse of Vanity," 108–38. It is not a matter of indifference here (see n. 29) that boredom, like acedia, is often opposed to joy (Saint Thomas, *Summa*, a.2, resp.). For a critique of this reprise of boredom, see J. Greisch, *La parole heureuse* (Paris, 1987), 274–84.

75. *Brief über den Humanismus, GA*, 325 [see Eng. trans., 205]. See the lecture ["What Is Metaphysics?"]: "Being-there means standing into the nothing" (*GA*, 9, 115) [see Eng. trans., 251].

76. Respectively, *GA* 9, 307 [see Eng. trans., 261] (see the Husserlian parallel in *Ideen III*, § 12, *Hua*, V, 75, above, chap. 5, § 7); Aristotle (*Metaphysics*, A, 2, 982b12) ["For it is owing to their wonder that men both now begin and at first began to philosophize"; Eng. trans., *The Complete Works of Aristotle*, ed. Jonathan Barnes (Princeton: Princeton University Press, 1984)]; and Plato (*Theaetetus*, 155d) ["This sense of wonder is the pathos of the philosopher. Philosophy indeed has no other origin"; Eng. trans., mod., in *The Collected Dialogues*, ed. Edith Hamilton and Huntington Cairns (Princeton: Princeton University Press, 1961)].

77. *Passions de l'âme*, § 53, AT, XI, 373, 5–13 [Eng. trans., Cottingham, Stoothoff, and Murdoch, in *The Philosophical Writings of Descartes*, vol. 1 (Cambridge: Cambridge University Press, 1985), 350].

78. *Was ist Metaphysik?*, *GA*, 9, 307 [Eng. trans., 261; mod.].

79. *Einführung in die Metaphysik*, § 28, *GA*, 40, 88 [see Eng. trans., 83].

80. *Sein und Zeit* § 4, 12, successively, lines 11–12, 4–5, 26 [Eng. trans., 32–33; mod.]. Other references above, chap. 4, § 6.

81. *Sein und Zeit*, § 4, 12, line 23 [Eng. trans., 33]. For an analysis of this "mineness," see above, chap. 3, §§ 6 and § 7.

82. *Brief über den Humanismus, GA*, 9, 319ff. [Eng. trans., 200]. It therefore seems difficult to identify the *Seinsfrage* with a being, even the privileged being: "Das Fragen ist selbst ein Seiendes" (*GA*, 20, 199); indeed, the claim here no longer exerts itself in the name of Being (but of the Father), nor with the destination or starting point of a being. Thus arises the pure form of the call.

83. *De Dieu qui vient à l'idée* (Paris, 1982), respectively, 245, 265. If the call comes down to an *à-Dieu*, one must necessarily conclude that "The alternative

between Being and nothing is not ultimate. The *à-Dieu* is not a process of Being" (264ff.).

84. See above, chap. 2, §§ 5–7.

85. E. Littré, *Dictionnaire de la langue française,* vol. 3, 133.

Index

251